ALSO BY WILLIAM SAFIRE

LANGUAGE

In Love with Norma Loquendi
Quoth the Maven
Coming to Terms
Fumblerules
Language Maven Strikes Again
You Could Look It Up
Take My Word for It
I Stand Corrected
What's the Good Word?
On Language
Safire's New Political Dictionary

POLITICS

The First Dissident
Safire's Washington
Before the Fall
Plunging into Politics
The Relations Explosion

FICTION

Sleeper Spy
Freedom
Full Disclosure

ANTHOLOGIES

Lend Me Your Ears: Great Speeches in History

(WITH LEONARD SAFIR)

Good Advice on Writing
Leadership
Words of Wisdom
Good Advice

WATCHING MY LANGUAGE

WATCHING MY LANGUAGE

Adventures in the Word Trade

William Safire

Illustrations by
Peter Kuper and Terry Allen

Random House
New York

Illustrations by Peter Kuper and Terry Allen

Grateful acknowledgment is made to *The New York Times* for
permission to reprint 76 "On Language" columns by
William Safire from the May 5, 1991, through January 24, 1993,
issues of *The New York Times Magazine*. Copyright © 1991, 1992, 1993
by The New York Times Company. Reprinted by permission.

Library of Congress Cataloging-in-Publication Data

Safire, William.
Watching my language: Adventures in the Word Trade / by William Safire.
p.   cm.
Includes index.
ISBN 0-679-42387-7
1. English language—Usage.   2. English language—Style.
I. Title.
PE1421.S2337   1996
428—dc20   95-3800

Random House website address: http://www.randomhouse.com/

Printed in the United States of America on acid-free paper

2 4 6 8 9 7 5 3

FIRST EDITION

For Mort Janklow,
from his first literary client
twenty-four books later

I do here, in the Name of all the Learned and polite Persons of the Nation, complain . . . that our Language is extremely imperfect; that its daily Improvements are by no means in proportion to its daily Corruptions, that the Pretenders to polish and refine it have chiefly multiplied Abuses and Absurdities. . . .

—JONATHAN SWIFT, *Proposal for Correcting,* 1712

INTRODUCTION

The early 1990's will be remembered not, as some economists say, as the Age of Affluence; nor as some environmentalists insist, the Age of Effluence; nor even, as Washington lobbyists insist, the Age of Influence. The linguists of tomorrow will call this the Age of *Euphluence.*

Don't run to your dictionary; I just made up that word to portray the power of the Prettification Patrol, and to deride its need to apply soft words to hard reality in the form of euphemism.

Prettification Patrol

Let's say you're trying to peddle some fake flowers. Do you call yourself a fake-flower peddler? Of course not; you're a *floral marketer,* artificial-flower division.

Now you look at your product—sometimes quite beautiful, petals made of silk or whatever—and you ask yourself, "Why *artificial?*" That's a word that turns buyers off. You brood about that, and come up with a fresh-as-a-daisy answer: You'll create a market for *permanent flowers.* That not only lends longevity to your produce, but it also knocks the noxious weeds turned out in hothouses and pesticide-ridden, inorganic, fertilizer-driven gardens as temporary flowers.

That's the art, or racket, of *euphemism,* from the Greek *eu-,* "good," and *pheme,* "speech." And it's been gaining speed ever since environmentalists were able to transform the damn *jungle* into the glorious *rain forest* (where you can get *wetlands fever*).

Some objects of green wrath, lumbermen and fishermen, counterattacked with euphemisms of their own. "The timber industry speaks of *harvesting* trees on public lands, the fishing industry of *harvesting* fish from the ocean," grumps Ray Sawhill of New York. "My understanding is that in order to har-

vest you have to have first reaped." Maybe he means *sown*; at any rate, if you have planted the trees, or raised the fish from caviar, you could then harvest them, although "harvest" is not a term that goes well outside the vegetable world. Thus, I would not use the headline, as *The New York Times* recently did, "Giant Maw for Fish Harvesting."

No newspaper can be held responsible, however, for the prose prettification in its advertising. If you're appealing to a snooty clientele, you hate to use the word *sale;* nice stores don't have sales. (In France, *sale* is a dirty word.) If it's cheap but it hasn't been marked down yet, call it a *special purchase.* Or, if you're the Atrium Gallery on Fifth Avenue, "Join us for our current anniversary exhibition of master jewelers and receive a 10 percent *accommodation.*" Hotels provide *accommodations;* what will they now call a lowering of rates on rooms?

Even the most innocent words, when they take on a taint, are quickly euphemized. The Miss America contest, eager to shed any hint of royalism, now forbids the use of *reign* to denote the period in which here-she-comes holds the title; her once-reign is now "a year of service."

No longer need Shakespeare's Edmund, in *King Lear,* cry, "Now, gods, stand up for bastards!" As Ben J. Wattenberg has written of those born on the wrong side of the blanket: "It was once called *bastardy.* Then *illegitimacy.* Then *out-of-wedlock birth.* And now, frequently, wholly sanitized, *nonmarital birth.*" (He left out *love child.*)

"Do you do euphemisms?" writes Ben Bradlee, *The Washington Post*'s vice president at-large. (In my view, the hyphen makes the words mean "not confined to a specific assignment"; without the hyphen, it would mean "sought after by the police.") He cited a broadcast by Peter Jennings of ABC when Yasir Arafat's plane was missing: "if something has befallen him *in a terminal way*. . . ."

Because the word *lying* is off-putting to some, we have seen some prettification under oath. Oliver North denied lying to Congress, but admitted he had "provided input which differed radically from the truth." And Roger Le Locataire notes from Ponders End, London, that British officials caught telling half-truths or otherwise deceiving the court admit they have been *economical with the truth.*

In the general derogation of politically correct terms, some euphemism has been parodied: Nobody seriously uses *vertically challenged* for "short," or holds that a bad speller is *orthographically impaired;* Clyde Haberman of *The New York Times* was writing tongue-in-cheek when he described a rotund Turkish political figure as *kilogramically endowed.* But some writers have rejected *prostitute* for the less pejorative "sexual worker," and the person in charge of waste disposal (formerly garbage) for the township of Montclair, New Jersey, refers to herself as "senior sanitarian."

In politics, the Clinton Administration has made it linguistic policy to refer to the taxes necessitated by its health plan as *premiums,* which most people associate with insurance policies. Others say that if the payment is mandatory, it's a *tax,* which has become a political dirty word.

Almost as dirty as *guns.* When Richard Nixon, a year before his death, came out with "Guns are an abomination," advocates for unrestricted sale of the things that shoot bullets searched for a euphemism. A reader of a Minneapolis city magazine, *Mpls. St. Paul,* wrote to the editor to assert that "thousands have saved themselves, contrary to the myth of the danger of a *home-protection weapon.*" Jason Zweig of *Forbes* magazine objects to this euphemism: "I don't think it can transform a gun into a mom-and-apple-pie product. You can call a bullet a *criminal-impairment projectile,* but that will never blind the mind's eye to the ferocious furrowing of metal through flesh and bone." (Mr. Zweig, an old-school Hyphen Harry, agrees, however, with the letter-writer's use of the hyphen in *home-protection weapon.*)

We cannot leave this subject without a look at *dysphemism,* defined in the

Random House Unabridged, revised second edition, as "the substitution of a harsh, disparaging or unpleasant expression for a more neutral one." It turns euphemism on its head.

When Dick Gregory titled a book *Nigger,* he bit down hard on a painful slur, turning it to his advantage. In the same way, the word *queer*—like *queen* and *fairy,* long used as a derogation—is being stolen by homosexuals for their own use.

"The vivid representation of identity," Edmund White said in a speech to the Center for Lesbian and Gay Studies in New York, "is especially important for the *queer* community." As reprinted in *The New York Times,* the word seemed shocking until Mr. White repeated it: "Until recently, there were few openly *queer* films or publications."

Is *gay* passé? If *queer* is now acceptable, its etymology deserves a look: Hugh Rawson's *Devious Derivations* tracks *Queer Street,* a condition of financial impecunity, to the 1811 edition of Grose's *Classical Dictionary of the Vulgar Tongue,* meaning "Wrong. Improper." Before that, the word *queer*— perhaps rooted in the Greek for "oblique, off-center"—was used by pickpockets and con men to mean "out of order," as in "queer as Dick's hatband." Until recently, *bent* was the term many homosexuals preferred as the antonym to *straight,* but the new usage has queered it.

I think of this essay on the euphluentials as an apt introduction to a compilation of timely but timeless "On Language" columns in *The New York Times.* But the word *introduction* spooks me; nobody reads introductions. Most readers want to get to the meat of a book and scorn the *foreword,* even when misspelled *forward.*

In the spirit of the age, consider this a *prolegomenon.*

WATCHING MY LANGUAGE

1 WATCHING MY LANGUAGE

Agent of No Influence

I called the C.I.A. and put it to them hard: Did you guys ever send any agents into the Atlanta branch of Bank Lavoro to find out about funny financing of loans to Iraq?

The spook on the phone immediately went on background, so I cannot identify him or quote him directly.

Why do you keep calling our people *agents,* he asked (not for quotation). The F.B.I. has *agents;* we have *operations officers* and *case officers* working for us. To the C.I.A., *agents* refer to people we recruit abroad who become part of our *assets.* What's the difference between an *agent* (a spy providing *humint,* or "human intelligence") and an *agent of influence*?

That's a Russian term, he replied, still on background, but attributable in a general way, not in quotes. When a K.G.B. man found a source, even one that took no money and would have been furious to be considered helpful to a foreign power, he would claim to have developed an *agent of influence.* It made the K.G.B. man look good in his reports, as if he had half-recruited a well-placed American.

I almost forgot the original purpose of my call. It was not for a language column, but was about guilty knowledge of loans to Iraq. I had been struck by the frequent use of the phrase *we have no evidence.*

In *Informing Statecraft: Intelligence for a New Century,* Angelo Codevilla, a longtime Senate aide, writes that the most common sentence starter in National Security Estimates is *we believe,* and that "the second most common phrase is *we have no evidence . . .* that is longhand for 'no.' "

A tricky phrase, *we have no evidence.* It says "no," but guards against the consequences of being wrong; it leaves an opening for a switch to "yes" if somebody else comes up with evidence to the contrary. Listen for it.

The phrase "we have no evidence" reminds me of the phrase in statistical inference that there is "not sufficient evidence" to reject a (null) hypothesis. In other words, the experimenter would not risk making a Type I error, which would be the mistake of believing something that is not true (for example, finding an innocent person guilty), a possible consequence of rejecting the null hypothesis. However, by not having sufficient evidence to reject the null hypothesis, the experimenter (the spook) risks making a Type II error, which would be the mistake of not believing something that is true (for example, finding a guilty person innocent). Thus, your essays are challenging Type II errors (you believe an alternative hypothesis, or that the guilty should be found guilty) while the spooks are not.

I'll just keep reading those essays, expecting more profound evidence to the contrary, which would make the probability of committing a Type II error minute or even infinitesimal!

David Bernklau
Brooklyn, New York

The Arch Triumphalist

Triumph Without Victory is the title of a *U.S. News & World Report* book about the Persian Gulf war. A nice differentiation of synonyms: In current usage, a *triumph* is a spectacular *win,* as of a single battle; *victory*—rooted in the Latin *vincere,* "to conquer"—often has the connotation of the successful culmination of a war.

Back in the days of the cold war (no, I'm not being nostalgic), the word *victory* was frowned on in accommodationist circles. General Douglas MacArthur's stern 1951 statement to a joint meeting of Congress, "In war there is no substitute for victory," seemed unduly final to many seeking a settlement of the Korean conflict; a decade later, Senator Barry M. Goldwater used the word to provoke his liberal critics in the title of his book *Why Not Victory?*

Meanwhile, perhaps to conceal ambitions of global domination, Soviet propagandists put forward the notion of *convergence,* a meeting of the Communist and capitalist systems on some undefined common ground; the notion of *winning* the cold war was considered bellicose and not in the spirit of détente. Caspar W. Weinberger, Defense Secretary for Ronald Reagan, was criticized for using the verb *prevail* in predicting the outcome of a nuclear war, but could have pointed to William Faulkner's use of the term about mankind in a Nobel Prize lecture.

Then Eastern Europe spun off from the Soviet empire, and the Soviet Union itself began to come apart; after the Communist party was banned in Russia, it became apparent that the West had actually *won* the ideological struggle with the bipolar bear. But when some unreconstructed hard-liners

wanted to run out in the streets to celebrate, reconstructed soft-liners pointed to the impropriety of gloating, as in the words of Rear Admiral John Woodward (Jack) Philip at the battle of Santiago in 1898: "Don't cheer, men, those poor devils are dying." A word was needed to attack the exultant winners for their offensive desire to celebrate.

The word was waiting, having been coined in 1964 in a nonpolitical, religious context. In a book on the Vatican Council, *Observer in Rome,* Robert McAfee Brown wrote, "I am greatly impressed by the recognition of human failings in this prayer and by its exclusion of the '*triumphalism*' that has often seemed to characterize the church." The use of quotation marks may have been the act of a self-conscious coiner, or more likely the author's use of a neologism in the Roman air at that time. The context shows it was an attack word on those confident of the rightness of their faith, which critics saw to be the proud and rigid certitude of religious authority.

In 1968, Wayne H. Cowan, managing editor of a liberal Protestant journal, was quoted in *The New York Times* as saying that a pastoral letter "mutes the *triumphalism* of the past." The word, perhaps a suitable euphemism for "arrogance" or at least "haughtiness," was too useful to be limited to any one field. In *The New Yorker* in 1975, Tad Szulc called the contrast between wealth and poverty in Brazil under President Ernesto Geisel "understandable, given what critics of the regime have labeled '*triumphalism*'—something that goes way beyond mere ostentation on a colossal scale."

Most dictionaries up-to-date enough to include the word are still defining it in religious terms: "the doctrine or belief that the teachings of a particular faith are eternal and indestructible" is the definition in the *Third Barnhart Dictionary of New English,* adding correctly that the term is "usually used in a pejorative way." Architecture took a whack at it: "In architecture and interior decoration," wrote *The Economist* in 1977 about Spain, "the shoddy '*triumphalism*' of the 1950's has given way."

But the temporal has now overtaken the spiritual and architectural; in London, *The Observer* wrote in 1983 that certain conservative journalists "fed readers and viewers a diet of *triumphalistic* pap." The same year, Fidel Castro warned that "an air of *triumphalism* reigns in the Reagan Administration," an attitude that he equated with adventurism.

Attending a 1991 conference headed by Graham T. Allison Jr. of Harvard, who was then working on a "grand bargain" to ease Soviet transition to a freer economy, Edward Mortimer of *The Financial Times* wrote, "The high point for me came when a text I had drafted on 'America's role in the new international order' was criticized, by an American, for its 'excessive *triumphalism.*' "

Victory, which John F. Kennedy said had a thousand fathers, is sweet, but its headiness can lead to unsteadiness. I recall the euphoria after the 1972 Nixon election; when some of my hotly partisan colleagues rubbed their hands in anticipation of a grand sweeping-out of losers, the speechwriter Raymond K. Price cautioned, "There is the 'sore winner' problem."

Winners—especially of landslide victories or ideological conflicts—do well to remember the words of Mark Antony when viewing the body of Julius Caesar: "Dost thou lie so low?/Are all thy conquests, glories, triumphs, spoils,/Shrunk to this little measure?" There are always those spoilsports around, loaded down with sour looks and wet blankets, and they now have a hefty verbal javelin to hurl at the celebrants at the victory party: *triumphalist.*

As you say, in current usage (pronounce that "uzij") the word triumph *means a win. In Roman times, however, it referred to the ritual procession to the Capitoline Hill in celebration of the victory.* Triumphalis *meant the decorations and pomp in connection with the parade, an important part of which was putting down the losers who marched in the procession enslaved and in chains.*

Even today, my Collins Anglo-American dictionary does not make the first meaning of triumph a victory, but rather the feeling of happiness and exultation that results from it.

> Arthur J. Morgan
> New York, New York

You misquoted President Kennedy as having said that "success has a thousand fathers." Quick like a bunny, on the same day as that grievous dereliction, I wrote to you to point out that what Kennedy had actually said (on April 21, 1961, after the Bay of Pigs debacle) was: "There's an old saying that victory has a hundred fathers and defeat is an orphan." I further pointed out that this was apparently borrowed (consciously or unconsciously) from a virtually identical remark by Count Galeazzo Ciano, Mussolini's son-in-law and Foreign Minister, in his Diaries *(published 1946): "As always, victory finds a hundred fathers but defeat is an orphan." (Both quotations are in Bartlett.)*

Lo! in today's "O. L.," you quote Kennedy to the effect that "Victory . . . had a thousand fathers." This time, you've got "victory" right, but you show the same giddy intoxication (redundant?) with high numbers. I warn you that if you father a thousand misquotations, I will write you a thousand letters.

> Louis Jay Herman*
> New York, New York

An Article Article

We do not call the Ukraine the Ukraine anymore. As disunionists have long maintained, Ukrainian nationalists think that the article "the" relegated them to regional status, while the name standing alone helped their cause of standing alone and independent.

Not everyone accepts this gracefully. Kevin Donahue of Albany, California, writes, "It's the Bahamas, the Congo, the Gambia, the Ivory Coast, the Netherlands, the Philippines, the Sudan—and the Ukraine, dammit!" He left out the Lebanon and the Hawaiian Islands.

A place should be called what the people there want to call it, is my libertarian view. But Louis Jay Herman (who, with Arthur J. Morgan, has just entered the Lexicographic Irregulars Hall of Fame) writes of the new name for Byelorussia: "It seems *Belarus* is how the folks say it in that neck of the tun-

---

*Mr. Herman, one of my favorite and most frequent correspondents, died on May 13, 1996.

dra. Fine, then let's be consistent and make it *Rossiya* and *Ukraina.* Head due west, and you find yourself in Polska (capital: Warszawa). From there, southward ho, and you're in Ceskoslovensko (capital: Praha)."

He adds this "advice to geographical nomenclaturists who feel an urge to scrap our traditional English renderings in order to humor the locals: You're opening a can of worms. Forget the whole thing."

Which leads to Safire's Law of Place Names: "You Cannot Fish in Global Waters Without Opening a Can of Worms." Or, "When in Roma . . ."

1. You left out one of the most conspicuous of the "the" locales—The Bronx.

2. A parallel to the problem mentioned last in the column—that of the selective use of the local, rather than the English, geographical name—is especially obtrusive here in the Los Angeles area. Local television newsreaders often pronounce Spanish-language geographical designations the "Spanish" way. It would not occur to these same people, of course, to say "Paree" for Paris or "Moskva" for Moscow, thank God—for such a practice if consistently applied would patently result in a perfect hash; but the Latino names, in an admittedly English-language newscast, must still be given their Politically Correct shading.

> Paul Bogrow
> Glendale, California

I say, "Open that can! Give those worms their rightful names!"

For years I have waged a depressingly solitary campaign to have place names written and pronounced as closely to the local version as foreign tongues and alphabets permit. Maybe Mr. Herman has never found himself driving in northern Italy looking in vain for road signs to "Florence"—or, farther north, missing Suomi entirely because he's heading for a country called "Finland." Maybe he, as a local, finds it logical to hear "Nueva York" or "Caroline du Sud," and has never questioned why the city of Lyon has been pluralized by the Anglos.

Your (and my) libertarian view—that a place should be called what the people there want to call it—needs to be imposed relentlessly on mapmakers and geographical publishers everywhere. Start now! Join the campaign! The fact that the French are even worse than we are (they translate not only places but famous people—like Michel-Ange and Le Grec) is no excuse for perpetuating our own linguistic chauvinism.

> Susan M. Seidman
> East Hampton, New York

Banausic Ain't Banal

The Supreme Court struck down New York State's "Son of Sam" law, which would have denied profits to perpetrators from writings about their crimes; as a First Amendment freak, I read with fascination the text of *Simon & Schuster* v. *New York State Crime Victims Board.*

Justice Sandra Day O'Connor, writing the Court's opinion, quoted Henry Hill, a gangster now in the Federal Witness Protection Program and the subject of Nicholas Pileggi's 1985 book, *Wiseguy: Life in a Mafia Family* (as the Court opinion put it, "hereinafter Wiseguy").

Although Mr. Hill admitted pulling off the largest cash robbery in United States history, the 1978 theft of $5.8 million from Lufthansa Airlines, Justice O'Connor wrote, "Most of Hill's crimes were more *banausic.*"

That word was new to me (and to Robert D. Sack of Gibson, Dunn & Crutcher, who called the case to my attention). *Banausic* (pronounced "buh-NAW-sik") is defined in *Merriam-Webster's Ninth New Collegiate* as "concerned with earning a living." It is rooted in the Greek *banausos,* "artisan," a word that then had a pejorative connotation: Working with the hands was considered a grubby thing to do by the types who strolled about in sheets.

On further review, as they say at football games, the adjective *banausic* now has two senses: One is "banal, spiritless, having no character or zip"; the other is "mechanistic, mired in routine, lacking in creativity." The *Oxford English Dictionary*'s supplement notes that the word (which comes after *banana*) is no longer rare, evidence of a pickup in usage, but adds no new definition to its original "merely mechanical."

What did Justice O'Connor mean? I shot her a postcard: "Was your meaning *banal* or *mechanical?* Have you used *banausic* before?"

"I intended it to mean 'mundane,' " she replies. "I have not used the word previously in an opinion, but once in a while it is satisfying to include a word that is not overused."

Mundane has two senses: "prosaic, commonplace, workaday," as the context of Justice O'Connor's opinion suggests, and the less common "materialistic, temporal" as opposed to "spiritual." I would drearily go into the etymology of *mundane,* but that would be (what's the word that follows *banana?*) banausic.

"Banausic" is commonly used in current Greek to denote cruel and barbarous behavior ranging from linguistic boorishness to extreme mental and/or physical brutality toward persons or objects. The term is routinely cited in court in "unfriendly" divorce and child abuse cases.

For the ancient Greeks, artisans of the type that cut and carried the Parthenon marbles were banausoi, *i.e., exhibited banausic behavior by performing (and internalizing the ferocity of) inhumanly hard labor.*

Ironically, if a Greek journalist were to read today Justice O'Connor's opinion as quoted, his conclusion would be the exact opposite from the one she intended—Hill must have killed at least a half-dozen people!

In short, even if we make allowances for drastic changes in meaning when words travel from one language to another, this latest transformation is nothing short of banausic.

> Eleni Mahaira-Odoni
> Belmont, Massachusetts

Hannah Arendt examined the historical grounding of the word in her 1960 essay, "The Crisis in Culture."

> *. . . to be a philistine, a man of banausic spirit, indicated then as today, an exclusively utilitarian mentality, an inability to think and to judge a thing apart from its function or utility.*

> Thomas Fitzgerald
> Ann Arbor, Michigan

Before Country Was Cool

The language of country music, a unique American art form, has not been given the sort of scholarly attention it deserves. The device of ironic interplay is worthy of a heavy doctoral thesis; while someone works on that, many of country's best lines have been compiled by Paula Schwed, a Gannett News Service reporter.

The title of her paperback is *I've Got Tears in My Ears From Lyin' on My Back in My Bed While I Cry Over You,* from a 1949 song by Harold Barlow.

Other favorites include "If the phone doesn't ring, it's me" (Buffett/Jennings/Utley) and "Ever since we said 'I do,' there's so many things you don't" (Slate/Lane), the latter probably based on a 1950's comedy routine. And then Daniel and Ruby Hice wrote, "Worst you ever gave me was the best I ever had," and John Schweers combined metaphors with "You snap your fingers and I'm back in your hands."

This wording is far more linguistically complex than the old June-and-moon rhymings and often raunchier than rap, which I will not illustrate here.

One common denominator is the juxtaposition of contrary ideas: "I miss you already and you're not even gone" (Rainwater/Young). Another is the use of contrasting nouns: "He gives me diamonds, you give me chills" (Goodman/Kennedy). A third, written by Averal Aldridge, is the counterpoint of opposite verbs, and it sums up the way I feel about country music: "I hate the way I love it."

Belittling the Diminutive

If Governor Clinton is elected, will he sign international treaties *Bill*? If Governor Wilson of California is the Republican nominee in 1996, will he insist on *Pete*?

We had this problem of diminutives in the 70's. Jack Rosenthal, editorial page editor of *The New York Times*, noted as a guest columnist in this space that the "strained first-name informality" of politics turned James Earl Carter Jr. to *Jimmy*. To this, Jody Powell, who was President Carter's press secretary, took exception, arguing that Miss Lillian elected to use the diminutive long before her son entered politics.

"The same process made Joseph Lester Jr. into *Jody* before I was old enough to respond to either one," Mr. Powell wrote Mr. Rosenthal, who became editor of this magazine in January 1993. He noted that the motivation was not the desire to present an informal, voter-friendly image but was the presence of a dozen Joseph Powells, all related, within a twenty-five-mile radius of Vienna, Georgia. "All the traditional means of distinguishing one from the other—*Big Joe, Little Joe, Joey, Joe Lee*, etc.—were in use."

The calculated inclination of politicians to adopt the informal diminutive as the formal moniker has been noted in this space before; call out "Robert!" on the floor of the United States Senate and neither Bob Dole nor Bob Packwood will turn around. And if you call Senator Gore "Albert," he will suggest you mean his father; his own name is plain old *Al*. This practice not only directs informality outward, but can have an effect on the person named: "Harriet we changed into *Hatty*, and then into *Tatty*," wrote Charles Dickens in the 1857 novel *Little Dorrit* about a girl in an orphanage, "because as practical people, we thought even a playful name might be a new thing to her, and might have a softening and affectionate kind of effect."

The free and easy use of such shortenings or alterings has been a trend in journalism, too: Meg Greenfield of *The Washington Post* was born Mary Ellen, and her initials—M.E.G.—became her name, *Meg*, and the most recent speechwriter to have turned into political sage, born Margaret Noonan, goes under the byline *Peggy*. And at *The Post*, Elizabeth Graham Weymouth, against the advice of pretentious pundits, hangs in there with *Lally*.

But the use of hypocorisms, terms of endearment derived from baby talk, is on the decline (only my Aunt Dorothy is still called *Toots*), and terms of endearment have come under suspicion ("Call me *Dollboat* or *Sweetie-Pie* one more time, Mr. Snodgrass, and you've got a harassment suit on your hands"). Mr. Powell, now a Washington public relations executive, detects a countertrend in the making:

"Why is it that people who have been known all their lives by one name," he wonders, "suddenly decide, when they hit thirtysomething, to be called something else, which no one who knows them recognizes?" He grants that if the discarded name is a nickname like *Doogie, Possum* or *Pinhead,* a change to a more dignified appellation is understandable, but if it is reasonably acceptable, like *Jack* or *Jimmy* or *Jody,* why bother? "Some might say" (former press secretaries like that arch formulation) "that it goes with the strained and pretentious formality adopted by those who feel the need to marshal all available evidence to prove that they really should be taken seriously."

Jack Rosenthal wrote back: "Given that my given name is Jacob, I gladly accept and acknowledge your point. There surely are many reasons people rename themselves. I did so in childhood because, as an immigrant, I was determined to sound more American (only to discover in later life that many baby boomers now favor 'Jacob' as a name for their sons)."

I've noticed that, too: A new pride in ethnicity has repopularized Benjamin, Jonathan and Sarah among Jewish Americans, Carmen, Dolores and Anita among Spanish-Americans and Andrea and Theodore among Greek-Americans. Could it also be that the reason for a growing preference for the formal name is not mere pretension, but reflects a desire for a new formality?

It is in the nature of pendulums to swing back. Jack Rosenthal recalls, as a young reporter in Oregon, attending a 1960 Nixon-Lodge rally to greet the patrician Senator from Massachusetts, Henry Cabot Lodge, on his first visit. It featured a banner draped across the street, reading, WELCOME TO OREGON, DICK AND HANK. When Lodge arrived, he looked up and asked, "Who's *Hank?*"

What the "father of his country" called Martha, his wife, was "Patsy."

Here's what he wrote to his wife about having been made Commander-in-Chief of the American Army in 1775: "You may believe me, my dear Patsy, that so far from seeking this appointment, I have used every endeavor in my power to avoid it. . . ."

And he ends his letter: "I am, with the most unfeigned regard, my dear Patsy, Your affectionate George Washington."

Arthur J. Morgan
New York, New York

Beyond Chutzpah

Like shooting stars, Russian words streak across the English language. But the *perestroika* and *glasnost* of the 80's are fading fast.

In *It Takes One to Tango,* a superb, anecdote-studded memoir that reveals how five Presidents dickered with the Soviets, General Ed Rowny tells of a day when a Soviet interpreter explored a Jackson Hole, Wyoming, supermarket during arms-reduction talks.

The Russian asked a saleswoman: "Do you know any Russian?" She replied, "No, I know only one word—*vodka.*" He pressed: "Haven't you ever heard of *perestroika*?" She smiled kindly: "No, I'm a teetotaler."

(General Rowny, our best Russian-speaking negotiator, does not supply the etymology of *teetotaler;* it is an 1834 emphasis on the *t* in *total,* for "total abstinence from alcohol"; a modern analogy would be *zeezero* for "zero mistakes.")

Glasnost, "openness," has not fared any better than *perestroika,* "restructuring," a modernization of "reorganizing." It may soon be superseded: In Moscow today, reports Celestine Bohlen of *The New York Times,* "People use the word *naglost,* meaning 'brazen insolence,' to sum up the prevailing atmosphere. *Naglost* applies equally to the Moscow drivers who think nothing of running red lights and to the state factory director who drives a Mercedes with government plates to a meeting where he attacks the government for failing to provide adequate subsidies to his floundering industry."

At last—a word to take synonymists one calibration beyond the Yiddish *chutzpah* for "sheer effrontery."

The "Bizarre" Bazaar

"I think it's shocking and frightening," said Marlin Fitzwater, a man not easily shocked or frightened, "to see that kind of *bizarre* behavior."

The President's press secretary was talking about Ross Perot's investigation of Mr. Bush's sons. Barbara Bush agreed: "I think it's *bizarre . . .* particularly for someone who did come and spend a day with us." Soon afterward, Vice President Dan Quayle joined in the attack on Mr. Perot, whose betrayed supporters Mr. Quayle now seeks to attract, for "nullifying representative democracy with a *bizarre* scheme of government by polls."

If memory serves, Mr. Bush used *bizarre* during the initial stages of Watergate, to describe the activities of the group that broke into Democratic headquarters. However, now he is into weirdsmanship: "This has been a tough, *weird* political year at home," he said, and on another occasion refused to go on "those *weird* little talk shows," as his rivals were doing.

In Spanish, *bizarro* has meant "brave," sometimes "handsome," perhaps an adaptation of the Basque word for "beard"; in Italian, *bizarro* became a dialect word for "angry"; in French, *bizarre* began as "brave, soldierly" and then

took on the senses of "odd; fantastic" that carried over into English. Its first use in our language dates back to 1648, as Edward Herbert, a British philosopher, wrote, "Her attire seemed as bizare as her person." Horticulturists use the adjective to describe variegated flowers, like striped tulips. It has no connection to *bazaar,* which comes from a Persian word for "market."

Weird has a wonderful history; it is a word that began in power and has come, like many politicians, on hard times. The noun in Old English, as found in *Beowulf,* meant "fate, predetermination"; the word evoked the power of destiny, and Allan Ramsay, a Scottish poet, wrote in 1718, "It's a wise wife that kens her weird." This usage developed into the sense of the supernatural: "magic, enchantment," picking up a connotation of evil, as a punishment inflicted by way of retribution.

As an adjective, *weird* took the supernatural quality of the noun, influenced by the three witches called "the weird sisters" in Shakespeare's *Macbeth.* (The *First Folio* uses the spellings *weyard* and *weyward,* probably influenced by *wayward.*) The modifier was shaped by poets like Shelley ("mutable as shapes in the weird clouds") and Keats ("steep her hair in weird syrops, that would keep her loveliness invisible") into the sense of "extraordinary, fantastic"; this meaning then broke down to the more everyday "unusual, odd." Today, the word has at least two senses: From the supernatural, with its ominous overtones, comes "eerie, ghostly, spooky, unearthly," and from its milder extension, "outlandish, peculiar, aberrant, oddball."

In contrast to the *bizarre, weird, strange* behavior of his opponents, Mr. Bush offers not nostrums but normalcy—"not experiment but equipoise," as Warren G. Harding liked to alliterate—stressing steadiness and stability while professing to be an agent of nonradical change.

Although the President has also used the synonym *strange*—"it's *strange* out there"—he has not yet turned to *far out* and *off the wall,* which are modern slangy, and has stayed far from *kinky,* with its experimental-sexual connotation, and *queer,* now a self-mocking term taken up by militant homosexuals. *Wacky* and *crazy* are too blunt and carry no ominous connotation, and *zany*—applied mainly to comedians—conveys a likable, whimsical feeling, hardly Mr. Bush's intention. *Grotesque* is too highfalutin and *eccentric* too bookish, recalling the definition, "An *eccentric* is a nut with a million dollars."

The Democratic nominee, Bill Clinton, has not yet joined Mr. Bush in systematically using the synonymy of strangeness. His preference in derogation is noticeably milder, bemused but not disrespectful, not yet with a note of alarm; when I called him for a reaction to a Perot notion, he called it "kinda *goofy.*"

Goofy, which first appeared in *Collier's* magazine in 1921 and was later popularized by the Walt Disney cartoon character, may have been based on the African *goofer,* a "witch doctor" who cast a spell; the *Oxford English Dictionary* notes that *goofer dust* is a powder used in such conjurations. Weird.

On the etymology of "bizarre"—is there a possibility that the Edward Herbert line has been misinterpreted? Perhaps rather than reading "Her attire seemed as bizare [odd] as her person" it should be read: "Her attire seemed as [soldierly] as her person"?

Some 35 years ago I came across mention of Richard Randolph (a cousin of

John Randolph of Roanoke and related somehow to Thomas Jefferson) and his Virginia plantation called "Bizarre." It seemed an odd, if not bizarre, name for the place one lived, and being in the middle of working on a project at the New York Public Library anyway, I began to consult their extensive collection of 18th-century dictionaries. All of them, in English and Spanish, listed the definition as being "brave" and "handsome," a much more likely name for a plantation. My curiosity aroused, I kept on reading dictionaries. It was not until the 19th-century editions that the meaning shifted to its current connotation of oddity, incongruity and sensational contrast.

I turned to reading about Mr. Randolph. During the latter part of the 18th century he lived on "Bizarre" plantation with his wife, Judith, her sister Anne Cary, aka Nancy, a few other kin and the requisite number of slaves. Nancy became pregnant and delivered a baby in the middle of the night. The body of the infant was discovered shortly afterward and Ms. Nancy and her brother-in-law Richard, named as the father of the child, were brought to trial for murder. Their defense attorneys were no less than Patrick Henry and John Marshall. Amid complaints about the wealthy and powerful getting a different brand of justice, the case was dismissed.

As might be expected there were headlines throughout Virginia (if not the rest of the colonies) about "The Bizarre Murder Case." I became convinced that this was what brought about the change in definition of the word "bizarre." And the next edition of Webster's a decade or two later had the change in definition to its current one.

Incidentally, after years of ostracism in Virginia, Ms. Nancy went north and eventually married Gouverneur Morris, the author of the Preamble of the Constitution. He was a man of the world, having lost his leg under a carriage while being chased by an irate husband in France. He knew her story and loved her anyway. Sic transit ingloria.

Brenda Brody
Westport, Connecticut

There is a Hebrew word, zar, which literally means "something strange" or "a stranger." It is a fairly common biblical word and it would not seem to me to be very far from the word bizarre, which in common English usage also means strange.

Walter B. Weitzner, M.D.
Brooklyn, New York

The Bloopie Awards

Now for the moment all Madison Avenue has been waiting for. The copy-writers are lined up, nervously tittering and editing among themselves; the nominations have been pouring in from irate consumers; the judges have called in their judgment calls. We're ready for the coveted 1992 Bloopie Awards.

Never has the competition for the Most Egregiously Misplaced Modifier Bloopie been hotter. Among the candidates:

Lufthansa: "In both classes, you'll find people committed to serving you with an unsurpassed European standard of elegance." The subject is *you*, and you cannot be in two classes at once. The modifier *in both classes* is intended to modify *people*, and the line should read, "You'll find people in both classes committed to serving you" et cetera, which would bring the copy up to an American standard of grammar.

Stayfree Ultra Plus pads for women: "So incredibly thin, you'll barely know it's there!" I suppose "Ultra Plus" is intentionally redundant, perhaps even a sophisticated play on *ne plus ultra,* of which there is nothing greater. But *you* is the subject, and by misplacing the modifier, the pad maker suggests that the reader is "so incredibly thin." (You can't be too rich or too thin or too correct; on second thought, you can.) That copy could be amended to include the hap-pily pudgy by putting an *It's* at the start, making the pad, not the person, so desirably slim.

Kellogg's Special K: "This diet isn't just for any body." The writer was so entranced with the wordplay on *body*—"any *body*," get it?—that he or she fell off the scale on the placement of *just.* "This diet isn't just" could suggest that the regimen is unfair, as so many are; the ambiguity may be dispatched with "This diet isn't for just any body." (Mazda's writers also have the slipping *just:* "It just feels right" could be read to imply "But it doesn't work right"; better change that to "It feels just right," not exactly the same meaning, but copy-writing isn't for just any auto body.)

Lands' End, the Direct Merchants, on their bathing attire: "We can fit you in a swimsuit that fits and flatters—right over the phone!" The swimsuit flat-ters over the phone? (I had a swimsuit like that once; the minute I put it on, it stopped fitting and flattering and fell silent, sneering.) Better to swing the end of the sentence to the front, where the pronoun to be modified can be found: "Right over the phone, we can fit you" et cetera.

And here's a juicy one from Minute Maid: "Help today's U.S. Olympic Hopefuls become tomorrow's Olympic Champions by purchasing Minute Maid Quality Products." Athletes do not become tomorrow's champs by pur-chasing anything; swing the end around to the beginning and attach it to a *you:* "By purchasing . . . you can help" et cetera.

The winner in this category? The envelope, please: It's Honda Motor Cars, with its wildly swerving claim, "While pleasing to your eye, the air passing over and around the body hardly notices it." Air is not "pleasing to your eye"; the car's *body* should come immediately after the modifying phrase. Thus: "While pleasing to your eye, the body is hardly noticed by the air passing over and around it." That formulation would not make a whole lot of sense, either, but at least the modifier would be attached to the right noun.

In a related category, Misused Modifiers, first runner-up is W. R. Grace & Company: "Some of our businesses don't fit us any more." *Any more,* separated into two words, should be used as an adjective, as in "I don't want to buy any more airlines." But *anymore,* when used as an adverb modifying a verb like *fit,* should be a single word: "don't fit us anymore."

The coveted Bloopie, however, goes to Dimetapp Cough Elixir for its hacking "Works as good as it tastes." You can say "tastes as good as it looks," because the adjective *good* is used with the linking verbs *taste* and *look,* but you cannot say "works as good" when *works as well* is the meaning. The copywriter made this error consciously, of course, to play back off *tastes good,* but it helps subvert the language of cold sufferers, who have enough trouble making themselves understood with a code in the node.

This year's Parallel Structure Bloopie, coveted like thy neighbor's wife, was closely fought over. The Harvard Business School asks, "What's innovative, time-tested, diverse, intense, global, and develops leaders?" Not the English department at Harvard, evidently: The last item does not lie flat like the rest. Because the parallel construction *leadership-developing* is awkward, an innovative leader racing around the world might try a separate sentence.

But not three sentences. (No sentence fragments.) Spirit Soap advertises: "It's like three soaps in one. Cleans. Moisturizes. Deodorant Protection." That last item clanks. I would change it to "Keeps you from smelling bad," but that sort of straight talk loses clients. Perhaps "Provides Deodorant Protection" would be more acceptable; it's at least parallel.

The Parallel envelope, please. The winner is Dr. Antonia C. Novello, Surgeon General of the United States, for her widely printed warning: "Smoking Causes Lung Cancer, Heart Disease, Emphysema, and May Complicate Pregnancy." The parallel object "Pregnancy Complications" would adopt the strong verb *cause* rather than the tentative *may complicate,* so she should take a deep drag and give her warning another shot. Either make sure that each object has a verb or add *and* before *emphysema* to cure the problem.

The Excess Comma Bloopie is shared by two airlines competing for the comma customers. USAir: "And, 2,000 miles for new members. . . ." American Airlines: "And, you will also continue to earn full mileage credit. . . ." Plus, *also* is redundant.

Finally, when it comes to this year's Pronoun Bloopie, *The New York Times Magazine* dominates the field. An ad for a wedding supplement advises "who to invite from the office"; *whom* is right, but *who/whom* is not my strong suit, either. Here's the bigger Bloopie: "Regular readers of *The New York Times Magazine* (like yourself) are always looking for objects to enhance their homes." The reflexive pronoun *yourself* should be used to reflect the same subject as object (I'm outdoing myself on this). In this case, all you need is *you:* "Regular readers (like you)." Purists would demand *such as you,* but not me. (They'd also insist on *not I,* which is better than *not myself,* but not as good as *not me.*)

I felt you were a trifle hard on the Harvard Business School. Admittedly, the line quoted ("What's innovative, time-tested, diverse, intense, global, and develops leaders?") is hardly brilliant, but to me it doesn't look like Bloopie-level egregiousness. Indeed, what you consider "awkwardness" might even be defensible, in this case and others. In defense of "faulty" parallelism, let me quote Mary P. Hiatt, from her fascinating book Artful Balance—The Parallel Structures of Style *(Teacher's College Press, New Humanistic Research Series, 1975):*

> *. . . insofar as we regard any departure from symmetry as some sort of violation of desirable order, we tend to consider any departure from strict parallelism as "faulty" parallelism. We should be careful about using the pejorative, however. We do not adversely criticize a rock for being "lopsided." We do not say of Medea that she should be sensible and accept her lot; rather, we are fascinated by her very excesses. We do not condemn John Steinbeck for "faulty" parallelism when he writes, "Here was himself, young, good-looking, snappy dresser, and making dough." (John Steinbeck,* Sweet Thursday, *p. 156.) . . . An obsession with order can be comfortable and totally stultifying. It is the little disorders that will attract attention, whether they are deliberately conceived or not.*

> *Tom Storer*
> *Paris, France*

Blowout!

The one-word headline of New York *Newsday* read: BLOWOUT!

To some, this meant *landslide,* which had replaced *avalanche* in political parlance for "overwhelming election victory." To political lexicographers, it meant that an old word had a new meaning.

Blowout began in the language as a synonym for *quarrel,* and was used alongside *ruction* and *ruckus.* When automobiles came along at the turn of the twentieth century, it was a depiction of the bursting of a pneumatic tire. (Electricians, heart specialists and oil-well drillers: Do not send angry post-cards about the suppression of arcs, aneurysms and the uprush of fluids; we're dealing here with the general lingo.)

In this generation, the most common slang meaning of *blowout* was "rau-cous party, swinging shindig"; in the new *American Heritage Dictionary,* the citation is from *Vanity Fair:* "Lunch was a billion-calorie blowout beside the pool."

Meanwhile, the expression *to blow away* took root, meaning "to overpower, to crush all resistance"; extending the metaphor, a music lover could be "blown away" by the latest hip-hop.

Somehow, these two locutions intersected. The political meaning of *blowout* is now "landslide"; in a political blowout, the opponent is blown away. (Strictly speaking, the noun should be *blowaway,* but nobody speaks slang strictly.)

Was the 1992 result a *blowout?* No; although no objective standard exists, especially in a three-way division, a difference of ten points in the popular-vote percentages would be indisputably a blowout; in the Electoral College, the number 400 might be a blowout point. Many newspapers went for *decisive* as the defining adjective for the Clinton victory; those who went for *landslide* and *blowout* added that they meant in the Electoral College. (At NBC, an assistant producer of *Today,* Chris Brown, reminded those on the air that *electoral* was pronounced "e-LEC-ter-ul," not the voguish "e-lec-TOR-al.")

Use all current meanings in a sentence: On the way to the blowout after the blowout, the victors' motorcade had a blowout.

The expression "blowout" may have come to politics by way of sports, where it is commonly used to mean a game with a lopsided score.

Michael Cargal
La Mesa, California

Born to Set It Right

"I'm not agonizing; I'm not delaying," Mario Cuomo told Sam Donaldson of ABC, as the New York Governor wrestled with the decision to run for President. "When you run out of time, then you make the decision. I'm not yet out of time."

"Hamlet act real old," gibed *Newsweek*'s Conventional Wisdom Watch. Leslie H. Gelb of *The New York Times* also scored a hit, a very palpable hit, in a headline alluding to Hamlet's most famous line: "To Cuomo or Not to Cuomo."

In the gross and scope of my own political harangues, I too have compared the way the native hue of Governor Cuomo's resolution has been sicklied o'er with the pale cast of thought. In my mind's eye, I saw this politician in an inky cloak, the skull of poor Yorick in hand, using a rhapsody of words to make infinite jests about the decision-making process, and I judged him *Hamlet-like.*

Was this fair? Forget fairness to the Governor, whose public cudgeling of his brain was a matter for political commentary; in linguistic affairs, as we equate the compound comparative *Hamlet-like* with indecision, usually synonymous with "pigeon-livered," we must consider fairness to Shakespeare's most famous character.

"You do Mario Cuomo too much honor and Hamlet too little," writes Jacques Barzun, a member of my Board of Octogenarian Mentors, "when you compare the governor to the prince. If you will reread the play, I think you will see how wrong the common opinion is about Hamlet's 'vacillation.' "

This master of the house of intellect holds that (1) Hamlet, in the midst of a palace intrigue, is being actively plotted against, and knows he would face his father's fatal fate if he were to act imprudently, and (2) because he is an educated, thinking, modern man, he does not accept his father's ghost's accusatory words without verification.

"It is a new awareness of self and moral choice that keeps Hamlet from acting like a headstrong brute," Professor Barzun argues. "The play includes the impetuous, thoughtless Laertes precisely to mark the contrast. What would we think of Hamlet if he did *not* weigh truth, revenge and killing, but promptly dispatched king, queen and royal clique, dagger first and questions afterward?"

We would reject such sweaty haste, as Governor Cuomo surely did and does, as unworthy of a serious person. Why, then, do so many of us think of Hamlet as afflicted with some craven scruple, an Elizabethan wimp?

"He tells us his thoughts, and that is the reason people have stereotyped him as a vacillator. Skip the soliloquies and see how steadily and bravely he acts," Professor Barzun concludes. (John Mitchell, as Attorney General, used to say, "Watch what we do, not what we say," a sinister extension of "Deeds, not words"; in an action-loving world, enterprises of great moment may be pithed or pitched away by thinking about them aloud.)

At least one language authority sees the word *Hamlet-like,* then, as "self-expository," with no negative connotation of indecisiveness; however, this intellectual interpretation is nose-wrinkling caviar to the general public, which sees a tide in the affairs of men leading on to fortune and prefers a decisive Caesar to a thoughtful Hamlet.

Nobody is going to cast Arnold Schwarzenegger in a movie titled *The Ambivalator.* That is why it is not such a hot idea for a politician to look at the mess in Washington and say, "O cursed spite, that ever I was born to set it right!"

When serving as a judge on the Iran-U.S. Claims Tribunal, I looked for a word to describe the pathology of the inability to decide. I desired to express my concern for delays.

The enclosed was the result: "dyscrinia (inability to make a decision), teleophobia (fear of making definite plans), abulia (lack of will power to make a decision), decidophobia (fear of making a decision), and social abulia (inability to select a course of action)." Are there any other appropriate words?

> Richard M. Mosk
> Los Angeles, California

It is good to know through your flattering column that you found enough merit in my view of Hamlet to consider it seriously. You are the third person to do so in half a century. The first was a Boston architect, now deceased, and the second, John Silber, a friend. Octogenerally speaking, people to whom I impart the good news say: "Yes, of course, you're right"; and at the first opportunity relapse into: "vacillating like Hamlet." This shows the need for a conventional figure to reinforce the puny adjective and establish oneself as a firm decision-maker.

Jacques [Barzun]
New York, New York

Britishisms Lying Doggo

"Is *doggo* to become the new sleeping dog of punditry?" asks Duncan Morrow of Springfield, Virginia. Readers who closely follow the usage of the chin-pulling set know that Britishisms and Southernisms abound; in this case, two syndicated columnists with Southern roots were caught using a Britishism.

Edwin Yoder Jr. speculated that Saddam Hussein's military strategy was to dig in, "protecting his military assets and lying *doggo* while U.S.-allied air power breaks over him."

James J. Kilpatrick dealt with those who would remove religious books from public-school libraries: "So far as the record discloses, no child ever even looked at the potentially dangerous books. The books just sat there on the shelf, *doggo,* on the outside possibility that someday some 11-year-old might want to learn a little bit."

That British slang term means "in concealment"; comparable American slang is "in the weeds" or "playing possum." John Algeo of the University of Georgia (who with his wife, Adele Algeo, conducts the "Among the New Words" column in *American Speech* magazine), informs me: "It is probably from *dog* plus the suffix -*o,* which is voguishly used in British slang, for example in *boyo* and hence *yobo.*" (*Yobo,* pronounced and often spelled *yobbo,* is *boy* spelled backward with an *o* attached.) "The rationale would then be 'to lie quiet, like a dog in hiding.' "

The eminent neologistician has citation files from Professor Allen Walker Read including this World War I American entry: " 'Sometimes the man isn't dead, but a perfectly live Boche patrol lying *doggo.*' [R. D. Holmes, 'Yankee in Trenches' (1918), page 80] [with a page 210 glossary entry:] Doggo—Still. Quiet. East Indian derivation." (Now, that's how to do a citation: Oll Korrect. It's a pleasure to deal with old pros.) Professor Algeo guesses that the expression "may have been an Irishism that spread via the British Army in India." Perhaps that's because the first citation is from Rudyard Kipling in 1893.

Because most of my in-laws are Brits, I have been using *loo* as a synonym for "john, can, little boys' room, facilities." This makes me feel affected but gets me the necessary directions in London. The etymology is usually listed as "obscure," but I received this fanciful leap from John L. Lowden of Wilmington, North Carolina: "Pay toilets in England required the deposit of two half-pennies, called *ha'pennies* (rhymes with *tape knees*) before one could enter a stall. The door's handle and the two side-by-side drop slots looked like this: LOO." Before spending a penny on that speculation, I ran *loo* past Mr. Algeo, who called it the product of an "incontinent imagination." He thinks the most probable origin is from the French word, *lieu,* "place"; the *lieux d'aisances* are translated as "places of convenience," perhaps the source of our "public convenience," or non-pay toilet.

Professors Algeo and Read wanted me to know, by the way, that I had been "oddly idiosyncratic in your recent statement that *Britishism* is 'preferred' to *Briticism.*" This is a gentle way of saying, "Where does a pop grammarian come off representing his personal foibles as the preference of most users?"

Their point is keen; the passive *preferred* should be used only to mean "this is what most educated users use," thereby to denote an objective report or description of the world as it is. The active "I prefer" is something else, meaning "this is what I use, after having given the matter more thought than most people have time for or interest in, and you might want to use it, too, if you have any taste or trust mine." That's what I meant, and should have used "I prefer" forthrightly and prescriptively, even if it causes linguistic heavy hitters to smile and say, "Listen to the popgramm try to sell the usage he prefers."

Granted, *Briticism* is used in the United States on the analogy of *Gallicism,* but the *-icism* ending is usually of words that end in *-ic,* like *Gallic,* or *critic,* with the final *c* being pronounced as an *s* before the *-ism.* But with words that end with *-ish,* like *British* or *Amish* or *Yiddish,* it seems to me more natural and communicative to say *Britishism, Amishism, Yiddishism.* (John Algeo himself uses *Irishism,* not *Iricism.*)

That's what's great about the usage dodge; not only can a cat look at a king, but a king can look back at a cat. "Preferred" may be preferable to a majority, but "I prefer"—accompanied by logic and a catchy cartoon in a literate publication—may affect the educated majority's judgment. In the weeds of slang and wetlands of usage, the possibility of improvement lies doggo.

The notion that the phrase "playing possum" is an American equivalent to "in concealment" is the product of an incontinent imagination. "Playing possum" has nothing to do with concealment; it has to do with mitigating the results of the failure to conceal. The possum, when discovered by an attacker, goes into a state mimicking death which causes the predator to lose interest in him. He is definitely not *lying* doggo.

John P. Boylan
Los Angeles, California

One of my cockney friends swears this is how the derivation of "loo" came about. In Europe and elsewhere, that facility is often referred to as a "water closet." In a variation of rhyming slang, when asked where he was heading, a cockney would reply: "To meet my Waterloo." In due course, that expression became, simply, loo. Sounds reasonable to me.

> Fredric C. Hamburg
> Bethesda, Maryland

As an expat Brit who has not entirely forgotten his early grounding in the language, I remember that "loo" was said to be derived from the French "l'eau," as in the expression, "Gardez l'eau" (meaning, look out for the water). This was a precautionary shout given from the upper windows of a house, before voiding the night's contents of the commode into the street gutter below.

> Michael T. Wells
> Greenwich, Connecticut

The Random House Dictionary of the English Language, Unabridged Edition, *very pertinently notes that this cry formerly used in Scotland to warn pedestrians when slops were about to be thrown from an upstairs window is derived from the French for* gare *(de)* l'eau—*beware of the water.*

> Martin M. Bruce
> Larchmont, New York

Dear Bill,
   Regarding your research on "loo," I was amazed that no one gave the source I heard in England: that the first flush toilet for the public was in Waterloo Station, ergo "loo."
   One of the euphemisms for going to the W.C. in use in England in the fifties was "spend a penny," so I was amused by your "before spending a penny on that speculation."

> José [Ferrer]*
> New York, New York

*José Ferrer died on January 26, 1992.

I had always supposed that with a mixture of delicacy and whimsy, the descent was from water closet *to* Waterloo *to* loo. *No evidence, but seems plausible, doesn't it?*

> Marshall D. Shulman
> Sherman, Connecticut

Let "lying doggo"s sleep!

> Steven Gruntfest
> Teaneck, New Jersey

Bubble, Bubble, Toil and Transition

Out with the old! In with the new! That's the message we're getting from the American language about the presidential succession.

What was the old word used to denote that awkward eleven-week period between Election Day and Inauguration Day—when the person serving as President is not re-elected?

Interregnum was the grand old word. It signified the interval between the reigns of kings when a country had no sovereign. It's true that *interregnum* didn't quite fit American government: We don't have a king, or in Latin, *rex,* and the old President does not leave office until a few minutes before the new one takes the inaugural oath. But most people were aware that, in the American context, it meant "the period between presidencies."

Forget it. The new word is *transition.* Not strictly new—Clark Clifford was said to have been in charge of the transition between the Eisenhower and Kennedy administrations—but never before given such official status. I'm not fighting the change; rooted in the Latin for "going over," *transition* is perfectly respectable, but someone should put in a moment's silent respect for *interregnum,* which after the Carter defeat was briefly known as the "interreaganum."

That's not the only noticeable linguistic change in Washington. Back in the Kennedy years, we had a *foe:* "Let the word go forth," the young President said at his inaugural, "to friend and foe alike." Those were the days when it was O.K. to acknowledge an *enemy;* indeed, Lyndon Johnson minced no words about the characterization of those ranged against the free world. Nixon speechwriters, eschewing confrontation, preferred the word *adversary,* except when North Vietnamese intransigence caused the President to write in the harsh word *enemy.*

In his first formal statement as President-elect, Bill Clinton evoked the

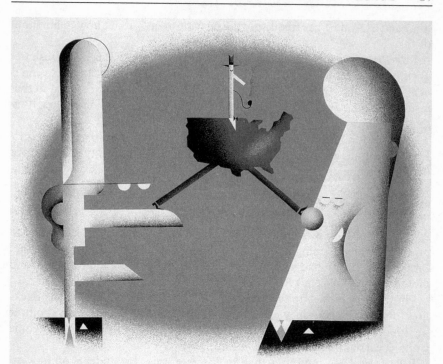

memory of John F. Kennedy and brought back the indeterminate *foe:* "I urge America's friends and foes alike to recognize, as I do, that America has only one President at a time." Covering all bases, as he seems eager to do, Governor Clinton followed up with the softer word: "The greatest mistake any *adversary* could make would be to doubt America's resolve during this period of transition." (No interregnum.)

Now to the most striking vocabulary change of all. Remember the *cocoon,* that protective coating of Secret Service agents, granite-faced White House police, surrounding sycophants, chauffeurs who never stop for red lights, and the aura of unapproachable power that separates the Man from the people who chose him?

Forget *cocoon,* unless you're collecting butterflies. The sometimes invisible but always palpable barrier is now called the *bubble.* "Will we see you in the streets of Washington a lot jogging?" a reporter asked the President-elect at his first post-election news conference, adding: "Are you frustrated by the *bubble?*" Mr. Clinton was not puzzled at the usage; he knew only too well what the *bubble* meant, and said he hoped to "maintain some greater level of ongoing personal contact with folks than is typically the case."

A few days before, Adam Nagourney in *USA Today* cited an earlier use of the word by the President-elect. "As long ago as August, Clinton was complaining about the barriers between a President and the public—he called it 'the *bubble*.' And he has frequently talked with friends about how to burst out of that."

Ross Perot was fond of the metaphor, too, applying it to President Bush frequently. "Everybody out there except the White House knows the recession is here," he told the lively Larry King in late October, "and if you lived in that insulated *bubble* they've created for the President, you wouldn't know it either."

The transition from *cocoon* to *bubble* was noted in the *Los Angeles Times* by Kenneth Turan, its film critic, who described an air of unreality hanging over the Bush campaign due "in considerable part to the bubble-like, enviably efficient security cocoon the President must travel in to ensure his physical safety."

I suspect, though I have no citation handy to prove it, that the recent use of *bubble* in this sense was rooted in the name for the transparent shield used to protect Presidents riding in open cars; it was widely noted, for example, that President Kennedy had scorned the available plastic bubble before his fatal motorcade in Dallas in 1963.

The military picked up the figure of speech. "The trick is to spot the Backfires [bombers] before they get within missile shooting range," a naval officer was quoted as saying in *Business Week* in 1982, "and force them to come within a carrier fleet's protective '*bubble*.' "

It has also been used in a slightly different sense by students of Edward Hall's studies in proxemics, more generally called "personal space." This is defined as "the zone around an individual into which other persons may not trespass." This self-imposed zone, Charles J. Holahan writes in *Environmental Psychology,* "has been compared to a *bubble* surrounding the individual, creating an invisible boundary between the person and potential intruders." The person blowing the bubble of personal space around himself can vary its scope, depending on his hermithood or the relationship he has with different friends and family.

The most profound definition of its current political sense was offered by a *Washington Post* reporter, David Maraniss, on the last day of the 1992 campaign. "The *bubble* is what surrounds the traveling road show of any Presidential campaign," he wrote. "It includes the candidate, the staff, the press, the plane, the bus and all the electronic gear of the 20th-century hustle . . . yet it is not so much a tangible phenomenon as a metaphysical one, a way of looking at things, at once cynical and cosy . . . where you find both the real story and yet an utterly false one, a speed-blurred picture of a very large country."

The words, they are a-changin', and the interregnum isn't even over yet. (I know it's a transition, but the old ways die hard.)

In the Kennedy years we had a foe, *but JFK did not call him an* enemy. *In his inaugural address he substituted the word* adversary *for* enemy, *at the suggestion of Walter Lippmann, who had been shown an early draft of the speech. And* adversary *it remained from then on. So Nixon was following JFK usage, as is Clinton. LBJ, as usual, made his own rules.*

Ronald Steel
Washington, D. C

The statement "Forget cocoon, *unless you're collecting butterflies," appears in your column.*
In general, it is only moths, not butterflies, that spin cocoons.

David D. Dickey
Knoxville, Tennessee

I recognize you as a perfectionist, and take the liberty of pointing out that although "Cocoon is for butterflies" is almost okay, cocoons are popularly and correctly associated with moths.
Many winged insects, in the last larval stage before their final moulting (ecdysis), spin cocoons for the pupal period. The pupa for the True Butterfly is known as a chrysalis, and a cocoonlike but rudimentary silken larval nest is formed by only a few species of True Butterflies, notably the far northern Alpines (genus Erebia).
As you know, butterflies and moths are different groups within the insect order Lepidoptera *(lepis-*scale, *and* pteron-*wing). The moths are, generally, nocturnal, while the True Butterflies (*Papilionoidea) *and the Skippers (*Hesperioidea) *cavort, generally, in daytime.*
After True Butterflies do it, in daytime, the female lays eggs, which yield larvae (caterpillars), which then pupate into a chrysalis that is not surrounded by a cocoon.

Douglas Sutherland Dodge
Guilford, Connecticut

The Man in the Big White Jail

Objection has been taken about the origin of the metaphoric place now occupied by our new President: *to be in the bubble.*

Comes now Philippa Brophy, literary agent: "My client, Richard Ben Cramer, author of *What It Takes: The Way to the White House* (Random House, 1992), is the journalist who coined the phrase *in the bubble,* not the two reporters you mentioned. In fact, both these guys called Cramer yesterday to point out the error."

Sure enough, here it is in the book, predating my citations, describing the way George Bush had been cosseted and cocooned in comfort by four hundred people devoted to his security, who made it possible for him to "leave his office, board an airplane, travel halfway across the nation, land in another city, travel overland 30 miles to a ball park and never see one person who was not a friend or someone whose sole purpose it was to serve or protect him. This is living *in the bubble.*"

That's where William Jefferson Clinton is living today, whether he likes it or not. The incarcerated feeling is not new: Harry Truman once pointed to the White House and said, "There is the big white jail." But *the bubble* is new; I speculated that its origin may be the protective plastic bubble over an open-top car in which the President sometimes rides during motorcades.

A half-dozen Lexicographic Irregulars pointed to a different origin: "Emotional isolation was the major theme," Mark S. Jackson of Rochester writes, "of a made-for-television movie, *The Boy in the Plastic Bubble,* which aired in 1976." Martin Ostrow of New York also remembered the case on which that John Travolta movie was based: "That young child whose immune system was so delicate that he spent his entire youth in a plastic room or what doctors and the press referred to as a 'plastic bubble.' " (David, the boy from Texas whose life inspired the film, died in 1984 at the age of twelve.)

That image was the source of this passage in *What I Saw at the Revolution,* the 1990 best-seller about the Reagan Administration by Peggy Noonan. This evocative speechwriter (who later wrote George Bush's first convention acceptance speech, the most memorable time that insulated figure broke through to a wide audience) was trying to get some anecdote from Ronald Reagan to make a speech more personal:

"Do you ever feel like the boy in the bubble?" Ms Noonan asked.

"Who was that?" Mr. Reagan replied.

"The boy who had no immune system," said his speechwriter, "so he had to live in a plastic bubble where he could see everyone and they could see him, but there was something between him and the people, the plastic. He couldn't touch them."

"Well, no," Mr. Reagan said.

Then he thought it over: "No, but there are times when you stand upstairs and look out at Pennsylvania Avenue and see the people there walking by.

And if I wanted to run out and get a newspaper or magazine, or just to walk down to the park and back . . . you miss that, of course."

His speechwriter observed, "What I think I perceive is not a feeling of estrangement but a wistfulness about connection."

Now to political etymology: The source of this metaphor of presidential isolation appears to be the fictional story (based on true circumstances) of the boy in the TV movie, picked up and used in Ms Noonan's memoir, and popularized in the coverage of political campaigns by Mr. Cramer.

A variant is *on the bubble,* a sports term: "College basketball prognosticators," writes Robert Hochschild of Brookline, Massachusetts, "have for several years used the phrase *on the bubble* to describe teams that are in a gray area in terms of ability—talented, but not necessarily deserving of a berth in a tournament. . . . I believe I once heard Peter Jennings describe several candidates as being *on the bubble* of legitimacy in voters' minds."

Everyone in Indiana knows that "on the bubble" refers to the precarious position of the qualifier for the last place in the field of 33 cars in the Indianapolis 500 auto race. The qualifying period ends at 6:00 P.M. on the Saturday prior to the race. A driver who has qualified for the 33rd place at, say, 5:00 P.M., but whose time is likely to be beaten by a later qualifier, is said to be "on the bubble."

Aruid Sponberg
Department of English
Valparaiso University
Valparaiso, Indiana

Buffalo Bill Not Defunct

"I'm not going to be *buffaloed* into appointing independent counsels," declared Attorney General William P. Barr, derided as the Cover-Up General by the Iraqgate implacables, "by political clamor and by the views of editorial writers."

In the same week, the colorful Americanism found its way into a *Newsweek* subhead: "Don't get *buffaloed*" was its advice to President-elect Bill Clinton, who had made a concession to the Senate majority leader, George Mitchell. (That was followed by "He'd better wise up or he'll get *steamrolled* again." The more familiar slang term is *steamrollered;* perhaps the writer wanted to play on being "rolled," taken advantage of, as well as being flattened by being run over by a steamroller.)

The meaning of *to be buffaloed* is "to be overawed, intimidated or confused." Do not confuse it with *bulldozed,* which means "pushed aside roughly" and is synonymous with *steamrollered.* The origin of *buffaloed* may be in "to be cowed," or frightened into submission; *buffalo* has long been used for "a cow without horns" as well as for the bison.

The *Dictionary of American Regional English* cites an 1896 *Dialect Notes* entry, "Buffaloo: to confuse, 'rattle.' " In 1929, *American Speech* reported, "When a cow becomes confused it is *'buffaloed.'* "

That is no longer the common usage, nor is the verb used in the active voice. In current use, *to be buffaloed* is to be daunted, spooked, unnerved. It is nice to see this fine old bit of folklore on the rise in Washington, where the skies are no longer cloudy all day.

But Who Won on Language?

After the first 1992 presidential debate, not a single *spinmeister* worked the pundit crowd on the subject of the best use of language. Thus, wholly uninfluenced, and with the all-unimportant English teacher vote at stake, I will undertake the linguistic (in contrast to the political) analysis.

1. *Split Infinitives.* Only the cultural elite goes out of its way to avoid inserting an adverb between the leaves of an infinitive. The people—ultimate arbiters of usage—happily split away, and all three candidates were willing crassly to pander to this inclination.

Bush: *"to significantly cut* defense spending." Clinton: *"to fully fund* the act named for that wonderful boy Ryan White." Perot: *"to clearly understand* the backgrounds of each person." (This practice leaves open the question: Do people who split their infinitives split their tickets as well?)

2. *The Offing of "On."* This preposition is becoming an endangered species. Mr. Bush spoke of "N.I.H. working the problem" of AIDS, rather than working *on* the problem; Mr. Perot had earlier eschewed the preposition with "How does this impact our children?"

Mr. Clinton ducked the *on* issue, but had his own preposition trouble: In his "work with them instead of manipulate them," he violated an idiom. *Instead of,* according to my associate, Jeffrey McQuain, aiding me in this debatese watch, takes a gerund—"manipulating," in this case—as its object, and not a verb like "manipulate."

However, the general Clinton usage showed careful rehearsal: *"whom* I've seen" took my breath away, as did "100,000 or slightly *fewer* [not *less*] troops." Not perfect yet: *"over* 150,000" AIDS deaths should have been *more than,* used with all figures except ages.

3. *Word Choice.* Perot erred on "historical event," which should be *historic;*

any past event is *historical,* but only the most memorable ones are *historic.*

Clinton talked of family values "transmuted from the elders to the children"; he may have meant "changed for the better," or "transformed, converted," but his context suggests he meant *transmitted.*

Bush used the unnecessary "the fact that" and put forward the inelegant "was when" but chose his other words with care.

4. *Alliteration.* Clinton trotted out "heartbreak and hope, more pain and more promise," and referred to the "Perot prescription"; Perot repeated his "gridlock government"; Bush may have intended to repeat the Republican derogation of "deadbeat dads," but misfixed it to "deadbeat fathers." However, the President came out on top in assonance, the repetition of vowel sounds, in the long *o*'s of "global slowdown."

5. *Homespun Phrases.* Perot walked away with this event, from "third shift in a Dairy Queen" to his familiar "not playing Lawrence Welk music" to "five-star migraine headache," presumably felt by Harry Truman toward General MacArthur. His "international competitors that are cleaning our plate," however, may be a euphemism for *cleaning our clock,* which slanguists suspect has sexual overtones. (I wonder why.)

6. *Use of Quotations.* "My wife, Hillary, gave me a book about a year ago," Clinton said, "in which the author defined insanity as just doing the same old thing over and over again and expecting a different result." When I asked Clinton's communications director, George Stephanopoulos, for the source of this quotation, he was unable to come up with it, and he said Hillary Clinton, asked about the source, could not remember the book because she passed along so many.

Clinton's brother once had an addiction problem; I called Alcoholics Anonymous, where two people confirmed that the saying is often heard at A.A. meetings. The expression stresses that alcoholism is a disease, like mental illness, and does not show a lack of willpower. An A.A. archivist was unable to find a print citation; however, he remarked that he had been asked about this very phrase about ten days before the debate.

Perot said, "Words are plentiful, deeds are precious"; there are many such comparisons of words and deeds in quotation books, including the sexist slogan of Maryland, *Fatti maschii, parole femine,* "Deeds are masculine, words are feminine." (My home state should do something about that.)

7. *Grammar.* "Till the military tell me," in the Bush usage, suggests that *the military* is to be construed as plural, like *the media;* I think *the military* is a collective noun to be construed as singular, and I think the military is with me on that.

Perot had a problem with pronoun-antecedent agreement: "A little child before they're eighteen months learns to think," which he could fix without breaking a sweat. (That famed Perotism is based on *breaking into a sweat,* but the clipped form is correct because it is an idiom.) Agreement was a headache, though not of five-star migraine intensity, to Clinton as well: "There is certainly dangers" and "There is certainly other trouble spots" suggest there is certainly difficulties for him in the area of subject-verb agreement.

I'm being a wise guy, here, of course; it should be noted that any three linguists, debating for ninety minutes on national television, would probably make as many mistakes as these three political campaigners. The spoken language cannot be held to the standard of the written language, except when it comes to pronunciation.

8. *Pronunciation.* Clinton said "la-MENT-a-bly" rather than the "LAM-en-ta-bly" preferred by purists, who also put the emphasis on the first syllables of *despicable* and *hospitable.* If Clinton goes on to victory and uses "la-MENT-a-bly" in news conferences, the lexicographers will have to fall in line. His mistake on *patriotism*—calling it "praytriotism"—may turn out to be a forward fumble, if taken to be an unconscious portmanteau coinage meaning "the fervent application of religious principles to political affairs."

Perot had repeated difficulty with *deteriorating,* which he pronounces "duh-TEER-ee-ate-ing." He might be better off with *degenerating, disintegrating, decomposing* or the simpler *crumbling.*

Bush frowned on "the tax-and-spend route," which he pronounced "ROWT." That is not incorrect; John Walker in 1791 decried the English tendency to use the French "ROOT." Most of us, however, have come to use "ROOT" to mean "way, itinerary, journey, map," spelled *route,* and pronounced the same as the root of a plant. We use "ROWT" to pronounce the word spelled *rout,* meaning "resounding defeat; disorderly flight from battle; electoral debacle."

A sandpapered-fingertip sensitivity to pronunciation was shown by the debate's moderator, Jim Lehrer of PBS. In his introduction, he said the program originated in St. Louis, "Miz-oor-uh." In his conclusion, he said good-bye from "Miz-oor-ee."

Caught out in this straddle, the author of *A Bus of My Own* confesses: "I did it deliberately. I went to the University of Miz-oor-uh. 'Miz-oor-uh! Tigers!' That was a signal to my friends that I knew that's the way it's pronounced there.

"But everybody else says 'Miz-oor-ee,' " says the national broadcaster, "so I closed on that."

Dear Bill:

At present, Mizura *is the spoken form used by natives of the State, also widespread in neighboring states, while* Mizuree *is the form used by those who follow the spelling, the printed form. Since that is familiar to the greatest part of the country and is the school form, the "outside" pressure on the native or "inside" form,* Mizura, *is very powerful. I would guess that Lehrer is from the local area, and* Mizura *was his natural spoken form, used at the beginning of the broadcast, but that later he yielded to "educated" pressure and said* Mizuree.

The name was that of a Fox (Algonkian) Indian tribe living at the mouth of the river. Precisely how the Indians in the seventeenth century said it we do not know. The French first recorded it in spelling, and that became established and was adopted into English. Now we feel we must pronunce the name as it is spelled. But who should know better than the natives how they want to say the name of their state? The spelling Missoura was recorded as late as 1838 and Missourah was still in use in 1910. The -ah pronunciation was firmly established by 1840 or 1850—we have evidence to support that, and it was used very widely, even in New England as late as the 1930s. One East Texas native informant (1936) reported, "I have never heard [ĭ] as the final vowel in East Texas," and from Bowling Green, Kentucky (1960), "It's always Mizurah here." The eastern Carolinas and Georgia are the Southern exception, but one third of speakers there say Mizurah. The difference is not a clear or marked case of "class cleavage"; Mizurah is used also by upper-level people of the region; but the force of the spelled or printed form, strongly favored in schools, is winning the contest. And Lehrer is a typical victim!

Fred [Cassidy]
Editor
Dictionary of American
Regional English
Madison, Wisconsin

For the most part, the presidential debates consisted of trite and almost predictable rhetoric. Still, the television stations insisted on providing a needless half-hour analysis afterward.

At least you provided a useful critique of the debates with discussion about which of the candidates was grammatically correct.

John A. Matcovich
New York, New York

For you to nitpick about the three presidential candidates' grammar and use of words during the televised debates seemed a waste of time. Considering that these men were speaking in front of television cameras, responding to a barrage of questions on numerous subjects and, at the same time, virtually fighting for their political lives, it was amazing that they were as coherent, cool, and calm as they managed to appear.

Jessica M. Paroly
Bronx, New York

The pressures of the 1992 campaign season were such that the use of language by George Bush, Bill Clinton and Ross Perot became more tarnished by the day. In a speech following the debate on October 15, Bush compared himself to the pennant-winning Atlanta Braves, saying that politics is like baseball: "It ain't over till the last batter swings." The relevant baseball saying is "It ain't over until the fat lady sings." Perhaps he was being careful not to offend any overweight voters.

Clinton was guilty of awkward language. I heard him speak of "growing the economy" and "growing jobs," as if he were running for national groundskeeper. Perhaps, because of the "character" or "trust" issue, he wanted to reassure skeptical voters by planting an image of Clinton the caretaker.

Perot, for his part, committed another racial gaffe in the October 19 debate. Referring to the savings and loan scandal, he said, "Nobody touched that tar baby till the day after the election in 1988." But unlike the infamous "you people" remarks, Perot's slur largely was ignored by newspapers and TV.

Dexter K. Flowers
Baltimore, Maryland

Dear Bill:

You say that "Only the cultural elite goes out of its way to avoid inserting an adverb between the leaves of an infinitive." You thereby perpetuate the common misconception that a so-called "split infinitive" results from "splitting" something by "inserting" an adverb between its parts, a misconception that results from the popular belief that the to *of* to go, *etc., is part of an infinitive rather than an adornment that is added to an infinitive. (It is a mystery to me why that belief about English* to *has gained such wide acceptance while no such beliefs about its German counterpart* zu *and its Dutch counterpart* te, *which are used exactly the same way, though not in such a broad range of syntactic contexts, has gained much currency.)*

In any event, English has both an infinitive with to *(as in "They forced him to leave") and an infinitive without* to *(as in "They made him leave"); my identification of the bare verb form in the latter examples as an infinitive is supported by the fact that not only does every English verb have exactly the same form after* to *as it has in the contexts that require a bare form of the verb without* to, *but precisely those verbs that lack an infinitive with* to *are also excluded in the latter contexts, namely modal auxiliary verbs (you can't say, "Nothing requires him to can play poker" nor "Nothing makes him can play poker," though "Nothing requires him to be able to play poker" is OK). The* to *is in fact an accompaniment of a whole verb phrase (i.e., a verb plus whatever objects and/or modifiers it may have), as can be seen from the possibility of using a single* to *with a conjoined verb phrase ("They ordered him to clean out his desk and turn in his keys"). In a so-called "split infinitive," the* to *is simply added to a verb phrase in which a modifier precedes the verb.*

Jim [James D. McCawley]
Department of Linguistics
University of Chicago
Chicago, Illinois

You note that Perot's "cleaning our plate" may be a euphemism for "cleaning our clock." But maybe the more appropriate idiom for which Perot's phrase substitutes is "eating our lunch." When someone "eats your lunch" you've been pretty soundly beaten, and your plate has been cleaned.

John J. Di Clemente
Tinley Park, Illinois

Who's a Fatti?

The state of Maryland's slogan, *Fatti maschii, parole femine,* is Italian for "Deeds are masculine, words are feminine." Because deeds are always considered better than mere words, the slogan is blatantly sexist, recalling the book of a century ago, *Great Men and Famous Women.*

Recently, in a fit of liberality, I called attention to this anachronism and urged my home state to do something about it.

Marylanders are creative traditionalists. The motto has been on the state seal since 1648; rather than fiddle with the seal itself, the House of Delegates is considering a proposal to change the English translation in the state's law books to "strong deeds, gentle words." This translation is not of the Italian motto, found on the crest of the Calverts, Maryland's founding family, but a loose rendering in reverse order of an entirely different Latin saying, which used to be Dwight Eisenhower's motto: *Suaviter in modo, fortiter in re.*

Richard Tapscott in *The Washington Post* called this a "don't-raise-the-bridge, lower-the-river" approach to problem-solving. It suggests a whole new way to treat discomfiting foreign words and phrases: Leave the original, just change the translation. Diplomats are following this development avidly: A word means, as Lewis Carroll had Humpty Dumpty say, just what I choose it to mean—neither more nor less.

You were a bit unfair when you made fun of my suggestion for a new translation of the Calvert family motto.

To be fair to the Calvert family motto it is important at least to acknowledge that George Calvert's usage and meaning may have been profoundly different than that of most of his contemporaries (the great translator and linguist John Florio excepted).

I was wrong to put deeds first. Tuscan scholars assure me that George Herbert's contemporary translation "words are women, deeds are men" is a more accurate rendering of the prevalent 17th-century English usage and meaning from the Italian. But was I wrong to remove the gender altogether?

Whether "Gentle in Words, Strong in Deeds," is an acceptable alternate translation indeed may be subject to dispute, but at least it is rooted in more than political correctness or some ill-conceived effort to please all. In 1599 John Florio tried to convince the world that the motto was and should be gender neutral. I tried to do the same in 1993. Perhaps we both failed, but I am neither ashamed of the effort, nor of the scholarly company I keep.

Edward C. Papenfuse
State Archivist and Commis-
sioner of Land Patents
Maryland State Archives
Annapolis, Maryland

You are wrong to criticize the Maryland legislature's proposal to retranslate the state's motto, "Fatti maschii, parole femine." "Masculine" and "feminine" in the motto clearly function metaphorically. But what is the metaphor? The exhorter is not urging that Marylanders act or speak in ways that are typical of men and women as they actually are (in his or her presumably sexist vision). That is, Marylanders are not being told to "Drink too much beer and trade catty gossip!" Rather, they are being exhorted to live up to the virtues that are allegedly characteristic of the sexes at their best: Men's deeds are strong, women's words are gentle. A literal translation ("Walk like a man, talk like a girl"?) would no longer convey the same meaning to a generation that recognizes that women can be strong (Sigourney Weaver) and men sensitive (Alan Alda). The proposed solution conveys the exact sense of the original motto, sacrificing metaphor, true, for plainer speech. But since the metaphor no longer works in any event, the less literal translation (and more literal advice) is preferable. Assuming Maryland still likes the content of the motto (and why not? it's pretty good advice), there is no reason to change it.

Gerard E. Lynch
Professor of Law
Columbia University
New York, New York

Campaign Trailese

"Bill Clinton is good at *sophistry,*" sneered Jerry Brown, who surfaces every sixteen years to win a few late primaries on the solipsism platform. "It means 'to make the weak word stronger,' " he added to reporters unfamiliar with coverage of a vocabularian. "Look it up."

I did. *Sophistry* means "false argument; fallacious reasoning." It can be extended to "scholarly-sounding deception; the abuse of learning to mislead." Perhaps some dictionary somewhere can be found to back up Mr. Brown's meaning, but that sense is not in the history of the word in the *Oxford English Dictionary.*

The Sophists—the word rooted in the Greek for "wisdom"—were ancient Greeks who imparted instruction for pay. They were often contrasted with the philosophers—rooted in "love of wisdom"—who handed out their learning free of charge. (A modern example of sophistry is a logical-sounding explanation of why a flat tax is less regressive than a progressive tax.)

Candidate Clinton slammed back with several colorful locutions. He accused Mr. Brown, who had accused the Clintons of collusion in the awarding of Arkansas legal business, of "jumping on my wife." There was no sexual innuendo to this charge. The Northern dialect equivalent to *jumping on* would be *picking on,* meaning "harassing, concentrating on unfairly."

Governor Clinton went on to disparage former Governor Brown's populist message by referring to his opponent as a scion of wealth "standing there in your *fifteen-hundred-dollar suit.*" A decade ago, we had a spate of usages about a four-hundred-dollar *suit;* more recently, in the trial of the Mafioso John Gotti, that derogation of lavish living was upped to a *fifteen-hundred-dollar suit.* (Since attention was called to his sartorial splendor, Mr. Brown has been appearing in loud zippered jackets worn by union members.)

According to a Clinton supporter, the Governor's wife, Hillary Clinton, took her husband aside just before a debate and told him: "If Jerry Brown goes off on some wild tangent against you, just remind him he's from California and what they say out there is *chill out.* Just tell him to chill out."

Sure enough, as Mr. Brown started to inveigh against the Clinton civil rights record, Mr. Clinton interrupted cheerfully with "Jerry, chill out! You're from California—chill out. Cool off a little." That became the sound bite used on all the evening news shows the next day. Note how Governor Clinton slipped in the definition, "to cool off," so that non-Californians would understand.

Another Clintonism has a more obscure origin: He said in February 1992 that he wanted people to see him "working hard, reaching out to them and fighting *until the last dog dies.*"

Philip J. Bergan of New York recalls that his father, the grandson of Irish immigrants in the hard-coal region of northeastern Pennsylvania, would say of neighbors who had been the last to leave a late-night party that "they'd stay *till the last dog was hung.*" Joan Hall at the *Dictionary of American Regional English* has a citation of *until the last dog was hung* from a 1902 novel, set in Michigan, by Stewart Edward White; she tracks this Northern and Western United States dialect phrase further to a 1721 proverb in the *Oxford Dictionary of English Proverbs:* "Give a dog an ill name and hang him," which was used to describe the calumny heaped on a political candidate.

We have come full circle. This usage is apparently unrelated to *hangdog,* an adjective originally meaning "abject, cowed" and now also "gloomy, chopfallen." The Clinton use of *until the last dog dies* suggests a canine Custer making its last stand, and is an enrichment of the revelers' or loyalists' "stay until the last dog is hung." This snippet of today's political lingo seems related to the lexicon of political smears used over two centuries ago.

An earlier opponent in the primaries of 1992, Paul Tsongas, sought to play on the verb *to pander* by using as a symbol the *panda bear.* The accusation was that Mr. Clinton was telling people what they wanted to hear while he, Mr. Tsongas, was telling them the harsh truth about capital-gains taxes.

· The noun *panda* comes from the Nepalese name for a bamboo-eating bear or raccoon, like the pair Hsing-Hsing and Ling-Ling now sitting in the National Zoo and refusing to procreate.

Pander is an eponymous word, from Pandarus, the name of a sleazy archer in the Trojan War. According to medieval legend used by Chaucer in his poem "Troilus and Criseyde," Pandarus procures Cressida for Troilus; in his play *Troilus and Cressida,* Shakespeare reflects the change of a name to a noun: Pandarus, Cressida's uncle, offers her to Troilus, thus: "Let all pitiful goersbetween be call'd to the world's end after my name; call them all Panders." The noun then meant "go-between in love affairs," but soon became "pimp." It now means "one who caters to others, thereby exploiting their weaknesses."

More troublesome to Mr. Clinton than the *panda-pander* pun is a sobriquet that has followed him for years: *Slick Willie,* made famous by the bank robber William Sutton, presumably so called because he slicked down his hair, though it may have been because he was a smooth talker. (When asked why he robbed banks, Mr. Sutton replied, "Because that's where the money is," an answer of such stunning clarity it is still cited in finance courses.) *Slick,* as well as its variant *sleek,* is rooted in the Greek *leios,* "smooth," and has two connotations: "well-groomed" and "slippery." A politician worries about the latter.

"Some of my critics say that I'm slick," said Governor Clinton, taking the charge head on and turning it against his primary opponent's flat-tax proposal. "I'll tell you what: If anybody can pull this proposal over the eyes of the voters of New York, they'll be the slickest politicians to ever come along. . . . We can grease the wheels of the Long Island Rail Road from now to kingdom come with the slickness it would take to shove this down the throats of the American people."

The Democratic national chairman, Ronald H. Brown, deplored what he called Jerry Brown's "scorched earth policy" of launching verbal attacks on Mr. Clinton's character and record. "Scorched earth" was popularized by reports of Stalin's call to his armies in World War II to leave no grain or supplies intact for the invading Germans. It was first used in the Sino-Japanese war in the 1930's; the Chinese word *zhengce* means "scorched earth," and the first citation in the *O.E.D.* supplement is from a *London Times* story in 1937: "The populace . . . are still disturbed . . . by wild rumors of a 'scorched earth policy' of burning the city before the Japanese enter."

And the campaign has only just begun. (A *solipsism,* by the way, is an example of extreme self-absorption. A solipsist believes that his self is the most important thing of all; this belief often fuels the "fire in the belly" that drives politicians to great heights or to scorched-earth policies.)

Apology of Safire

Ragemonger Jerry Brown was corrected in this space for his definition of *sophistry,* which most of us think means "tricky reasoning," but which he defined as "to make the weak word stronger."

Classicists have sprung to his defense. In Paragraph 18 of Plato's *Apology* of Socrates, that Greek philosopher is on trial for his life and makes his defense. (The word *apology* originally meant "defense"; later it gained a connotation of "expression of regret." The formerly courageous *apologist* is now perceived to be not so much a resolute defender as a sleazy cover-upper.)

Socrates is quoted as telling the jury that his attackers, drawing on comments by the playwright Aristophanes, have accused him of being a wise man (*sophos*) "who makes the weaker argument the stronger"—that is, who corrupts youth by showing them how to persuade people to do the wrong thing. Many classicists think that this twisting of language is where *sophistry* comes from—using skills gained by the wise to refute wisdom.

The problem is the word *logos,* which can mean "word" (as Jerry Brown translates it) or "argument" (as most translators prefer in this context). Barth Pollak, professor of mathematics at Notre Dame, writes: "Perhaps when Jerry Brown said, 'Look it up,' he had something a tad more scholarly in mind than a dictionary." He adds: "Mathematics, not classics, is my shtick so I'll leave further investigation to others," but, having provided the citation from Plato's *Apology,* he asks, "Don't you owe one to Mr. Brown?"

Sure, and here it is. I don't get worked up about these things.

Confederacy Rises Again

When the C.I.A. was still persuaded that the Soviet gross national product was growing, a former high official of that agency called me with a contrarian tip: "You want to consider the possibility of the first disintegration of a superpower." My nameless (actually, he has a name), my unidentified (he has an identity, too), my publicity-averse source added: "Some disunionists like you should give some thought to methods for the republics to confederate."

Confederate? I have written extensively about *Confederates,* capitalized, as the Southerners called themselves during the Civil War, and have a few confederates of my own, though these peer-groupies now go by the name of *colleagues, associates* or *confrères.* However, I had never used the word as a verb; as is my wont, I asked my source what the difference was between *confederate* and *federate.* He said only to mark his words (actually, to stop marking his words), that the Soviet internal monolith would one day break up.

(Why am I still protecting my source? Sources these days are eager to be identified. This one is Herbert Meyer, now publisher of Storm King Press in Friday Harbor, Washington, formerly Bill Casey's favorite analyst at the C.I.A. All of us in the pundit dodge have to re-examine our oaths in the Era of Credited Leaks and give names to the sources who were right; the other guys I forget.)

So now all we hear is how the former Union of Soviet Socialist Republics, then the Union of Soviet Sovereign Republics and now who knows what to call it, has become *a loose confederation of states.* The adjective *loose,* formerly married to *woman,* is remarried to *confederation* in all chin-pulling Kremlinology. (There's a dead word, along with *Sovietologist;* what are we going to call the tea-leaf readers now? Russia-watchers? Disunionologists? Gorky Parkers?)

Years too late for a world beat, here is the difference between the verbs *federate* and *confederate.*

From the Latin *foedus,* "compact, league," akin to *fidere,* "to trust," we have *federate,* which means "to unite," or more precisely, "to form a union." Our founders knew this; having been together under the Articles of Confederation from 1781 to 1789, they felt the need "to form a more perfect Union"—"perfect" in the sense of "complete, finished, whole"—and so they drew up the Constitution to federate the states.

But to *federate* is not to amalgamate, lump, blend or meld; the word carries the meaning that each of the signatories retains internal management of some of its affairs. The great pre-Johnson lexicographer Nathan Bailey nicely defined *federation* as "a covenanting," with its biblical overtones, agreeing to form a bond that permits each of the covenanters some freedom and individuality within the unity.

Con- is a Latin prefix meaning "together," which makes *confederate* redundant—to unite together—but instead of strengthening the union, the *con-* weakens it. To *confederate* is to form an alliance, a league, a compact for the purpose of acting together as a group, but not as one.

Thus, a *federation* is a single sovereign power; its component parts may have all sorts of rights, but not sovereignty. A *confederation* is an association of sovereign states, each of which may delegate rights and powers to a central government but does not delegate its sovereignty.

In 1789, the United States went from a *confederation* to a *federation* in the minds of the Northern states, but still retained the characteristics of a confederation to Southerners, who thought in 1860 that the union could be dissolved. When the Southern states seceded, they called their own grouping a *confederation* to make this very point, but did not put a right to secede in their own Constitution; the ambiguity was noted in the North. This suggests a lesson to confederators in Moscow, Kiev and the other republic capitals: Decide clearly at the outset about the state sovereignty that includes the right of secession.

In the synonymy of political togetherness, *union* and *united* are strongest; *federation* is sovereign but not so tightly united; *confederation* is an alliance of separate but interdependent sovereignties; *commonwealth,* originally an autonomous political unit (Massachusetts), is now a loose association of sovereign nations with a sentimental common allegiance (as to the British crown), or can be a sovereign political unit voluntarily linked to another power (Puerto Rico); *league,* now recalling "of women voters" rather than "of nations," has been replaced in diplomatic usage by *organization* (U.N.O., NATO, O.A.S.) and is like a club, not easy to get into but easy to leave; *conference* is both loose and temporary, even if it creates a bureaucracy to last for decades, and *community,* now usually economic, is the most amorphous of all.

The striking linguistic note in all this is the uniqueness of the word *loose.* No synonym, like *free,* comes close; the other synonyms say what its opposite is not, like *unbound, unfastened, unattached, unconnected.* Therefore, if you want to say "a loose confederation" but do not want to use a phrase in vogue, forget your squeamishness and say "a loose confederation."

Cordialities and Crushes

The confirmation hearings of Clarence Thomas continue to have linguistic and grammatical reverberations.

Trying to reconcile the differences in testimony, a puzzled Senator Hank Brown of Colorado said, "Most members are like I." The nation winced; the preposition *like* requires the object *me.*

"Were any one of these conversations repeated more than once?" asked asked Senator Senator Biden Biden. Not only was this redundant, but also the plural verb *were* disagreed with the singular subject *one*. When grammarians in the audience snickered aloud—or someone else laughed or applauded a witness—Joe Biden, desperate to get on the right side of the nation's English teachers, warned he would be "removing whomever does," but he tried too hard; the subject he had in mind was *whoever*.

Senator Howell Heflin of Alabama added a syllable to *vindictive;* he pronounced it "vin-DIC-a-tive," which may be indictive of a feel for local dialect, but when the nominee said he had his *dander up,* the Senator repeated it as "your dander off." *Dander* began as an alternative form of *dandruff,* loose scales on the scalp; when one becomes angry, the hair rises and the dander flies upward, at least metaphorically. *Up,* not *off,* is the only correct word to follow *dander* in this expression.

Denials were *categorical.* As originally used by Aristotle dealing with logic, it meant "affirmative," opposed to negative; later logicians used the word (rooted, curiously, in the Greek for "accusation") to mean "absolute, without condition." In choosing intensifiers for his denials, then-Judge Thomas at one point used "unequivocally, uncategorically"; he was probably searching for a parallel *un-* adverb, and *unconditionally* did not pop to mind; he meant *categorically.*

The adjective Judge Thomas chose with care to describe his relationship with his former aide Anita Hill was *cordial.* That term, from the Latin *cor,* "heart," also the root of *coronary,* now means "kindly and courteous" but is more hearty than heartfelt. In closing letters, *cordially* is the formal way of expressing friendliness, a significant step short of *warmly* or *affectionately,* not as backslapping as *genially* or as breezy as *amiably.* It is a safely distant or businesslike expression of warmth.

A slightly old-fashioned slang term, but one that everyone recognized, was used by Phyllis Berry Myers, a witness attesting to the Thomas rectitude. Senator Heflin, his dander off, asked, "Are you saying that . . . set of circumstances made you to believe that she had a sexual interest?" She changed his phraseology to make it understandable and less grim: "That she had a *crush* on the chairman? Yes."

Crush, in its romantic sense, may have bloomed in Thomas Moufet's 1599 line "the hart-breake crush of melancholies wheele." The modern sense of "infatuation"—a strong but passing attraction—originated in the United States about a century ago. Isabella Maud Rittenhouse wrote in 1884 that "Wintie is weeping because her crush is gone." A decade later, J. S. Wood wrote in *Yale Yarns:* "It was a 'crush,' you see, on both sides," and by 1913 *Dialect Notes* defined the term as "to be conspicuously attached to some one." (The same feeling, but concealed, is called a *sneaker.*)

Some innocent words gain sinister overtones. Senator Alan Simpson spoke darkly of being sent letters and faxes warning about what he called Anita

Hill's "proclivities." Senator Edward Kennedy denounced this word by pro-nunciation—that is, putting it in verbal quotation marks and sneering.

I joined him in this reproof of his colleague, because the word was used sneakily to hint at homosexuality, much as *preferences,* spoken with an arched eyebrow, takes a phrase meant to avoid offense—"sexual preferences"—and uses the noun to mean what the whole phrase euphemizes. In its original sense, *proclivity* (rooted in the Latin *clivus,* "hill," and signaling the slope or incline of that hill) meant "inclination, tendency, propensity, leaning"; it now carries a connotation of behavior or thinking disapproved of or considered abnormal by the speaker.

Alienists were alienated by the lay use of psychological terms. *Schizo-phrenic* was used when "split personality" or "dual personality" was meant; this common error is caused by the clinical term beginning with what sounds like a schism, or divide.

Fantasize also drove them up the wall: Around 1325, long before Freud, a song lyric went, "This worldly blis/Is but a fykel fantasy." *Fantasy* with an *f* meant "caprice, whim," while *phantasy* with a *ph* meant "product of the imag-ination, vision, dream"; now the *f* has triumphed, the meaning of *fantasy* is "dream" and the clinical meaning is "an imagined event stimulated by an un-fulfilled psychological need." The intransitive verb *fantasize,* first used in 1926, means "to indulge in fantasies."

When Senator Biden used the phrase "Hell hath no fury like a woman scorned," he identified the source as Shakespeare; within an hour he was cor-rected by a colleague and announced the source to be William Congreve, who wrote in 1697, "Heaven has no rage like love to hatred turned,/Nor Hell a fury like a woman scorned." The Senator self-mockingly said, "Not that I think that Mr. Congreve would ever plagiarize Shakespeare," and added that his staff would search in Shakespeare for an earlier use.

Such a search would be fruitless; the Biden researchers would do better to look in the playwright Colley Cibber's 1696 *Love's Last Shift:* "We shall find no fiend in Hell can match the fury of a disappointed woman," a sentiment that would surely be defined today as sexist. Congreve evidently stole the fa-mous line from Cibber, probably after seeing the play the year before; the Sen-ator was right to suspect at least the possibility of plagiarism.

I would say that repeating a conversation is one of many things that a person can do many times, including more than once. I don't know what you mean by its being redundant. For example, if I say the same thing six times, then I've re-peated it five times, which is certainly more than once.

Thomas D. Stowe
New York, New York

Crack That Code

The second sentence of Article IV of the Armed Forces Code of Conduct states: "I will give no information or take part in any action which might be harmful to my comrades."

This sentence, memorized by so many cadets and midshipmen, is important for members of our armed forces to keep in mind if taken prisoner. Maybe we should fix its grammar.

1Lt (that's "First Lieutenant" in militarese) Wesley Chang at Randolph AFB (that's "Air Force Base") in Texas (that's "TX") writes: "I've tried unsuccessfully to have this problem corrected from my level. Your support could make a big difference."

Here it comes, from a level that once reached the heights of corporal: "I will give no information or take part in any action" does not march. Changing the *or* to *nor* would help, but the formulation is awkward because the *no* is not parallel to the *any.*

Left-oblique, hut. Make it: "I will not give any information or take part in any action which might be harmful to my comrades." Now change the *which* to *that* because the final clause is restrictive: "I will not give any information or take part in any action that may be harmful to my comrades."

Good luck, 1Lt Chang, on your travels up through channels.

Crisis Crisis

The use of the word *crisis* as an attributive noun should be noted. In the old days, *crisis* was the noun being modified, as in *Cuban missile crisis.* Now it is doing the modifying.

Irene S. Pollin, M.S.W. (that stands for Master of Social Work), spoke at a recent meeting of the Linda Pollin Foundation in Bethesda, Maryland, discussing controversies about counseling the chronically ill. Her subject was the evolution of the curriculum in medical *crisis counseling.*

Joseph J. Sisco is a veteran diplomat; when I ran into him on a street near the White House and asked what he was doing these days, he said he was in *crisis assessment.* This is political and economic risk analysis for companies thinking of doing business in hot spots.

Here's an announcement from Clifford A. Miller of Burbank, California, whom I used to know as a great public relations man, but whose new shingle reads "Strategic Counsel" (presumably, how to stay out of trouble) and *"Crisis Management"* (what to do if you didn't listen to the first advice).

Vice President Quayle, like President Bush before him, is chairman of the *crisis-management* team that assembles in the Situation Room on not-so-dull days. (Why isn't that basement conference room called the Crisis Center? Because the White House does not want the public to get excited every time it is put in use. "I don't think we met down there during the Cuban missile crisis," says McGeorge Bundy, who was President Kennedy's National Security Adviser in 1961, when the communications center was named the Situation Room. He does not recollect who named it that, nor does Ted Sorensen, a Kennedy aide. The widow of Bromley Smith, then the executive director of the National Security Council, promises to dig around in this historical lexicographic quest, but if anyone else can shed light on the sit-room situation, holler.)

The first use of *crisis* as an attributive noun in my recollection was by Dr. Morton Bard, a psychologist working with the New York Police Department in the 1960's on what he called *family-crisis intervention.*

Crisis is the critical new modifier; one of these days we will see a strategy maker (former policy maker) come up with *crisis engagement.*

Dig Those Digerati

A white puff of smoke has gone up over Lexicon Central: We have a coinage!

"I call your attention," writes Jason McManus, editor in chief of Time Warner, "to a neologism to me: *digerati.* This occurs in the *New York Times* Business section in an article by John Markoff, who refers to George Gilder's writings as being 'taken seriously among the computer digerati.' It did make me smile with appreciation in the trust it was Mr. Markoff's invention to lighten up a highly technical story."

Literati, Italian for the Latin *litterati,* "learned," means "the intellectual set." In the late 1930's, a portmanteau word was formed to blend the world of glittering celebrities with these intellectuals: *glitterati.*

Now all that glitters is *digital,* from the Latin for "finger," and later applied to a number that can be counted on the ten fingers. Hence, *digerati,* "computer intellectuals," a word sure to flash through the world's electronic mailboxes.

My colleague Mr. Markoff confirms that the term was first used in his story, but—honest fellow—attributes coinage to the usually anonymous "backfield" editor, Tim Race.

The coiner has the right to set down the definition. According to Mr. Race, it goes: "**Digerati,** *n.pl.,* people highly skilled in the processing and manipulation of digital information; wealthy or scholarly techno-nerds."

Please tell Mr. Race that the correct term is "technerd."

I'll take this moment to remind you of the coinage I submitted in autumn: "Prestalgia."

It means "longing for the days that haven't happened yet" and is common among the digerati.

> *Gary Arlen*
> *Bethesda, Maryland*

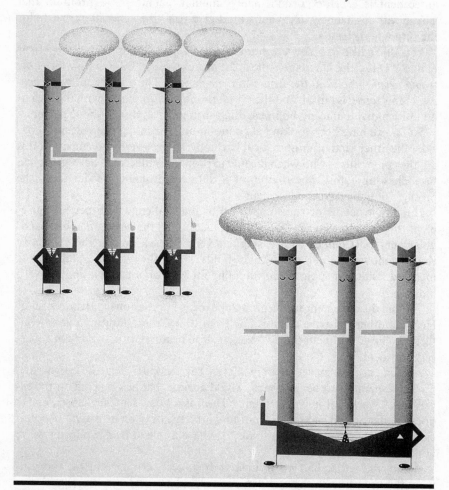

Disagreeing to Agree

MTV, the cable network playing the music that appeals to young minds, had a good idea: It would make its facilities available to candidates for President, thereby appealing to pulsing brains as well as tapping feet.

"Tonight on MTV," headlined the proud network's full-page ad in some of the nation's most prestigious newspapers, "Bill Clinton faces the generation that holds the future in their hands."

Members of a straitlaced, out-of-it generation looked at that ad, shook their heads and said, "In *its* hands." The word *their* is a pronoun, which is a word that substitutes for a noun; that pronoun must agree in number with the noun for which it substitutes, which we call its antecedent. But in this case, the antecedent is *generation,* undeniably singular, calling for a pronoun that agrees with it—namely, *its.* That would give you "the generation that holds the future in its hands."

You don't like *its*? You are hooked, as a sensitive copywriter, on "their hands"? O.K., the language is flexible; make it read "Bill Clinton faces *the young people* who hold the future in *their* hands." The antecedent word *people,* in this sense, is plural, and the plural pronoun *their* agrees with the idea of all those individual teeny-boppers, thigh-drummers and saxophone players.

So far, we have been looking at pronoun-antecedent agreement; now consider the other kind of grammatical harmony, subject-verb agreement. In this ad, the copywriter—who when it came to pronoun-antecedent agreement had been chewing gum to the rhythm of a different drummer—twice faced the problem of subject-verb agreement.

Happily, twice he or she stepped up to the challenge with perfect agreement: In the main clause ("Bill Clinton faces . . .") the writer matched a singular subject (*Clinton*) with a singular verb (*faces*), and in the restrictive clause following *generation* ("that holds . . ."), the writer equally tidily matched a singular subject (*that* standing for *generation*) with a singular verb (*holds*).

The big disagreement problem, it appears, is in pronouns and antecedents. Here's another full-page ad, this one from Blue Cross, shouting out its conflict: "If the government thinks it has a role in health reform, we've got a message for them."

Agreement junkies would immediately say, "For *it*." But the copywriter, trying desperately to be idiomatic, would answer that he's playing on the expression "We've got news for them." *Them* is a good sentence-closer, and *it* doesn't quite sound right. O.K., not to worry, the flexicon is ready: "If politicians (or government leaders) think they have a role in health reform, we've got a message for them."

Again, the writer had no trouble with subject-verb agreement: "government thinks" works in the singular, as does "it has," and "we (have) got" also matches plural subject with verb.

Few people would argue with the agreeable didactives above. Now let's get into agreement trouble. Here is a note from J. Bennett Johnston, Senator from Louisiana: "Would my favorite song of yesteryear, 'To Each His Own,' now be 'To Each Their Own,' or is everyone entitled to their own opinion on that issue?"

Very tricky double question, Senator. You are asking first: When gender is indeterminate (*to each*), why should we go with the male (*his own*)? If "To Each His or Her Own" doesn't exactly make music, how about a neutral plural instead, like *their*? Then you ask the second part: When *everyone* is the antecedent, should the pronoun be singular or plural? (All this on one postcard—with proper stamp, not corruptly franked.)

First to sex: I would not break the rule on pronoun-antecedent agreement just to make a political point. Pressure from feminists to do so is understandable, and writers from Jane Austen to Sydney Smith have done it, but as sexual equality is achieved, the need to stretch syntax will let up. I suggest a politics-grammar deal: Let half the Senate be women and let the male pronoun embrace the female.

Now to the controversy raging among usagists about notional and formal concord. In our irenic, friendly field, on this subject there's blood all over the floor.

Notionalists, the swingers in this scrap, concentrate on meaning; formalists, on grammatical concord. Take the indeterminate pronouns *anybody* or *everybody, somebody* or *nobody:* Notionalists say each one may be plural, but formalists treat the words as singular.

Formalists say *everybody is,* meaning "every single body," and *nobody is,* meaning "not one body"; notionalists go along with the subject-verb agreement, but part company with the formalists on pronouns and antecedents. The meaning of *everybody,* say the notionalists, is not the singular *person* but the plural *people;* therefore, *them* or *their* agrees with the antecedent *everybody,* not *him* or *his.*

"The plural *they, their, them* with an indefinite pronoun as referent is in common standard use," reports *Merriam-Webster's Dictionary of English Usage,* waving the notionalist banner, "both as common-gender singular and to reflect notional agreement." One example it gives is from the great modern novelist Bernard Malamud, who had a character "look around . . . to see if *any* of the girls playing in the street was her, but *they* never were." Then, with sly glee, the laid-back usagists cite a prescriptive sentence of mine: "Whenever *anyone* uses the pressure of usage to force you to accept the nonsensical and swallow the solecism, here's what to tell *them.*"

That was my mistake; I should have matched *anyone* with *him.* But I wasn't thinking of one person, any one body; I was thinking of all those loosey-goosey guys who go with the usage flow, and so—drat!—I followed the meaning rather than the form and used the notional *them.* Now I have to ask myself: If I meant *them,* why not say *them*? Shouldn't form follow function?

Almost everybody who reads this column respects the moorings of grammatical form and resists the temptation to wallow in linguistic ambiguity (note how *almost everybody* takes the singular verb form *reads, respects* and *resists*), but they—damn, there I go again, using *they* when the form calls for *he.* Is it worth it? Do I feel like a jerk, trying to conform to good order? After all, I say *none is* when I mean "not one of them is," and *none are* when I mean "not any of them are."

O.K., that's it—fight's over for me; we're going to slip that mooring. My new rule: The writer or speaker using indeterminate pronouns should go with the pronoun that fits the meaning of the antecedent in his own mind.

I still consider nouns like *generation* and, in American usage, *government* to be singular collectives that take the pronoun *its.* But for pronoun-antecedent agreement of indeterminate pronouns, my determination is: Let everybody do *their* thing, when the meaning of *everybody* is the plural "all people," and to each *his* own, when the sense is singular. Consistency counts; after all, as Senator Johnston's favorite song goes, a rose must remain with the sun and the rain or its lovely promise won't come true.

It was once acceptable, of course, to say, "If a person feels sick, he should see his doctor." ("Man embraces woman," as waggish grammarians used to put it.) However, that is now politically incorrect.

The obvious solution is to use the plural. ("If people . . . they. . . .") Of late, however, I have noted a covert operation designed to redress the grammatical balance by letting woman embrace man. Last year, for example, the Times *columnist Anthony Lewis wrote: "Every time an American moves or changes jobs, she is likely to find herself with a different health-insurance carrier." Just recently, a (male) professor discussing computerized college testing in a letter to the editor of* The Times *noted that "the student will immediately receive a score earmarking her prospects for life."*

In neither case was there a female antecedent anywhere in sight. What you had was linguistic politicking at its sneakiest.

> Louis Jay Herman
> New York, New York

As a card-carrying "agreement junkie," I find that I must disagree with your conclusions.

Nouns of multitude such as "generation" and "government" and the intermediate pronouns "each," "everybody," "nobody," "anyone," etc. are without question singular and must, necessarily, take the singular verb form and should be followed, if appropriate, by singular pronouns and possessives. As for your new rule, it is true that writers and speakers should use pronouns, possessives and verbs that fit the meaning (and the notion) of the antecedent. But for crying out loud, if the writer or speaker has a plural meaning for his or her antecedent, a singular intermediate pronoun should not have been used in the first place. If by "anyone" you mean "all those loosey-goosey guys," say it.

It is interesting to note, however, that if one were to defer judgment to Fowler's Modern English Usage, *the formalists' guide to good grammar, one would find that the "agreement problem" in each of the advertisements you discuss is not the actual problem, but rather the* result *of a misunderstanding and a subsequent misuse of nouns of multitude. Of such nouns* Fowler's *states, "they are treated as singular or plural at discretion—and sometimes, naturally, without discretion." In this light the problem is not, in MTV's advertisement, antecedent-pronoun disagreement, nor is it, in Blue Cross's statement, subject-verb disagreement; in each case, followers of* Fowler's *would hold, the disagreement is caused by a lack of discretion.*

I found the Bernard Malamud quotation used by Merriam-Webster's *as an example of notional use to be a strange choice. Mr. Malamud is a novelist who may have his characters speak any way he likes. Nonetheless, it does not help* Merriam-Webster's *case (pun intended) to use a sentence that exhibits not only antecedent-pronoun disagreement (which it defends), but also another violation of the rules of grammar. Mr. Malamud's character should not have "looked around . . . to see if any of the girls playing in the street was her . . ." The character should have instead looked to see if any of the girls was* she.

Darius Wadia
Weehawken, New Jersey

I was surprised and disappointed in your easy capitulation to sloppy usage regarding pronoun-antecedent agreement.

The main cause for the offending practice is the desire to appear gender-neutral when using the singular person where personal pronouns typically are gender-related. The offenders are either too lazy to cast the sentence with a plural antecedent or too weak-spirited to let the masculine pronoun serve the generic role it traditionally has. For example, if one hesitates to say, "Any child can avoid trouble by listening to his parents," he (not "they") can say, "Children can avoid trouble by listening to their parents."

Jerome Kurshan
Princeton, New Jersey

I would like to add my own experience with the use of the plural pronoun to blur a singular antecedent, what you refer to as notionalism.

I am the editor of the Oxford Student's Dictionary for Hebrew Speakers *and the* WEBSTER+ *trilingual electronic dictionary, plus a number of phrase books and language teaching materials. My credentials should place me right in the middle of this controversy.*

In 1987 Collins published a new English learner's dictionary called the Collins COBUILD English Language Dictionary. *Its two most prominent innovations were the arrangement of definitions according to frequency as determined by analysis of a 20-million item database and a style of definition which used full English sentences. Thus, the definition itself would provide an example of usage.*

One of the editors' decisions was to use the third person plural pronoun for indefinite antecedents, such as "someone," disregarding what you call formalism in your article. This was also intended to avoid the possible sexism in using a singular pronoun.

Fine. But then I noticed their definition of "masturbate."

masturbate . . . *If someone* **masturbates,** *they stroke or rub their own genitals in order to get sexual pleasure.*

I wrote to the managing editor, Patrick Hanks, a personal friend, and said that surely here was a case where "he or she" would have been more appropriate. The next edition, a slightly condensed one, left out the entry entirely.

Three years ago, Professor Sir Randolph Quirk, the leading expert in EFL teaching (he was knighted for his work in English grammar) was given an honorary degree by our university. During his stay here he gave several lectures on English grammar and mentioned the development of the plural pronoun use for indefinite singular antecedents.

In the discussion period after the lecture I mentioned the Collins COBUILD *definition of "masturbate" and said that masturbating in the plural bothered me more than sexism in language. Sir Randolph replied, "You're behind the times."*

> *Joseph A. Reif*
> *Bar-Ilan University*
> *Ramat-Gan, Israel*

Your column "Disagreeing to Agree" reached me yesterday morning, July 4th. As I was reading the Declaration of Independence that evening (what an abnormal and totally un-American thing to do! I should have been watching the fireworks on TV), I was much chagrined to find in that document an error of the pronoun-antecedent-agreement variety.

The mistake-riddled sentence is the very first in the document, and many schoolchildren in days of yore knew it by heart: "When, in the course of human events, it becomes necessary for one people to dissolve the political bands which have connected them with another, and to assume among the powers of the earth, the separate and equal station to which the laws of Nature and of Nature's God entitle them, a decent respect to the opinions of mankind requires that they should declare the causes which impel them to the separation." In the beginning of the sentence the colonials are represented as one people, *but later on are variously referred to as* them *or* they.

Is Tom Jefferson's mistake excused under your new policy of pronoun-antecedent leniency? I would think not, since he modifies "people" with "one," specifying its singularity.

I forgive him anyway.

> Jared Hertzberg
> Norwood, New Jersey

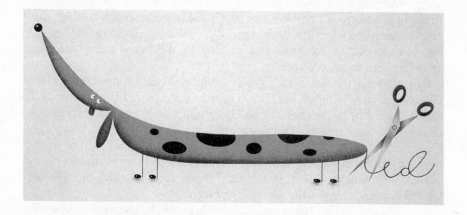

The Disappearing -ed

"Your column is a pack of damn lies," writes a concerned reader, referring to work I do in a political mode. That comment troubled me; should it be *damn* lies or *damned* lies?

If meaning is to determine spelling, the *-ed* is necessary; *damned* is the past participle of the verb *to damn,* and is used by my irate reader as an adherent adjective—that is, it is a modifier stuck on before its noun. That is why Benjamin Disraeli quoted Mark Twain as saying, "There are three kinds of lies: lies, *damned* lies and statistics."

But if pronunciation determines spelling, the final *-ed* is dropped; few of us pronounce the concluding *d* in *damned* when using it before another word. Although we will say, "I'll be damned," with the final *d* coming through, and we expect Shakespearean actors playing Lady Macbeth to enunciate the *d* in "Out, damn'd spot," the normal dry cleaner saying the same phrase will address a stain with "Out, damn spot."

Which standard are we to apply—the traditional one of meaning or the looser one of pronunciation?

As we have seen, that issue is seldom a problem when the word is not used as a modifier, or comes after the word modified. I'm *old-fashioned;* I pour a jigger of bourbon over a piece of sugar in an *old-fashioned* glass, add two dashes of bitters and a splash of soda, garnish with a slice of orange and a maraschino cherry, stir and sip my *old-fashioned.* Read the preceding sentence aloud; you will pronounce the *d* the first and third times, but not the second; that's because the adherent adjective in *old-fashioned glass* lends itself to the pronunciation "ol-fashionglass." (Erudite mail on this column will begin, "Why are you putting all that garbage in an old-fashioned?")

But the problem of the disappearing *d* or *-ed* manifests itself in that second usage, when the spelling does not match the pronunciation. *Old-fashion* looks funny in print before a noun—"served with old-fashion peach cobbler," as it says on the menu—but it sounds right. Why should we insist on the *-ed* ending, when we readily accept *ice cream*? After all, we do not mean "the cream of the ice" but mean *iced cream.*

"Throughout the centuries," Professor John Algeo of the University of Georgia tells me, "English has tended to reduce a group of consonants at the end of a word by losing the last one." For example, a thousand years ago, we pronounced the *b* in *lamb,* and really hit that *g* in *long* (as a few Lawn Guy-landers still do). "So some English speakers today, in the vanguard of continuing the process of change, drop the final consonants in words like *world* and *blind,* which come out 'worl' and 'bline.' Judging from the past, those are advanced pronunciations—the wave of the future."

The final *d* or *-ed* is getting kicked in the head by the rise of the attributive noun—that word for a thing that is used to modify another thing, like *killer* whale, *fashion* color, *lead* pencil and *call* girl. No wonder so many people follow that analogy to dispense with the *d* in making similar phrases, using stripped-down participles as if they were attributive nouns: *corn beef, whip cream, toss salad, skim milk, barbecue chicken, candy apples,* even *string instrument* and *stain glass.*

This brings us to the controversial rap singer Ice-T. Politicians complaining about violence in his lyrics miss the significant cultural controversy in his name—namely, should he be "Iced-T"? Nobody, of course, pronounces the *-ed* in *iced tea;* as Professor Algeo notes, "Since *-ed* in the first stands for the sound of *t,* it is lost before another *t* sound, just as *for goodness' sake* is usually pronounced like *for goodnesake,* with the final *s* sound of *goodness* lost before the initial one of *sake. . . . Iced tea* and *ice tea* would usually be pronounced alike in speech of normal tempo, thus inviting the simpler spelling."

Does this change mean we must adopt pronunciation as our standard in spelling, and reject meaning? No. We do not write *for cry sake,* though that is our pronunciation of *for Christ's sake;* even when we write *for Chrissake,* we retain enough of the original meaning to remind readers that Jesus is being invoked.

Ears are sloppy and eyes are precise; accordingly, speech can be loose but writing should be tight. If it has taken a thousand years to lose the *b* in *lamb,* let it take a couple of generations at least to drop the -*ed* in the written *whipped cream.*

I will continue to eat *processed* cheese in my *queen-sized* bed, eschewing crackers. Denny's restaurants offer "smaller-size portions at reduced prices"; I suggest they change that to *smaller-sized* portions lest they drift toward *reduce* prices.

You don't have to be a nut about retaining the -*ed* in print. The corn popper in my office spews out *popcorn*, not *popped corn;* if I butter it, however, it is *buttered popcorn*, not *butter popcorn*. Similarly, with no rationale other than linguistic *Fingerspitzengefühl*, I will choke down a *microwave dinner* but reject a *bake potato*. Yes to *cream cheese*, no to *cream broccoli* (I say it's *creamed spinach* and I say to hell with it).

"Do I contradict myself?" Walt Whitman asked in "Song of Myself" in 1855. "Very well then I contradict myself. (I am large, I contain multitudes.)" Same goes for language; let it change at its own good pace; force nothing into tidy little boxes.

Government's latest acronym is *Istea*. It stands for "Intermodal Surface Transportation Efficiency Act of 1991." It's pronounced "ice tea," but I still think of it as *iced tea*.

As we all know, "skim" is a verb, referring to "the act of skimming." Therefore, it should not be modifying the noun, "milk."

Perhaps the manufacturers who perpetuate this grammatical flaw argue that space does not permit them to add the "ed" and turn "skim" into an adjective. More likely they said to themselves, "What the hell. Everybody else is using verbs to modify nouns, so why shouldn't we?"

Burling Lowrey
Washington, D.C.

Don't Call Her Madam

William F. Buckley Jr., my senior colleague in columny, has written his most intimate and self-revealing book, which proves that even right-wingers have feelings. *Winding Down* is the title, suggesting an end to his long-sailing affair with the sea, and underscoring that phrase's meaning as "a slowing and relaxing," distinct from the more abrupt *winding up*.

Mr. Buckley, "Bill" to his friends, does not like to be called by that diminutive, or even the full "William," by strangers. He has taken the position that the spread of first-namism not only is an affront to good manners but also subtracts from the value of a first-name relationship between people who know each other. When he says, "Call me Bill," that is an invitation to greater intimacy, or an acknowledgment of an informal relationship, and should not be presumed by a recent acquaintance or a pushy kid.

Most politicians go the other way. They are eager to first-name every potential voter and be first-named in return because that establishes a bond of immediate familiarity. Not so Barbara A. Mikulski, Democratic Senator from Maryland, who heads a subcommittee on housing. When addressed as "Barbara" by Jack F. Kemp, Secretary of Housing and Urban Development—an outgoing and informal soul who is on a first-name basis with every contemporary he meets—she wrote to him that she prefers to be known as "Madam Chair."

Why the formal notification? "That was a perfunctory thing," she told Jason DeParle of *The New York Times,* using a word that means "automatic" or "mechanical." She added, "A lot of people ask how to address me." (The honorific was spelled "Madam" in the newspaper, reflecting the American pronunciation; it is spelled "Madame" only when the French pronunciation is intended.)

Hail to thee, dignified spirit! The liberal "Madam Chair" and the conservative Mr. Buckley have at least that thoughtful formality in common.

But this thought intrudes: What if Barbara Mikulski is elected President? Only a spouse could call her Barbara in public; all others would adopt "Madam President." But does that reflect modern usage? Would there not be a movement to call her "Ms President," more directly parallel to "Mr. President"?

Madam and *Sir* are parallel, and we do not use "Sir President"; *Mrs. President* would be incorrect, as she would not be married to the President, and even if that were the case, "Mrs." is not our usage in front of titles. Nor, if the President were a single female, would "Miss President" do.

We must think about *Ms President* and *Ms Chair.* Like *Sir, Madam* is too formal as an American title; the words may be used in passing—"Excuse me, sir or madam, you're sitting on my eyelashes"—but not before a name or title. We have elevated *Ms* (I write it without a period because it's not an abbreviation for anything) to standard usage, correct except when the person signifies a preference for revealing marital status with *Mrs.* or *Miss.* The time has come to use it in titles. I live in Maryland, so maybe it's O.K. to call Senator Mikulski "Barbara"—constituents have privileges—but for the rest of you, let's make it *Ms Chair.*

You may be right that "Madam President" for a woman president may not fly today, despite the usage of "madam" for "Mr." in the legislative and executive branches of government for many years. Even today we hear Madam Speaker (for a woman Member presiding temporarily over the House) and Madam Secretary downtown. And yes, when Ms. Mikulski is presiding over the Senate, she is addressed as Madam President.

You may not know how the Supreme Court resolved the issue when Sandra Day O'Connor was appointed to the Court: by discontinuing the traditional "Mr. Justice" and "Mr. Chief Justice" in favor of the simple "Justice O'Connor," "Chief Justice Rehnquist," etc. Thus, it is possible that a future president may be called just "President Mikulski."

There is a good reason, however, not to follow the Supreme Court's precedent: the use of "Mr." for presidents, members of Congress and Supreme Court justices stems from the first days of the Republic, to emphasize that American political leaders were to be common men, not men of nobility or title. It is a revolutionary term that should not be dispensed with unthinkingly.

Both Mrs. and Ms. (with the period) are used in the House and Senate, apparently at the option of the Member, when referring to a female representative or senator by name, rather than title. But that doesn't translate to a woman president. I therefore vote for Madam President.

Joseph E. Ross
Director, Congressional
Research Service
The Library of Congress
Washington, D.C.

Double Dip or Dead-Cat Bounce?

Rosey Scenario, that always-cheerful economist, may soon be jilted if we are indeed in a *double dip.*

That dread prospect first found expression in *Business Week* in February 1975, attributed to an unidentified Ford Administration economist: "What is now likely is a '*double-dip recession,*' as one Administration economist puts it." Three months later, it reported a scenario that "portrays a *double-dip recession* in which the economy recovers in the second half of 1975 but lapses into decline again in 1976." (This did not happen.)

The threat is back; whistling past this graveyard a couple of weeks ago was Jerry Jasinowski, president of the National Association of Manufacturers, who reported a poll in which "only 3 percent expect a *double dip.*"

The meaning is "two declines in rapid succession" or "aborted recovery"; this sense is quite different from *double dipping,* defined in my 1978 political dictionary as "income, in the form of salary or pension, from two government sources." When Admiral Stansfield Turner retired from the Navy to become Director of Central Intelligence in the Carter Administration, I zapped him

as a "ring-knocking double dipper," which some bird watchers took to be a rare specimen of woodpecker but old Washington hands knew was an Annapolis graduate drawing a Navy pension and government salary simultaneously.

Dip and *deep* are related words. *Double dip*'s earlier sense—of excess, or at least lavishness—is based on the metaphor of a clerk in an ice-cream store digging deeply twice into a container to come up with two scoops to be placed on a single cone. (I always ask for *sprinkles;* Midwesterners were first to call the topping *jimmies;* files of the *Dictionary of American Regional English* include *shots, hundreds and thousands, nonpareils* and even *bedbugs.* This is taking me far afield of economic jargon, but in a recession, there's no more satisfying pick-me-up than a double dip of chocolate and butter pecan with multicolored sprinkles.) The old slang sense of excess has been shunted aside by the new sense of "two downturns."

A more graphic synonym for that worrisome news is *dead-cat bounce*. I first heard that phrase in 1991 from Laurence Tisch, the CBS chairman, who told me over a power breakfast at the Regency Hotel in New York that this vivid description of a fearsome scenario was being bruited about in the nation's boardrooms. I opened a file; about that time, *The Vancouver Sun* in British Columbia reported: "Is the recession really over, or is it a '*dead-cat bounce*'? The latter, we're told, is the market jargon for a false sign of recovery—gruesome, but graphic."

Gruesome is right. The feline metaphor, surely distressing to animal lovers, was first used by a departing member of Franklin D. Roosevelt's Administration, Hugh Johnson of the National Recovery Administration, who described his exit as being amidst "a hail of dead cats," by which he meant widespread criticism. Dr. Seuss, when a political cartoonist for the newspaper *PM* in the 1940's, used cats with X-marks for eyes as symbols of denunciations of politicians.

The earliest citation I have is *dead cat bounce,* unhyphenated, although the first two words should be hyphenated as a compound adjective modifying *bounce.* On December 7, 1985, Chris Sherwell in Singapore and Wong Sulong in Kuala Lumpur reported in *The Financial Times* that investment analysts "said the rise was partly technical and cautioned against concluding that the recent falls in the market were at an end. 'This is what we call a *dead cat bounce,*' one broker said flatly."

A year after this Far Eastern citation, an Associated Press dispatch from New York quoted a broker, Raymond DeVoe Jr., on oil stocks as advising, "Beware the *dead-cat bounce.*" The broker gave this explanation of the macabre phrase: "This applies to stocks or commodities that have gone into free-fall descent and then rallied briefly. If you threw a dead cat off a 50-story building, it might bounce when it hit the sidewalk. But don't confuse that bounce with renewed life. It is still a dead cat."

The phrase—born in the Far East, savored in Britain, adopted on Wall Street—has nine lives. Lexicographer Paul Dickson's 1990 *Slang!* preserved it for posterity with this definition: "Small increase in the market averages after a substantial drop." Recently, Reuters resuscitated the phrase in a piece about the sad days of British yuppies: "Like any clique, they had their own impenetrable language. '*Dead-cat bounce*' was when shares crashed, then rose but failed to recover to anything near their previous values."

In chapter 6 of Mark Twain's 1876 novel, *The Adventures of Tom Sawyer,* Tom sees Huckleberry Finn carrying something, and Huck explains that it's a "dead cat."

"Say—what is dead cats good for, Huck?"

"Good for? Cure warts with."

Dustbins and Garbage Heaps

As Mensheviks departed from the 1917 Congress of Soviets, the Bolshevik Leon Trotsky shouted after them: "Go to the place where you belong from now on—the dustbin of history!" He may have taken this from Augustine Birrell's 1887 phrase, "that great dust heap called 'history.' "

In 1991, both the philosophy of Communism and the Soviet Union were consigned, rhetorically, to the dustbin, ash heap and garbage heap of history. Which is it—where do the discards go?

Dustbin is British English; the American translation is *garbage pail.* (A *dustman*—Alfred Doolittle's occupation in Shaw's *Pygmalion*—used to be a *garbage man* and is now a *sanitation worker.*)

A word was needed to cover both British and American usage, and to reflect the throwing-out of metal statues of Communist leaders. The International *Herald Tribune* came up with it in a banner headline about the "junking" of Lenin's power structure: SCRAP HEAP OF HISTORY.

"Dustbins and Garbage Heaps," yes; "Scrap Heap of History," no.

Being third generation in this dodge of recycling, I have had opportunity to observe the tags applied to metal scrap and, alas and gotcha, I think you've tripped up.

"Scrap" is usually used correctly today, that is metal (or other materials) which will be recycled. In the case of metals, the scrap is always *recycled by being* remelted *into new metal.*

Dustbins, yes. Garbage heaps, yes. Waste, yes. Rubbish, yes. Junk, possibly, but this word is sometimes used as a pejorative for "scrap."

The distinction between "scrap" and "waste" is not entirely theoretical and Safirean. This is a national and indeed international debate on whether scrap should be included in the laws covering waste, that is the waste coming out of households and municipal dumps. It should not.

> *Michael Suisman*
> *Chairman, Suisman &*
> *Blumenthal*
> *Buyers, Processors and Sellers*
> *Aerospace, Non-Ferrous and*
> *Ferrous Scrap*
> *Hartford, Connecticut*

Electability

"Clinton's campaign is not about ideology," Renee Loth wrote in the *Boston Globe,* "it's about *electability.*"

"I think that the press should pay attention to someone with good ideas," Paul Tsongas said before winning the New Hampshire primary, "and not just look at *electability.*"

"All this talk about '*electability*,' " said Governor Mario Cuomo, waving his hand dismissively (we were talking on the phone, and I could hear him waving his hand). "Whoever wins New Hampshire gets a presumption of *electability*." (I think he hoped I wouldn't believe it.)

In the linguistic contest between *electability* and *winnability*, it's *electability* in a landslide.

Winnability had a good press early in that campaign, especially after supporters of Dwight Eisenhower used it against Robert Taft, Ike's competitor for the 1952 Republican nomination. As the *Oxford English Dictionary* supplement notes, it was a concern expressed by Richard Nixon during his mid-60's comeback. (The "can't win" theme was first used against Henry Clay in 1840 by Thurlow Weed, the Albany kingmaker who supported William Henry Harrison.)

But *winnability* has been clipped to *winnable,* and is applied to elections rather than candidates, as in "You know, if we have a triple-dip recession, this election is *winnable.*" Its use in a negative form, *unwinnable,* dates back to John Bellenden's translation in 1536 of a history of Scottish warfare: "This crag is . . . *unwynnabill.*"

Meanwhile, the more staid and less zingy *electability* has maintained its franchise dating from the 1879 coinage of *electable.* "Hart plans to stress the '*electability* issue,' " wrote *Time* magazine in 1984, and the candidate had a point: His opponent, Walter Mondale, seems in retrospect to have been unelectable after his loss to President Reagan. But the prediction of defeat implicit in that "issue" does not always come true: In August 1987, Senator Bob Dole said, "*Electability* is going to be an issue," but George Bush was deemed—and proved to be—capable of being elected.

Can *winnability* (always with two *n*'s, to differentiate it from the defeatist *whine-ability*) make a comeback and upset the entrenched *electability*? It's available. (But who, besides Governor Cuomo, can remember *availability*?)

El Niño

El Niño de Navidad is Spanish for "The Christ Child"; a current of warm sea water that sweeps across the Pacific Ocean and down the coast of Peru every decade or so is called El Niño by fishermen because it usually appears at Christmastime.

This ocean current, which pushes aside the cold Humboldt current and results in a poor catch of anchovies, is then blamed for every rained-out picnic in the world. It affects the jet stream, causing trade winds to blow the wrong way, wet conditions in dry areas, floods and a rise in world protein prices.

Because it has great allegorical resonance, I write a profound political thumbsucker about the El Niño (pronounced "NEEN-yo") current every time around. This year I equated its return to the inexorability of recessions; it's as good as the dartboard theory of stock selection.

This time, I have upset the Squad Squad, which has a representative of its anti-redundancy crusade at the news desk of the *Times*'s Washington bureau. He is Irv Molotsky, who drops this in my electronic mail (I check my "box" every month or so, when I finish with the real mail).

"You wrote the other day of 'the El Niño current.' Since *el* is the Spanish for 'the,' aren't you saying 'the the child'?" Arguing by analogy, he adds, "When you were a young man about town with Tex and Jinx, I bet you went to El Morocco, not to *the* El Morocco."

Memories of dazzling Eileen Ford models against zebra-striped nightclub banquettes flood through my mind like warm sea water. I dash the icy Humboldt in my face to ask: Did I say, "I can't afford El Morocco; how about Hurley's Bar?" or "I can't afford *the* El Morocco; how about the Studio Club in Mount Vernon?"

Irv is right: I couldn't afford (no *the*) El Morocco in its New York heyday. But when I did get lured there, I stole *the* El Morocco ashtray, and snatched up *the* El Morocco matches, and leered at *the* El Morocco hatchick (now called a coatroom attendant in successor nightspots). The name "El Morocco," in all those cases, is an attributive noun phrase modifying *ashtray, matches* and *hatchick;* "the El Morocco whatever" is, therefore, not redundant, and the same goes for "the El Niño current." This use of a doubled *the,* however, should occur only when one of the definite articles is foreign; never give "the The Bronx cheer."

And so to the frequent cry of "Gotcha!" I can in this case reply, "Gedoudahere."

Dear Bill:

Your item on "El Niño" got the pronunciation almost but not quite right. You said (if I remember correctly—I can't find the clipping) that the word was pronounced "NEEN-yo," which puts the syllable boundary in the middle of what is really a single sound (a palatalized "n") and encourages the reader to use the non-palatalized "n" that English has in such words as "vineyard"; it would have been much more accurate to give the pronunciation as "NEE-nyo."

At least, though, The Times *printed some sort of an approximation to the tilde on the "ñ," which is better than what* The Times *usually does with diacritics, although far below the typographical standards observed by hole-in-the-wall printeries in East Harlem that make business cards and wedding invitations for the Puerto Rican community. Actually, I've been meaning to write to you about diacritics for some time, but the relevant* NYT *clipping, which now has serendipitously turned up, kept disappearing into heaps of paper before I composed the letter. Most American newspapers and magazines, even* The New York Times, *follow the disgraceful and slovenly practice of omitting diacritics in foreign names. This is a policy that you might want to try to get your colleagues to change: the fact that even such a prestigious institution as* The New York Times *makes little attempt to reproduce orthographic distinctions that do real work in many foreign versions of the Roman alphabet encourages the common attitude in this country that might be described as linguistic solipsism: the belief that only one's own native language is fully real.*

The Times *at least keeps the diacritics in French and German, but many other publications ignore them even in such unexotic languages. A ludicrous case of omitted diacritics showed up in both Chicago daily newspapers for several months, when one of our two Spanish-language television stations was carrying a telenovela entitled* Los Años Perdidos, *that is, "The Lost Years." However, the TV listings in both the* Tribune *and the* Sun-Times *gave it as* Los Anos Perdidos, *which means "The Lost Assholes."*

> Jim *[James D. McCawley]*
> *Department of Linguistics*
> *University of Chicago*
> *Chicago, Illinois*

Engagement Party

Governor Bill Clinton, searching for a new and different word to describe his foreign policy—not isolationist, but not too interventionist—floated out "a new strategy for American *engagement.*" The choice, he told the Foreign Policy Association, was "whether we will *engage* or abstain."

Eyebrows shot up at the Heritage Foundation, a conservative think tank. Kim R. Holmes, its foreign-policy chief, had only the week before circulated a speech centered on "Selective *Engagement:* A New Global Strategy."

And a month before that, Secretary of State James A. Baker 3d titled a portion of a speech "From Containment to Collective *Engagement.*" The early cold war strategy called *containment* of Communism, promulgated by George (Mr. X) Kennan, was to be replaced by a policy of *collective engagement* that Baker defined, in a burst of turgidity, as "nations taking concerted action to pursue common interests and solve common problems."

(Note that the State Department still uses the word *policy;* at the White House, and at think tanks that incubate future national-security advisers, the only word to use is *strategy.* Policy is bookish; strategy is fun.)

Where did the Baker State Department get its use of *engagement?* Not from the Pentagon, which considers an engagement a battle, and is not seeking to engage an enemy without at least a half-million troops in place and the fervent support of the American people. No, this noun comes from the frequently used verb *engage,* as used by diplomats in "engage in a dialogue." That is steeped in the French *gage,* a token or pledge given to insure performance, and is the source of *engagement ring.* ("She's lovely. She's engaged. She uses Ponds" was the slogan back when cleansing cream was cold cream. We used to wonder how many of those models went ahead and got married.)

The immediate source of the current run of lovely *engagements* in diplolingo is, I think, the 1988 campaign platform of Gary Hart. With a nice touch of alliteration, he spoke of *enlightened engagement,* which would disentangle the United States from outdated alliances and foolish adventurism without withdrawing from useful associations and necessary interventions.

Disengage that clutch of fear: Abstinence from global responsibility does not make the heart grow fonder. Hawks and doves alike have adopted *engagement* as the strategy of the future. Now, says the waitress: How do you like your engagement? *Selective, collective, enlightened . . .*

Dr. Chester Crocker, now a professor of politics at the University of Georgetown, was the man who, I think, was responsible for the introduction of the word "engagement" in the diplomatic vocabulary.

In 1981 he became Assistant Secretary of State for African Affairs when Ronald Reagan took office as president.

He elaborated a new political strategy to deal with South Africa and the growing war between South Africa and its neighbors, which he dubbed "Constructive Engagement."

Joao Santa-Rita
Fairfax, Virginia

Enjoy!

In Donna Adele, an authentically Italian restaurant in Washington, an Italian headwaiter took my order, ripped the page off his order book with a flourish, handed it to the Italian waiter, adding a few words in Italian, and said to me cheerfully, over his shoulder, *"Enjoy!"*

That's not Italian. The same concluding good wish was offered on the island of Maui, in Hawaii, by a waitress in a grass skirt (she was from Seattle, but the uniform called for grass skirts). Again, not *Aloha* or *Mahalo,* not even the French *Bon appétit,* but *Enjoy!*

I suspect we may be seeing the worldwide spread of an Americanism that one day could rival the ubiquitous *O.K.* The last time an expression born in the New World made an impact in many foreign languages, it was the proliferation of *No problem.* Can we trace the origin and track the spread of *Enjoy!* as a verb without a stated object? *Nyet problemy.*

In his 1986 book, *Yiddish and English,* Random House lexicographer Sol Steinmetz cites this 1968 quotation of furrier Jacques Kaplan by Marylin Bender in *The New York Times:* "It's a dancing over the volcano attitude, an enjoy-enjoy philosophy." That reduplication is typical of Yiddish—*Es, es* means "Eat, eat"—and the friendly command of *Enjoy!* comes from *Hob anoe,* a Yiddish phrase derived from the German *hob,* "have," and the Hebrew *hanoe,* "enjoyment."

Curiously, the Yiddish phrase from which *Enjoy!* is derived is not the expression most often used at the dining table by those who speak Yiddish or Hebrew. *Es gezunterheyt,* literally "Eat in health," is Yiddish, and *Leteavon,* "For appetite," is Hebrew.

If *Enjoy!* is to go global, it will have stiff competition. The French *Bon appétit,* the Spanish *Buen apetito* and the Italian *Buon appetito* each mean "Good appetite," as does the German *Guten Appetit* (though many German waiters will say *Mahlzeit!,* "Mealtime!"). The Russians are also fixed on a pleasant appetite—*Priyatnovo appetita*—but the Japanese have a variant: *Takusan meshiagatte kudasai,* "Please eat a lot."

Restaurant personnel do travel, however, and the new expression contains a polite imperative, putting the server on a more nearly equal basis with the customer.

Is *Enjoy!* likely to make inroads on the good-appetite translations, or to become standard without an object? "To use *enjoy* without an *it* or a *them* is perhaps cute," writes John David Grayson, a linguistics professor at Concordia University in Montreal, "if everyone recognizes the expression as Yinglish and playful. It is a disaster when English-speakers think that such an expression is standard usage."

I dunno. Purists and slobs can agree that the object of the verb *enjoy* in this usage is the unspoken but clearly understood *your meal.* As they set down their plates before us, the members of the waiting game are using the transitive verb, *enjoy,* in a way that grammarians call "absolutely"; that is, the verb takes an object, but the object is implied, not directly stated. (The transitive verb *like*—I like this—may also be used absolutely; the question "You like?" and its response "I like," with no objects stated, are current examples of absolute use that began with the Shakespearean expression *if you like.*)

The earliest example of the absolute use of the transitive *enjoy* comes from an essay by English author John Ruskin in *The Eagle's Nest,* in 1872: "It is appointed for all men to enjoy, but for few to achieve."

Not such a disaster; the syntactic crowd, which thinks positively, could learn to live with *enjoy* employed absolutely. The burning question in the kitchens of the restaurant world is: Will French traditionalists stand for it? *Certainement,* traditionalists in the Académie Française, where the language is defended against assaults from the barbarians, a furious assertion of *Bon appétit* will be heard. But cool heads will point out that the English verb *enjoy* comes from the Old French *enjoir,* "to make or give joy," and French waiters who were offering a taste of a fourteenth-century Bordeaux (great century) might have been comfortable with "*Enjoyez!*"

We will keep an eye on the spread of this expression, and on its competition with the declining, decaying evocations of good appetites. Will the Yiddishism, now firmly established as New Yorkese and taking root as an Americanism, be contained within these shores? Or will citations be sent in from the centers of haute cuisine and the humble beaneries around the globe?

Because this linguistic prairie fire will be fun to watch, a certain expression comes to mind—but, sorry, you're not my table.

Enjoy was first used in connection with the presentation of food to a diner by the Jewish waiters at the famous Lindy's on Broadway.

*They were also the originators of another expression, "*You're entitled.*" This was used when a patron refused the dessert course although included in the luncheon price.*

> Ralph Costantino
> New York, New York

Most native speakers of German would probably offer this translation only when requested to translate literally. Otherwise they would be likely to tell you that "Mahlzeit!" stands for "Gesegnete Mahlzeit!", which translates as "[Have a] blessed meal!" (and reminds me of a prayer used in the United States: "Bless us, oh Lord, and these thy gifts which we are about to receive . . ."). *I heard the full German phrase quite frequently during my youth in rural Austria, and it is still in use. This is not to suggest that today the expression "Mahlzeit!" necessarily has a spiritual connotation; however, it does connote a wish along the lines of "Have a good meal!" or "Bon appétit!" and is not the meaningless exclamation or, worse, command that your translation suggests.*

> Rosemarie Rogers
> Cambridge, Massachusetts

Maybe we should look for the origin of enjoy! *in another expression, namely:* genist! *(literally: enjoy!) which was still used in the 1930's at least in Eastern Galician, Bukovinian, and Bessarabian Yiddish, as an exhortation to partake of refreshments offered at the table.*

> Mordkhe Schaechter
> Executive Director
> Yiddish-language Resource
> Center
> League for Yiddish, Inc.
> New York, New York

Although "Buen apetito" is a direct translation of "Bon appétit," it is seldom heard in South America, never in Spain. There, the courteous "Buen provecho" that precedes a meal is literally translated "[take] good advantage/benefit," which brings it close enough to "Enjoy!" for one to wonder (in this quintocentenario year) about the Murano/Converso influence!

> Audrey A. P. Lavin
> Ruth Fuquen
> Canton, Ohio

You say the Spanish equivalent of bon appétit *is* buen apetito, *which is literally true. But in much of Latin America that phrase is seldom if ever heard. Where it does appear, it is mostly an upper-class phrase (e.g., in Argentina, where emulation of the French is a long-standing cultural aberration). The working-class phrase is* buen provecho, *often abbreviated to* provecho. *This is totally idiomatic. It means something like "eat it well" in the sense of "wear it well."*

> Arthur M. Shapiro
> Davis, California

The Evolving Moment

"He's very, very intelligent," said Barbra (only two *a*'s) Streisand about the tennis star Andre Agassi, "very, very sensitive, very evolved; more than his linear years. . . . He plays like a Zen master. It's very in the moment."

Much food for thought is set forth in this display of the language of the superstar subculture. Weakness is shown in the overuse of *very,* the adverbial crutch, and *sensitive* has become a cliché in the feminist praise of other-directed males, but *evolved* to mean "advanced in social awareness" is a new one on me.

At least that is the meaning the context seems to indicate. To evolve is to change through growth; both homo sapiens and the apes are descended from a common ancestor, evolving differently. One sense is "to derive," another "to develop," a third "to improve," a fourth "to emerge." A more recent sense has been applied to political positions: "to mature in a way considered positive by the observer"; in this meaning, Dan Quayle's embrace of the centrist Pennsylvania abortion statute is seen by abortion-rights activists as an evolution of his previously uncompromising position.

Its change from active to passive voice—from "He *evolved from* the Missing Link" to "He *is evolved*"—was probably influenced by the adoption of *involved* as a compliment. Some of us who still shudder at memories of Watergate can recall the sinister implication of the question "Is he *involved*?"; now, *to be involved* is to be a fully fledged participant in the action and passion of the times. Relatedly, thanks to the well-reported compliment of Ms Streisand's, we are seeing the transformation of "His positions have evolved" to "He is an evolved person"—describing not just a tennis player, but a human being sensitized right down to his sandpapered fingertips.

"More than his *linear* years," however, is a mistake. *Linear* means "direct, uninterrupted"; it has gained a pejorative vogue sense of "unimaginative," as in *linear thinking,* in contrast to insightful, inspired leaps of genius. I think what Ms Streisand had in mind was "beyond his chronological years," which is better expressed as simply "beyond his years." You can see what she was getting at—the years lined up in an orderly fashion—but even in the anything-goes world of show-biz lingo, not everything goes. Strike the set on *linear.*

"*It's very in the moment,*" though, is not to be scorned. This *very* calls attention to the use of a preposition or a noun as a modifier, as in "It's very *in,*" or "It's very *New York,*" or the ultimate fashion compliment, "It's very *you.*"

To be very *in the moment* (perhaps a variation of *of the moment* or *up to the minute*) appears to be a loose translation of the French *au courant,* variously translated as "up to date, fashionable, with-it," or in some other way closely in tune with the *Zeitgeist.* On this one, let us not rain on Barbra's parade: People who love language are the loveliest people in the world.

As quoted, Streisand says, "He plays like a Zen master. It's very in the moment." "It's," in the quote, refers to Agassi's tennis—his tennis is very in the moment. "In the moment" refers to the ability of a player to achieve such a high level of concentration during each point of play that he is able to block out every-

thing else. Martina Navratilova refers to this as "staying in the present"; other professional tennis players have similar phrases to describe the intense level of concentration needed.

Mark Rosoff
Scarsdale, New York

Evolving in the Moment

Barbra Streisand, the political activist and singer, was quoted here as saying about her friend Andre Agassi, the tennis star, that he was "very *evolved;* more than his linear years . . . very *in the moment."*

I carefully—perhaps linearly—traced the evolution of *evolved* to mean "maturing in a way considered positive by the observer; advanced in social awareness." This definition triggered a refutation from people, mainly Californians, who have a more evolved understanding of new-age terminology. Peter Norton, the computer utilitarian of Santa Monica, defines *evolved* as "not 'advanced in social awareness' but advanced in spiritual evolution, in the Buddhist and Hindu sense." My icon-happy correspondent adds drawings of a straight arrow to indicate *linear years,* and of an arrow with a loop in its shaft to denote *spiritual years.*

Alan Alda, the actor, has long been a Lexicographic Irregular; he knows the difference between a *skit* and a *sketch,* and knows the unlikely meaning of *apple box,* which I do not. Mr. Alda writes that "Both words and crystals are put to uses in California that seem odd to people in the East. Rather than having the connotation of 'social awareness,' I think the term *evolved* is used here in a more spiritual context.

"I remember first hearing the word *evolved* used in this way several years ago when people would say that someone was 'very evolved spiritually,' " Mr. Alda continues. "This was a compliment derived from the belief—fashionable for a while in this country, especially in California—that with every incarnation you improve as a person until you evolve into a model creature. Agents and other meat-eaters were considered to be recent entrants into this process." He concludes that the passive *is evolved* is rooted in that onward-and-upward assumption—now considered erroneous by nonlinear thinkers, often vegetarian—that humans are at the top of the evolutionary scale. "So, to say that Agassi is 'very evolved' is to say that spiritually he's tops."

This Alda interpretation is reinforced by Tama Starr of New York, author of *The "Natural Inferiority" of Women,* an excoriation of misguided males: "The rather complex idea packed into *evolved* is that while all souls journey from incarnation to incarnation, acquiring spiritual wisdom along the way,

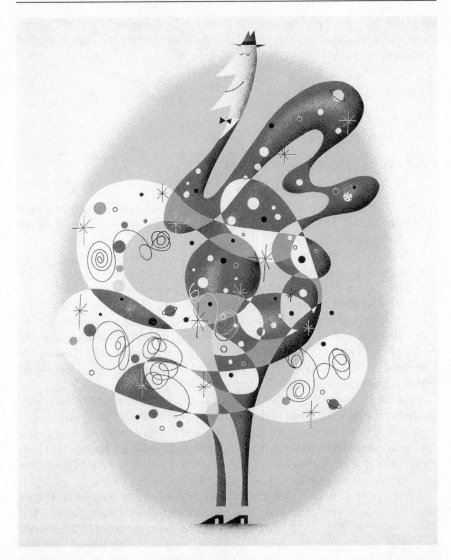

some (called 'old souls' in the jargon) have had more of these opportunities than others . . . and thus have become more *evolved.*" Ms Starr adds: "I am not inventing or hallucinating this. It is a cliché from the Middle New Age (circa 1971)."

As a merry old soul who enjoyed the linear performance of Mr. Alda's father, Robert, in *Guys and Dolls* in 1950, I reacted to the torrent of new-age mail by directing an October query to Ms Streisand about her meaning. She wrote back: "Thank you for the offer to respond. If you vote for Clinton, I just might." (I did, but she did not do what she said she might; this double-cross augurs ill for the new Administration, whose pre-election promises I now have specific cause to distrust.)

Others, however, have come to my aid in the matter of *in the moment,* which I treated as a variant of *up to the minute* or the French *au courant.*

"She used *in the moment* in the way it is often used by actors and acting teachers," writes George Cuttingham, president of the American Academy of Dramatic Arts. "A performer's desirable state of total, relaxed commitment to (or concentration on) the moment at hand, free of concern with previous or future moments." He notes the application of the precepts of Zen Buddhism to Mr. Agassi's profession in W. Timothy Gallwey's book *The Inner Game of Tennis.*

"A person who is *in the moment,*" writes David Smith, a Harvard graduate student of history, "is one who avoids the common tendency of dwelling on the past, the future or anything extrinsic to the moment at hand . . . similar to experiencing an Eastern state of transcendental immanence." Contrariwise, "one who is *au courant* is probably at great pains to heed the dictates of contemporary fashion."

Linda Healey, a copy editor at the International *Herald Tribune,* agrees that *in the moment* has nothing to do with being "up-to-date or in tune with the Zeitgeist." She considers the practitioner to be "totally absorbed . . . in each instant as it happens, like a practitioner of Zen who aims to eliminate the barrier between ego and experience." Karen Duktig of Haverstraw, New York, calls it "the feeling of time being suspended, of nothing else in the world right now except this tennis game, this ball and this racquet. No score, no spectators, just arm and racquet and ball and net . . . this is called 'flow.' Focused. 'Lost in the moment' really describes it, but 'lost' sounds so negative." That sense applies to dance as well. Writes Elizabeth Zimmer, dance editor of *The Village Voice,* "It more likely means 'present,' in the sense implied by the New Age mantra 'Be here now.' "

Obviously this Buddhist thinking has had an impact on the stage. Konstantin Stanislavsky, the Russian director and acting theorist, urged actors to behave as if the action were actually taking place at the time of performance. "In the post-Stanislavsky experiments of the 1960's and 70's," writes Richard E. Kramer of New York, "this concept was expanded to include the notion that the performance itself *is* really happening now, and the actor is also a real person in the presence of other real people, the audience."

Which brings us back to Alan Alda for his analysis of this Zen phrase's application to acting: "You have to be acquainted with the concept of acting 'moment to moment.' This means when you are playing a scene you try to deal with what is happening right now. You don't bring a predetermined attitude onstage. . . . You do not pretend to be listening; you listen. You stay in the moment."

It's easy enough to spoof new-age jargon and its persontras, but language mavens should concentrate on what the speaker or writer means, and not blithely assume it to be what the reader or audience brings to it. That was my error; I applied my own logic to Ms Streisand's words, a reading that turned out to be a type of folk etymology that linguists should guard against.

"We tend to lean toward theories of derivation that tie in with our own personal experience," goes Mr. Alda's mash note, in gentle reproof to my derogation of show-biz lingo as an anything-goes world. "I often wonder how many definitive statements of how a word or phrase got that way simply reflect a comfortable feeling on someone's part that it sounds like a duck so it must be a duck.

"If someone on a set asked you for a half-apple and you started peeling a piece of fruit," he zings, "you might hear a colorful word or two about Potomac Pundits."

"Explicit" Is Not a Dirty Word

In a "parental advisory," many record companies now include these words of warning on their adult offerings: "*Explicit lyrics.*"

"I take it," writes Peter Wood of Boston University, "that this is not intended to warn consumers that the lyrics were enunciated with precision, or that the listener might be overwhelmed by an encounter with clear statements."

David A. Santogrossi of West Lafayette, Indiana, has the same problem: "The word *explicit* means 'straightforward, openly stated rather than implied.' But I can imagine a time when I will ask a woman to 'be more explicit'—and get a slap in the face."

We have here a word that was keeping company with a modifier, and when the modifier ran out, the word was left in the lurch with the modified meaning. That happened with *male chauvinist;* a *chauvinist* was a nationalist zealot, like the soldier named Chauvin who fervently followed Napoleon. Then *Time* magazine in 1950 coined the term *male chauvinist,* to mean "misogynist, woman-hater" or more specifically "male supremacist"; after a while, militant feminists used *chauvinist* without the *male* modifier to make their points. The noun had absorbed the connotation of the phrase, ruining the noun for any other meaning.

Same thing is happening to *explicit,* a word rooted in the Latin for "unfolded." The adjectival phrase was *sexually explicit,* until the premodifying adverb *sexually* was lopped off by frequent users. That left *explicit* to carry on alone, abandoned by the modifier that got it into trouble. Now the word has the odor of obscenity or pornography about it, while its pristine senses—of clarity and openness—are left out in the cold. This argues for the sanctity of the marriage of modifiers, but go tell that to the promiscuous phrase splitters.

The premodifier is not always the guilty party. Take the noun phrase *adult entertainment.* When we were kids, *adult* meant "grown-up, mature," but now its association with the go-go world of show biz has given it a sense of "not suitable for children." As a result, the word *adult* has gained the sense of *risqué* (French for "risking offense in polite conversation") or outright *pornographic* (from the Greek for "the writing of harlots") or *erotic* (from the Greek *Eros,* god of love), which means "arousing sexual desire." *Amateur,* by the way, is based on the Latin *amare,* "to love," and has come to mean "doing something not for pay but for the love of it."

Now, after all this grammatical ground-pawing, we get to the hot part. "Starring in Tonight's Erotic Video: The Couple Down the Street" is a five-column headline in *The New York Times,* above a story about "amateur adult videotapes." The star in this booming new industry is a thirty-seven-year-old Kentucky lawyer and mother of two who "refuses to allow her real name to be made public," writes Michael deCourcy Hinds, "but has revealed nearly everything else in five or six erotic tapes."

Mr. Hinds reports that the big hit is titled *Mary Lou the Stud Finder,* based on a visit to the lawyer's home by a couple of carpenters to repair the porch. One sense of *stud* is "an upright in the framing of the walls to which paneling or laths are fastened," and a *stud finder* is an instrument that detects these uprights without tearing open the wall. A slang sense of *stud,* taken from a stallion used for breeding, is "a posturing male," as in the nickname of the hero in James T. Farrell's trilogy, *Studs Lonigan.*

Now to what has happened to the old-fashioned noun *swinger* and the participle *wife-swapping,* which many assumed would change to *spouse-swapping.* That did not happen; according to reporter Hinds, "Mary Lou said she and her husband attend conventions around the country of people interested in swapping sex partners, which participants refer to these days as '*consensual non-monogamy.*' "

Curious term; let us consider each of its parts.

Why *consensual,* not *consenting,* as in "consenting adults"? A case can be made that *consenting* applies to one-way consent (though two partners can give it simultaneously) while *consensual* denotes a two-way arrangement; besides, there is a nice play on *sensual.*

Monogamy means "one mate at a time." We tend to think of *monogamy* as the opposite of *polygamy,* which means "more than one mate at a time," but they are not precise antonyms because they deal only with the number of mates, not with the absence or presence of mates. (I use *mates* rather than *spouses* so as to include the rest of the animal kingdom.) In human affairs, *polygamy* becomes the crime of *bigamy* when it involves the contract of marriage to more than one person; presumably that is why the consensualists choose the fuzzier *non-monogamy.*

I do not consent; if you prefer a Goldwynism, when it comes to *non-monogamy,* consensual me out.

Non-monogamy is a cop-out, a word coined to avoid the use of a more direct term. The "A-word," as it is called in politics, is *adultery,* "intercourse between a married person and someone not his or her spouse." That's what Mary Lou and her husband assert to be their recreation, and it is not for grammarians to pass moral judgment, but when it comes to grammatical judgment, what they are saying is wrong, wrong, wrong. As a married couple, they are practicing *consensual adultery;* if they were unmarried but still a couple, they would be fairly described as *polygamous* because the adjective does not carry the same specificity as the noun, *polygamy.*

Frankly—and today's column is nothing if not frank—I see nothing wrong with the term *swinging couples,* which has the widely understood meaning easily diagramed by anyone who understands how to rotate automobile tires in such a way as to distribute wear evenly. Unblessed or unburdened by marriage vows, the non-adulterous participants would be engaged in a simple *orgy,* from the Latin word for "secret rites" akin to the Greek *ergon,* "work," which some world-weary types claim it is. Here we go again: *Orgy* originally meant "wild revelry," as at the parties of Dionysus, and can still be applied to any licentious or passionate activity, but its frequent linkage with *sex* has given *orgy,* standing by itself, a meaning of "unbridled intercourse."

The alert reader will have noted two uses of the same abandoned and abused noun in the past two paragraphs. That is *intercourse,* which once meant general "dealings between individuals or groups," and still does in non-swinging dictionaries, but which most people take to mean *sexual intercourse.* If consensual non-monogamists ask, "Was there intercourse at the orgy?," few carpenters would take the meaning to be "Was there any cultural or commercial communication during the revelry?"

Left at the altar by the adjective *sexual,* the innocent *intercourse*—standing by itself—is connotatively damaged goods. *Explicit* knows just how it feels.

I have an explicit, adult comment to make. The English word orgy *is not "from the Latin word for 'secret rites' akin to the Greek* ergon, *'work.' " It is (see etymological note in* Webster's New World Dictionary*) from the Greek word for "secret rites" akin to the Greek* ergon, *"work" (which is in turn akin to the English word* work*). The politically and militarily dominant Romans borrowed thousands of words from the culturally dominant Greeks and eventually passed them along to the various European languages. Nearly all English words of Greek origin were therefore acquired through the medium of Latin, but that doesn't make them any less Greek.*

Louis Jay Herman
New York, New York

While "polygamy" may mean "more than one mate at a time," this specifically seems to apply to one (1) male with several females; one (1) female with several males is generally referred to as "polyandry" in the human or other biological pairings.

Felix Schnur
Scarsdale, New York

Family Values

"Integrity, courage, strength"—those were the *family values* as defined by Barbara Bush at the 1992 Republican convention in Houston. She added "sharing, love of God and pride in being an American." Not much controversy in that definition.

But on "family values night," as Marilyn Quayle described the session dominated by Republican women, the values took on an accusatory edge: After recalling that many in the baby boom had not "joined the counterculture" or "dodged the draft," the Vice President's wife made clear to cheering conservatives what she felt was at the center of family values: "Commitment, marriage and fidelity are not just arbitrary arrangements."

Pat Robertson, the religious broadcaster who sought the presidential nomination in 1988, eschewed such innuendo and slammed home the political point: "When Bill and Hillary Clinton talk about family values, they are not talking about either families or values. They are talking about a radical plan to destroy the traditional family."

We have here the G.O.P.'s political attack phrase of the 1992 campaign. When Mario Cuomo stressed the words *family* and *values* in his speech to the 1984 Democratic convention, he used them in a warmly positive sense. But this year, packaged in a single phrase, the terms are an assertion of moral traditionalism that carries an implicit charge: The other side seeks to undermine the institution of the family by taking a permissive line on (a) abortion rights, (b) homosexual rights and (c) the "character issue," code words for marital infidelity.

Sometimes pot smoking is included, but sex is most often the common denominator, and the pointing finger includes women who do not center their lives inside the home: The defeated candidate Pat Buchanan includes "radical feminist" in his angry denunciation of those who lack what he considers to be family values.

The use of *family* as an attributive noun in its modern sense can be traced back to the eighteenth century, as in Samuel Johnson's 1781 sales pitch for his dictionary: "This Lexicon . . . might become a concomitant to the Family

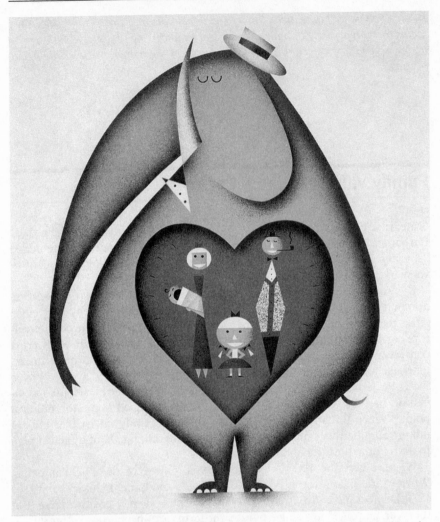

Bible." In that decade, *family man* was coined, followed a generation later by *family circle.*

The word *family* is based on the Latin *famulus,* "servant"; in 1400, a man's servants included his wife, children and domestic help. "His family," goes a report of a 1621 Star Chamber case, "were himself and his wife and daughters, two mayds, and a man." You do not have to be a radical feminist to know that this sense has been lost. The poet John Milton first used *family* in the sense of "parents and children" in *Paradise Lost* in 1667, with Jesus as the head of the family of Man: "As Father of his Familie he clad/Thir nakedness."

The family being used as the attributive, or modifying, noun today is the *traditional family,* by which is usually meant a father and mother (of opposite sexes), legally married, with children under eighteen living at home. According to the Census Bureau, 26 percent of American households now meet these criteria.

This group is also known as the *nuclear family,* a coinage of the anthropologist George P. Murdock in 1949—"a married man and woman with their offspring"—perhaps taken from the 1913 "nucleus-complex" discussed by the psychoanalyst Carl Jung, combining the lust of sons for mothers and lust of daughters for fathers. (How did we get here? Back to politics.) In 1966, Daniel T. Jenkins wrote of "the extended, as distinct from the nuclear, family," and Barbara Bush in 1992 used that term to expand her meaning of family: "When we speak of families, we include extended families. We mean the neighbors, even the community itself."

The earlier term for something similar to *family values* was *social issue,* a 1970 coinage by Richard M. Scammon and Ben J. Wattenberg in their seminal work, *The Real Majority.* The authors argued that rather than being primarily concerned with the old *bread-and-butter issue* of economics, the voters were turning their attention to the drug culture, angry dissenters and changing moral standards.

Like the *social issue,* the term *family values* calls attention to a cultural rather than an economic interest, as Republicans are especially eager to do this year; the difference is that the use of *family values* focuses more sharply on abortion, gay rights and the pre- and extramarital activities that go under the name of *playing around* or *hanky-panky.* (Another sexual issue, harassment, is not included in most definitions of *family values,* presumably because it usually takes place at the office and not within plain sight of the family; besides, opposition to sexual harassment is a cause more associated with feminists and libertarians than with traditionalists.)

And now, for etymologists at least, to the jackpot question: Who is the coiner of *family values* in its current sense? The earliest use of the phrase I can find is in *The Education of Catholic Americans,* a 1966 book by the Reverend Andrew M. Greeley and Peter H. Rossi: "Marriage and *family values* do show some relationship with Catholic education; however, the relationship is in most instances not a strong one." (Greeley, now also a well-known novelist, titled one of his books *Wages of Sin,* taken from a grammatically disagreeable line in the Book of Romans: "For the wages of sin *is* death.")

The first official political use of *family values* was in the 1976 Republican party platform: "Divorce rates, threatened neighborhoods and schools and public scandal all create a hostile atmosphere that erodes family structures and *family values.*"

Lexicographic Irregulars are invited to submit earlier citations; more to the point, however, is the search for the modern political operative who first sent his principal a memo about how the public can be distracted from slow economic growth by a concentration on family values. Even the most confidential White House interoffice memorandums will be accepted in this purely lexicographic quest.

The campaign theme is powerful, but it can backfire. At the Houston convention, as a score of the members of the Bush family gathered around the President and Barbara Bush to display family values in all their solidarity, the background music inexplicably chosen for this moving moment in the Astrodome was "The Best of Times" from *La Cage aux Folles,* a Broadway musical that broke new ground in the straights' acceptance of homosexuality.

Folklore Alert

"Analysts on television programs like 'Nightline' berated themselves for considering such a sordid topic," wrote John Tierney of *The New York Times* about self-conscious media handling of a story about Philip Andering. "The passionate discussions usually began with a disclaimer that carried all the moral authority of 'We can't go on meeting like this.' "

Nice line. But unlike the often-used *shocked, shocked*—a reference to a hypocritical comment by the Claude Rains character in the movie *Casablanca*—the phrase *we can't go on meeting like this,* now a jocular cliché, is not readily attributable.

In Noël Coward's film *Brief Encounter* in 1945, a desperate Laura tells Alec after their affair is almost discovered, "I can't go on any longer." That may be a clue—but perhaps the Lexicographic Irregulars can come up with the source of the *meeting like this* phrase.

The Game's the Thing

I was sitting in the Washington bureau of *The New York Times* and schmoozing with Maureen Dowd and Andrew Rosenthal, two of our White House correspondents. They informed me about a parlor game in the nation's capital: the Shakespeare Campaign of 1992.

The idea is to match characters in the Bard's plays with real people in today's political whirl. For example, you say, "*Iago,*" and the other player selects a current figure who could fit that role (Richard Darman, our brilliantly devious budget director). Then you do it the other way: Somebody says, "Hillary Clinton" or "Marilyn Quayle," and the respondent says, "*Lady Macbeth*" or "*Portia,*" as the case and the political judgment may be.

Shakespeare '92 may have started with the frequent comparison of Mario Cuomo with Hamlet. *Rosencrantz* and *Guildenstern*? Sam Skinner and Bob

Teeter. And now the other way: Take George Bush or Bill Clinton or some other political player and fill in the Shakespearean counterpart. Ross Perot? *Brutus. Laertes?* Jerry Brown.

The game gets political conversation going on a literate level and compares our transient cast of characters to eternal role models. (The trick is to compare *to,* showing similarity, rather than compare *with,* which is to show difference as well.) Lex Irregs are invited to send in their castings. You can spill over to pundits, too: I can think of three candidates for *Polonius.*

Damned Spot

In the Washington parlor game of identifying current political people and forces with Shakespearean characters, readers have concentrated on (1) Ross Perot and (2) the news media.

Michael Dowd of Washington nominates Coriolanus, the Roman general, as Perot "because he, too, wanted to be begged to serve." Most entries, however, agree with Munroe A. Winter of Lake Bluff, Illinois: "Surely the prosperous Ross Perot is Prospero." Goodwin G. Weinberg of New York finds a nonpunning rationale for Perot's Prospero, "who'll subdue the Caliban budget deficit and mayhap tame magically a few other monstrous ills."

John F. Andrews, president of the Shakespeare Guild, in Washington, takes a different tack but comes out with the same Shakespearean character from *The Tempest:* "And who does Ross Perot think he is if not Prospero? The rhyme is irresistible, and the personality fits too. He's secretive, manipulative, testy, self-righteous, autocratic and persuaded that he alone possesses the magic required to control our isle's unruly Calibans."

Estelle Gelshenen of East Meadow, Long Island, suggests that "Frivolous political gossipmongers who delight in digging up dirt" could play "the Gravediggers from *Hamlet,* who are also referred to in the play as Clowns."

The most unkindest cut for those of us in the information-mediating dodge comes from Daniel Patrick Moynihan of New York, who is chairman of a Senate subcommittee that is responsible for "Water Resources, Transportation and Infrastructure." He nominates the Washington bureau chief of *The New York Times* to play Thersites, a "deformed and scurrilous" character in *Troilus and Cressida.* Moynihan quotes Thersites as saying, "Lechery, lechery, still war and lechery, nothing else holds fashion."

The reason for the infrastructing Senator's pique? "Try—just try—to get a follow-up story on the Intermodal Surface Transportation Efficiency Act of 1991. Widely acclaimed as the most important legislation of its kind in a generation!" Senator Moynihan is right: In politics and the press, nothing beats war and lechery.

The Gauge Gouge

"A Japanese friend and I went to rent a car," writes Kevin P. Kearney of San Francisco. "We sat in the parking lot trying to decipher all the doohickeys and thingamabobs on the Pontiac Bonneville. She pointed to the second of two words in 'system gages' and asked, 'Is that correct?'

"When did the variant spelling of *gauges* become acceptable? It looks wrong no matter how long I look at it."

Gauge is a hard word to spell. The temptation is to invert a couple of letters to make it come out *guage,* the last syllable in *language,* or to simplify it—as did the makers of the new Pontiac rented by Kearney's friend—by spelling it the way it is pronounced, *gage.*

But that would be wrong, as Richard Nixon used to say. The word spelled *gage,* means "token," and is akin to the Old High German for "wed." The word spelled *gauge,* from Old North French, means "a standard of measurement," with a bunch of senses that flow from that.

For some five centuries, people on occasion have dropped the *u* in *gauge;* that's long enough to make it a variant, which is how philologists say "sort of correct" when a mistake is made often enough for long enough. But most people have hung on to the *u,* and I would not abandon it just because some officious or wrongheaded supervisor at General Motors likes to mislead our Japanese friends by printing his own variant on the dashboards of Pontiak Bonnyvilles.

General Motors has enough problems these days without being wrongheadedly labeled wrongheaded or officious.

Having spent many years working at quality improvement, I have acquired an intimate acquaintance with gages, but as a language lover, I have winced, shuddered, fumed, and fulminated on encountering guage. *Had you been exposed to that atrocity as often as I have, I expect you would have abandoned the* u *as quickly as I did and adopted* gage *as the preferred spelling in specifications, manufacturing and testing procedures, memos, and other shop paperwork.* Gage *is a hard word to misspell, which is reason enough to favor it.*

Gage *is hardly a "simplified spelling" (like* lite *or* thru*), nor is it some GM supervisor's "own variant."* RHD 1 *says, at* gauge, *"Also,* esp. in technical use, **gage.**" OED *gives* gage *as an acceptable secondary spelling.*

OED *also notes, "The spelling* gauge *prevails in this country [the UK] except in sense 5 [a nautical term]. The more normal* gage *has been adopted in more recent American Dicts. The form* guage *is a mere blunder."*

The history of gage *is old and honorable. The correct answer to "When did the variant spelling of* gauges *become acceptable?" is 1677.* OED *cites Marvell in a* Letter to Mayor of Hull: *"The gager shall always leave with the Brewer a note of his gage." In the sense of a graduated measuring instrument, there is a 1688 citation from Burnet (*Letters on the Present State of Italy*): "There is a Gage, by which they Weigh the Water, . . ."*

Our Japanese friends should be able to cope with gage *at least as well as our French friends do. In 1952, a French company, Hispano-Suiza, compiled an English-French Technical Dictionary to help their people understand English documents for aircraft engines licensed from Rolls-Royce. It includes this entry:*

Gauge (gage) *. . . Voir aussi <<gage>>, mesure, jauge, calibre (In Modern French, the g- of the Old North French* gauge *has been softened, and the spelling changed accordingly, to* jauge.*)*

Walter Siff
Fairfield, Connecticut

The meters in the automobile in your article that measure speed, RPM, oil pressure, etc., are "gauges." The word "gauge" is used when referring to any device that measures a quantity. A "gage" on the other hand is a tool that is used to determine the accuracy of a feature on an item. For example: the diameter of a hole would be measured with a plug gage, the radius or fillet of a corner would be measured with a radius gage, the overall height of an object can be measured with a height gage, one would check the gap of a spark plug with a feeler gage.

Chris Locovare
Bay Shore, New York

Get It?

A battle cry of the women's movement, especially concerning the issue of sexual harassment in the workplace, emerged from the controversy that swirled around the nomination of Clarence Thomas to the Supreme Court.

"The times they are a-changin'," said Representative Patricia Schroeder, recalling a 1964 Bob Dylan song as she marched on the Senate, "and the boys here *don't get it* on this issue."

My *Times* Op-Ed colleague Anna Quindlen wrote: "The need for more women in elective office was vivid every time the cameras panned that line of knotted ties. 'They just *don't get it,*' we said, as we've said so many times before, about slurs, about condescension, about rape cases."

This is based on a locution first used in America by Mark Twain in his 1892 "American Claimant," in which a character says, "I don't know that I quite get the bearings of your position." This was followed by a Jack London 1913 usage, "D'ye get that?" It's a stretch, but the sense of *get* as "to understand or acquire knowledge" might be in John Wyclif's 1388 translation of Proverbs 4:7: "In al thi possessioun gete thou prudence"; six years earlier, he had used "purchase" instead of "gete thou."

The most familiar modern use of *get* meaning "understand" comes at the end of a joke that lays an egg, when the lame comic asks, "Get it?" That led to "I don't get it," as when Fred Astaire told *Newsweek* in 1975, "This nostalgia bit—I don't get it." At the same time, *getting it?* was gaining a sexual connotation, though not as strong as *getting any?* has.

A nuance was added with the word *just* and with the import directed toward others: "Some bosses *just don't get it,* especially when it comes to

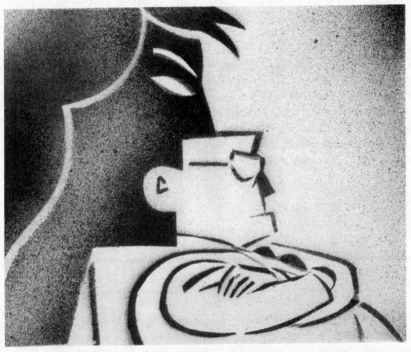

women's rights," Mary Sit wrote in the *Boston Globe* on November 25, 1990; this usage picked up a phrase current among feminists, which was amplified in the Thomas controversy. The meaning is "beyond mere lack of understanding; a total missing of the point."

Several terms lost their taboo as a result of the televised hearings. One was *dong,* as in "Long Dong Silver," the stage name of a pornographic film "actor" of the late 70's and early 80's. Accounts vary, but one pornographer tells me (and I don't even own a pornograph) he was an elderly man with a freakishly long sex organ; films of him were played on a loop in the rear of sex shops. The name was a rhyming play on "Long John Silver," the pirate in Robert Louis Stevenson's *Treasure Island.*

The penis has been called the *dong* since the 1920's, first cited by *American Speech* magazine in 1930; it appeared in John Steinbeck's 1939 novel, *The Grapes of Wrath,* with Tom Joad saying to the one-eyed man in the auto junk-yard, "Tell 'em ya dong's growed sence you los' your eye." In the 40's, it was used as a mild vulgarism, not as mild as *weenie,* similar to *wang; dong* was considered coarse, but not quite as shocking as other old slang terms. The word was coined, though not in this sense, by Edward Lear for a character in an 1877 lyric, "The Dong with a luminous nose." Because the *penis* (Latin for "tail") can be compared to a tongue of a bell, the ringing of which is echoically expressed as "ding-dong," it has been called both a *dingus* and a *dong.*

Perhaps because the nation was being bombarded with terms and images never before considered suitable for broadcast, editors became more permissive. In a *New York Times* opinion piece by Peggy Noonan, the speechwriter known for "a kinder, gentler nation," J. C. Alvarez, a special assistant to Clarence Thomas at the Equal Employment Opportunity Commission, was described admiringly as "a person who if a boss ever sexually abused her would kick him in the gajoobies and haul him straight to court."

Slang lexicographers are familiar with *bullets, chestnuts, clangers, jewels* and a hundred other terms for the human testes, but *gajoobies* was a new one to me. From the context, I presume this is a variation of *cojones,* the Spanish word for testes, frequently used by John Wayne and Reagan Administration aides. It was perhaps influenced by *gazoo,* a locution for an area leading to the intestines, used previously by Senator Alan Simpson and quoted widely.

Psychological terms abounded. *Schizophrenia* was misused; the meaning intended was "split personality." *Delusion* was tossed around by me and others; it means "any belief held despite convincing proof against it," and in psychiatry, "a misjudgment based on projection," which is "an attribution to another of an impulse thought by yourself."

Fantasize and *level of comfort* will be explored in a future column, but *erotomania* needs immediate work. Eros is the Greek god of love, and *mania* is "madness"; the 1858 term was originally applied to one carried away by sexual imaginings, then was more seriously taken to mean the madness caused by an excess of passionate love. Now, as reported by Felicity Barringer of *The New York Times,* it is "the psychiatric term for a condition in which otherwise competent and rational people harbor a fixed romantic delusion . . . plausible, although wrong, and the person's behavior is not otherwise odd or bizarre." Its best use was in *The Listener* magazine's 1967 reference to the leering Groucho Marx: "The erotomaniac gleam at the tip of the phallic cigar."

Pronunciation was the talk of the town. I ran into Justice Antonin Scalia at a dinner party and asked him about the question most often put to me: how to say *harassment.* For days, my own answer to frantic inquiries from broad-casters on this controversy was "I prefer to accent the second syllable, which

I will not pronounce for fear of giving offense." (Somebody has to stand up for prudery.) Justice Scalia pronounced it the other way: "HAR-ass-ment." I promptly cross-examined him on *lamentable, despicable, hospitable*—he was consistent and principled, stressing the first syllable in all cases, as we were once taught to do.

He's not incorrect, but he is no longer in the mainstream of pronunciation preference. The increased preference for "ha-RASS-ment" is unmistakable, and has been reflected in the change in most leading dictionaries. Professor Anita Hill repeatedly changed her pronunciation, using both "HAR-ass-ment" and "ha-RASS-ment"; Dan Rather of CBS and Peter Jennings of ABC went with the more modern "ha-RASS," but Tom Brokaw tossed the *NBC Handbook of Pronunciation* into the ashcan and went with the traditional "HAR-ass."

Harass is rooted in the excitation of hounds, leading to the Middle French *harer,* "to excite hunting dogs"; the word, perhaps influenced by the English "harry" and "raze," was first used by Sir Walter Raleigh before 1618: "burnt and harrazed the Countrie." Sir Francis Bacon wrote in 1622 of attempts "to harrasse and wearie the English."

Today, the original "HAR-ass" remains British English; the newer "ha-RASS" is preferred in American English. From these transfixing hearings, Americans learned to pronounce it either way, but not to do it.

I don't have any information on the origin or currency of the term gajoobies, *but your discussion would certainly have been enlivened by a reference to a scene in the 1982 film* Tootsie. *In the movie Dustin Hoffman, in his role of Michael Dorsey, who's in his role as Dorothy Michaels, who's in her role as Emily Kimberly, a soap-opera hospital administrator, talks to Jessica Lange's character about a doctor who has been sexually harassing the nurses. "I'm going to issue every nurse on this ward an electric cattle prod," Hoffman/Dorsey/Michaels/ Kimberly says, "and instruct them to just zap him in the badoobies."*

I think you dropped the ball on this one.

Eric Newman
Hackensack, New Jersey

I can always count on you to prefer the blue-collar pronunciation, as in "harass-ment." But since I've worn a white collar since I was six, I'm invariably on the other side.

Arthur J. Morgan
New York, New York

Get with the Program

"The most difficult thing to teach players," said the basketball coach Pat Riley to the columnist Dave Anderson of *The New York Times,* "is how to get away from being themselves and *get with the program.*"

The same week, in a piece about the cooperation among nations to safeguard copyrights and trade names, *Time* magazine intoned: "Countries that don't *get with the program* are asking for trouble."

"Rather an apt phrase, I think," writes Rob Slocum, passing on these recent citations. My file on this phrase is bulging. (Why do all files *bulge*? Will computer files bulge, too?) The earliest slip noted its frequent use by Sharon Davis, a Republican campaign worker in Santa Barbara, California, in the 1968 presidential campaign; it struck Easterners as a Westernism.

The *Los Angeles Times* is a frequent user: In a headline about related children swimmers (nicely punning "sibling revelry"), the *Times* writes, "Swimming: it seems as if everybody's brother—or sister—*gets with the program.*" And on the editorial page: "Why don't we tell the Kuwaitis to *get with the program*?"

The first question is: What's the *program*? With computer programming now a part of the language, the temptation is to assign this word to computer lingo, but the sense of *program* as "routine, pattern, cooperative endeavor" antedates that. In his 1972 *Black Jargon in White America,* David Claerbaut notes that *program* has a sense of "lifestyle, behavior pattern"; Joan Hall of the *Dictionary of American Regional English* speculates that *"get with the program* is a suggestion that you modify your own behavior patterns to fit some other style."

In sports, it often means "repress your desire to be an individual star to become a useful member of the team." In social work or international affairs, it means "take advantage of this organized opportunity." In business, it means "conform or else," and among political-party disciplinarians, "eschew deviationism."

The phrase has staying power, recently given a new boost by the vogue of the verb "to program." I have not been able to determine if the phrase *get with it* is a clip of the longer phrase, or if *the program* later became a way of defining *it.* But it is surely an important addition to the language of lock step, and those linguists who are fighting the problem should adapt to the new regimen.

You fail to distinguish the source of this statement, which is the 12-step program of Alcoholics Anonymous, founded in 1935. For the record, "to get with the program" means to work the principles (12 steps) of the A.A. program.

> Joan White
> Pearl River, New York

Use of the phrase "get with the program" predates 1968 California politics by at least four years. Undergoing Army basic training at Fort Leonard Wood, Missouri, in the summer of 1964, we grunts heard that admonition from drill instructors daily, from reveille to taps.

> John F. Hogan
> Chicago, Illinois

In the late 1950s Marine Corps drill instructors used it frequently and vociferously. In fact they used it frequently and vociferously with reference to me—me, whom everybody loved (to borrow a poetic allusion once used by Governor Pat Brown of California, who may have been more of a reader than people gave him credit for).

> Michael M. Short
> Chief of Bureau
> Associated Press
> Boston, Massachusetts

In 1953 when I was an aviation cadet, quite often an upperclassman and cadet officer would bellow at an individual underclassman or entire squadron of us at rigid attention, "Are you hot for the program?" The appropriate response was a very loud "Yes, sir!"

Whenever a cadet made a mistake or failed to pay attention, he was also admonished loudly that he'd better "get with the program, mister!"

While I heard the expression (and used it myself later as an upperclassman and deputy aviation cadet group commander) in 1953, I daresay its use can be traced back earlier, very likely to at least World War II when we had to produce thousands of pilots, navigators and bombardiers through the aviation cadet program.

> Jon Lewis Allen
> Dallas, Texas

It's unlikely that the phrase "get with it" is clipped from the longer version. Get with it was jazz and "cool" talk in the 50s or earlier, meaning to support, follow, join in with, or appreciate a context, style, or situation (program?). I seem to remember it being used earlier.

But the phrase to "be with it" antedates this by decades; it's colorful carny (carnival) slang of the 20s (and probably earlier). To be "with it" was to be a carny, a part of the show or the carnival world of traveling tent shows, an insider in that world, such as a roughneck, jointee, concessionaire, talker or artiste. Saying something like "I'm with it," was often a sly signal of identity to another carny, something that outsiders wouldn't understand, not unlike the 40s phrases "M.O.T." (Member of Our Tribe) used by some American Jews, or the Pig Latin "O-fay" (foe, enemy) used by some blacks to refer to non-blacks. Carnies were also big users of Pig Latin and other "with it" ways of excluding and belittling rubes and marks.

Philip S. Goodman
New York, New York

Gifts of Gab

"With all thy getting," the publisher B. C. Forbes liked to quote from Proverbs 4:7, "get understanding."

With all thy quoting, get a quotation book. The old editions are good, but the new ones are better because people are making new quotations every day.

The heaviest hitters in the field are *Bartlett's Familiar Quotations,* Sixteenth Edition (Little, Brown), edited by Justin Kaplan, and the *Oxford Dictionary of Quotations,* New Edition, edited by Angela Partington. (It's the Fourth Edition, duly noted on the title page; I don't know why the publishers prefer the vague "new edition" on the jacket.) If you have a very large Christmas stocking, get both, because each has its separate virtues. If you have to choose, the best buy for Americans is *Bartlett's.*

That's not only because the publisher offers 1,400 big pages for $40 while Oxford falls short of 1,100 pages for $35; the reason for *Bartlett's'* dominance of the field is its scholarship and zest. When Mr. Kaplan quotes Margaret Fuller's "I accept the universe," he footnotes Thomas Carlyle's comment, "By God! She'd better." *Oxford* does it the wrong way around, under Carlyle, making it harder to look up.

In selections from the Book of Job, an interest of mine, *Bartlett's* has twice the text; *Oxford* leaves out lines like "He is a king over all the children of pride." Both stick to the familiar King James Version of 1611; *Oxford* should consider shifting to its own beautiful and more accurate Bible translation in future editions.

Mr. Kaplan is a careful man: He lists "There's no such thing as a free lunch" under the economist Milton Friedman. I wrote to Milton about the origin of that adage some years back, and he cheerfully acknowledged it had not been original with him; that's why the quotologist adds a careful "attributed" next to the line.

Oxford is more specific about dates, however, and shows better judgment on the selection of the sayings of Ronald Reagan. Both books cite *evil empire,* but *Bartlett's* goes beyond Reagan's 1983 usage to its origin in the 1977 George Lucas film, *Star Wars.* (Both also have the line "Go ahead, make my day," delivered first by Clint Eastwood, but only *Bartlett's* has the right citation. *Oxford* cites the 1971 film *Dirty Harry* as its origin; instead, it started in that film's 1983 sequel, *Sudden Impact,* written by Joseph C. Stinson.)

"The only thing necessary for the triumph of evil is that good men do nothing." If you want to find out how some of us have broken our heads to find the coiner of that, get *Nice Guys Finish Seventh: False Phrases, Spurious Sayings and Familiar Misquotations* by Ralph Keyes (HarperCollins, $18). It wasn't Edmund Burke, and if you were there when it was first said, speak up.

Mr. Keyes's title is drawn from the way the sportswriter Frank Graham edited Leo Durocher's "The nice guys are all over there. In seventh place." We remember it as "Nice guys finish last." (Who said "Show me a good loser and I'll show you a loser"? In a mean-spirited moment years ago, I attributed that to Henry Kissinger, but it wasn't his coinage. Keyes suggests Knute Rockne, but Richard Nixon credits his college football coach, Chief Newman.)

Then there's *Dickson's Word Treasury: A Connoisseur's Collection of Old and New, Weird and Wonderful, Useful and Outlandish Words* (have you noticed how subtitles are getting more hard-sell lately?) by Paul Dickson (Wiley paperback, $14.95). His chapter on journalese offers such gems as *densely wooded area,* defined as "where most 'badly decomposed' bodies are found," and *flawed,* "used by critics in reviews in which they actually enjoyed the film, play, book or whatever but feel compelled to say something negative lest their boss think that they have gone soft in the head." A section on phobias is useful: A copy was sent to me with *levophobia* tagged; it means "fear of things on the left."

Stephen Glazier, who died just before his chef d'oeuvre was published in 1992, was a modern Peter Mark Roget—a putter-together of word lists. *The Random House Word Menu* (guess what publisher, $22) combines dictionary, thesaurus and glossary in an original way that is of great use to writers. Look up *cooks,* for example, to find *baker, barkeeper, confectioner, publican* ("*manager of tavern*") and, among many others, a solution to the waiter-waitress-waitron problem that some linguistically correct types have posed: *server.*

Under *grunts,* as a category of speech many other word books neglect, the writer may select from a range including *aah, harrumph, la-di-da, oof, ta-da, unh-unh, varoom* and the ever-popular *yech.*

Palindrome freaks, a small category of word lovers who like to read back and forth, will snap up the slim and somewhat overpriced paperback *If I Had a Hi-Fi* by William Irvine (Laurel, $5.99), which includes *We panic in a pew* and *Desserts, I stressed* and the ambitious *Some men interpret nine memos.* (Gary Muldoon of Rochester, in the course of explaining to me that the word *mnemonic* comes from the Greek goddess Mnemosyne, contributes a palindrome of interest to parents proud of their grown-up offspring: *Diapers repaid.*)

For serious linguists, the gift of the year is a reprint of Otto Jespersen's 1924 *The Philosophy of Grammar,* with an introduction and a new index by James D. McCawley (University of Chicago Press paperback, $17.95). When I recently offended who-whomniks by opining that *than* was a preposition, not a conjunction, Professor McCawley rode to my rescue by citing the great Danish linguist Jespersen's conclusion that so-called subordinating conjunctions are prepositions with clause objects. (Anybody still there? Helluva book.)

For librarians of major Wall Street investment houses—not a huge audience, but somebody has to look out for their interests—here's *The New Palgrave Dictionary of Money and Finance* (Stockton Press, three volumes, $595). General readers will find more than they want to know about *takeovers, leverage* and the *quantity theory of money,* but word freaks will be titillated by such entries as *contango,* "a fee paid by the buyer who wants to postpone delivery," a sultry dance by the buyer of futures options that is the reverse of *backwardation.*

The *Wizard of Oz* entry by Hugh Rockoff was an eye-opener: This children's story by L. Frank Baum is explicated as an 1890's allegory about bimetalism. The Yellow Brick Road is the gold standard (an ounce of gold); the Cowardly Lion is William Jennings Bryan, derogated for lack of courage by free-silver populists; President William McKinley, friend to financiers, is the Wicked Witch of the West, and the Wizard in Emerald City (Washington, D.C.) is Mark Hanna, the Republican leader. *The New Palgrave* does not say who Dorothy's dog is supposed to be.

Finally, for word lovers who appreciate an example of simple and lucid writing on a subject of infinite complexity, try the new edition of Robert Jastrow's short classic, *God and the Astronomers* (Norton, $18.95). By running the big-bang theory backward, scientists must deal with the moment of cosmic creation, a subject usually confined to theologians. To describe the reach of Hubble's Law of the Expanding Universe, he writes, "It applies not only to the Cosmos, but also to inflating balloons and loaves of bread rising in the oven." The bigger the subject, Jastrow demonstrates, the more effective are homely words.

After discussing the merits of Bartlett's Familiar Quotations *and the* Oxford Dictionary of Quotations, *you state "the best buy . . ." Because you are com-*

paring one object with another, would it not be more correct to state "the better buy . . ."?

M. David Cohen, M.D.
San Francisco, California

I was struck by the seemingly random sequence of the two highly obscure words: "contango" and "backwardation."

I have come across these two words only once before, in Gilbert and Sullivan's penultimate comic opera, Utopia, Limited, *first produced in 1893. It has not been unusual for me to have expanded my vocabulary through Williams Gilbert and Safire, and I am guessing that the latter was aware that he was quoting the former.*

In Utopia, Limited, *an island king, King Paramount, eager to reform his tropical paradise into a commercial institution modeled upon Great Britain, invites six "Flowers of Progress" to his shores. These six gentlemen are each ". . . Representatives of the principal causes that have tended to make England the powerful, happy, and blameless country which the consensus of European civilization has declared it to be." Among these six is Mr. Goldbury, a company promoter. He is introduced to the utopian populace by the king's daughter, Princess Zara, (a Girton graduate) with the following lyric:*

A Company Promoter, this, with special education,
Which teaches what Contango means and also Backwardation—
To speculators he supplies a grand financial leaven,
Time was when two were company—but now it must be seven.

Thomas Z. Shepard
New York, New York

Gotcha! Gang Strikes Again

I have been unfair to Rudyard Kipling and the prophet Isaiah.

In a recent aside, I stated that novelist James Jones took the title of *From Here to Eternity* from "The Whiffenpoof Song," the ballad sung by poor little lamb-like Yalies from under the table down at Mory's.

That number, I am informed by J. F. Cooper of Poughkeepsie, New York, is based directly on Kipling's *Barrack-Room Ballads:*

> Gentlemenrankers out on the spree
> Damned from here to Eternity,
> God ha' mercy on such as we,
> Baa! Yah! Baa!

A *ranker* was an officer risen from the ranks; the Kipling use of slang was changed to *songsters* by the collegial bleating hearts of 1910.

The Gotcha! Gangster's letter (no, Mr. Cooper, there is no gang T-shirt) was addressed only to "Baa! Yah! Baa!" at the *Times* bureau; the news clerks, a hip group including Tim Sullivan, who is soon to become a reporter at the *Fort Worth Star-Telegram,* unerringly delivered it to me.

Now to honor the prophet: In discussing the derivation of *Eat, drink and be merry,* which comes from Ecclesiastes, I also quoted Isaiah as saying, "Let us eat and drink; for tomorrow we shall die."

But I was corrected by Michael Sanders of Monsey, New York. (Upstate New York is apparently a favored hangout of the Gotcha! Gang; Carl Strock of *The Daily Gazette* in Schenectady caught me giving *credence* when I should have given *credibility.*) Mr. Sanders points out that it was not the prophet who was eating flesh and drinking wine and calling on others to live it up; on the contrary, he was quoting others who would not listen to his warnings.

That's the second time I mistook a quotation of others by Isaiah to be his own view. Years ago, digging for the origin of *holier than thou,* I cited him in my political dictionary as the source of "Stand by thyself, come not near to me, for I am holier than thou" (Isaiah 65:5). But again, he was quoting and criticizing others, in that case pious hypocrites. Isaiah wasn't *holier than thou,* though he was surely holier than thou or me.

Rarely does one add to the language by attributing sayings to others. But hordes of TV rip-'n'-readers unconsciously quote him directly every day in the opening words of Isaiah 51:21: "Therefore hear *now this.*"

Your definition of a "gentleman ranker" as "an officer risen from the ranks" is one meaning of the term, but it is not the meaning intended by Kipling.

Editor Stanley Appelbaum in his notes on the poem in Gunga Din and Other Poems *(Dover, 1990), says:*

"The 'gentleman ranker' means a rank-and-file soldier who belonged to the gentry in civilian life."

When the title From Here to Eternity *was suggested to James Jones for his novel, according to a* Life *magazine piece at the time the book came out, Jones, too, thought it referred to a bunch of drunken college boys and didn't want to use it. Only when the origin of the line was explained to him did he relent.*

> *Rupert Welch*
> *Falls Church, Virginia*

You stated that the "ranker" in Kipling's poem "Gentlemen-Rankers," from the collection entitled Barrack-Room Ballads, *referred to an officer risen from the ranks. To the contrary, this particular "ranker" is a gentleman who, in happier circumstances, might have been an officer but who is serving in the ranks. He transgressed society's conventions and is paying for his sin, and possibly hiding from punishment, serving as an enlisted man. A variant on the theme of the remittance man.*

My father told of singing the Kipling poem as a Lieutenant of Marines during the "Days of the Empire," the Philippines in 1908. That was obviously prior to "The Whiffenpoof Song," on which, incidentally, Rudy Vallee secured the copyright. Perhaps that is why the Whiffs were "poor" little lambs.

> *Victor I. Morrison, Jr.*
> *Old Lyme, Connecticut*

> **thou:**   *pron. sing. nom. case*
> *poss. thy or thine*
> *obj. and dative thee*

So aren't you a little mixed up? Even if you (shame on you) accept than *as a preposition (instead of a coordinating conjunction), it should read "holier than thee or me." Likewise, as a conformist, I would say "holier than thou or I."*

> *Ruth Muller*
> *Clifton, New Jersey*

Grammar Scandal

Citizens infuriated by check-kiting at the House Bank would do well to consider the exaltation of the ignorance of grammar in the New York State Legislature.

"The members of the Legislature are not necessarily charged with a knowledge of the grammatical rules of the English language," asserts Section 251 in McKinney's Codes, the guide for interpreting New York statutes, "and in the interpretation of *their acts,* such construction is given the language as will best effectuate *their intent,* without reference to the accurate grammatical construction of words, phrases, and sentences." (Italics mine; confusion theirs.)

The reason the quoted sentence is incomprehensible is that the pronouns are disconnected from their antecedents. There's no firmly attached *their* there.

Does *their acts* refer to our intrepid *members*? I suppose so, even though it seems to refer to the *grammatical rules,* which comes between the pronoun and the intended antecedent.

Does *their intent* still refer to our slovenly legislative draftspersons, or to *their acts*? Only your Assemblyman knows for sure.

Far be it from me to indulge in an intentional fallacy, but I think what the drafters were trying to say was "Judge us not by what we say in cold print, but by what you can read of our minds." In the gloss on another section, 252, this is expressed as "the grammatical form of words must give way if it conflicts with the legislative intent."

What kind of way is this to run a government? Does Governor Mario Cuomo know about this trashing of the language, this contempt for the fundamental tool of law, in interpreting the statutes of his supposedly literate State of New York? Does a conservative State Senate approve of this laid-back laxity and wanton permissiveness as the basis for adjudication of disputes?

The sloppy solons of Albany, too lazy to reject a guide shot through with grammatical errors, evidently want their laws interpreted by divining rod, a desire that will lead to their undoing. (I know which antecedent that second *their* refers to—but does anybody else? Will I remember my intent in a week? Of course not. It's enough to force a language maven to vote for terms limitation.)

You say "a guide shot through with grammatical errors." The dictionary says "grammatical" means "in accordance with the rules of grammar." Therefore, "grammatical errors" equals "errors that are in accordance with the rules of grammar." That is an oxymoron.

Your error in grammar was in saying "grammatical errors" rather than "errors in grammar." You could have said also "grammar errors." You are correct in your title, "Grammar Scandal." You didn't say "grammatical scandal."

Your New York State Legislature quote says "a knowledge of the grammatical rules." This equals "a knowledge of the rules in accordance with the rules of grammar." That's confusing because two sets of rules are implied. The Legislature could have said, "a knowledge of the rules of grammar," or "a knowledge of grammar rules."

They do have one correct quote: "the grammatical form of words." That is the form that is in accordance with the rules of grammar.

I suspect that new, revised dictionary definitions will argue that it's O.K. to say "grammatical errors." That's an "exaltation of the ignorance of grammar."

Perry Anastos
New York, New York

Greenhorn

The heavy hitters of the East Hampton, Long Island, media-theatrical-legal establishment were supping at the beach house of Mort Zuckerman of *U.S. News.* When the conversation veered to the assimilation of minorities in America, Mort Janklow, the literary agent, used the word *greenhorn* to denote an immigrant from Eastern Europe at the turn of the twentieth century.

Richard Reeves, the columnist (this is beginning to read like a Liz Smith column; also present at the dinner were the irrepressible Peter Stone, author of the new Will Rogers musical, and the dour Lloyd Cutler, counsel to the President in the Carter Administration; dare I put the names in boldface and eat a peach?)—at any rate, Reeves asked, "What's the derivation of *greenhorn?*" Janklow guessed it had something to do with *animal husbandry,* an archaic phrase that many now take to be a derogation of married life. The group at Nuthin' Dune, too lazy to pick up a dictionary, sent the query to me.

Fortunately for them, I had just said to myself: The next interesting word that comes in will be the basis for a comparison of dictionaries. You have to be fair about this; some lexicographers, like star quarterbacks, get a hot hand on certain words, while others plunk along; yet on other terms, the plunkers turn to stars. Which word shall be the criterion? Close your eyes and open the mail: O.K., let's use *greenhorn.*

All good lexies depend on two basic sources for their definitions: the *Oxford English Dictionary* for the history of a word (with its supplement or CD-ROM for more recent usage), and their own citation files to determine the current senses. They also look at one another's latest dictionaries and try to be original in defining without straying too far from the norm.

Greenhorn, begins the *O.E.D.,* is "1. An appellation given to an animal, ? orig. to an ox with 'green' or young horns. *Obs.*" The question mark means they admit to guessing at the origin, same as the agent Janklow did; nobody has made a better guess. (Was there a fifteenth-century novice named Sam Greenhorn who gave his name to the word? Unlikely.) So we go with the *O.E.D.*'s presumed etymology. The first sense of "young ox" used in 1460 is obv. *obs.*—obviously obsolete.

The second historical sense is "a recently enlisted soldier; a raw recruit" with citations from 1650. Third is "a raw, inexperienced person, *esp.* a novice in a trade . . . ignoramus . . . simpleton." The best citation is from an 1831 Disraeli novel: "he execrated the greenhornism which made him feign a passion and then get caught where he meant to capture."

That's the *O.E.D.* history. If you're a lexie, you go to your own citation files to see how it's being used today. From my own citation file, I have this passage from David Ignatius's recent spy novel, *Siro:*

"Always close the drapes," says the smart-sexy heroine, a C.I.A. recruit, going by the book in a hotel-room meeting with her mentor. "We're in

Rockville," replies the veteran spook, "nobody cares." The novelist narrates: "Anna nodded. She felt like a *greenhorn.*"

(I don't really have citation files on this; I was reading that novel until the wee hours last night, after having started this piece, and the word popped up at me. Such coincidences always happen. Now close the drapes and we'll continue, knowing the word is currently used by novelists in the sense of "novice, newcomer," and by agents in the sense of "immigrant.")

How do three top American dictionaries handle the word? Here is how the definition appears:

> **green•horn** (grēn´hôrn´) *n.* [[orig. with reference to a young animal with immature horns]] **1** *a*) an inexperienced person; beginner; novice ★*b*) [Now Rare] a newly arrived immigrant **2** a person easily deceived; dupe
>
> *Webster's New World, Third College Edition*

> **green•horn** /-hȯ(ə)rn/ *n.* [obs. *greenhorn* (animal with young horns)] (1682) **1:** an inexperienced or unsophisticated person **2:** a newcomer (as to a country) unacquainted with local manners and customs
>
> *Merriam-Webster's Ninth New Collegiate*

> **green•horn** (grēn´hôrn´), *n.* **1.** an untrained or inexperienced person. **2.** a naive or gullible person. **3.** a newly arrived immigrant; newcomer. [1425–75; late ME; orig. applied to cattle with green (i.e., young) horns]—**green´horn´ism,** *n.*
>
> *Random House Webster's College*

At first glance, the entries seem much the same; *inexperienced* is used in the first sense every time, although it could be argued that the current sense (which should be listed first) is *naïve,* and there are plenty of people who keep having awful experiences but who remain hopelessly naïve. As to the word's animal origin, all three present as a certainty what the *O.E.D.* properly lists as a question mark and I would call informed speculation, logically deduced but unattested.

On close inspection, however, different judgments are made and features are offered. In the first entry, *Webster's New World,* the lexicographer offers two synonyms beyond *inexperienced*—*beginner* and *novice*—while Merriam-Webster adds only *unsophisticated,* and Random House chooses *untrained,* with a separate sense of *naïve* and *gullible.* I think Random House comes out best on that, because a difference exists between *inexperienced* and *naïve, gullible,* and it is useful to have the senses separate.

What about the *immigrant* sense? *Webster's New World* is the only one to list it as *rare;* obviously Victoria Neufeldt, the editor, doesn't hang out with aging media biggies in the Hamptons. But that little star before the reference to immigrants is a *WNW* exclusive: It tells us that the word in that sense is an Americanism; Random House wisely dropped the "slang" judgment in its unabridged dictionary. Of the three dictionaries' treatment of the new-immigrant sense, I prefer Merriam-Webster's broader definition: "a new-comer (as to a country) unacquainted with local manners and customs."

On pronunciation, all three agree the first syllable gets a slightly stronger stress, but Merriam-Webster uses a hyphen to send you looking up at other greens, and its schwas leave me schwach—that is, its linguistically precise pro-nunciation symbols are depressing to the amateur who never will read the in-comprehensible key on the lower right corner of every page spread. (This will be solved when we all get sound on the dictionaries in our computers.)

Webster's New World doesn't have a date for any sense; Merriam-Webster gives the date (1682) for the first use of the term in the "inexperienced" sense while the *Random House Webster* gives a vague range of years (1425–1475) for the word when it referred to young cattle (probably). On this, I want to know what Merriam-Webster gives me: coinage of the primary current mean-ing.

Give Random a point for adding the *-ism* (though you'd have to look in the spacious *Oxford* to discover its coinage by Disraeli) and for punctuating its entries with periods.

On the whole, I'd give the edge on this entry to *Webster's New World,* be-cause it separates the "inexperienced" slightly from the "new immigrant" and gives a separate sense to "easily deceived." When I work my way through a couple hundred thousand more entries, I'll decide which dictionary is best; don't hold your breath.

Therefore, when didactic people say to you, "According to Webster's," your proper riposte is: "Which Webster's? What do you take me for, a *greenhorn*?"

Dear Bill:

Not only has the term been widely used to mean "immigrants," but immi-grants themselves, as they became "Americanized," freely used the term to refer to succeeding waves of newcomers. I vividly remember my father, who had come here from Minsk as a 9-year-old before the turn of the century—he learned the language on his own, established himself as a businessman and "macher" in his local community—so referring to new arrivals. It was typical of his generation's prideful way of calling attention to their achievements, not yet equalled by the "greenhorns."

Bart [Hobart Rowen]*
The Washington Post
Washington, D.C.

* Bart Rowen died on April 13, 1995.

I thought you might be interested in the enclosed, in the 1927 Century Dictionary.

> **green•horn** *(grēn'hôrn),* n. *[In allusion to the immature horns of a young animal.] A raw, inexperienced person (as, "mere greenhorns, men unused to Indian life": Irving's "Captain Bonneville," vii.); a foreigner lately arrived; hence, one easily imposed upon.*

Harry H. Voigt
Chevy Chase, Maryland

I was surprised to find there was no mention at all of the Yiddish use of the term. My family and their friends used it somewhat derisively to describe and categorize those Jewish immigrants who came in a later wave.

. *As evidence I submit the Yiddish song "Meine Greena Cuzina" (My Greenhorn Cousin), who is charming and pretty despite her greenhorn status.*

I was about seven years old before I realized greenhorn *was not a Yiddish word.*

Harold Steinberg
East Hampton, New York

Growing Down Grows Up

During the late political unpleasantness, Governor Clinton promised to *"grow the economy."* President Bush derided this promise not on the basis of its syntactical formulation but in regard to its object: He accused his opponent of intending to *"grow government,"* and he pledged that if re-elected he would *grow down the deficit.*

"At first," writes a horrified Anthony Lanyi of McLean, Virginia, "I assumed these were slips of the tongue, since *grow* as a transitive verb is used only in an agricultural context, as in 'I grow tomatoes in my garden.' " In similar dismay, Esther B. Fein, a *New York Times* reporter reared in the tradition of fine distinctions, stopped me in the hall to say, "You *raise* cattle and *rear* children, but *grow the economy* and *grow down the deficit?*"

Grow to like it, because the transitive use of *grow* in a citified sense has deep roots in the language and is here to stay. "Whan David had regned vii yere in Ebron," William Caxton wrote in 1481 about Jerusalem, "he grewe and amended moche this cyte."

Fred Mish, editorial director of Merriam-Webster, says, "The transitive use of *grow* with inanimate objects like *business* is covered by the basic transitive definition, 'to cause to grow.' " The object of *grow* doesn't have to be limited to soybeans or a beard—it can logically apply to growing a business, an economy, a government or a deficit.

But what about *growing down*? This term is an oxymoron, a jarring juxtaposition of opposites, with an honored place in English dialect; the English lexicographer James O. Halliwell reported in 1847 that "to grow downward, i.e. to get smaller" was "a common phrase in the provinces."

Down is not used nearly so often in verb phrases as *up,* but we pay down loans, dress down illiterates and bring down Presidents; in the case of *grow down,* we are influenced by the recent *builddown* of forces, which played off *buildup.*

Be not horrified at what seem like daring or extended usages, even by politicians under pressure. The unfamiliar should not be presumed to be mistaken; that's how we grow the language.

Hard Line

"From the Reagan Administration's 'Prince of Darkness,' " reads the news release, "a novel of the cold war: *Hard Line,* by Richard Perle."

Now that *hard-liners* (the noun hyphenated like the adjective *hard-line*) find themselves advocating aid for Boris Yeltsin's Russia, *hard-liner* is losing its political meaning, which used to be "advocate of a confrontational or anti-concessional policy toward the Soviet Union." Before it sinks into history, let's nail down its etymology.

Hard lines was a British nautical expression meaning "bad luck"—*hard line money* was hardship pay—but that had little if anything to do with its political sense. Closer to its current meaning was *hard shells,* a faction of the Democratic Convention in 1848 that faced the "barn-burners," also known as the *soft shells,* perhaps after the local crabs. Local Baptist groups also had hard-shell and soft-shell monikers at that time.

The lexicographer Cynthia Barnhart has found a citation that antedates any of those in current dictionaries: In the *Britannica Yearbook* printed in 1955, Chester Bowles, the advertising executive turned diplomat, wrote about "the Stalinist *hard line.*" Two years later, *Time* magazine picked up the usage as a hyphenated modifier—"A few hard-line Polish Communists dismissed the display . . . as mere vulgar American ostentation"—in a piece about a United States exhibit at a fair in Poznan. By 1960 the magazine was using it as a noun as well, in discussing criticism of Nikita Khrushchev by "domestic *hard-liners.*"

Now the compound term is floating around, seeking a more general place in the language. I would drop the hyphen and use the solid word to mean "resistant to accommodation; strict." The trick is to be very firm about that definition; none of those fuzzy edges preferred by soft-line lexicographers.

#@/\()! =
Hash, At, Slash, Backslash, Open, Close, Bang

The prefixes *meta-* and *mega-* —no. Stop. Belay that. Something is bothering me and I cannot write on today's chosen subject.

That is because the first key I punched on my computer keyboard has an arrow pointing upward on it; in the typewriter era, before anybody who matters today was born, that was just the *shift key,* so named because it shifted the keyboard into uppercase. I call it the *bus-stop sign* because bus stops in Manhattan used to have signs in the shape of arrows pointing upward, but they're gone, presumably because people waiting for buses got stiff necks looking at the sky.

Most other people still call it the *shift key,* even though nothing moves mechanically, because it still changes the letters to capitals. The hackers have not changed it to *uparrow* because in an era they call "early ASCII"—that American Standard Code for Information Interchange—they used *uparrow* for the symbol you can sometimes find over the number *6,* which those of us in the language dodge who need help in pronouncing vowel sounds call the *circumflex;* more often, hackers call an upward-aimed arrowhead *control,* and most often of all, the simple *hat.*

(When used at the bottom of a line in proofreading, the same upward-pointing symbol for "insert here" is called the *caret,* from the Latin *carere,* "to be without." On my word processor keyboard, over the comma, I have a caret that is pointed to the left, which may mean "derived from" to dictionary-readers, but is now called a *less than;* over the period, or dot, it appears pointed to the right, and has been dubbed a *greater than.* People who call them *angle brackets* are considered < bright.)

@ any rate, as I was holding down the shift key, I hit the little *a* with the tail around it—it's on top of the *2*—because I have been instructed by Judith Wilner, Ed Gravely and their brave band of technologists at *The New York Times* that if I do not do so, nothing that I write will ever go anywhere.

The question hit me: What do you call that little *a* with the tail? I called Bob Costello, new editorial director @ Houghton Mifflin, publishers of the *American Heritage Dictionary.* He took a poll of lexicographers and replied: "It's called the *at* sign." Good name for a sign standing for "at," as in "two mainframes @ 400 G's a throw." Although some computer whizzes have been known to call the @ a *snail*, we can go with *at*.

What other unfamiliarly named symbols do I stare @ all day? We have previously discussed the *pound sign*, also called the *number sign, crosshatch* and *octothorpe*. What's the curved line that looks like a quizzical eyebrow? "That's a *tilde*," Mr. Costello said, "and it tells you how to pronounce the *n* in *señor*." It's a Spanish word from the Latin term for a tiny diacritical mark used to change the phonetic value of a letter.

"It's a *squiggle*," said Danny Hillis of Thinking Machines Corporation, producers of the world's fastest massively parallel computers, capable of performing nine billion calculations a second, which will be hooted at as leaden-footed in a few months. Mr. Hillis had written from Cambridge, Massachusetts, where thinking machinists hang out, to emend my piece on the pound sign, adding *hash* to the nomenclature: "For example, the cartoon expletive #@/\()! can be read as *hash, at, slash, backslash, open, close, bang.*"

He put his associate, Guy Steele, on the speakerphone. Nine billion calculations a second, and these guys don't have an extension phone. Guy (everybody in computering is on a first-name basis) is co-editor of *The Hacker's Dictionary*, and confirms that the tilde is often called a *squiggle*, but thinks a more common usage is *twiddle*. A few hackers will call it a *swung dash*, but these are the far-out types who call the @ a *strudel, whorl* or *snail*.

What do they call the asterisk? "*Star*," said Danny. "*Splat*," said Guy. Give me *splat* any day; it conjures a vision of an insect hitting my windshield and making a mark that has me looking for a footnote on my dashboard. *Star*, however, is the word being pushed by the phone companies. *Point* and *dot* are being pushed by programmers who can't be slowed by the three-syllable *period*. (A programmer at the Pentagon tells me if the missiles are coming in, he intends to retaliate with *star-dot-star*, a sequence of keyboard symbols to start an attack that wipes out the entire Milky Way galaxy and several of its neighbors. I think he means "asterisk, period, asterisk," but I have no need to know.)

What about the ampersand, that ancient sign used to connect partners, as in S. J. Perelman's accountants, Whitelipt & Trembling? "That's too silly a word to change," said Danny. Guy, from across the room, boomed, "You sometimes hear the *and sign*. Occasionally the *pretzel*." I'll stick with *ampersand*. It is silly; it is built out of "and *per se* and," meaning "the sign '&' by itself stands for 'and,' " which is a lot of etymological noise, but the old name has its charm.

Guy said he would fax me some pages of the next edition of *The Hacker's Dictionary*, and Danny put in: "There's a controversy about the word *hacker*. A few years ago, it was an endearing term for people who were interested in computers; lately it's been used in a sinister way, to describe people who break into computer files and steal information or plant viruses. They're stealing the meaning from us."

So what do good hackers call the bad hackers? "*Crackers,*" said Danny, "on the analogy of *safecracker.*" Let's give it a try; perhaps Georgians would be glad to give up the derogation. (I realize it sounds condescending to refer to my two ingenious sources by their first names, as if they were kids; in truth, they are rocket-scientist managers in a company with yearly sales over $60 million—that's a *buck sign*—and they probably will earn more in the next nanosecond than I will in the rest of my life. And I bet they come to work in jeans and shoes you pump up.)

What else do we have here? The simple, vertical line (I don't know where it is on your keyboard; I have enough trouble with my unenhanced version) is called a *pipe* or *vertical bar;* what we old-timers know as "parentheses" are now just *open* and *close,* or more descriptively, *left banana* and *right banana.*

The brackets with the nipple in the middle are called *bracelets* or *curly braces,* and here's the latest renaming of the < and > signs: Forget *less than* and *greater than.* It's now *left angle bracket* and *right angle bracket,* or *bra* and *ket* for short; this locution is in hot competition, according to *The Hacker's Dictionary,* with *read from/write to; suck/blow; crunch/zap;* and *comes from/gozinta.*

@ this . I)

In the above symbolic sentence, I was trying to say, "At this point I close." However, many hackers will translate that as modern poetry: "*Snail this dot I right banana.*" At nine billion calculations per second, they can figure something out.

The answer to the question "what do computer mavens call an asterisk" is easy. They call it an "asterik."

I use a program that occasionally requires the help of my "support system" in Silicon Valley. Often, one of the Debbies who answer the phone will give me the instruction "asterik period asterik." I have never had the temerity to correct her. (After all, I am the one who needs the support.) Recently, however, Debbie said "star dot star." Uncertain, I asked, "Is that an asterisk?" There was a moment of puzzled silence before she replied, "Yes, that is what is called an asterik."

I think I am going to go with star dot star.

Annette Henkin Landau
New York, New York

Before I retired and moved out here to New Mexico I too was in the computing dodge—at Long Island Jewish Medical Center—and I used to grit my teeth when I heard programmers call the "*" an "astrik"! They lacked a classical ed-

ucation, so they couldn't have known that the word "asterisk" comes from the Greek "asteriskos," which means "little star."

I put a poem up on a wall that I thought might help. It didn't, but here it is:

> Mary had a little plane,
> In it she did frisk.
> Wasn't she a silly girl,
> Her little *.

Anyway, I welcome splat. *It's much better than* astrik.

Norman Gold
Rio Rancho, New Mexico

Many years ago, an erudite gentleman whose wisdom I would not question told me that / is a shilling bar. Nor did I ask why. Your column roused both my hackles and my curiosity. I hied me to my dictionary, to learn that either said gentleman was in error or I misunderstood.

It is a shilling mark.

> **Shilling mark/,** *a virgule, as needed as a divider between shillings and pence:* One reads 2/6 as "two shillings and sixpence" or "two and six." *Also called* shilling.
> Random House Dictionary of the English Language
> *Unabridged Edition (1966)*

Milton Riback
White Plains, New York

I am a bit surprised that you passed up the opportunity to remind everyone that the names "bra" and "ket" for the < and > symbols were introduced into quantum mechanics by P.A.M. Dirac, circa 1930. I attach herewith a copy of pages 18 and 19 of the fourth edition (1956) of his Principles of Quantum Mechanics *(Oxford, Clarendon Press, first edition, 1930) for ready reference.*

Ramachandran Bharath
Marquette, Michigan

As an historian of English usage, you may be interested in a precursor of the hackers' bra *for* < *and* ket *for* >. *The third edition of P.A.M. Dirac's book on quantum mechanics introduced those names to the vocabulary of physics in 1947,* bra *for* <| *and* ket *for* |>.

Dirac's book in its three editions is arguably the most influential physics book written in this century, and his notation and nomenclature caught on immediately. I don't know whether the computer people borrowed bra *and* ket *from the physicists or reinvented them. Computing was in its infancy in 1947, and word processing was unknown, at least to me. The small computing community was dominated by physicists and mathematicians, and the transfer of jargon would have been natural for several decades.*

Murray Peshkin
Elmhurst, Illinois

You call tilde *"a Spanish word from the Latin term for a tiny diacritical mark used to change the phonetic value of a letter," omitting to mention the word's rather interesting etymology.* Tilde *is a quaint Spanish corruption of Latin* titulus, *whence our word* title. *If you want to get diacritical about it, we have a second derivative of* titulus, *namely* tittle, *which survives chiefly in the phrase "not one jot or tittle" (see Matthew v, 18). While I'm in the mood for tittle-tattle, I may as well tell you that* jot *is derived from* iota, *the Greek name of the letter* i *(see the phrase "not one iota").*

Louis Jay Herman
New York, New York

As to "squiggle": this too is a popular standard item of physics, chemistry, and mathematics, and is not *to be associated with "tilde." A tilde must be accompanied by the letter it modifies. Squiggle stands alone, should be at the center of the line, and means "on the order of," or some acknowledged degree of approximation. (This letter will take ~1 week to get to you.)*

And finally "dot": I agree it is a convenient shortcut for "period," but there is another important context. Most people having a mathematics as a second language are likely to interpret "dot" to mean a line-centered dot (as in A·B) as compared with the usual position of a period (A.B). As such, it means "multiplied by" in some sense, often just as a convenient separator of factors.

Robert S. Knox
Professor of Physics
University of Rochester
Rochester, New York

I call your attention to the fourth paragraph, in which you write about the carets that point left and right. You state ". . . now called a less than . . ." and ". . . dubbed a greater than." I take exception to the word now. As a math major in high school—way back when—those signs appeared often in the geometry courses, and they meant then exactly what they mean today, i.e., 7 < 9 (seven is less than nine) and 9 > 7 (nine is greater than seven). I think they are the only signs on the computer keyboard that are called still what they always have been called.

> Carol Jenkins
> Kew Gardens, New York

You would have to have been taking a very long view to say that the symbol < "is now called a less than." The symbol was introduced with that meaning long enough ago that the definition was written in Latin: a < b significet a minorem quam b (that is, "let a < b mean a less than b"). This was in Thomas Harriot's Artis analyticae praxis *of 1631. The corresponding use of > to mean "greater than" was introduced at the same time. Both symbols had been generally adopted by mathematicians more than two centuries ago.*

You can check this information in several histories of mathematics, perhaps most conveniently in F. Cajori, A History of Mathematical Notation, *Vol. I (Chicago, 1928), p. 199.*

Though your computer people didn't know it, the angle bracket is not the same as < in most technical typesetting; it looks like this: ⟨.

> William C. Waterhouse
> Professor of Mathematics
> Pennsylvania State University
> University Park, Pennsylvania

My little girls discovered on their first home computer that the large key on the right was the last one you hit to make the programs run, so they called it the "do-it" key, not the enter or return key. It was interesting to observe that when they instructed their playmates to "hit the do-it key" the correct key was invariably selected just as my fellow employees have always been able to discern what I meant by "right caret" and "left caret."

> Doug Lindsay
> Stillwater, New York

To the statistician, the difference between a circumflex and no circumflex (I'll go with cap instead of hat for alliterative reasons) is the difference between a statistic and a parameter!

Re your prefix usage: You write "in the next nanosecond" and elsewhere "nine billion calculations per second." Since the reciprocal of one-billionth (nano-) is one billion, you could have gone with "nine gigacalculations per second" and get cited for a coinage that might have led to a trend. (Just imagine President Bush talking about "a kilopoint of light"!)

David Bernklau
Brooklyn, New York

When I was young in the Fifties and worked weekends as a proofreader at Newsweek, it was our wont to show up for work on 42nd Street where my overseer, Robert Austerlitz, had us read aloud to one another every single word that went into the magazine.

This required a certain lingual shorthand. To say, for instance, "Best & Co.," we would say out loud "quote up Best jigger up Co stop unquote."

Thus the ampersand was called a "jigger." A period was "stop." An exclamation point was a "screamer." "Up" meant a capital letter. And one said "Co" not "company" because "Co" it was. A comma was "com."

This sign, ^ a circumflex, was referred to as a "dingbat." Mr. Austerlitz and his companion friend reader, whose name I have forgotten, called each other "Dingbat" and "Screamer."

Liz Smith
New York Newsday
New York, New York

You might have mentioned the growing use in electronic mail sent between computers of the colon, dash, right parenthesis, otherwise known as the sideways happy face.

:-) is used in e-mail to indicate joy, or that the writer doesn't mean for a statement to be taken seriously. There is a family of these faces, covering a range of emotions— :-) :-| :-(—and, in a tongue-in-cheek mood, there is the winking happy face ;-).

Stephen Clark
Poughkeepsie, New York

Techno-dweebs such as myself, writing computer programs and impatient with the inherent limitations of the Dvorak keyboard, have gobbled up every spare key in order to have a way for the computer user and the software to communicate. ("A fool there was and he made his prayer/Even as you and I") Tildes, stars, and pipes are hot and smoking today largely because everyone and his doctor's dog is becoming "computer literate" and taking courses that we in the techno-dweebs union are happy to teach. When referring to the "control characters" or "control codes," one cannot keep saying "that squiggley thing"; students lose all respect.

"Pipe," for example, is called a pipe because in the UNIX operating system (favored not by harem guards but by Bell Labs researchers, who originated it) a pipe connects one program with another, to pass it data or commands. Yes, it does look a tiny bit like a pipe; but I would wager that this new usage is techno-talk that has climbed out of the window of the lab and gone to town. Saying "money | safire" would run the computer program called "money" and send all the messages and output and so forth into a file (or another program) called "safire." This is not the same thing as "program trading."

And when your Pentagon correspondent threatens to destroy the world with star-dot-star, people who use IBM PC-DOS smile knowingly. (International Business Machines, Personal Computer, Disk Operating System is the one you use if you don't use UNIX—but you knew that.) In the MS-DOS world, *.* meant "all the files," and typing DELETE *.* was the ultimate nihilist act, since it would immediately and ruthlessly erase every single thing your computer ever knew. The words that the average computer user employed at this point often did not appear in dictionaries.

When you tailed off with your wonderful "@ this . I)" I smiled. Anyone active in the world of recreational online computer messaging systems (coinage needed: such a mouthful!) would have read the last character as a "smiley" or smiling face. Due to the limitations of computer screen display, these faces are most commonly typed and read sideways, as shown below.

> :-) *smiling face*
> :-(*frowning face*
> ;-) *winking smiling face*
> 8-) *eyes goggling in astonishment*
> d:-) *smiling face wearing a Red Sox cap*

These act as "body language" and can soften the blow when one writer is "flaming" at another. Though it can give the average spell checker electronic fits.

James Held
Forest Hills, New York

Heads Up!

An elliptical command (one with the verb understood) became an adjective and is now becoming a noun. You have to keep track of these usages before one of them pops you on the noggin.

Israel's Housing Minister, Ariel Sharon, had an appointment to meet his United States counterpart, Jack F. Kemp, at the Housing and Urban Development office in Washington. This displeased Secretary of State James A. Baker 3d. "Baker, while on the road, learned of plans for the Kemp-Sharon meeting," wrote *USA Today,* "and sent a '*heads up*' to the White House, saying it was 'inappropriate' and 'a little awkward' to see Sharon officially when he was working to defeat President Bush's policies."

The words in single quotation marks came from a State Department source. As a result of what Secretary Baker or his spokesman called a *heads up,* Mr. Sharon had to meet Secretary Kemp outside the office, on neutral ground, in this case the Israeli Embassy. (This rebuke caused Israelis, who are sharply divided about Mr. Sharon, to rally behind him, a result that could not have been what Mr. Baker intended.)

Obviously, a *heads up*—the noun—is part of today's official parlance. It has a nicely nuanced meaning, halfway between a bland *prior notification* and the more dire *warning.*

Heads up has two possible roots. One is "lift up your heads, do not let your eyes be downcast"; in a 1914 citation from *Collier's* provided by Sol Steinmetz at Random House, a character says, "Heads up, you guys! . . . We ain't licked yet." A synonymous expression in this sense is the imperative "Look alive."

A more specific derivation is in baseball. I recall staring at the dandelions in right field in Van Cortlandt Park in the Bronx when the center fielder shouted at me, "Heads up!"—not to cheer me up, but to suggest I look at a baseball coming my way before it caused injury.

That warning continues in military slang: In a recent Department of Defense dictionary, *heads up* is defined as "In air intercept, a code meaning 'Enemy got through (part or all).' " The baseball usage of the phrase led to the formation of a hyphenated adjective in *heads-up ball.* Maurice H. Weseen's 1934 *Dictionary of American Slang* defines that phrase as "good baseball playing." A *heads-up* player was one who was not only literally keeping his eye on the ball in the air, but also figuratively staying alert.

Only recently has the phrase turned into a noun. I am frequently called by collegial colleagues who say, "I just wanted you to have a *heads up* on this, but tomorrow will I give you a pop in my column." We now have enough written citations, especially from Foggy Bottom, to include the latest sense in dictionaries. Definition: "friendly, informal warning."

I have a heads up for you. There is another sense of heads up, *now military jargon, which should be noted. At jet-fighter speeds, it could be quite dangerous for a pilot to take the time to look down at the instrument panel. Current technology enables an image of a gunsight, bombsight, instrument reading, etc., to be projected into the pilot's line of sight, so it can be seen while looking straight ahead. This is called a* heads up display. *Within the next few years, it will probably show up in your automobile to display the speedometer reading (and perhaps other instruments as well) and so pass into the general language.*

Walter Siff
Fairfield, Connecticut

Hyphenated Americans

Justice Thurgood Marshall, in the news conference he held after announcing his retirement, sent a stylistic tremor through copy desks everywhere. Asked whether the state of "black people" had improved during his twenty-four-year Supreme Court tenure, he replied: "In the first place, I am not a *black people.* I am an *Afro-American.* Now, do you want to talk about *Afro-Americans?*"

A *New York Times* reporter, Neil A. Lewis, observed: "Justice Marshall has long avoided using the term *black,* preferring *Negro* or, more recently, *Afro-American.*" Jesse Jackson has been pressing the appellation *African-American,* which has been catching on in the black community more than *Afro-American;* however, the studied rejection of *black* by the former chief counsel of the NAACP Legal Defense Fund at a much-publicized event made *African-American* the designation of choice among most journalistic style makers.

But there's a problem, which has more to do with space than race: The longer form does not lend itself to headlines. *Black leaders* fits; *African-American leaders* crowds the verb off the page, or costs precious milliseconds of network time. For this reason, we can expect *black* to remain the description in the second reference, as in "Justice Marshall, an 82-year-old African-American, told other black leaders and the N.A.A.C.P. membership that . . ."

The National Association for the Advancement of Colored People is not going to change its name, despite the current treatment of *colored person* as old-fashioned (though *person of color* is up-to-date); that's because the N.A.A.C.P.'s initials are more familiar than its full name, and many people cannot recall what the second *A* stands for, anyway. (Same thing for the *C* for *Congress* in A.F.L.-C.I.O.)

Thus we have come from *blacks* to *colored people* and *Negroes* (at first *negro,* later *Negro),* then back to *blacks*—"black power" and "black is beauti-ful" were slogans of the 1960's—and now to *Afro-* and *African-Americans.*

The purpose of the current self-description may be to emphasize geo-graphical rather than racial roots, stressing a similarity of overseas heritage with other immigrants to America. Moreover, it gets the word *American* right there in the name, as *Irish-Americans* and *Italian-Americans* do. At the turn of the twentieth century, *hyphenated American* was a term of contempt used by nativists to demean the allegiance of immigrants; now such hyphenation is sought-after.

I'm for going along with calling people what they prefer, provided the des-ignation does not mislead or confuse. *Native American,* adopted by many American Indians, causes semantic difficulty because all citizens born here are native Americans, as against naturalized Americans; indeed, *nativism* means "immigrant-baiting," directly derived from the nineteenth-century Na-tive American party, official name of the secretive Know-Nothings.

You can't call an American Indian an *Indian-American,* because that refers to an immigrant from India; the accurate term for the descendant of tribes-people here before the Europeans arrived is *aboriginal American,* unhyphen-ated, meaning "here first," but neither that nor its hyphenated shortening, *Abo-American,* is catching on.

American Indian remains a proud and dignified term, as does *black Ameri-can,* but both may be relegated to second-reference status in coming years. Or perhaps not; in the lexicon of self-identification, usage calls the shots.

Dear Bill:

The replacement of black *by* Afro-American *or* African-American *leaves us without a way of separating race from nationality:* blacks *can take in not only* black Americans *but also* black Canadians, *black Brazilians, and black British people, but* African-Americans *can't. Do you know how Justice Marshall refers collectively to the black persons of the western hemisphere?*

> *Jim [James D. McCawley]*
> *Department of Linguistics*
> *University of Chicago*
> *Chicago, Illinois*

Many of us prefer black *as a primary designation. I prefer it not because of any objection to* African-American *(or* Afro-American*) but because* black *is pre-cise and inclusionary rather than exclusionary; it has universal application. There are millions of blacks who are residents of the U.S. but who are nationals* *of other countries. Therefore,* African-American *as a primary reference has the potential for creating artificial barriers.*

I believe both terms, along with Afro-American *and* people of color *(which has been around at least since the 1820s and which I now hear some people use to include Asians and Latinos), will be used interchangeably, at least in public discourse. But I think* black *will continue to be the primary reference; I hardly ever hear* African-American *used in ordinary conversation.*

> *Doris F. Innis*
> *New York, New York*

Hypothalamus High

Brain Work: The Neuroscience Newsletter, an educational publication of the Eleanor Naylor Dana Institute in New York, includes a brief article about a study by Dr. Simon LeVay of the Salk Institute that found a region of the hypothalamus to be smaller in homosexual men than in heterosexual men; some see this as evidence that sexual orientation is inborn.

The serious, scientific newsletter duly reports scientists to be cautious, with some calling the results "inconclusive," but goes on to note: "What was conclusive was the leap of *hypothalamus* into pop lingo—as in a recent issue of *Time* magazine."

Time quoted a popular radio talk-show commentator beginning a broadcast with "Greetings, conversationalists . . . this is Rush Limbaugh, the most dangerous man in America, with the largest *hypothalamus* in North America."

In the same issue, in an article about sexy Calvin Klein advertising, *Time* wrote about a previous campaign with Brooke Shields that "sold a lot of jeans and spawned a *hypothalamus-numbing* host of imitators."

We have here the popularization of a new symbol of virility. In Greek, *thalamos* is "an inner chamber"; the *hypothalamus* is the region of the brain that controls temperature and appetite, produces hormones, and presumably induces scorn for quiche and causes backward to reel the mind of trendy *Time* writers. Be the first caller-in to Mr. Limbaugh to pronounce it correctly: accent on the *thal.*

If by Whisky . . .

When pursuing a story about equivocation in high office, I was told, "He gave an *if-by-whisky* speech." My source, asked about his curious compound adjective, said he thought it was a Florida political expression.

That triggered a call to Richard B. Stone, now a Washington banker but a former United States Senator from Florida familiar with that state's political patois. He immediately recognized the phrase, meaning "calculated ambivalence," and provided the etymon: Fuller Warren, Florida's Governor in the 50's, was running for office in a year that counties were voting their local option on permitting the sale of liquor. Asked for his position on wet-vs.-dry, he would say:

"*If by whisky,* you mean the water of life that cheers men's souls, that smooths out the tensions of the day, that gives gentle perspective to one's view of life, then put my name on the list of the fervent wets.

"But *if by whisky,* you mean the devil's brew that rends families, destroys careers and ruins one's ability to work, then count me in the ranks of the dries."

If Not by Whisky

The great political straddle exemplified by the *if-by-whisky* speech was attributed here to Governor Fuller Warren of Florida in the 1950's. An earlier and richer formulation was submitted by Norman L. Simpson of Syracuse, who found an undated and unattributed clipping in his family archives; he dates it to the 1920's, during discussions of the repeal of the Volstead Act prohibiting the sale of liquor:

"I'll take a stand on any issue at any time, regardless of how fraught with controversy it may be. You have asked me how I feel about whisky; well, Brother, here's how I stand.

"If by whisky, you mean the Devil's brew, the Poison scourge, the bloody monster that defies innocence, dethrones reason, creates misery and poverty, yea, literally takes the bread out of the mouths of babes; if you mean the Evil Drink that topples men and women from pinnacles of righteous, gracious living into the bottomless pit of despair, degradation, shame, helplessness and hopelessness—then certainly I am against it with all my power.

"But if by whisky, you mean the oil of conversation, the philosophic wine and ale that is consumed when good fellows get together, that puts a song in their hearts, laughter on their lips and the warm glow of contentment in their eyes; if you mean that sterling drink that puts the spring in an old man's steps on a frosty morning; if you mean that drink, the sale of which pours into our treasury untold millions of dollars which are used to provide tender care for our little crippled children, our pitifully aged and infirm and to build our highways, hospitals and schools—then, Brother, I am for it. This is my stand."

The *if-by-whisky* technique is still in active use. Asked by Jonathan Alter of *Newsweek* if he was not too sensitive to criticism, Governor Mario M. Cuomo of New York replied:

"If by thin-skinned you mean very, very quick to respond—that's what I've done for a lifetime. I'd been a lawyer for more than 20 years. You can't let the comment from the witness pass.

"If [by thin-skinned] you're talking about being personally sensitive to criticism, that's a lot of [expletive]."

Phrasedick Alert

Here's a flash from the campaign to find the origin of the classic *if-by-whisky* speech, a parody of a politician taking both sides of an issue. Coinage goes to Judge Noah S. (Soggy) Sweat Jr. of Corinth, Mississippi (the nickname "Soggy" based not on his last name but on "Sorghum Top," referring to the way his hair resembled the tassel that grows atop sugarcane).

In 1952, as wets and drys were debating local prohibition of booze, Judge Sweat, now sixty-nine years old, copyrighted his speech: "If when you say whisky you mean the Devil's brew . . . but if when you say whisky you mean the oil of conversation. . . ."

On another etymological front, it was reported here that the coiner of the now-ubiquitous phrase *the peace process* was Henry A. Kissinger, then Secretary of State, in the mid-1970's. To double-check, I sent a note with the citation to my old friend Henry in New York, who replies: "I honestly don't know if I coined the phrase *peace process*. But have I ever refused credit for anything?"

I can't resist joining the "if-by-whisky" search.

My contribution uses "demon rum" and is set during Prohibition. This version appears in Carl Carmer's popular 1934 work, Stars Fell on Alabama. *The unnamed speaker is the governor of Alabama and is described as having the booming voice heard on the radio that declared the votes Alabama gave to fellow-Alabamian Oscar Underwood in the 1924 Democratic convention. At any rate, the speaker is now haranguing an audience at "a combination political rally, singin' and barbecue" (86). I have copied for you the relevant page of dialogue, beginning with a critic who demands that the governor take a stand on the "liquor question."*

> *"When I think of all the homes the demon rum has ruined, when I think of the hearts of pure women and little children—broken by a husband's accursed habit, when I think of the lives alcohol has snuffed out in their prime—then, ladies and gentlemen, I'm* agin *it. . . .*
>
> *"But," thundered the voice—"but—when I rise on a chill mornin' and pull the window down an' hug the fire and shiver an' I can't get warm nohow—an' my wife says to me, 'Ol' man, how about a bit of toddy to warm your innards?'—THEN, BOYS, I'M FOR IT." . . .*
>
> *Tennant chuckled. "He's the world's champion fence-straddler."*

Scott Culclasure
Greensboro, North Carolina

Impregnating the Pause

Alcibiades, the ancient Greek orator whose name is pronounced "Al Si-BY-a-deez," is quoted less often these days than Al Capone. Granted, the gangster got off a great line, cited by eminent strategic planners as well as young punks: "You can get much farther with a kind word and a gun than you can with a kind word alone." Alcibiades, however, is best remembered for what he did not say.

Robert Byrd of West Virginia, guardian of the United States Senate's sense of history, rose in that body recently to call our attention to the lesson of the Greek who was the ward of Pericles.

"Alcibiades is not exactly a paragon of good living," the Senator cautioned. That's putting it mildly: Alcibiades was the paragon of recklessness and treachery, who sold out his native Athens for a place in Sparta, and is remembered for opinions like "As for democracy . . . nothing new can be said about an acknowledged foolishness."

But the man could speak, and he had a trick that caused audiences to hang on his words: "Plutarch tells us," Senator Byrd said, "on the authority of the prince of orators, Demosthenes, that Alcibiades often hesitated in the midst of a speech, not hitting upon the word he wanted, and stopped until it occurred to him." Why, the Senator asked rhetorically, don't we do that anymore? "I think there can be an art in the use of a pause. And I find nothing wrong with a pause. It does not have to be filled in with *you know.*" This pestiferous phrase "betrays a mind whose thoughts are often so disorganized as to be unutterable—a mind in neutral gear coupled to a tongue stuck in over-drive."

Although grease monkeys in garages across the land would rise to raise a point of metaphoric order that *overdrive* arranges gears to produce greater speed with less power (the drive shaft to the wheels may turn four times for every three revolutions of the engine's crankshaft), the term has been used as a verb in the King James translation of Genesis 33:13 and is used figuratively today as a noun rooted in automotive mechanics to mean "heightened activity potentially leading to the stress of overwork."

Although the Senator's mechanical metaphor is sustainable, is his complaint sound—that is, is the ubiquitous *y'know* a nervous filler used by speakers too embarrassed to pause when the appropriate word does not come to mind?

Only sometimes. We are now into what Demosthenes, Alcibiades & Company would call *embolalia*—"em-bo-loll-ya"—from the Greek for "the insertion of chatter." Modern linguists led by Leonard Bloomfield in 1933 call these "hesitation forms"—the sounds of stammering (*uh*), stuttering (*um, um*), throat-clearing (*ahem!*), stalling (*well, um, that is*), interjected when the speaker is groping for words or at a loss for the next thought.

You know that *y'know* is among the most common of these hesitation forms. Its meaning is not the imperious "you understand" or even the old interrogatory "do you get it?" It is given as, and taken to be, merely a filler phrase, intended to fill a beat in the flow of sound, not unlike *like,* in its new sense of, like, a filler word.

Similarly, *I mean,* as most frequently used today, has ceased to mean *I mean*—in its former sense of "for me, this denotes, expresses, represents," or "here is my import, sense, significance, message." Ironically, often the new sense of *I mean* is no sense at all: It is intended to convey meaninglessness, a habitual, annoying filler phrase synonymous with the unknowing *y'know.*

But I want to suggest that the words and phrases dismissed as hesitation forms are sometimes used for purposes other than to moan or to stammer with socially acceptable grunts while groping.

All three of these staples of modern filler communication—*I mean, y'know, like*—can also be used as "tee-up words." In olden times, pointer phrases or tee-up words were *get this, would you believe?* and *are you ready?* The function of these rib-nudging phrases was—are you ready?—to make the point, to focus the listener's attention on what was to follow.

That attention-impelling function, or "articulated colon," today belongs to *I mean, y'know* and *like,* as in "That girl is, *like,* kooky; that guy is, *I mean,* gnarly—*y'know,* far out to the point of spaciness." (Do not confuse this articulated colon with another interjection, known tentatively in the linguistic dodge as "the nail-nibbling self-reassurance"; in the 70's, *O.K.?* was interjected to mean "Are you listening? Am I making sense?" Today, *y'know?* with a rising inflection often serves this nebbishistic function.)

And that's not all, as the man says. (*As the man says, so to speak* and *as it were* are apologies for clichés; for some reason, *the man* has replaced *they.* These are self-conscious interjections related to hesitation forms but considered more adult.) Another purpose of hesitation forms is to dissociate yourself slightly from the harsh reality of what is to follow. ("Darling, I'm, like, involved with this other person.") It is the articulation of a slight grimace.

By the use of a beat of time filled with a meaningless interjection, uncommitted people who are "into distancing" make a little space between themselves and their words, as if that lessens their impact. Thus, when we hear one of the ubiquitous trio of hesitation forms, we should ask ourselves: Is this being used as (1) a purposeful tee-up, (2) a cowardly disengager or (3) a mere filler to cover a grope?

If the purpose is to tee up or point, we should accept *y'know* and its friends as a mildly annoying spoken punctuation, the articulated colon that signals "focus on this." If the purpose is disengagement, we should pity the noncommitter. If the purpose is to grab a moment to think, we should allow ourselves to wonder: Why are filler phrases needed at all? What motivates the speaker to fill the moment of silence with any sound at all?

Now we are back to the Alcibiadean pause. Did the sneaky Greek orator really pause because he was seeking the right word—or did he use that refreshing device, as Churchill later did, to pull listeners to the edge of their seats?

I recall a session that a roomful of image makers held with a presidential candidate before a televised news conference. The problem was that the candidate anticipated all the questions, knew all the answers and tended to pop out the reply the moment the question was asked; it made him seem like a smart aleck, too glib.

The sage advice was this: On at least one question, cross 'em all up with a pregnant pause. Stop. Pause a moment or two—like maybe three whole seconds, driving sound-bite specialists crazy with the waste of costly network time—as if the question caused the interviewee to think his position over. No need for *well, y'know, I mean* or any such filler, though a thoughtful *hmmm* might be permissible.

It worked. Attention was paid. The ghost of Alcibiades . . . smiled.

In a manner unusual in classical Greek, Alcibiades also had a fondness for beginning many sentences with the Greek equivalent of the English conjunction and. *This is strikingly similar to the fondness of President Bush, as you first pointed out in a brief study of his inaugural address, where the President began 11.1 percent of his sentences with the lowly* and.

A classicist, Michael Vickers, of the Ashmolean Museum of Oxford University, who is writing a biography of Alcibiades, pointed out to me in my study of

President Bush's prose that the resemblance between the two leaders is only stylistic.

"How unlike Alcibiades is George Bush," said Vickers. "Alcibiades was an amalgam of J. F. Kennedy, Oliver North, Vidkun Quisling, and John Belushi."

For more pregnant pauses—

E. Leo McMannus
Venice, Florida

Your article brought to mind a word I had learned many years ago but have had little opportunity to employ, namely:

Aposiopesis

I. Martin Spier
New York, New York

You offer a few ideas in response to Senator Robert Byrd's rhetorical question about pause-fillers in speech. Yes, they're used to buy time for thought, and other purposes.

But I think they're so common now because we've lost the art of respectful listening. So eager we are to get in our point of view, so tempted to interrupt, we don't allow pauses to go unfilled. Grow up in a household where your sentences are met with impatient, c'mon-spit-it-out, I-have-somethin'-more-important-to-say inattention, and you'll sprinkle into your discourse enough y'knows and uhs and likes *to ultimately say what you set out to say, developing an unpleasant habit. They serve, however annoyingly, as muzzles on would-be butters-in.*

In ancient Greece, perhaps, one dared not interrupt, and a speaker could, as Alicibiades did, pause with dignity and aplomb.

Taj Harvey
Huntington Station, New York

As a driver shifts through the gears from low (first) to overdrive (fifth), the gears in the transmission are recombined to turn the drive shaft with increasing speed but with decreasing torque—*not power.*

Torque *is twisting. You apply torque when you open a jar of peanut butter or tighten a bolt or turn down the volume on your teenager's stereo. Technically, torque is that which causes or tends to cause rotation.*

Power, *on the other hand, is the rate (over time) at which energy is generated* or work is performed (i.e., energy is used). Power is equal to torque times rotational speed (and times a fudge factor to adjust for the units in which these quantities are measured). For example, for a drive shaft to transmit 100 horsepower (HP) to the wheels at a speed of 1,500 revolutions per minute (rpm), it requires 350 foot-pounds (ft lb) of torque, but if the transmission gears are shifted so the drive shaft turns at 3,000 rpm, it needs only 175 ft lb of torque. (Aside: in engineering practice, periods are not used in abbreviations of units of measure.)

Specifically, overdrive refers to a transmission gear ratio less than one-to-one, so that the driven shaft rotates faster than the driving shaft. Since an automobile can't run in overdrive until it is moving fairly fast (in my car, about 40 mph), half of Senator Byrd's metaphor, ". . . a tongue stuck in overdrive," aptly represents nonstop speech. The problem is in the other half.

Neutral is the position of the transmission gear shift lever at which there is no connection at all between the engine and the drive shaft—that is to say, they are uncoupled—and each can operate independently of the other. Thus ". . . a mind in neutral gear . . ." frees the tongue to say whatever it damn well pleases. It is here that Senator Byrd's mechanical metaphor for an inherent contradiction misses the mark.

His intent would have been better served had he said, ". . . a mind running at idle speed coupled to a tongue stuck in overdrive." Such a combination in an automobile would cause it to stall, and it is not inappropriate to play on that word when y'know and its equivalents are used to fill time until the next idea comes along.

All of which brings to mind the notice, neatly lettered, that I sometimes see hanging in engineering offices: "Please be sure brain is engaged before putting mouth into motion."

Walter Siff
Fairfield, Connecticut

With reference to "You can get much farther with a kind word and a gun than you can with a kind word alone," I believe this statement should correctly be credited to John Dillinger and not Capone. In fact, Capone's attempts to promote the image of a law-abiding businessman belies the suggestion that he would have uttered the aforementioned phrase. To wit, it was Dillinger, the avowed bank robber, who made this brash statement.

Joseph A. Keane
Sparkill, New York

Inside the Circumferential Highway

As other Democratic hopefuls. . . . (That's a cliché. Hopefully, we can dispense with the transformation of the adjective *hopeful* into a noun. Begin again.)

As Democrats pressing their candidature. . . . (Academics will like that word, but it's in the same prissy league as *governance* and *polity;* besides, what's wrong with *candidacy*? Begin again; this is your last chance.)

As those guys panting after the Democratic nomination began to show primary results, the telepundit Mark Shields said of Governor Bill Clinton, "He won the *inside-the-Beltway* primary."

The Beltway in this usage is the Capital Beltway, a circumferential highway that enables traffic to skirt, or bypass, the city streets. In many American small towns, such a traffic-reliever is called a *bypass.*

In Britain, the term is *ring road* or *ringway,* though some wish to gentrify that to *orbital road.* The heart of Moscow is circled by the *Sadovoye Koltso* (*sadovoye* means "garden"; *koltso* is Russian for "ring").

Mr. Shields was not, of course, referring to a primary held in Washington, D.C. *Inside the Beltway* is not a place but a state of mind; used as a compound adjective, the prepositional phrase means "having the conventional wisdom held by self-described political insiders."

The political term first appeared in *The Washington Post* atop a fishing story in 1977: "*Inside-the-Beltway* Trout Fishing Nears." But not until 1983, according to my Nexis search, did its political-insider sense come to the fore. In a *Newsweek* article an anonymous Democratic campaign manager was quoted as refusing to derogate the possibility of a return by former Senator George McGovern: "If he's perceived as a man on a fool's errand, that's still *inside the* [Washington] *Beltway,* not the world as a whole."

Two years later, the phrase still required a bracketed explanation. A United Press International report from Washington quoted Mark Russell, the humorist, making this assessment of Senator Alan Simpson of Wyoming: "Simpson epitomizes the Western disdain for '*inside-the-beltway*' [Washington know-it-alls]." In 1991, Senator Charles Grassley of Iowa used the phrase in the Clarence Thomas hearings: "ordinary American people, who look at things differently than are looked at here *inside the Beltway.*"

A few now use the phrase to describe "the real inside skinny"; it is the title of a gossipy news column in the *Washington Times.* Most prefer the sense of "showing insular thinking, removed from the heartland." John Leo, the stylish essayist in *U.S. News & World Report,* assessed the opinions of a group of opinionators about Pat Buchanan by pointing out that "Almost every one . . . comes from the same tiny hothouse: the *inside-the-beltway* punditry industry."

The phrase reflects a populist disdain for central government, though it is most often used by people who live in its environs. Part of the general run-ning-against-Washington movement, it is more anti-ineffectual than anti-intellectual.

Hyphenate the phrase when used as a modifier before the noun it describes. Capitalize the *B* when making reference to the Washington Beltway, as you capitalize the *M* in Washington Monument, a rule that covers most use today; ultimately, this important new bit of political slang will lower the case as it takes on a meaning of general insiderness.

Two related phrases:

Beltway bandits are consultants, usually to the defense industry, who prac-tice inside the Beltway; use is lessening because defense contracts are no longer the ripe plums they used to be.

In the loop, a place George Bush denied being during the Iran-contra affair, means "among those consulted," usually a tight circle. *Loop,* or circle, was used in Chicago at the turn of the century, when the titan Charles Tyson Yerkes built the railway known as the Loop around the downtown business district; the area itself is now known as the Loop. By analogy, the District of Columbia may well become known sometime in the next millennium as the Beltway.

If you check out some of the older "gyrenes" at "8th and I," you'll find they used the term "skinny" 30 years ago to refer to "real inside, inside story." Modify "skinny" and you're redundant. Don't know why they call Marines "gyrenes," though.

John A. Sullivan III
Caldwell, New Jersey

In Your Face

Basketball, the game that brought the general language *one-on-one, tossup* and *full-court press,* has done it again.

In a single recent issue of *The New Yorker,* one film critic described a movie as "the worst kind of *in-your-face* farce"; another hailed actor Al Pacino for his "persuasive portrait of a pesky, *in-your-face* romantic" in the movie *Frankie and Johnny,* and John Updike, in a review of two novels, praised the "slangy, *in-your-face* prose styles" in which the narrators—both white women in Africa—discussed their bowel movements "with a frankness new to ro-mantic heroines."

"What does this expression mean?" asks Daniel M. Klein of Great Barrington, Massachusetts. "Where have I been? And what are all these things doing in my face?"

Intimidating you, that's what. Carl Ladensack of Lancaster, Pennsylvania, found the expression in *You'll Never Eat Lunch in This Town Again* by Julia Phillips: "You were ignored, but she managed to be *in your face* at the same time." He notes: "The context and tone suggest something like *bold, arrogant, bothersome* or *audacious.* . . . Is this a new vulgarism that will soon sweep across the media and like a nasty slap strike all of us in the face?"

It may sound like a euphemism for a vulgarism, similar to *stick it in your ear,* but the suddenly popular compound adjective *in-your-face* has a nonvulgar derivation.

Richard A. Spears, a leading slanguist, suggests that "it sounds like the reverse of *get out of my face,* which tells somebody to move away." This locution, which seems to be formed on the analogy of *get off my back,* soon replaced *back off* as the preferred slang in calling for physical or symbolic withdrawal. The first citation in the *Dictionary of American Regional English* is from 1931: "Git out *o' my face,* or I'll slap ye into the middle of next week!" *DARE* reports that its use is especially frequent among black speakers.

The allusion is confrontational. Mr. Spears observes that "*in your face* would reverse *out of my face,* to mean 'getting in front of people to bother them.'"

Face, like *cheek,* has long had a sense of "brazenness." In the 1851 *Polly Peablossom's Wedding,* a collection of stories edited by Thomas A. Burke, a character asks, "How can you have the *face* to talk to me arter saying what you sed?" The defiant sense exists in the verb as well: *face up to* and *face down.*

The definition of *in-your-face,* the term now in vogue, was put forward in 1982 by Tim Considine in his book *The Language of Sport:* "aggressively challenging, disrespectful or disdainful." His example was "scored with an *in-your-face* slam dunk."

(A *slam dunk,* as sports fans know, is not a method of ingesting coffee performed vigorously with a doughnut; it is a basketball term meaning "a forceful dunk shot," in which the ball is dramatically pushed down, or stuffed, into the basket by a leaping player. You don't see many gentle dunk shots anymore; this is the age of slam.)

Thus has *outta my face* given rise to *in your face.* "As a modifier, this phrase has catapulted overnight into the cliché Hall of Fame," writes Allan M. Siegal, assistant managing editor of *The New York Times.* He also comments: "To my ear, it's crude, and that's exactly what recommends it for most of the uses to which it's put. Even if the crudeness doesn't offend, the triteness—attained with record speed—does."

Evidence: the *Times* editorial about the recent primary election, during which Bill Clinton learned that campaigning down New York streets could be a character-building experience, was entitled "The *In-Your-Face* Primary."

Governor Jerry Brown, a *Times* reporter wrote, used "headlong rhetoric . . . well suited to the *in-your-face* style of New York politics." In all, the phrase appeared in this newspaper twenty-eight times in a two-month period; editor Siegal's complaint about triteness may slow it down.

Aggressive, assertive, militant, contentious, combative, belligerent, arrogant—all these words and more are available to us. Not pushy enough for you? *Quarrelsome, truculent, offensive!* Slam! Dunk! *Disrespectful!*

When I first came upon "in your face," I didn't find it all that new. Somehow in the distant haze of memory, perhaps seventy years ago, I heard my Yiddish-speaking father say "in eier punim" (translated, in your face) when he meant to direct a sharp put-down to his adversary. Still later, when English came easier to him, he turned from "in eier punim" to its English equivalent, "finger in the face, facts."

Charles Ansell
Sherman Oaks, California

It's a Rain Forest Out There

What's happened to the *jungle*?

It's disappearing. This once-popular word was first used in 1776 in Nathaniel B. Halhed's translation of a code of Hindu laws: "Land Waste for Five Years . . . is called Jungle." It is respectably rooted in the Hindi *jangal* and the Sanskrit *jangala,* "wasteland, desert." After a century of use in this dry sense, the word was applied to uncultivated tropical land, overgrown with grasses and teeming with snakes and creepily wet wildlife; Thomas Macaulay wrote in 1849 of "a vast pool . . . overhung with rank jungle."

As recently as a generation ago, the word was doing fine. Rudyard Kipling wrote *The Jungle Book* in 1894, and coined *the law of the jungle,* cruel but fair in its way. A children's play structure was called a *jungle gym* in 1923; *jungle warfare* was taught in all the best military schools after World War II, and the metaphor was extended to *The Asphalt Jungle,* a 1950 John Huston movie (which brought Marilyn Monroe to prominence) about the fierce city, while Evan Hunter's 1954 novel about city schools was titled *The Blackboard Jungle.* Harried executives told the joke of Tarzan swinging on a vine into his treehouse and telling Jane, his mate: "Whew! It's a jungle out there."

All gone. *Jungle* is no more, at least not in sophisticated usage. The *rain forest* has taken over.

It started to grow slowly. The German botanist Andreas Franz Wilhelm Schimper first used *Regenwald* in 1898; William Rogers Fisher translated it literally in this 1903 publication in English: "The *Rainforest* is evergreen, hygrophilous in character, at least thirty meters high, but usually much taller, rich in thick-stemmed lianes, and in wood as well as herbaceous epiphytes."

That was what used to be a *jungle;* in those days, a somewhat drier woodland that attracted lumberjacks was a *forest.* Now they're both forests; the dripping one with the quicksand and weird birdcalls is a *tropical rain forest* while the nice woods with reasonable rainfall that Hansel and Gretel would go trooping through is a *temperate rain forest.*

This is the environmentalists' greatest linguistic triumph. Because a *jungle* was fearsome, nobody would want to preserve it. But a *forest* has a nice ring to it—there was Robin Hood with his merry men robbing the rich in Sherwood Forest—and the word lent itself to persuasion for preservation. If a pollster asks, "Is it O.K. to mow down the *jungle?*" the answer will be "Sure, who needs it?"; if the same pollster asks, "Do you approve of destruction of the *rain forest?*" the answer will be "No, it will lead to global warming or a new ice age."

Get off that jungle, Jim. When they colorize that John Huston movie for television, we will see Marilyn Monroe in *The Asphalt Rain Forest.*

Jump-Start Those Animal Spirits

"What this economy needs," *The Wall Street Journal* exhorts, "is more risk-taking, more *animal spirits.*" A few years ago, the investor Warren Buffett found that "Leaders, business or otherwise, seldom are deficient in *animal spirits* and often relish increased activity and challenge."

Not everyone agrees with the need for, or the meaning of, these *animal spirits.* "We really did have a genuine bubble in real estate," says Richard Syron, president of the Boston Federal Reserve Bank, "and it was driven by *animal spirits.*" He means that property values were inflated by overspeculation, and uses the phrase in the sense of "misplaced optimism."

From what vasty deep were these spirits summoned, and why does the cliché afflict economists particularly?

"Physitions teache," wrote Bartholomew Traheron in his 1543 translation of a surgery text, "that there ben thre kindes of spirites, *animal, vital* and *naturall.* The animal spirite hath his seate in the brayne, and . . . is called *animal,* bycause it is the first instrument of the soule, whych the Latins call *animam.*" (You wonder why copy editors want hazardous-duty pay for this column?)

The poet John Milton used the image in his 1667 *Paradise Lost:* "If . . . he might taint/Th' *animal Spirits* that from pure blood arise." Writing a few

decades before Milton, the French philosopher René Descartes held that these spirits were triggered by the sight of a frightful figure that in turn would jolt the nerves "and dispose the legs for flight." Most writers, though, preferred an ebullient sense: "She had high *animal spirits,*" Jane Austen wrote in *Pride and Prejudice* in 1813, and Benjamin Disraeli in his novel *Coningsby* in 1844 wrote, "He . . . had great *animal spirits,* and a keen sense of enjoyment."

The economists, however, had already staked their claim. In his 1719 *Survey of Trade,* William Wood reported "the Increase of our Foreign Trade . . . whence has arisen all those *Animal Spirits,* those Springs of Riches which has enabled us to spend so many millions for the preservation of our liberties."

Enter John Maynard Keynes, never noted for sprightly writing, with his monumental *General Theory of Employment, Interest and Money.*

"Most, probably, of our decisions to do something positive," he wrote in 1936, ". . . can only be taken as a result of *animal spirits*—of a spontaneous urge to action rather than inaction, and not as the outcome of a weighted average of quantitative benefits multiplied by quantitative probabilities." Don't overlook this human element, the first Keynesian cautioned: "If the *animal spirits* are dimmed and the spontaneous optimism falters, leaving us to depend on nothing but a mathematical expectation, enterprise will fade and die."

We are all animal-spiritists now; the phrase has come to mean "risk-taking, entrepreneurial zeal," a willingness to roll the dice and open a plant when others read the charts gloomily. A Syracuse University economics professor, Douglas Holtz-Eakin, calls this concept "the dividing line between economists who favor the fundamentals and those who believe the fundamentals may be tainted by short-run swings of optimism or pessimism."

But what about the time when *animal spirits* are not enough to dispose our legs for flight? That's when another great cliché kicks in: "President Bush met his economic advisers," *The Christian Science Monitor* wrote, ". . . to encourage more bank lending to *jump-start* a stagnant economy." The *Monitor* likes that metaphor, and no wonder: That is where the extension of the metaphor appears to have begun.

On March 26, 1982, Peter Grier, a business reporter for *The Monitor,* was covering a speech by the economist Milton Friedman, Nobel laureate and guru of the no-free-lunch. According to notes still in the reporter's possession, Professor Friedman said the recovery's "absolutely essential condition is reduction in the size of government. Nothing else will do it." Mr. Grier enlivened his copy by using a metaphor, and it appeared in the newspaper this way: " 'The triumph of the policy Ronald Reagan has been following is that he is making [Congress] talk seriously on his terms,' Friedman said. The President's policies will effectively *jump-start* our stalled economy. 'Nothing else will do it,' he said."

I asked the reporter, who continues to cover business in Washington for the newly invigorated *Monitor,* how he came up with the historic metaphoric extension. "I was having trouble with my Honda at the time," he recalls. "Hard to start, stalling—one day the whole engine fell out on Massachusetts Avenue. *Jump-start* was on my mind as I went to cover Friedman's speech."

The compound verb is raging through economic reporting and commentary. "Closing down Washington and sealing it off until November 1992 like some plagued medieval city would undoubtedly *jump-start* the economy," mutters *The Wall Street Journal,* which much prefers *animal spirits* to such government intervention. Bob Dole, the Senate Republican leader in this medieval city, writes, "I am questioning whether any so-called tax-cut plan could *jump start* a $5.6 trillion economy." He prefers no hyphen.

The metaphor is that of giving an automobile, with its battery dead, a surge of electricity that causes a spark to start the engine. To do this, a *jumper cable* connects a source of electricity through the dead battery's terminals to the starter. One sense of *jump* is "to connect," as a spark jumps a gap, making the end receiving the energy leap as if to life. (If your engine has fallen out and is lying on Massachusetts Avenue, however, there is little a *jump-start* can do.)

The extended metaphor jumped into the language heavily in 1987 and did not land only in economics. "Only America can give Europeanization the *jump-start* it needs," Christopher Layne wrote in *Foreign Policy,* using it as a noun. In *Science* magazine, M. Mitchell Waldrop wrote of "a 'white hole' that so drastically pinches the curvature of space and time that it can give the new universe a kind of *jump start.*" From the cosmic to the comical: "In the current political parlance," Elizabeth Drew wrote in *The New Yorker,* "the question is whether [Senator Albert] Gore can '*jump-start*' his campaign in the South."

Nobody says *revivify, revive* or *revitalize* anymore; you rarely hear *rekindle* or *resurrect,* or even *enliven, quicken* or *awaken. Resuscitate* and *reinvigorate* are dead. Those who wish to avoid a cliché may consider *animate,* but the spirit is weak.

I enjoyed your bit on "jump start" but was surprised you did not mention its exact Depression antecedent, "pump priming." Down on the farm, you had to put a bit of water in the pump to get a flood of water out of it; in a more agrarian era pump priming was as resonant as jump starting is in a society approaching one car per capita.

The notion in the early years of the New Deal was that there was nothing wrong with the economy that a one-shot infusion of money wouldn't cure. As they learned that this did not work, modern fiscal policy was developed. The endless use of "jump start" shows that nobody remembers anything, especially Republicans. You can't jump start a broken engine.

Richard P. Rosenthal
Brooklyn, New York

Kinder Than Who?

When George Bush spoke of a "kinder, gentler nation," I reported that Nancy Reagan turned to a convention boxmate and tartly asked, "Kinder than who?" I added, "She knew when the cord was being cut, despite her grammatical lapse."

Purist who-whomniks hit back. In the course of a thoughtful letter on values, Neil Rudenstine, the president of Harvard, writes: "If we are thinking about the nation, then 'Kinder than what?' would probably have been right. But if the comparison seemed rather more personal, then 'Kinder than who?' is maybe clumsily correct."

Hermione Wickenden of Weston, Connecticut, writes, "If the question had been completed, it would logically read: 'Kinder than *who* (or Ronnie!) is kind?' " David Carney of Sag Harbor, Long Island, notes, "You obviously mistook *than,* a conjunctive adverb of comparison, for a preposition."

You bet I take *than* as a preposition, not a conjunction. The purists would ask "Kinder than who [is]?" and answer "Kinder than I [am]"; impurists, or non-stiffs, would answer "Kinder than *me,*" using the objective case, and substituting the objective *whom* for *me.*

Nancy Reagan's friend Peter Hannaford takes no position on the who/whom controversy, but points out that Mrs. Reagan did not listen to the speech from a convention box and doubts the accuracy of my report. Maybe it's apocryphal, though my source says not; if Mrs. Reagan said it, she used the words "Kinder than who?" and I am prepared to concede she has a legion of who-whomniks to support her grammar.

Dear Bill:

You touch on the question of what part of speech than *belongs to. The question of whether it is a preposition or a (subordinating) conjunction isn't a real question for someone who (like me) accepts Jespersen's conclusion (The Philosophy of Grammar, p. 89 [reprinted in 1992 by the University of Chicago Press]) that so-called subordinating conjunctions are prepositions with clause objects.* Than *is a preposition regardless of whether it has a clause object or a noun-phrase object (or any other kind of object: it can take an amazing range of things as its object, as can its congener* as*), and the issue is whether, when a clause object of* than *is reduced down to one item and that item is a pronoun, the pronoun's case is chosen on the basis of its role as object of a preposition (*whom, me, him*) or on the basis of its role in the reduced clause (*who, I, he, if it is the subject of that clause).*

The latter way of resolving the jurisdictional dispute between these two fac-

tors is regarded as praiseworthy by the generic purists to whom you refer, and the former way of resolving it as objectionable, which is their prerogative, but it is absurd for them to suggest that a person is being inconsistent if he says "kinder than whom" but "kinder than who is."

Jim [James D. McCawley]
Department of Linguistics
University of Chicago
Chicago, Illinois

Let Forthcoming Come Forth

"The emir and the crown prince were very *forthcoming,*" said Secretary of State James A. Baker 3d, using one of the most frequent words in the vocabulary of diplomacy. It means "open to new ideas, cooperative, willing to bring helpful suggestions to the negotiations."

In diplolingo, the antonym of *forthcoming* is *frank,* which in this limited sense means "surly, argumentative, intransigent and causing an obstacle to peace." A meeting described by a spokesman as a *frank discussion* is bad enough; a *frank exchange* verges on shouted recriminations and hints of war.

Forthcoming, however, is a compliment; in a recent political polemic, I fell into using it myself. That triggered this note from Sheila Davis of New York: "I've been saddened by the slow erosion of *forthright.* I was therefore stunned by your replacement of *forthright* by *forthcoming.*" She asks: "Is this a case of *anxious/eager?* Are we about to read a new entry in our dictionaries under *forthcoming*—'synonymous with *forthright*'?"

Don't be anxious; I am eager to straighten this out.

Forthright means "straightforward, candid, without hesitation or guile," and in the nondiplomatic sense, "frank."

Forthcoming, however, has a couple of meanings: One is "about to appear, soon to be available, approaching"; the second sense of the word is forthcoming in the following sentence. That is the "open, cooperative, helpful" sense in diplolingo, usually marked in dictionaries as "chiefly British."

Controversy rages over that British sense. In *American Usage and Style: The Consensus,* Roy H. Copperud (now the word columnist for *Editor & Publisher*) says, "The displacement of *forthright* (direct, straightforward) or, sometimes, *outgoing* (friendly, responsive) by *forthcoming* is regrettable and should be discouraged." Why? "It can cause ambiguity. . . . For example, 'The President's statement was forthcoming' could be understood to mean that it was about to be made, not that it was forthright."

I am ordinarily on the side of preserving distinctions, not because I am eager to please, but because I am anxious about fuzziness. The question before us is this: Does *forthcoming* in its "coming forth with ideas" sense fill a need for meaning that no other word offers?

It does. Let's say the emir, or whoever, is willing to go along with what you suggest. You, as a diplomat, cannot describe his attitude as *responsive,* which it is, because that makes it sound as if you are the one with the ideas and he's just sitting there, going along, responding to you. *Helpful* is patronizing, and too easily confused with *unhelpful,* a diplolingo staple meaning "I'm going to zap this guy for this"; *friendly* denotes the tenor of the talks but not the action of moving them forward.

If you want to indicate that the emir has also come forth with a helpful idea, or to cover his acquiescence in your proposal, the best word is *forthcoming.* It's best not because it contains no possibility for ambiguity—on the contrary, it does confuse at times, as Mr. Copperud points out—but because I cannot think of another word to describe the emir's willingness to help or even to be creative. Remember that it is used by diplomats to compliment the other guy in the meeting for his willingness to go along, or at least agree not to obstruct, while it also suggests that he came forth with an idea of his own.

Let lexicographers, then, drop the "chiefly British" (as the latest *Random House Webster's College* edition does) and forthrightly accept *forthcoming* with its two meanings. Let us hope that the forthcoming statement will show the emir to be forthcoming.

"Using one of the most frequent words. . . ." "Frequent" has an adverbial feeling. It is used to modify words that come from verbs. Frequent actions (act), exaggerations (exaggerate), meetings (meet), etc. "Words," having no verbal connection, resists "frequent." It wants "frequently used" or "found." Think it over, Safire.

Arthur J. Morgan
New York, New York

Let's Kill All the Copy Editors

"Here I am, the Rip Van Winkle of the world of words," writes Suzanne Garment of Washington, author of *Scandal: The Culture of Mistrust in American Politics.* "Having finished the manuscript of my book, I sent it off to a very good copy editor, confident that he would find little to change in such a grammatically conscientious text as mine."

Every writer knows the feeling, and what happens next: "But it came back to me all marked up and translated into a strange dialect," Mrs. Garment continues. And when she confided her consternation to her publishers? "They assured me that the editor had merely modernized my usage, which was twenty years out of date."

Modern copy editors and their stylebook conspirators have a case of the lowers, which is to say that capitalization is out. (No, leave it *conspirators;* to me, a *co-conspirator* is as redundant as a *co-equal.*) This has been a two-century trend in America; if Thomas Jefferson were writing today, the Continental Congress's Committee on Style would not permit "certain unalienable

Rights, that among these are Life, Liberty and the pursuit of Happiness" or even "mutually pledge to each other our Lives, our Fortunes and our sacred Honor." O.K., styles change, we don't wear powdered wigs anymore, and common nouns are not capitalized anymore except in German. (Forget the controversy over *unalienable* vs. *inalienable*—why didn't John Adams knock out either *mutually* or *to each other* before signing?)

But the decapitation momentum is entering a Reign of Error. "I was taught," reports my scandalous correspondent, "that there exist entities like the Democratic Party, the Army, the U.S. Attorney, and the Secretary of Labor. I was even told that I should clarify things for my readers by referring to, say, the Progressive Era, or the South. Now—that's all gone. Is there really no more Army-Navy game? Must I write about the 'Republican party,' which sounds like Saturday night in Kennebunkport? Is there no more Hell?"

Suzanne, your little copy-editing friends are wrong. We are not going to turn into slaves of e.e. cummings. Some of us still capitalize Hell, to gladden the heart of the Devil, when referring to a specific place and its genial host; only when using those terms in a derivative sense (what the hell, I'm devil-may-care) do we accept the lowercase. A Russian dressing is not a russian dressing; thus does capitalization differentiate. We have plenty of Washington monuments (Admiral Farragut, Clark Clifford) but only one Washington Monument. The Department of State, it seems to me, should not be half-decapped by writing it "State department," and the title "secretary of state," as some copy editors prefer it, is unnecessarily demeaning to james a. baker iii.

And why are we all so willing to become hyphenated Americans? "I can no longer write about *grass roots lobbying,*" broods Mrs. G. "I must say *grass-roots lobbying,* to save readers from a misinterpretation of which I can not even conceive. If I write *foreign policy deliberations,* will a reader really think that I'm referring to policy debates held abroad? Does he or she need to be protected from error by the hyphenated *foreign-policy deliberations?*"

We create new compound adjectives every day: Our *Iraq-bombing* President is pitted against the *U.N.-defying* Saddam. (No, it doesn't need the second name. I call him Saddam; he calls me Bill.) But after a certain length of time and amount of usage, a compound adjective ought to be given a badge of usefulness by dropping its hyphen. As a flack long ago, I used to cook up *public-relations stunts;* now, as stern pundit, I deride *public relations stunts.* The phrase stands by itself in expressing a meaning. Nobody is led to think of relations stunts done in public; the hyphen is understood.

"When it comes to nouns," adds Miss Van Winkle, "the newfangled (new-fangled?) practice is even more mystifying. Why must it be *whistle-blower* instead of *whistleblower?* Any day now they will succeed in turning the sinister *coverup* into a prissy *cover-up.*"

Nice distinction there, in the left-handed *sinister* and the palms-up *prissy.* For years, I have been searching for a reason to eliminate, once and for all, the hyphen in the word meaning "obstruction of justice, hiding of corruption, deliberate obfuscation so as to draw a veil in front of journalists who are courageously enlarging the public's right to know." Now we have it: a *cover-up,* hyphenated, means "a beach towel, sari or caftan grabbed by a person sunbathing in the nude when surprised by a gang of ogling children"; a *coverup,* unhyphenated, is "an impeachable act, sometimes masterminded by an unindicted co-conspirator." (The *co-* is O.K. there, for legal precision.)

"I can't even say *any more* any more," complains Rip. "They now insist on *anymore* (quoth the editor, 'Anymore!'). Who decided these things? When was the battle lost?"

I'll decide. (You want to decide? Set some day for your decision. Someday is now in my column, so I'll decide.) In its negative form—that is, in Standard English—the adverb *anymore* should be written as one word, as in the Yogi Berra–ism "That place is so popular that nobody goes there *anymore.*" However, in dialect—not yet Standard English—the word is often used in a positive form, as when the apologist for the coverup says, "Everybody does it anymore." That dialect form should also be one word.

Who says? Whaddya, some kind of dictator? (That dialect locution, using *whaddya,* is not a shortening of "What, are you some kind of dictator?" but means "What are you, some kind of dictator?"; the placement of the comma alters the meaning.) I accept the modern copy editors' compression of *any more* into one word because that identifies it as an adverb. When the *more* is used as an adjective or pronoun, it should be written as two words: "Here at Procter & Gamble, there won't be any more whistleblowing" (the *more* is an adjective modifying the noun *whistleblowing,* one word), or "No, little boy, I won't let you see any more" (the *more* stands for "additional parts of my naked body").

To differentiate the adverb from that two-word pronoun and adjective usage, I recommend the one-word adverbial form: "You won't have me to kick around anymore" (*anymore* in this case is an adverb, modifying the verb phrase).

Same with *some day/someday,* as used both ways above. As a noun meaning "an unnamed but specific day," it should be two words, as in "We'll agree to some day next month for the arraignment"; as an adverb, it is one word, as in "Roll your fingers on this ink pad, Snow White, and someday your prints will come."

Form follows function, not fad; in copy editing, style must have its reasons.

As a manuscript editor at a university press, I can confirm that you have it right: We editors are a snooty lot of aspiring Thistlebottoms. Overzealous editing, alas, is as much a sin of the age as is bad writing. Part of what drives editors to adopt sometimes arbitrary conventions of capitalization, hyphenation, punctuation and spelling is inconsistent usage by authors. The author who objects to my lowercasing "cold war" on page 26 may himself choose the minuscule on page 27.

I try not to stand in the way of the author's voice, especially if it is barreling down the page like a Mack truck. If the author has a nice feel for language and a sense of direction, I'm content just to point out the few bumpy phrases to avoid. But if the author shows herself to be clumsy with words, then we may both be in trouble. When she drives us over a metaphor, I shut my eyes in fear; later, looking ahead on the map, I encourage her to stick to the land route even if it takes us six sentences out of our way and over the most boring stretch of prose in the county. In short, I become phobic, and that is a lousy state of mind for good editing.

Editors and authors need to learn to cooperate. Rarely do an author and editor share a similar taste in writing style; rarely are they matched in writing skill. Each must gauge the other's strengths and weaknesses and play to the former. I know that this is possible: it amazes me when I think about it, but some of my best friends are authors.

> Richard Miller
> New Haven, Connecticut

I do not know Ms. Garment personally and so cannot comment on her behavior, but I am forced to wonder if she is truly scandalous or merely scandalized by the work of her copy editor.

> Mark Braun, M.D.
> Cranston, Rhode Island

I have no problem with republican party, chief justice, language maven. If you prefer The Congress rather than congress, then that is up to you (frankly, I prefer congress to The Congress any time). I think lower case letters are a capital idea. My personal preference is to use upper case for the names of people, streets and cities—I have no time to waste upper casing the initial letters of political parties, or the Rag Bag of Concepts in Your List of required Upper Casing.

> Jan R. Harrington
> New York, New York

I read with great interest and eager anticipation "Let's Kill All the Copy Editors." Not only did the title alone indicate to me that, as usual, we were seeing eye to eye on things, but I hoped you might cite as Specific Example No. 1 my favorite peeve in all the world—the deliberate lower-casing, and deliberate downgrading, of the most powerful office in the world, namely the presidency (o.k. there, perhaps) and the man who holds it, namely the president (abhorrent there) of the United States.

With a few notable exceptions such as The Times *and* Time *magazine, the fashionable trend ever since Nixon has been to deliberately diminish the office as much as possible, as I am sure you are aware. A recent example in* People *magazine, I believe it was, almost prompted me to write you—some hero of the moment had found that his fame took him to Washington where he rubbed elbows with "the Supreme Court, the Congress and the president." Later I was pushed over the edge by a picture of Jerry Ford, I believe it was, with Elvis Presley—"the president and the King compare notes."*

At which point, Constant Weader fwowed up.

The average citizen does not notice subtlety or realize, as you and I do, the deliberate, derogatory nature of it. But somebody ought to yell. It's vicious and it's intended to do exactly what it is doing, demean the office and the man who holds it. And whatever one thinks of the man, the office is the office, and it should not be treated like that.

Allen Drury
Tiburon, California

Are you absolutely certain the Continental Congress's Committee on Style would have forced Thomas J. to write "mutually pledge to each other our Lives . . ." etc.?

I like to think that H. L. Mencken had it right with his "Declaration of Independence in American," which graced one of the preliminary pages of American Language, *3d edition:*

> *When things get so balled up that the people of a country have got to cut loose from some other country and go it on their own hook, without asking no permission from nobody, excepting maybe God Almighty, then they ought to let everybody know why they done it, so that everybody can see they are on the level, and not trying to put nothing over on nobody.*

Lawrence D. Skutch
Westport, Connecticut

Linguistically Correct

What does "PC" stand for? If your impulse is to blurt out "personal computer," you have gone software in the head. If those letters evoke memories of the Peace Corps, you are antediluvian (from "before the Flood," which makes you at least as old as Noah). A percentage of postcards from hypochondriacs will insist that the initials stand for the Latin direction *post cibum*, "after meals," the only digestively conducive time to pop certain pills.

Those of us with slanguistic *Fingerspitzengefühl*, however, know that the initials stand for the most controversial phrase on college campuses today: *politically correct*.

In "Thatch," a comic strip by Jeff Shesol of Brown University, a heroic character slips on a cape and supermanly tights with "PC" emblazoned on his chest. It's not a nerd, it's not a plane, it's . . . Politically Correct Person!

Ralph Waldo Emerson held in 1841 that "Whoso would be a man must be a nonconformist." That use of *man* today, in the sense of "one who possesses what were considered 'manly' virtues, like intellectual independence and moral courage," is rightly taken to be sexist; whoso would be a conformist must be *politically correct*.

"There is a new McCarthyism that has spread over American college campuses," writes Max Lerner, an old-line liberal. "We call it 'political correctness.'" The new *Random House Webster's College Dictionary* (the use of Webster in the name of a dictionary is a form of marketing correctness) defines the term as "marked by or adhering to a typically progressive orthodoxy on issues involving especially race, gender, sexual affinity or ecology."

I would edit that definition to denote *politically correct* as "an adverbially premodified adjectival lexical unit used to attack liberal conformity on sexual, racial, environmental and other voguish issues." (Maybe I should write a dictionary titled "*Not* Webster's.")

Item: "At the State University at Binghamton," Frank Herron wrote in the *Syracuse Herald-Journal* in March, "a meeting of a group formed to resist the pressure to conform to 'politically correct' speech was crashed by about 150 students, some carrying sticks."

Distantly related item: "A professor at the University of California at Santa Barbara noted that *pet* had become a derogatory term," wrote Stephanie Schorow of the Associated Press, "at the insistence of animal rights activists. The politically correct term was now *companion animal*." When the professor facetiously wondered if some magazine centerfold models, now called Penthouse Pets, would soon be called Penthouse *Companion Animals,* fifteen women promptly filed sexual harassment charges.

Linguistically sensitive *Newsweek* warns students: "Watch what you say. There's a politically correct way to talk about race, sex and ideas." *The New Republic* rejects that discipline, seeing "the imposition of political correctness" as meaning "our universities, which should strive for an identity in contradistinction to the world at large, have become distillations of our bitterest social divisions."

The first citation I can find for the incendiary phrase dates from a December 1975 statement by Karen DeCrow, then president of the National Organization for Women. She claimed that a dissident faction felt that feminism was only for "white, middle-class, straight women" and insisted NOW was moving in the "intellectually and *politically correct* direction." The phrase began as an assertion by liberal (progressive, concerned) activists and then was turned into an attack phrase by conservative (right-wing, heartless) passivists.

The first word in the phrase is a "premodifier"—an adverb that modifies and then fuses with an adjective to form a compound modifying a noun. (I learned this at a thinly veiled, hastily called news conference.) As Quirk, Greenbaum, Leech, and Svartvik note in their *Grammar of Contemporary English,* such adverb premodifiers often express viewpoints: *politically expedient, artistically justifiable, economically feasible, theoretically sound, ethically wrong,* and as girls from Brooklyn said of boys from Bronx Science, *geographically undesirable.* Of all these married modifiers, *politically correct* has become the most tightly wedded.

The origin is in *correct thinking.* "Where Do Correct Ideas Come From?" was the title of a 1963 thought by Chairman Mao Zedong, one of those later collected in a little red book that sold in numbers that still make publishers sigh. The Chairman thought on: "Do they drop from the skies? No. Are they innate in the mind? No. They come from social practice, and from it alone."

The Maoist phrase was also translated as *correct thinking,* as shown in this 1977 use by Kenneth Turan of *The Washington Post* on the glories of Dr. Brown's Cel-Ray tonic: "This beverage not only quenches your thirst . . . but serves as a talisman and a cultural rite as well, a sign of goodness and correct thinking that even Chairman Mao would have appreciated."

To dedicated Communists, *correct thinking* was "the disciplined inculcation of a party line expressed in all forms of social and political intercourse." When it was adopted self-mockingly by conservatives in the United States, it meant usually "one of us." The columnist George F. Will described Irena Kirkland in 1985 as "a life-affirming person and one of Washington's dozen or so Correct Thinkers."

To both left and right, then, *correct* came to mean "reflecting the opinions of the group"; in the late 80's, when the right went after the conformity of the left on college campuses, the affirmation of *politically correct* became an epithet.

Briefly now to the issue of vocabulary vigilantes who try to enforce "correct" language. Examples of tabooboos can be found in the list compiled by fellows at the University of Missouri Multicultural Management Program: *feminine* "can be objectionable to some women"; *codger* or *geezer,* "an objectionable reference to a senior citizen"; *Jew,* "some people find use of *Jew* alone offensive and prefer *Jewish person*"; and *swarthy,* "avoid all unnecessary references to skin color, such as yellow."

A Syracuse law student, Dennis F. Chiappetta Jr., notes in a recent letter about all such lingo-policing: "From what I can see, the end they seek is the removal of all language that brings to anyone's mind a negative or in any form degrading image. Is this possible? Can any language be written so 'correctly' as to invoke only pleasant or neutral feelings?"

My correspondent, a profound rather than correct thinker, follows up: "With the removal of terms of derision, will the prejudices also disappear—or will these new terms adopt connotations that users of the old terms may have seen in those terms?"

The opinions of Lex Irregs are solicited; we'll limit the debate here to specific choices of words rather than diatribes about "correct" subjects and attitudes.

Some words of derision hurt; they should be identified as slurs in at least one sense and avoided. Others—from *pert* and *petite* to *soulful* and *wannabe*—are getting a bad rap from the hypersensitive. The communication question to be asked is not "Could this possibly offend?" but "Does this get the intended point across?"

It seems to me that political correctness has been around for quite a while. Indeed, consider the word orthodox *itself, which, according to the* Compact OED *(p. 2012), means "right in opinion. 1. holding right or correct opinions, i.e. such as are currently accepted as correct, or are in accordance with some recognized standard."*

> Richard P. Kubelka
> San Jose, California

Listing to Portmanteau

A portmanteau word is a blend of two words to produce a third. This is just a guesstimate, but I'd say hundreds of words—from *brunch* to *glitterati*—have been coined under the label of the old French suitcase, or *portmanteau,* that folded in the middle.

Now we have the portmanteau name. In olden times, a woman getting married—who did not like the idea of dropping her surname and taking her husband's—would keep her surname in hyphenated form: Charlayne Hunter-Gault of PBS, for example, was born Charlayne Hunter and married a man named Gault. Along came *Ms,* and you no longer knew whether the woman is using her married name or not. But those were baby steps toward what is now the complete merger.

"Valerie Jane Silverman, a daughter of Mr. and Mrs. Bennet H. Silverman of Hastings-on-Hudson, N.Y.," read a society-page item last month in *The New York Times,* "was married yesterday to Michael Thomas Flaherty . . . on the campus of Harvard University.

"The couple changed their surname yesterday to Flaherman. Mrs. Flaherman, 26 years old, and her husband, 27, are 1987 graduates of Harvard." The item goes on to say, "Mr. Flaherman will receive a master's degree in city planning from the Massachusetts Institute of Technology next month."

The portmanteau choice was plain: It would either be *Silverty* or *Flaherman,* and they went for the man's name first.

Will this become a trend? It's good to see that the Flahermans have made the ultimate commitment; they are obviously not even considering the nomenclature difficulties in event of a divorce.

Try it yourself, dear reader, if you are or have been married: See what your spouse-merged name would be, and whose name would come first. Now, if the couple break up, and each partner marries again to a mate who has had a similar experience. . . .

I read with interest your column on the couple who had combined their last names upon marriage, and thought you might be interested in how my wife and I approached the issue. Her name is Patricia Lund, mine Charles Yingling. As we both have professional careers, we each wished to keep our own names. However, we had to decide what to call the children, and rather than hyphenate, decided on a solution similar to the Flahermans'. Our son and daughter (now 11 and 9) are, so far as I know, the world's only two Lundlings. They are each very proud of having a name of their own, part from their Mom and part from Dad. The order was easily determined; Yinglund just didn't have the panache of Lundling. (I suspect the Flahermen [doesn't that sound better than Flahermans?] may have used a similar criterion, rather than one based on gender—Silverty just doesn't have that ring, either).

Our approach, of course, neatly sidesteps the divorce issue; were we to split, our children would still be ours, with names to match, and we would go on as always with our own names. I guess it could become an issue in the next generation, when one or another part of the portmanteau would have to be dropped to create a new one, assuming our children continued the pattern. It could prove quite challenging to future generations of genealogists.

Charles D. Yingling
San Francisco, California

Lying Low

Tar-Baby did me in; I should have listened to Brer Fox.

Beginning a pusillanimous apology in a political harangue, I wrote, "Another reason I laid low was. . . ."

"You have committed the most common grammatical error in the English language," retorted Marian Mumford Brown of Orleans, Massachusetts, "using *laid* as the past tense of the verb *lie.* The proper conjugation of *lie,* meaning 'recline,' is *lie, lay, lain.*"

Elizabeth Baird Saenger of Mamaroneck, New York, picks it up from there: "You meant and should have said, 'Another reason I lay low. . . .' *Lay* is the simple past tense of *lie,* an intransitive verb (I *lie* low today, I *lay* low yesterday, I have *lain* low for weeks now)."

Lie, I am instructed, when it is a verb meaning "to recline," is intransitive; that is, when you lie in the weeds, you are not committing any action against the weeds. My recent prediction on television that Mikhail S. Gorbachev will "*lay* there in the weeds, and he'll try to make a comeback," was a repetition of my error—he'll *lie* there in the weeds.

An entirely different verb is *lay,* meaning "to put, place," and it is transitive, as when you lay your hands on a villain, or lay odds on the unlikelihood that a language maven has a blind spot.

Now here's the point of confusion: As we have seen, when you change the present tense of *lie* to the past tense, you get *lay* ("I lay low yesterday"). But that same word *lay* is the present tense of the verb meaning "to put"; as Ms Saenger (I use no period) writes: "I *lay* down the newspaper now in order to write. I *laid* it down yesterday. I have *laid* it in the same place for weeks."

When I asked my grammatical aide, Jeffrey McQuain, how to get out of this without looking like a sap, he suggested, "If you were a hen, you could lay low in the nest, meaning lay the eggs low." I am not a hen. "Or you could say you were misled by Uncle Remus."

That's it: "Tar-Baby stay still, en Brer Fox, he lay low." The author, Joel Chandler Harris, misled generations of Americans with his dialect idiom; if the present tense for Tar-Baby was given as *stay,* then the present tense for Brer Fox should have been *lie.* Only if Tar-Baby *stayed* still—past tense—could Brer Fox *lay* low.

However, let's face it, "Brer Fox lay low" is the memorable phrase, and it is grammatically impeccable. The word I used, *laid,* can best be used in the past tense of *lay,* as in "I have just laid my cards on the table." And that's no lie.

Webster III (but so do other dictionaries) reproduces the common two-word verb "lay low." This is another transitive form of lay *(meaning that it takes a direct object—from "transitive," signifying "to carry," in this case onward to a direct object) that means "to strike, bring down, etc." An example, in the passive voice: The balloon was* laid low *by a fire in its gas bag. Or: The enemy* laid low *the balloon.*

It seems possible to me that in writing your sentence, "Another reason I laid low . . ." was that you might well have been inadvertently "reflexing" from "lay low" (tr.) by way of what linguists call making a "false analogy."

Albert L. Weeks
Sarasota, Florida

Mailbag

"Dear Postal Customer:" begins this communication from the United States Postal Service, formerly the U.S. Mail, forwarded to me by Phyllis Agard of Amherst, Massachusetts. "Recently you received a brochure from the U.S. Postal Service concerning the coming of automated sortation and the need for proper address hygiene."

We need not look askance, as Ms Agard does, at *automated sortation.* I would call it *automatic,* or *mechanical,* because it does not employ the principle of feedback (self-control by machine, as in a thermostat) that is the essence of *automation,* and *sorting* is preferred on historical principles. But these are matters of judgment and taste, and an outfit that eschews the plain word *mail* for the pompous phrase *postal service* is at least consistent in choosing the costly-sounding *automated sortation.*

But "proper address *hygiene*"? That word, derived from the Greek to mean "the science of maintaining health," is sickened by such usage. We can debate the difference between *healthy,* "being in good health," and *healthful,* "contributing to good health," but the stretching of *hygiene*—with its habits of brushing your teeth, taking a shower now and then, wiping the mouth of your pop bottle on your sleeve before handing it to your neighbor—into the realm of addressing envelopes is beyond the linguistic pale.

In choosing this term, our postal servants are not suggesting we refrain from licking stamps that others have previously licked—an unhygienic act— but are urging us to use ZIP codes to assist its machines and to abbreviate each state's name in a manner that is not confusing to them. (MA, written as USPS suggests, without a period, stands for Massachusetts, not for Maine or Mother.) "By using this address information correctly," the Postal Service writes, "it will enable new automation equipment to sort your mail to it's proper destination."

Unclean! Unclean! The introductory phrase containing a gerund, *by using this address information correctly,* cries out for attachment of the action to a person; following it with *it* leaves it hopelessly dangling. And there is no need to spend millions for computer software to catch the simplest grammatical errors; a large dog can be trained to sink its teeth into the hand of anybody inputting an apostrophe in the possessive *its.*

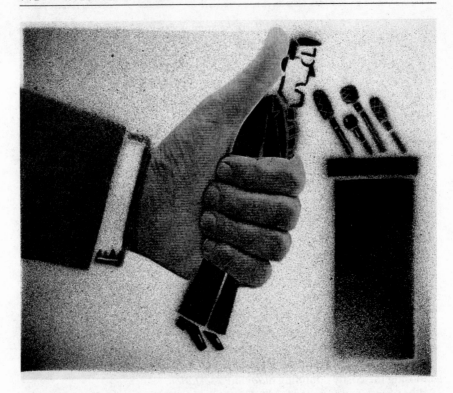

Manhandling the Handlers

Who's the most universal villain in politics? Not the *grafter* or *tinhorn;* not the *henchman* or *hack* or *hatchet man* or the *hanger-on;* not even the *gut fighter* or *black advance* or *dirty trickster.* The most despised, scorned and spat-upon person in politics today is the *handler.*

"Have you reconsidered the wisdom," Brit Hume of ABC asked President Bush, "of placing nominees at the disposal of White House *handlers?*"

Mr. Bush replied that it was demeaning "to suggest that *handlers* are telling everybody what to say or not to say." He preferred to call them "people trying to help." He continued: "Somehow I don't like the word *handlers.* Like the prizefighter—O.K., go in there and slug him again."

The President was partly right on his etymology. A *handler,* in boxing, is the chief second or the assistant second permitted in a boxer's corner between rounds, a trainer or manager known for telling his woozy fighter, "He never laid a glove on you," pushing in the mouthpiece and urging his man back into the ring, taking the little stool with him as the bell sounds for the next round. The word was first cited in this sense in a 1950 book by Jack Dempsey: "His handlers threw in the towel," which means that they "asked the referee to stop the fight."

Among the great boxing handlers were Jack (Chappie) Blackburn, who was in Joe Louis's corner; Angelo Dundee, who was the trainer of Muhammad Ali and Sugar Ray Leonard; and Cus D'Amato, who was more of a manager than trainer, but who handled Floyd Patterson and Mike Tyson.

But any socialite who has attended the Westminster dog show can tell you that the boxing term was derived from the showing of the points of a dog at a trial. A good handler settles the dog down emotionally, primps it physically and sensitizes it mentally before putting the show animal through its paces before the judges in public.

Same with candidates and their modern handlers. They prefer to be called *media consultants* or *policy advisers;* candidates tend to call them *aides, staffers* or *briefers.* Members of the media like to call them *handlers* because it derogates the candidate being advised, briefed or handled by putting him or her in the place of a dog, or at least in the role of a manipulated prizefighter.

In politics, the term is always used in a pejorative sense; nobody ever says, "I'm so-and-so's handler," any more than he or she says, "I'm the puppeteer and spin doctor." The sleazy characters doing the same thing on the opponent's staff, of course, are the despised *handlers.*

What about the people who help prepare journalists for appearances on television? They're *colleagues.*

Euphemism Watch

In the early 1970's, the dirty-tricksters who used to sabotage an opponent's rallies were called *the black advance;* because this technique was soon discredited, and because the phrase caused confusion among regular advance agents who were nonwhite, the umbrella term for those seeking to embarrass the other side, legitimately or not, was blanded out to *opposition research.*

Handlers are also trying to shake that pejorative term, taken from boxing, because it suggests that the candidate is a palooka taking orders from the trainer or second in his corner; they prefer *consultants* (preferred modifier: *campaign*) or *advisers* (preferred modifier: *key;* this term has replaced *intimate,* which may have a sexual connotation).

Adpeople (you can't say *admen* anymore) are faced with the negative connotation of *negative advertising;* the phrase, meaning "ads that attack the character or record of the opponent," is a downer. As image merchants themselves, the negative-ad writers and producers have come up with their euphemism: *comparative advertising.*

"It's fair game to be *comparative,*" says Sig Rogich, the Ambassador to Iceland who was summoned back to help the Bush campaign. The word brings up an image of fairness, as in comparing the speed of wash-day miracles, although that sort of commercial advertising occasionally descends to "Our car has great brakes; get into Brand X's, and you're dead."

"The biggest danger is not doing it right," Doug Watts, a former Reagan ad director, said to Richard L. Berke of *The New York Times*. The executive then used the most vivid figure of speech in the campaign's advertising lexicon to date: "You only get so many shots with the cream pie."

McQueen's English

President Bush, asked if his showdown with what he had called "powerful political forces" supporting a loan guarantee to Israel would cause damage, replied, "I don't think there's any damage." He added, "Lawsie, we'll be debating something else tomorrow."

Lawsie? Mr. Bush sometimes says "Lordy" as a euphemism of "My God," but this was the first time he has used this old Americanism in a news conference.

Harriet Beecher Stowe, in *Uncle Tom's Cabin* in 1851, had a slave say, "Law, Missis, you must whip me." Joel Chandler Harris in 1881 had a line in his Uncle Remus stories: "Lawdy mussy, Brer Rabbit! Whar my vittles?" At about that time, a diminutive of *Lawd* was used by Mark Twain in a letter: "A kind-hearted, well-meaning corpse was the Boston young man, but *lawsy* bless me, horribly dull company." He then put the term in the mouth of Jim in *Huckleberry Finn:* "But lawsy, how you did fool 'em, Huck!"

Perhaps the President has recently screened *Gone With the Wind* in the White House theater. Most Americans readily recall the actress Butterfly Mc-Queen, playing the character named Prissy, using this mildest profanity to introduce, in a voice high-pitched with panic, one of the most famous lines in movie history: "*Lawsie,* Miss Scarlett, I don't know nothin' 'bout birthin' no babies."

Medlex

Doctors often use language to establish what social scientists like to call power relationships. A University of Michigan sociologist, Renee Anspach, discovered that physicians present their own observations as factual—using verbs of objectivity like *note* and *observe*—while casting a hint of doubt on the symptoms reported by patients, who *admit, claim, state* or *deny* various pains.

It's easy to knock doctors for that professional uppityness, and for limiting the meanings of plain words; for example, to an anatomist, an *arm* starts at the shoulder and ends at the elbow, and a *leg* goes from the knee to the foot. But John H. Dirckx, M.D., in an essay on etymology in the front of Merriam-Webster's excellent medical desk dictionary, shows how doctors have used "lively and even poetic compounds" to identify old ailments: These include *frozen shoulder, bamboo spine, knock-knee, strawberry mark* and *the bends.* Instead of *patellar reflex,* or immortalization as *Gowers's reflex,* the discoverer of that test insisted on the plain-worded *knee jerk.*

Me: "Don't Finish My—." You: "Sentence."

When Charlotte Beers unexpectedly quit as chief executive of a large advertising agency in Chicago, she pointed to three younger executives and told a reporter: "These guys needed headroom. They began to finish all my sentences."

The meaning of *began to finish all my sentences* was "moved in on me, crowded me, assumed part of my authority." It is a metaphor for challenge or derogation, and is not meant to be taken literally.

On the same day Ms Beers finished her own sentence, Kirk Johnson of *The New York Times* wrote this lead from Hartford about a couple of state auditors: "It was perhaps inevitable, after twenty-five years in side-by-side offices poring over the same documents, that Leo V. Donohue and Henry J. Becker Jr. should start completing each other's sentences." He reported this exchange:

Mr. Becker: I guess we knew each other—.

Mr. Donohue: Since about nineteen—.

In unison: Fifty-five.

In this usage, the meaning of sentence-finishing is different: To complete each other's sentences is a sign of intimacy, of two heads that break as one.

The lexicographic question arises: When someone completes your sentence for you, are you being insulted or complimented? Is your interlocutor signaling that he is measuring your office for his favorite new carpeting—or that he is closely, even enthusiastically, attuned to your thinking and is merely demonstrating the depth of his understanding?

I chewed this over with Allan Metcalf at MacMurray College in Illinois; he's director of the American Dialect, uh. . . .

"Society. I find myself thinking of literary examples: Shakespeare's Queen Elizabeth who bitterly interrupts Richard III."

I looked that up.

King Richard: Now, by my George, my garter, and my crown—.

Queen Elizabeth: Profaned, dishonour'd, and the third usurp'd.

Richard: I swear—.

Elizabeth: By nothing; for this is no oath.

That is the sense used in Chicago ad agencies: She's interrupting him to put him down or crowd him out. The purpose is not to finish the sentence as the other person intends, but to finish it as the interrupter wishes.

I asked Professor Metcalf for a good source on this, and he directed me to Deborah Tannen, a linguistics professor at Georgetown University: "She's a real linguist, not an epigone."

Professor Tannen, currently in residence at the Institute for Advanced Study in Princeton, New Jersey, where very few epigones hang out, is author of the best-selling *You Just Don't Understand: Women and Men in Conversation.* (It has a real call-me-Ishmael opening line: "Many years ago I was married to a man who shouted at me. . . .")

"The two forms of completing another's sentence are *interruption* and *overlap*," she explained. "Either you may interrupt the other person, as in taking advantage of a pause, or you may chime in, in chorus with the other speaker."

Professor Tannen calls this type of conversation "high-involvement style," which includes standing close, talking loudly and leaping from topic to topic. Cultures that feature this style include Eastern Europeans, Mediterraneans, Africans and Arabs; women, Professor Tannen reports, finish others' sentences more often than men do.

"High-involvement style sends what I call a metamessage of rapport," she says. "The message is the words themselves; the metamessage is what is conveyed, such as showing that you understand the other person or showing the closeness of your relationship."

But what if you don't like having other people finish your sentences for you, even if they are trying only to show intimacy?

"Whether or not it's meant to be offensive doesn't matter. What matters is how the listener perceives the speaker's intention. The positive metamessage is 'I understand you so well.' The negative metamessage, if people don't like having their sentences completed for them, is 'You're putting words into my mouth.' "

She thinks it is more often intended to be positive than negative; I think it is more often received negatively. My conclusion is based on subjective data, sometimes called my own experience.

When I go on a television program to pontificate about the meaning of the current campaign, I sometimes start to say something and then stop for an instant to ask myself—is that what I really mean? I would not want to sell viewers an epigone in a poke. The host or hostess, aware that every millisecond sells for millions—and certain that at the slightest pause millions of viewers jab madly at their hand-held tuners—fills the horrible moment of contemplation with what may or may not be the intended end of my sentence.

And if there is one thing we low-involvement stylists hate, it is for people to, uh. . . .

Your column reminded me of Gilbert & Sullivan's The Gondoliers, *in which two brother* gondolieri, *who hold the republican belief that all men are equal, are informed that one of them is the only son of the late King of Barataria. They are summoned to the kingdom to reign jointly until the true King's identity can be ascertained.*

Their duet, which follows, is traditionally sung so that each brother finishes the other's sentences:

Marco:	*Replying, we—*	
Guiseppe:		*sing*
	As one indi—	
Marco:		*vidual,*
	As I find I'm a—	
Guiseppe:		*king,*
	To my kingdom I—	
Marco:		*bid you all.*
	I'm aware you ob—	
Guiseppe:		*ject*

	To pavilions and—
Marco:	*palaces,*
	But you'll find I re—
Guiseppe:	*spect*
	Your Republican—
Marco:	*fallacies.*

Once arrived in Barataria, the brothers elevate servants to the level of aristo-crats in furtherance of their philosophy. Neither brother, of course, turns out to be the real King, and their notion of equality is debunked by the end of the opera, as all conclude that "When everyone is somebodee, Then no one's anybody!"

> Paul H. Falon
> Washington, D. C

On sentence-finishing: Anacoluthon *is the rhetorical term dealing with the in-terruption of grammatical order in a sentence—including, at times, the unfin-ished sentence. (See J. A.* Cuddon, A Dictionary of Literary Terms, *and* Bernard Dupriez, A Dictionary of Literary Devices— *as well as, more exhaus-tively, H. Lausberg,* Handbuch der literarischen Rhetorik.*)*

Stichomythia *is a dialogue of alternating single lines, frequent in classical drama, Shakespeare, Molière, et al. (Again: Cuddon.)*

> Richard J. Schoeck
> Lawrence, Kansas

Meta-phor

"Lately I've heard several references to this *meta-* stuff," writes Gary Mul-doon of Rochester. *"Meta-process, meta-logue. Metamucil?"* He concludes with the Will Rogers line "I never meta-man I didn't like."

Meta- is the prefix of change, rooted in the Greek for "after, changing, with something else." Its most popular sense is "beyond," as in *metaphysics,* the study of the fundamental nature of reality and being, named for Aristotle's treatise that appears after "Physics" in his collected works. This is similar to "over, across," as in *metaphor,* from the Greek for "to carry across"—taking one figure of speech and applying it to another situation, as in "drowning in a sea of metaphors."

Another sense is "changing," as in the *metamorphosis* of a caterpillar into a butterfly. Then there's "later than, in succession to" (and while I'm there, an *epigone,* pronounced "EP-uh-gohn," is an imitator piggybacking on the work of a creative artist or scholar). Don't forget *meta-*'s meaning of "comprehending"—as a *meta-language* is a lingo used to describe languages.

That brings us to Deborah Tannen's *metamessage:* "a message beyond the message," one that conveys more than the obvious meaning of the words.

The Mocking "Do"

"I know you don't often 'do' punctuation," writes Rebecca Warburton of Victoria, British Columbia, "just as many domestics don't 'do' windows, but I notice you place periods and commas before a terminating quotation mark, regardless of whether the period or comma is actually part of the quote. Prevailing practice now seems to place all punctuation marks outside the quotes; is this a sign of ignorance?"

I have already taken a stand on the placement of periods. "Here's where I stand on period placement." In that case, the period goes inside, at the end of the quoted sentence. "Now let's try it with the period outside". That makes the period look like a lonely end; it's a no-go. What about this, though: "Here's my stand," say I, "on what punc-junkies call 'period placement'." Right in the middle, between the marks that end the inside quote and the whole quotation, because it completes the quoted sentence and, besides, it looks right.

Now here comes a more controversial one. Should it be: I won't go along with "the easy way". (Internal quote, period outside the marks.) Or: I won't go along with "the easy way." (Internal quote, period inside.)

I say: Take the "hard way". Instead of following an inflexible rule, use logic: A period is supposed to be placed at the end of a complete sentence. Put the period outside the quoted part if the quoted part is not a complete sentence.

Most copy editors in the United States do not agree with this commonsense, graceful British usage. As Allan M. Siegal, the *New York Times* panjandrum on style, has said, "American usage, sanctioned by all the major stylebooks, places all commas and periods inside the quotes and all colons and semicolons outside; in American usage, only the placement of exclamation points and question marks is governed by logic."

Enough of that controversy; the reason Ms Warburton's letter appears today is that she uses *do* in a mood we shall call the teasing transitive.

"Let's *do* lunch." (The stylebook and I agree the period goes inside.) That is the pseudo-invitation extended by Hollywood producers while kissing the air a foot from the cheeks of wrinkling starlets they want never to see again.

This usage of the transitive verb *do* usually has no article (*a, an, the*) between the verb and its direct object (*lunch*). Students *do homework* (including *doing fractions* to prepare for the arithmetic test), and recruits *do push-ups;* Rich Little *does impressions;* Liza Minnelli will *do requests* if she can get a cosmetician to *do makeup* and a hairdresser to *do hair.* Mike Tyson will *do time.*

Do followed by a direct object may have begun with *do penance,* a Roman Catholic locution, around the thirteenth century, soon followed by *do business.* Within seven brief centuries, the International House of Pancakes was advertising, "Nobody does breakfast like IHOP does breakfast." (That's where the stylebook puts the period; makes no sense.)

A curious turn came in this usage, perhaps after domestic servants began informing employers, "No heavy lifting and I don't *do* windows." (Logic suggests the period belongs outside the quotes because the quoted sentence is only a part of the complete sentence.) British students have long used "I *do* history" to identify their major.

When the movie industry made it a vogue usage, the ridicule began: "Book people, incidentally, still *have* lunch," wrote Jay Jacobs in the January 1985 *Gourmet* magazine, "in an era when other professionals speak of *doing* lunch." A year later, in *Science 86* magazine, Lynn Crawford wrote: "Cattleman Scott Kleberg is a modern-day cowboy. He has a secretary and an office. He *takes* meetings and *does* lunch." (Me: "Objection!" Stylebook: "Overruled.")

These citations were provided by Fred Mish at Merriam-Webster, who notes: "In print, at least, *do lunch* seems to be used somewhat mockingly to characterize the language of others, so it may be that unself-conscious use is waning. We have more from 1985–87 than from 1988–91." ("Obj——")

The lexicographer sees it as a special application of the "consume, use" sense of *do* that emerged in the 50's and early 60's, and here is the key: Like so many locutions today, this is rooted in narcotics lingo. "Do you *do* drugs?" began as a guilty insider's question, and led down to the Gehenna of doing lunches.

The teasing transitive may be on the wane in Hollywood, but it is doing fine in Washington, the other show-biz capital. Those who use it, however, are outnumbered by those who notice it and quote it to show its user's show-biz background. "We don't *do* touchy-feelie retreats and psychological profiles of each other," an unidentified White House official scornfully told Ann Devroy of *The Washington Post* recently. "We *do* politics. And right now," he added, in the light of recession statistics, "we *do* panic."

(Look, fellas, I did it three times running your way, with the period after a quoted phrase inside the quotation marks, and it puts form before function. H. W. Fowler ducked this controversy in his long entry on "stops," but as for me, not. Henceforth, whenever the quote is part of a longer sentence, I will put the period outside the quotation mark. Changing it to conform to the stylebooks will take a positive action on your part. After a while, you'll start missing some, and then word will get around it's O.K.—just as Ms Warburton has noted, and you'll never hold back the logical flood. Let me show you how natural it looks, and just this once let it go through.)

"And right now," he added, "we *do* panic".

Modifier's Lib

Retronyms have a relative: Andrew Tauber of Lexington, Massachusetts, calls them "liberated modifiers." These are the new nouns formed from adjectives modifying old nouns.

For example, at Nick & Tony's in Easthampton, Long Island, the people at my table ordered "one regular coffee, two decaf cappuccino, three decafs." I lay awake thinking about that.

"Liberation of a modifier occurs," writes Mr. Tauber, "when a new product achieves standing of its own but fails to dislodge its hegemonic predecessor." *Decaffeinated coffee* did not replace regular coffee; it became a competitor known by its clipped liberated modifier, *decaf.*

Has this phenomenon happened before? Here's the first that comes to mind: *op-ed,* a modified modifier for a noun, *page.* And in "zoological garden," the adjective *zoological* became the noun *zoo.* Sol Steinmetz at Random House has another: *prefab,* for "prefabricated house" (leading to the retronym, *stick-built* house). The dragnet is out for others; send them in with an order of *fries.*

Enclosed are more examples for your "adjectives-to-nouns" file.

oral exams	*orals*
final (contests)	*finals*
regional (games)	*regionals*
black-and-white prints	*black-and-whites*
glossy photos	*glossies (e.g., 8 × 10's)*
daily newspapers	*dailies*
automatic rifle	*automatic*
4-door cars	*4-doors*
convertible (-top) car	*convertible*
bell-bottom trousers	*bell-bottoms*

ad lib remark	*ad lib*
partial dentures	*partials (e.g., uppers)*
bifocal lenses	*bifocals*

Stanley A. Spatz, M.D.
Hallandale, Florida

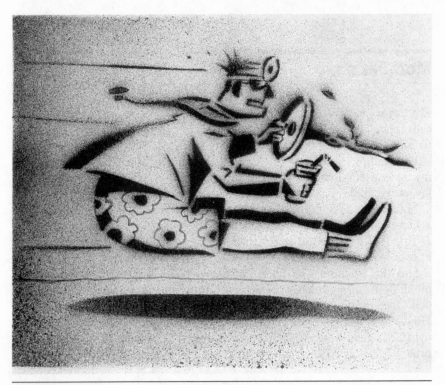

Modifier's Lib

I was watching a *soap* on *cable* and wishing it were a *western* when the thought struck: Will I need a *physical* to get *major medical*?

Native speakers have no difficulty with the foregoing. Liberated modifiers have swept through the language, and these adjectives and attributive nouns now stand alone; the words they once modified have been cast into what the Old Bolsheviks used to call "the dustbin of history."

Unsqueezed, the lead sentence of this item would read, "I was watching a *soap opera* on *cable television* and wishing it were a *western movie* when the thought struck: Will I need a *physical examination* to get *major medical insurance*?" But nobody talks that way; it takes forever.

Can you imagine the tediousness of talking about a movie actress putting on contact *lenses* and getting a facial *treatment* before making a cameo *appearance*? (Discard the italicized words; this is a fast-forward world.)

Those of us who write *op-eds* for *dailies* and long for *malteds* can hardly complain about our kids grabbing their *portables* and hopping in the *compact* or the *convertible* to go to the *condo* on the beach, where they promise to study their *electives*. (That gets rid of *pages, newspapers, milks, radios, cars, automobiles, apartments* and *courses*.)

After my first observation of this downsizing of our vocabulary, Joan Murray of Rochester wrote, "My *temp* got a *perm* after she met the *sub* from the *tech* wearing his *cords* at the *pub*." Lynn G. Zeitlin of Narberth, Pennsylvania, reported she saw "an obstetrician in *shorts* driving a *stick* and drinking a *soda*, having just delivered a *preemie*."

This condensation follow-up was triggered by a *spot* from my Dodge dealer shouting over the radio that "you can get *air* at no extra charge." To those of us who still think in terms of *aerial antennas*, rather than mere *aerials* sunk into the glass windows, that seemed aberrant, but sure enough, it was countered by Jeep-Eagle dealers: Their *wagons* (conductor, did I miss the *station*?) also come "with *air* at no extra charge." Apparently *conditioning* just died; the air is now free. (A *conditioner*, meanwhile, is what follows a shampoo. The *hair* is free.)

This is the living language at work, and I'm not complaining; just trying to keep up. Those of you who insist that *dirigible* means "capable of being steered" are undirigible; the *dirigible balloon* has cast off its *balloon* and is now simply a *dirigible*, an airship with cameras that peer down on a *dome*, formerly a *domed stadium*, in which the offensive team is the *offense* and does the *run-and-shoot* (no offense intended).

Time to store this; I'll kill anybody who spills *decaf* on my *floppy*.

You remarked on auto dealers' use of "with air." I am also struck by their use of "with automatic." For one thing, it seems to me that no other group regularly uses automatic *as a noun. In football, a change of play barked out by the quarterback at the line of scrimmage used to be called an* automatic, *but you cannot hear that anymore because it is now an* audible. *The main reason, though, is this irony: intended to save the word* transmission, *the use of "with automatic" actually wastes the word* with.

Alberto Guzman
Bronx, New York

Multi Multi-

Multi- is a prefix that has a special place in my heart. As a cub reporter for a column in the old New York *Herald Tribune,* I interviewed the Italian movie actress Gina Lollobrigida, then making her first splash in *Pane, Amore e Fantasia.* I was then short of all three—bread, love and dreams—and treasured a picture she gave me, which shows her posing in revealing rags and pouting defiantly, and is inscribed "*Molto simpàtico.*"

Multi-, like the Italian *molto,* is from the Latin *multus,* "much"; Miss Lollobrigida was offering fans much affection. Stuck on the beginning of nouns, like *multivitamin,* it means "more than one, several"; on the beginning of adjectives, like *multifaceted, multi-* means "many."

MULTILATERALS RAISE HOPES is the headline on a recent issue of the weekly *Near East Report.* The liberated modifier, *multilateral,* used to be part of *multilateral discussions;* now on its own, it was used here to refer to the talks between Israel and many Arab states about regional issues.

This figurative use of the adjective was started by Sir William Jones, the English jurist, in a 1784 letter to the conservative statesman Edmund Burke:

"The charter of justice . . . makes me *multilateral;* it gives me an equity side, a law side, an ecclesiastical side, a crown side, an admiralty side."

For some reason, Sir William was dissatisfied with *many-sided.* That early anti-manyism has caught on; although *few* is doing fine, *many* is in disuse. If Han Suyin were writing her Hong Kong novel today, she would change the title (and the subsequent movie and song) to *Love is a* Multi-*Splendored Thing.*

We used to be in a *bipolar world,* using a term Zbigniew Brzezinski popularized in the early 1970's after the term *polarization* was used to cluck-cluck at political partisanship. In fact, the world has always been *bipolar,* rotating as it does on an axis with north and south poles, but that geopolitical sense has led to the replacement of *bi-* (two) with *multi-* (count 'em).

With the dissolution of one of the two superpowers, the world has become *multipolar,* a word associated in the mid-70's with Henry Kissinger, whose clients today are *multinational.* (Such companies require *multilingual* interpreters, and hire *multimarket* executives who engage in *multitasking* rather than do anything themselves.)

The *multi-* boom was given a push by Clark Kerr of the University of California in 1963, when the *multidisciplinary* president scorned *uni-* for a *multiversity.* He probably lifted this from the philosopher William James, who wanted a word for the absence of order in the universe and came up with *multiverse.*

Now our *multitalented* singers recording on *multitrack* tapes are covered in *multicolumn* news stories by *multimedia* correspondents using *multisyllabic* words (such as *multisyllabic*). Detergents that used to claim to be *all-purpose* are now trendily *multipurpose.*

The controversy raging on college campuses is about *multiculturalism.* The adjective form of that noun was coined in a July 3, 1941, book review in my old *Herald Tribune,* a decade before *Pane, Amore e Fantasia* was filmed. Some book—I don't know the title—was described as "a fervent sermon against nationalism, national prejudice and behavior in favor of a 'multicultural' way of life."

When proponents of cultural diversity gained attention derogating Western civilization in the 1980's, *multicultural* became a college curriculum code word for "not dominated by whites." The historian Arthur Schlesinger Jr., writing in *The Wall Street Journal* last year, blasted the views of "high-minded but wrong-headed *multicultural* zealots."

The former gossip columnist for the *Washington Times,* Charlotte Hays, reported in a recent *New Republic* article about her old employers that Arnaud de Borchgrave, now editor-at-large, was up-to-date on usage even in thank-you notes: "For something Arnaud particularly liked, there was a gallant *'multithanks.'* "

In the general gentrification of inclusive words with *multi-,* beery Joe Six-pack, who used to watch the games on TV in his undershirt, went out and bought a *multiband* radio to listen to commentary about his team's *multiflex* defense, replaced his old cable system with a *multidirectional* antenna, snacks on *multigrain* cereals and has changed his name to Joseph *Multipack.*

As the use of the prefix multiplies, its meaning is demeaned. Like a hot stock with low earnings, it soon loses its multiple. (*Poly*-want a cracker?)

"Harry is a multimillionaire," goes an instructive joke. "No, Harry is a millionaire, maybe, but not a *multimillionaire.*" First man insists, "*Multimillionaire.*" Skeptic asks, "How much does he actually have in the bank?" First man says, "Ten thousand dollars." Skeptic admits, "You're right—he's a *multimillionaire.*"

You credit Zbig Brzezinski with having "popularized" the term "bipolar" in the 1970s.

I would suspect that the term was used even earlier, but it was discussed at some length by W.T.R. Fox in his book The Superpowers *published in 1944 and by Morton Kaplan in his book* System and Process *published in 1957. Since we discussed the concept endlessly when I was a graduate student at Yale in 1947–51, whatever Zbig did with the concept in the early 1970s can hardly be called popularizing!*

> *Roger Hilsman*
> *Institute of War and Peace*
> *Studies*
> *Columbia University*
> *New York, New York*

Name That Disease

An Irish physician named Robert James Graves, poking around various glands in 1835, may not have been the first to describe the exophthalmic goiter, but he gave the most accurate early account of what we now call a hyperthyroid condition; as a result, the imbalance of secretion from which President Bush has been suffering, and which led to his heart fibrillation, is called *Graves' disease.*

I think the grammatical diagnosis is wrong. A second opinion: Punctuate it *Graves's disease,* with an apostrophe followed by an *s.* No matter what it says in *Merriam-Webster's Medical Desk Dictionary* or in *Webster's New World Dictionary,* the possessive of a proper name ending in *s* should be formed by adding an apostrophe and another *s.* Maintain standards, as they say at the

Court of St. James's. (Lowercase the *d* in *disease;* the lexicographers have that right.)

You have to watch these doctors when it comes to naming diseases, treatments and medications; it's sometimes hard to tell what motivates them. As a longtime political hawk, I liked the choice of the name for an anticoagulant discovered when University of Wisconsin researchers were examining spoiled sweet clover as the cause of hemorrhage in cattle; the doctors called it *warfarin,* and it was officially so named by Du Pont. But it had nothing to do with a war on bleeding; the bellicose *warfarin* is based on the acronym WARF, from Wisconsin Alumni Research Foundation.

Nurse, hand me those *Kelly clamps;* I want to filter a few of the names of individuals perpetuated in the names of disorders, instruments and procedures through my *Gooch crucible.* There are *Cushing's syndrome* to describe an overactive adrenal gland, *Wernicke's encephalopathy* (what too much booze and too little food can do to the brain), *Hodgkin's disease, Hansen's disease, Parkinson's disease* (I'm not describing the ailments anymore because they're depressing) and scores of others.

At Johns Hopkins Hospital alone, they've coined *Osler's nodes, Whipple's disease, the Blalock-Taussig operation, the Welch bacillus* and *the Gott shunt.*

It's nice that all these dedicated types get their recognition, but a countertrend has developed: naming newfound diseases by place. Lawrence K. Altman, M.D., the medical correspondent and columnist of *The New York Times,* reported a few years ago that "Many otherwise obscure places have been immortalized by the custom of identifying microbes and diseases by the geographic area in which they were first recognized." The practice is especially virulent in virus-naming. He listed *Coxsackie viruses,* causing the worst kinds of sniffles in a town in upstate New York, and *Junin virus,* causing a hemorrhagic fever linked to a town near Buenos Aires.

At a time when General Motors advertisements were calling for customers to get "Pontiac fever," a bacterial infection spread in Pontiac, Michigan, and immediately became known as *Pontiac fever.* In summertime, we face the bloodsucking, parasitic menace of ticks (spelled with a *k,* contrary to what you read in "tic-and-flea" catalogues; a *tic* is a twitch); these carry *Lyme disease,* originally *Lyme arthritis,* named after the town in Connecticut where the flu-like symptoms were first observed. Lyme is nowhere near the Rocky Mountains, where spotted fever, also carried by ticks with a *k,* was supposedly confined; in fact, more cases of Rocky Mountain spotted fever occur in the East. (Citizens of Lyme in New Hampshire—where Lyme disease is rare—are still wondering why they were hit by the name.)

Initialese and acronyms also pulse through medicine's nomenclature. William Kouwenhoven at Johns Hopkins popularized the term *CPR,* for "cardiopulmonary resuscitation" (which led to the jocular definition of *barium:* "what you do when CPR fails").

AIDS is the best-known acronym, for "acquired immune deficiency syndrome"; earlier, it was called *GRID,* for "gay-related immunodeficiency disease," but it was soon realized that the virus was not limited to homosexuals or to men. *AIDS* as a name is also on the way out, being replaced by *H.I.V.* infection—not an acronym, with the letters pronounced individually—which stands for "human immunodeficiency virus," cause of the disease.

Further research into the Self-Labeling Disease Syndrome is sorely needed; some medical journal should solicit learned articles on how germs and viruses are labeled, and whether the direction is toward human names, place names, or abbreviations. Groucho Marx tried to make light of the macabre subject with a famous crack: "I've got Bright's disease, but not to worry—he's got mine."

Graves' disease was also described at the same time and independently by Professor Basedow in Vienna. Actually, most of the enlightened world in Europe, the Soviet Union and many countries in Asia, including Israel, call it Basedow's and not Graves' disease. It was also described by Parry 100 years before Graves, except that Parry did not publish it to carry his name, but only described it in the college annals. Otherwise the disease would have been called Parry's disease.

Graves' disease, as originally described, is hyperthyroidism and bulging of the eyes (proptosis).

HIV infection does not mean AIDS disease. There are people who have HIV infection; they carry the virus but do not have AIDS disease.

Heskel M. Haddad, M.D.
New York, New York

We are slowly starting to drop the possessive "s" in eponymous diseases (e.g., Down syndrome), so the day may arrive when you can abandon your campaign.

Sally R. Sacks
Senior Editor, Consultant:
The Journal of Medical
Consultation
Greenwich, Connecticut

I, too, have "named a disease"—though I doubt that many will have heard of it.
A number of years ago, while working in a children's hospital, a clinical staff member (physician) undertook to shape me into a clinician. One of the early lessons to be learned by Ph.D. scholars is that everything in medicine must have

a name—no matter how ambiguous or uninformative. Once on a clinical visit, I was asked to complete the diagnosis and enter it on a "consult" form. The young patient—it seemed to me—was nothing less than a rotten kid, spoiled, and disrespectful of authority, and not requiring any "medical attention." When forced to find an appropriate syndrome, I gave birth to the "Wilder-Chaye Syndrome." Both sides of the hyphen would trigger associations to persons familiar with neurology, but my intention was to capture the Yiddish meaning of a "wild animal." Two marvelous results followed: (1) the chief of neurology proudly announced weeks later that a computer listing indicated our hospital correctly diagnosed "this rare and most interesting syndrome"; (2) months later, at a professional meeting, a colleague from Chicago paraded about with a hand-made button with "P.O.W." in large type, and in fine print: the Society for Parents Of Wilder-Chaye.

The syndrome remains a serious concern for the quality of many lives, and someday, I am sure, I expect to be fully recognized for my contribution.

David I. Mostofsky, Ph.D.
Professor of Psychology
Boston University
Boston, Massachusetts

I refer to your statement that "AIDS as a name is also on the way out, being replaced by H.I.V. infection. . . ."

The two terms are not interchangeable! People who are H.I.V. positive are often far healthier than even our present President; not to mention our First Lady or even our First Dog! People with AIDS are always desperately ill.

H.I.V. is the cause and AIDS is the sad result. No one can be infected by AIDS, because the term refers only to the syndrome that is the culmination of the destruction of the immune system. Just so, no one dies of the H.I.V. infection, per se. They die of the diseases that take advantage of the fact that the immune system is destroyed.

John T Pieret
Centereach, New York

Fibrillate

While in the medical mode, we should take on *fibrillation,* the ailment that caused such consternation before it was learned that the heartbeat irregularity was caused by a hyperthyroid condition.

Fibrillate, coined in 1839, comes from the Latin *fibra,* "fiber," the same term now in vogue among dietitians and moralists. When the muscle fibers of the heart contract irregularly and rapidly, a disparity develops between the pulse and heartbeat rates; this is *fibrillation,* not to be used synonymously (as I did, and got a lot of free medical advice—lend me your shunt, Gott) with *flutter,* which in its medical sense usually means a rhythmic spasmodic contraction. In lay terms, a *fibrillation* goes "thump, thumpathump, thump," while a *flutter* can go "thumpathumpathumpathump." (Some doctors will feel impelled to denounce this definition; the urge to correct is called *Safire's syndrome.*)

By definition, atrial fibrillation is irregularly irregular. Atrial flutter is regular. Thus, the "thumpas" are not correct.

          Robert L. Erickson, M.D.
          Montclair, New Jersey

The New Omics

Realpolitik—pronounced "ray-ahl-pol-ih-TEEK," so as not to confuse it with "real politics"—was coined by Ludwig von Rochau in 1853 to describe Bismarck's hardheaded policies in the years leading to German unification. In American political usage, it means "international diplomacy based on strength rather than appeals to morality and world opinion" and—with Tony Lake, a key Clinton adviser, apparently on the way in—it may be on the way out (the policy, not the word).

A coinage based on *realpolitik* is likely to be used in think tanks and academic seminars if the Clinton-Gore ticket wins. That term is *realeconomik,* set forth by Susan and Martin Tolchin in a book that a new Administration's insiders would be reading, *Selling Our Security: The Erosion of America's Assets* (Knopf). The approach rejects the "Nations have no friends, only interests" summation of Viscount Palmerston's remark; instead, they write, "The U.S. needs a new vision, a *'realeconomik'* that addresses its need to regain economic ground; otherwise, its role as a world leader will surely diminish over time."

The popularity of another coinage will be inevitable in a Clinton Administration: *Clintonomics.* For the *omics* suffix to work, the President's name must end in an *n.* This all began when some of us in 1969 began pushing *Nixonomics.* (Although *Johnsonomics* would have been an effective neologism, it was not used, suggesting that *Nixonomics* was the form's first presidential use.) Although there was some straining for *Fordonomics* and *Carternomics,* neither got off the ground because of the lack of the concluding *n.*

With Reagan came, of course, *Reaganomics.* In 1992, Democrats wishing to criticize George Bush's economic policies did not want to evoke the popular former President's name, and there was no *Bushonomics;* they had to settle for *trickle-down economics,* a coinage probably used first by Democrats in the 1932 campaign against Herbert Hoover. (The theory under attack was also expressed then as "feeding the sparrows by feeding the horses.")

Now we are likely to have *Clintonomics,* described breathlessly at first as a new approach, and hailed when the economy turns upward; then, when the business cycle pushes the pendulum back the other way, Republicans will seize *Clintonomics* as their term of attack. Some linguistic trends are predictable.

Nifty Gifties

During the holidays I am overwhelmed with the urge to plug language books. These are not the *bodice-rippers* (novels with heaving covers) piled up in *dumps* (cardboard display cases) at the front of bookstores; these are the bodice-soothing books about words tucked away in the back that the language lover's lovers, searching for the appropriate gift, must ask for.

Here's what to ask for this season, preferably in an assertive tone, followed by "Whattya mean, 'out of stock'—you call yourself a bookstore? Order it now!"

If ever you have made a mountain out of a molehill, you have staggered into the world of the cliché. The lexicographer Eric Partridge used to collect them, but now Christine Ammer has added a dimension of etymology in *Have a Nice Day—No Problem!* (NAL/Dutton, $25). The English equivalent of the French *faire d'une mouche un éléphant*—make an elephant out of a fly—is first cited by the *Oxford English Dictionary* in John Foxe's *Book of Martyrs* in 1570 (though James Rogers's 1985 *Dictionary of Clichés* provides an earlier use in Nicholas Udall's 1548 *Paraphrase of Erasmus*).

One of the nicest dedications of any language book was in the classic *Modern English Usage*. Henry W. Fowler dedicated it to his brother, Francis George Fowler, "who shared with me the planning of this book, but did not live to share the writing." The giant of usage went on: "I think of it as it should have been, with its prolixities docked, its dullnesses enlivened, its fads eliminated, its truths multiplied. He had a nimbler wit, a better sense of proportion, and a more open mind, than his twelve-year-older partner." This poignant note in a prescriptive work is recalled in an appreciation of the Fowlers by Robert Burchfield, who was chief editor of the Oxford English dictionaries, in one of the essays in his deliciously literate *Unlocking the English Language* (Farrar, Straus & Giroux).

The most modern use of the word *bra*, as motor enthusiasts know, is the nose mask or protective device or radar-eluder on the front of cars. This new sense of the clip of an old word—*brassiere*, from the French for "bodice" (see *bodice-ripper*, above), derived from *bras*, "arm"—was spotted and cited by John and Adele Algeo, America's foremost neologists, in *American Speech* magazine. They have drawn together all the installments of the new-word section of that publication in *Fifty Years Among the New Words*, with a useful unified index (Cambridge University Press, $60).

After an article in this space cruelly titled "Let's Kill All the Copy Editors," I received heart-rending letters from many of these underpaid indispensables. In expiation, I recommend *The Fine Art of Copyediting* by Elsie Myers Stainton (Columbia University Press, $25). To those authors who complain of "nit-picking," she suggests copyeditors (one word, she says) reply mildly, "But who wants nits?"

A participle, as thinking people know, is often a verb acting as an adjective to modify a noun, like "thinking" in this sentence. Now: Don't condemn *dangling participles* when you mean *misplaced participles*. In *The World Almanac Guide to Good Word Usage* (in which the insertion of *Word* in the phrase "good usage" is confusing), the authors, Martin Manser and Jeffrey McQuain, cite examples of misplacement like "Startled by the noise, the book she was reading fell to the floor"; the participle modifies the wrong word. To

truly dangle, however, they point out that the participle must have no attachment to the subject at all, as in "Lying in the sun, the heat felt good." ("To
truly dangle . . . they" misplaces rather than dangles.) Skimming through this
good usage handbook from Avon, I was glad to see it costs only $8.95 in
paper. ("Skimming . . . I" is properly moored.)

How many software programmers does it take to screw in a lightbulb? Answer: None; that's a hardware problem. This joke, which draws blanks from
normal people but causes much thigh-slapping among hackers and wonks, is
cited in a serious study of the language of the new technocracy titled *Tech-
nobabble* by John A. Barry (M.I.T. Press, $22.50). The same publisher offers a
sprightly lexicon by Eric S. Raymond, *The New Hacker's Dictionary* ($10.95
in paper), which competes with the more sobersided *Random House Personal
Computer Dictionary* by Philip E. Margolis ($10 in paper). Acronyms are very
big in this field; according to hacker Raymond, a Wombat is a "Waste of
Money, Brains and Time."

If you can afford a great reference work that makes all American lexies
proud, get Volume II of Fred Cassidy's *Dictionary of American Regional English,* published this year [1991] (Belknap Press of Harvard University Press,
$59.95). *DARE* examines American dialect in all its richness and glory; what
do you say about an unmarried young person whose younger siblings are
married? That unfortunate is *dancin' in the hog trough.*

For the heavy linguistic hitters—scholars, Chomskyans and anti-
Chomskyans, the deep-structure crowd—the big book completed this year is
James D. McCawley's masterly, two-volume *The Syntactic Phenomena of English* (University of Chicago Press, $39.90 in paper). The man is living in syn-
tax; it's an honor to get a postcard from him blasting my pretensions to
grammatical authority.

Guides to writing—some in print, others in software—continue to prolifer-
ate; the best-written this year is *The New Oxford Guide to Writing* by Thomas
S. Kane (Oxford University Press, $19.95). But nothing helps the aspiring
writer more than reading fine writers in action; here are four new books on
disparate subjects—beauty, free speech, nature, human nature—whose prose
is worthy of emulation: *Nature Perfected: Gardens Through History* by
William Howard Adams (Abbeville Press, $49.95); *Make No Law* by Anthony
Lewis (Random House, $25); *The Moon by Whale Light* by Diane Ackerman
(Random House, $20), and *Jefferson Davis,* a towering biography by William
C. Davis (HarperCollins, $35).

Finally, with holidays in prospect, we can use words assembled in the form
of a salute with glass in hand. Not the hedonistic "Let us have wine and
women, mirth and laughter,/Sermons and soda water the day after" proposed
by the boozing, womanizing Lord Byron, and anthologized by Paul Dickson
in *Toasts: Over 1,500 of the Best* (Crown, $18). Better, on your way to the
bookstore, to remember the lifted glass of Thomas Tusser: "At Christmas,
play and make good cheer/For Christmas comes but once a year."

Night Arrant

Frederick B. Lacey, the retired federal judge hired by the Justice Department in the Iraqgate affair—who raised some eyebrows by styling himself "the independent counsel"—blasted the media and the Congress on his way out the door. His characterization of corruption charges, delivered in a voice quavering with outrage: "*arrant nonsense.*"

Arrant has long been fused to *nonsense* in impenetrable cliché. These are wedded words, like *unmitigated gall, limpid pools* and *fugitive financier.* In *The Washington Post* report of Mr. Lacey's spoken statement, the words were written "errant nonsense."

A senior Justice Department official, whose background insights made in calls to me were denounced by the Attorney General's defender as "gross distortions" (another example of wedded words), called to ask: Which is correct, *arrant* or *errant,* when modifying *nonsense?*

Arrant means "flagrant; notorious; thoroughgoing," as in Hamlet's "We are arrant knaves all, believe none of us" (Shakespeare's Second Quarto drops the *all*). It started out as a variation of *errant,* which means "wandering, roving, especially in search of adventure." Both words are rooted in the Latin *errare* and the Old French *errer,* "to wander," which has a second sense: "to err, or wander off the proper path."

The senses split, and different meanings became assigned to each. A *knight errant* was a fellow in clanking armor wandering about looking for damsels in distress (more wedded words); *arrant nonsense* was outright gibberish mouthed by sensation-seeking solons and scriveners.

Noblesse Largesse

"The *largesse,*" Keith Bradsher of *The New York Times* wrote about payments to farmers, "will be far less than the impression created by the President." On the same day in the same paper, Michael Wines wrote, "While President Bush politicked across the Great Plains early last week, handing farmers some $1.8 billion in Federal *largess. . . .*"

Such action was cause for fury from skinflints, a source of pleasure to local recipients, the usual thing to cynical old pols and a source of puzzlement to me: Was this lavish expenditure of public funds to be spelled *largesse* or *largess?*

The Old French word is, of course, *largesse,* meaning "bounty, abundance," rooted in the Latin *largiri*, "give freely." (The earliest uses of the English adjective *large* meant "liberal in giving," leading to "ample" and finally to "big.") The word in French means "generosity, liberality," but in English has gained a patronizing overtone, like a gift bestowed by a superior to an inferior with a pat on the head.

The problem is the spelling. The earliest editions of Shakespeare spelled Richard II's complaint about his budget deficit both ways, with the First Folio using the longer spelling: "Our Coffers, with too great a Court/And liberall *Largesse*, are growne somewhat light." In 1832, the poet Tennyson clipped it: "I have not lack'd thy mild reproof/Nor golden *largess* of thy praise." But in 1888, the poet James Russell Lowell used the ending with the *e:* "I could not bear to see those eyes/On all with wasteful *largesse* shine."

The *Oxford English Dictionary* identifies "at his *largesse*," with a final *e,* as an obsolete English term for "at liberty," and it is probably the source of "at large" for wanted criminals.

The dictionaries don't take a strong position. The superb third edition of the *American Heritage Dictionary* (which elevates its editor, Anne H. Soukhanov, to *Lexicographer Regina*) lists "largess, also largesse"; *Merriam-Webster's Ninth* says "largess or largesse," as does *Webster's New World;* no clear-cut preference should be inferred from the listing of the shorter before the longer form.

That leaves the spelling up to you and me. And if I know you, with everything else you have on your mind, you'll leave it up to me.

If we want to stress the Frenchiness of the word, we leave the *e,* just as we do in the French phrase *noblesse oblige,* "the obligation of nobility" or "the kindness and gentility expected of the cultural elite, except when in campaign mode."

If we want to save space, as headline writers always do, then we clip the final *e.* But if we do that, why do we always spell *finesse* with a final *e?*

I say, ignore the newspaper stylebooks and go with *largesse.* It has more panache (not "panach") and seems to encourage the speaker to eschew the soft *g* and use the French *zh.* If we are using a word to attack the pose of royalty, let's use the French word spelled the French way. Vwala!

You incorrectly translate the French phrase noblesse oblige *as "the obligation of nobility."* Noblesse oblige *is actually a complete sentence, in which* noblesse *("nobility") is the subject and* oblige *("obliges") is a verb. "Nobility obliges" means, of course, "Nobility imposes obligations."*

Louis Jay Herman
New York, New York

No Picnic

What is the latest put-down of a person who is *not all there*—whose *elevator does not go all the way to the top,* whose *oars are not both in the water*?

Sally Quinn, whose latest novel is the entertaining *Happy Endings,* reports this sighting: *his belt does not go through all the loops.* A variant formulation, describing inadequacy in a situation rather than in an individual (and probably based on *an hour late and a dollar short*), is *one sandwich short of a picnic.*

These are transient phrases; the definition of dottiness that has shown generational staying power is *out to lunch.* It is, of course, taken from the sign on an establishment's door meaning "temporarily gone"; although the more officious signs state, "Open 9–12, 2–5," with the new sense of fogginess, those signs more often say cheerfully, "Be right back," or for the less industrious proprietors, "Gone fishin'."

But in its sense of "gone bonkers," *out to lunch* has achieved a place in the slang Hall of Fame. "Members of Congress who support these bills are *out to lunch,*" Tom Schatz of Citizens Against Government Waste charged last month; in 1984, candidate Walter Mondale told a Michigan labor group, "The Reagan Administration is *out to lunch.*" The earliest use so far sighted/cited is in *Science Digest* in August 1955: " '*Out to lunch*' refers to someone who, in other years, just wasn't 'there'—and he is told immediately to 'Get with it!' " This phrase, which may have originated in the scientific community, was adopted in its sense of "crazily distant; profoundly out of touch; once removed from reality" in Britain. "Dostoyevsky notwithstanding," wrote *The Times Literary Supplement* in 1983 about a crime novel, "it's not always a good idea to have a central character who's *out to lunch* most of the time."

This is by way of advertising for the coiner of the slang phrase now achieving the stature of a classic. If you have a pre-1955 written citation, send it to me. I'll be in.

Not!

"This usage occurs more often in spoken than in written communications," writes Franklin L. Noel, magistrate judge of Federal District Court in St. Paul. "Rather than using the ordinary syntax, the speaker will express a negative by making an affirmative statement, followed by a brief pause punctuated by the word *not.*"

As a good judge should, he includes a citation: On a recent *Today* show,

Jane Pauley, the former co-anchor, made an appearance to plug a new program that will not be called *Real Life with Jane Pauley,* the title of her most recent show.

"In describing the as-yet-untitled new show," writes the judge, "Ms. Pauley said that her daughter had suggested it be called 'Real Life with Jane Pauley . . . Not.' My law clerks often use this mode of expression, and I fear that my ignorance may be generational." (Judge Noel is forty years old.)

I have been keeping a *Not!* file ever since the pundit George F. Will, writing about pork-barrel legislation (now simply called *pork*) in the House Appropriations Committee, commented: "Bush will kill that program. Not." (George handled it in a declarative rather than exclamatory fashion, but he's a conservative.)

This reversing addendum, or pseudo-Gallic negative, is a syntactical device popularized by Mike Myers and Dana Carvey, the comedians who play the cable-TV talk-show characters Wayne Campbell and Garth Algar on *Saturday Night Live.* It has exploded into the language in connection with the promotion of the Paramount movie *Wayne's World* and is likely to be with us until it disappears into Hula-Hoop land.

A nonbook of the same title, published to ride the movie's popularity, offers a helpful glossary of exclamations used by the comedians usually referred to, like Olsen and Johnson of *Hellzapoppin,* as "the zany pair."

Not! is defined therein as "Used at the end of a statement of fact, expressing denial, negation or refusal." Parenthetically, the popularizers explain, "Similar to how a negative symbol at the beginning of a mathematical subset renders that subset negative regardless of any possible positive integer within said subset."

This glossary also defines "*He shoots! He scores!*" as "He is victorious. He is successful." That nonce acclamation is taken from a sportscaster's excited report of a successful shot in basketball, patterned after the baseball announcer Mel Allen's "How 'bout that!" after a home run, a generation or so ago. The glossary adds the regurgitory *hurl,* which was included here recently in a general roundup of barfmanship without reference to the source of its popularization.

Stories about the comedians invariably use their lingo. "We told friends they had impeccable taste—NOT!" writes Linda Shrieves of *The Orlando Sentinel.* "We told the boss that he was a stupendous manager and a real motivator—NOT!" She concludes (using the device about the zany pair, as TV critics do about the movie), "Wayne and Garth—experts in the field of logic. NOT!"

I write "popularize" rather than "coin" about *Not!* because NBC, faithful to etymological standards, rebroadcast a 1978 *Saturday Night Live* episode in which the comedian Steve Martin uttered the word in the belated-negation context used today. Playing Chaz the Spaz, Martin told Gilda Radner, playing Lisa Lupner, who had developed a dial-a-toaster, "That's a fabulous science fair project." He paused and sneered, "Not!"

Perhaps the usage is rooted in the French *ne . . . pas,* which forms a negative around a verb; *je sais,* "I know," becomes *je ne sais pas,* "I know not." The heavy emphasis on the *pas* could be the source of the American nonce term. Or not.

Relatedly, consider this headline over an Associated Press dispatch in *The New York Times,* sent in by William G. Clotworthy of Westport, Connecticut: "Blacks Are Urged Not to Buy Japanese Cars." He wonders if this should not be corrected to read "Blacks Are Urged to Not Buy Japanese Cars."

Not to buy or *to not buy?* Hardly a knotty problem. *To not buy* may be rhetorically preferable, as it is more urgent an urge than *not to buy,* but that usage is not the practice of the native speaker. You want pedantry? Here's pedantry: In most cases of an infinitive following a transitive verb in the passive voice, the negating word precedes rather than splits the infinitive. (I just made that up to assuage the dismay of purists.)

The reader expects this item to conclude with some outrageous statement followed by an arch use of *Not!* Refraining from its use is a double reversal.

Thank you for clearing up the mystery of the word Not! *appearing at the end of a statement. My husband and I couldn't figure out where our 8-year-old daughter picked this up. We're reassured to know that it's a generational phenomenon and will soon "disappear into Hula-Hoop land." Not! Well, maybe.*

> Wendy H. Hashmall
> New York, New York

It is my thought that the use of Not! *at the end of a sentence is the verbal equivalent of the international symbol for "no" that you see on so many signs. It seems to be an interesting example of the post-literate realm crossing over into the literate one.*

> Elizabeth B. Perry
> Philadelphia, Pennsylvania

The surprise factor may—or may not—support your theory of the basis in French ne . . . pas. *In Old French,* ne *was the only negative necessary (as in Latin* non). *The* pas *was a noun (related to English "pace") used, among several other nouns (*mie—*crumb,* point—*jot,* gote—*drop, etc.), to reinforce the unstressed* ne. *So the French "je ne sais pas" may be more analagous to "I don't know at all" than to "I know not."*

In modern spoken French, the stress is on the final syllable of any group of words. You are right to hear the emphasis on pas, *since the* ne *is never the final syllable of a group.*

> Barry Judd
> Somerset, New Jersey

Dear Bill:

Concerning the end-of-sentence use of "Not" to express denial, my educated guess is that the usage is much more likely to be rooted in Yiddish than in French. Here's why:

Yiddish is distinguished by its inversions of word order. A typical Yiddishism is the transposition of a predicate adjective or adverb to the end of a declarative sentence. For example: "Shakespeare this play is not." "Funny, he is not." "A plumber, maybe he is; but a doctor? Not." Notice how syntactically close the last example is to the Wayne and Garth collocation, "Madonna is my girlfriend—Not!"

I base my conjecture partly on the fact that the usage was introduced by Steve Martin and Gilda Radner, who knew French—Not! But Yiddish? Certainly Yes!

Hence I would refer to this usage as a possible "pseudo-Yiddish negative" but "a pseudo-Gallic negative"—Not!

> Sol [Steinmetz]
> Random House
> New York, New York

In my youth in southeastern Pennsylvania (1930s and 1940s), many of my contemporaries and particularly our elders spoke Pennsylvania Dutch, and consequently their spoken English was affected by that language structure.

The suffix "Not" was in common usage but never to reverse the meaning of a statement. "Not?" effectively replaced the prefix "Is it not true that . . . ," turning a statement into a question. It can be used with great emphasis, making the question a powerful challenge.

This Pennsylvania Dutch usage of "not" makes a lot more sense than the puzzling usage in your circles. Not?

> James N. Reed
> Brookline, Massachusetts

Your article on the post-ultimate "NOT" rolled around the crevices of my mind for a few days until I finally located its predecessor—a particularly fine poem by e. e. cummings (XIV in the collection 1 × 1) which begins

> *pity this busy monster, manunkind,*
>
> *not. Progress is a comfortable disease:*
> *your victim (death and life safely beyond)*
>
> *plays with the bigness of his littleness . . .*

This is not likely the source of the current linguistic fashion, but it is a good example of its effective use.

Jonnie Breyer Stahl
La Jolla, California

I recalled a relevant paragraph in a humorous story by Ellis Parker Butler titled "Pigs Is Pigs."

Suspending my regular explorations into the novels of P. G. Wodehouse, the plays of Maxwell Anderson and the McGuffey Readers, I reread "Pigs Is Pigs" and found the following passage: " 'Cert'nly, me dear frind F'annery. Delighted!' Not!"

The story was originally published in 1906 by McClure, Phillips & Co.

Martin F. Schwartz
New York, New York

When I was growing up in Montreal, at age 10 in the early 1950's, television broadcasting was not yet available in Canada. Public broadcasting of sporting events was limited to radio.

The only sports that I can recall being regularly broadcast were baseball, hockey and football. Although I am relating to Canada, I don't believe that professional basketball, even in the United States, had reached a level of being broadcast publicly at that time.

Because the hockey broadcasts were limited to radio, the announcers' inflections played a large role in the audience's following of the action. Particularly in hockey, a shot at the net very often took place at a high speed of movement of both the player and the hockey puck. Thus, if a goal was scored, it was very common for the announcer to exclaim excitedly, "He shoots! He scores!"

For another important source that the expression originated with hockey and not basketball, I remember that at that time one of the most popular books for boys in the juvenile section of our public library was a book exactly with that title, He Shoots! He Scores! Unfortunately I don't remember the name of the author and whether it was published only in Canada. The book consisted of a series of brief biographies of famous hockey players of that era (1940's and 1950's).

Barry Skolnik
Scarsdale, New York

During the thirties and forties, and perhaps into the fifties, Foster Hewitt, hockey's answer to Mel Allen, at least in Canada, was the announcer of the Saturday night broadcasts of the Toronto Maple Leaf games from Maple Leaf Gardens. It was known as "hockey night" to Canadians, as it was broadcast across the country on the CBC network.

"He shoots! He scores!" was said without any audible pause, particularly if the Leafs were doing the scoring. Hewitt broadcast, as he put it, from "up in the gondola."

Hockey, in turn, borrowed the term "hat trick," which had its genesis in cricket. It referred to a bowler's taking of three wickets from the opposing team with three straight balls. According to the OED *his club then presented him with a new hat.*

George R. Holloway
New York, New York

No Score

The National Hockey League has taken umbrage at my speculation that the vogue expression *He shoots! He scores!* might be rooted in basketball.

"The phrase was coined by the Canadian broadcaster Foster Hewitt," writes Stu Hackel, the N.H.L.'s broadcasting director, "who pioneered radio play-by-play of the sport beginning in 1923. *He shoots! He scores!* is always invoked with great enthusiasm (thus the exclamation points), since scoring in hockey is relatively infrequent in relation to attempts to score."

He continues with a full-court press: "Pity the poor basketball announcers, were it in fact their phrase, who would have to shout it over 100 times in a broadcast."

Not Me

In an article about personal bankruptcy, a *New York Times* business writer quoted F. Scott Fitzgerald as having remarked to Ernest Hemingway, "the rich are different than you and I."

"You have people to look this up," writes Miriam Hurewitz of Westport, Connecticut. "Did Fitzgerald really say it that way? Different than you and *I*? My students of copy editing at N.Y.U. would be interested in your reply."

My students of researching would pick up a copy of the *Harper Book of*

American Quotations, or the *Oxford Dictionary of Quotations* (Fitzgerald's version is not in Bartlett or Bergen Evans; that's strange), and find it excerpted from Fitzgerald's story "The Rich Boy," published posthumously in his 1960 collection, *Babylon Revisited:* "Let me tell you about the very rich. They are different from you and me." (*The Crack-Up* records Ernest Hemingway's snappy if shallow rejoinder—"Yes, they have more money"—but rarely do we read Fitzgerald's explanation of how the very rich are different: "They possess and enjoy early, and it does something to them, makes them soft where we are hard, and cynical where we are trustful, in a way that, unless you were born rich, it is very difficult to understand.")

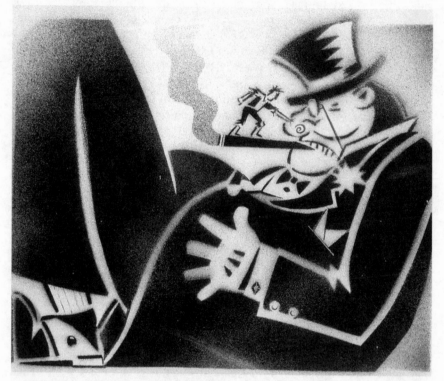

The point is that Fitzgerald wrote "from you and *me,*" which was misrecollected as "than you and I"; why the *I?* Let's not get drawn into the *different from/than/to* controversy (*from* is preferable but not solely correct), because the subject today is what follows *than.* Purists—people who defend the ramparts after their honorable position has been outflanked and overwhelmed—want to follow *than* with *I.* Never "than *me.*"

Nobody doubts that the objective *me* should follow a preposition; between you and me, not even the most outdated pedant can get away with *between you and I.* The question: Is *than* to be treated as a preposition or as a conjunction? If it's a preposition, like *in, on, by* or *to,* its function is to form a phrase that will serve as a modifier of a noun or verb; if it is a conjunction, like *and, but* or *because,* its purpose is to connect words or groups of words. Let's cut to the chase: If you treat *than* as a preposition, you'll say "than me"; if you treat it as a conjunction, you'll say "than I."

To test the waters of usage on this locution, I slipped a controversial usage into an otherwise mild-mannered political column placing myself on the side of what President Bush came to call a "hostile horde." I referred to a report by a *New York Times* colleague who, I asserted, "is far more evenhanded than me."

The first call was from the shoe-leather pundit Rowland Evans: "I was shocked, shocked to read your piece about the Middle East," he said, shocked. "Never have I disagreed with you so completely. To follow the comparative conjunction *than* with *me*? For shame."

This note from Bernard Kalb, now a fellow at the Freedom Forum Media Studies Center at Columbia University: "*Me?* I! Why? Gotcha, Bernie."

"Are you starting to objectify yourself?" asks A. Posner of East Lansing, Michigan. Melissa Weissberg, a writing tutor at Yale, wonders, "Was this solecism meant simply to demonstrate—graphically—the collapse of grammatical standards?" Rabbi Jonathan Gerard of Dover, New Hampshire, wishes me a happy new year with "Shouldn't it be 'far more evenhanded than I [am]'?" Robert Hay of Wilmette, Illinois, adds: "I have always considered the word *than* a conjunction, but you apparently have the backing of *Merriam-Webster's Ninth New Collegiate Dictionary* when you follow *than* with the objective case. Maybe you're wiser than me (than I am)."

I haven't had so much mail since I wondered where "the wind that shakes the barley" comes from. (That file is all in one closet; I'll get to it one of these days, when I need the closet for an overcoat.) The Gotcha! Gang was out in force; the tone of the "than me" correspondence is expressed by "You, of all people" and "I cannot tell you with what dismay . . ."

The only support for the *me* came in a clip sent in by Jeanne Schonberg of New York; she spotted this statement by Lady Antonia Fraser, the historian and wife of the playwright Harold Pinter, who was curious about being identified as a *writer* while Michael Holroyd, the biographer, was labeled an *author.* Said Lady Antonia: "I was baffled but intrigued. What does *writer* mean? Will Michael Holroyd get to be a writer in three years' time? He's three years younger than me."

I'm with you, Lady Antonia; you write better than him. (I mean, of course, "than he does," but I do not write *than he,* because I treat *than* as a preposition, taking *him, her, them* and *me* rather than *he, she, they* and *I.*) Lady Antonia and I are writers; we have an ear attuned to native speech; we can tell when the tide has turned, the conjunction has prepositionated and the writing must follow the speaking. If not us, whom? (Make that "If not us, who?" But not "If not we" anything.)

Why is "than me" better than "than I"? Not only does it sound less strained to native speakers, but also it saves the reader or hearer from having to figure out the unstated verb: "who is more evenhanded than I [am]." (The *I* is required only when it affects the meaning of the sentence: "She knows him better than I" means that she knows him better than I know him. "She knows him better than me" means that she knows him better than she knows me.)

Even Shakespeare came down on the side of using *than* as a preposition. In *Julius Caesar,* the conspirator Cassius describes the Roman leader to Casca as "A man no mightier than thyself, or me."

These days the objective case is beating out the nominative in other areas as well. Purists are the only ones who say, "It is I," although *I* is technically correct as the predicate nominative (a noun or pronoun that follows a linking verb like *is*). The stuffy-sounding "It is I" has been replaced by the breezier "It's me," and who is to resist breeziness? Not me.

Consider the most famous murder confession. In the early accounts, the fable went this way: "Who killed Cock Robin? 'I,' said the Sparrow, 'With my bow and arrow, I killed Cock Robin.' " In a modern courtroom, would the defendant Sparrow have said, "I"? Of course not; he would have said: "Me. I killed Cock Robin." Today's judges would not accept any confession made in the nominative case.

Let me tell you about the very grammatical. They are different from you and me. They get their habits ingrained early, and it does something to them, makes them rigid where we are flexible, and cynical of usage where we are trustful, in a way that, unless you were exposed at an early age to a severe English teacher, it is very difficult to understand.

Those who fail to learn from history are doomed to repeat it.

The specific epoch to which I am referring is the Norman Conquest—those roughly three centuries of French infiltration of our great and marvelous native tongue. Thus one cannot truly consider any grammatical aberration without first determining which set of rules, that is, French or English, applies.

I happen to agree with the premise that "than" is a conjunction and not a preposition. According to good Anglo-Saxon grammar, it should then be followed in all cases by a subjective rather than an objective personal pronoun, so that "than I" would be the only acceptable combination. Unfortunately, that rule was compromised in 1066, and English was never able to recover fully from the French influence, not the least of which was the notion of "strong" and "weak" personal pronouns, regardless of case.

Both regular subjective and objective pronouns are weak in French, viz. je/me, tu/te, il/se, etc., and so they have a tidy little list of strong ones to insert whenever strength is desired, to wit: moi, toi, lui/soi, etc. In English we are taught to say properly, "It is I," but in French we are taught to say "C'est moi!" Of course, we all say, "It's me," and no one but effete, arrogant recalcitrants and the very grammatical say, "It is I."

Now that the Channel is about to open, shouldn't we step forward and admit after, lo, these six hundred years that the influence of French persists to such an extent that we should admonish pedagogues everywhere English is taught to cease attempting to disabuse our collective residual linguistic consciousness of its borrowed but well-founded notion of the existence of strong and weak personal pronouns in English, not to mention to acknowledge the predisposition of many Anglophones to their use? Strong rules once broken can still stand, whereas weak rules over time are eroded and finally forgotten.

I have not yet accepted the fact that this is also why my nine-year-old son says, "Him and me are going to the movies." The supposition of course is that "he and I" are weak, but that "him and me" are strong, and if "him and me" are strong, then, they are certainly strong enough to go to the movies. Can you tell me then, is my son smarter than I, than me, or than all of us?

> *Peter Rutenberg*
> *Los Angeles, California*

Your column, nicely titled though it is ("Not Me"), seems to me to deal inadequately with the I/me problem. The tension between pedantry and common usage is too fundamental and pervasive to be resolved by asserting that, in the context of that particular misquotation from F. Scott Fitzgerald, "than" is not a conjunction but a preposition.

The reality is that when English is spoken naturally, a stressed first-person pronoun will be "me" or "us," not "I" or "we" (and similarly, her, him and them rather than their nominative counterparts). This is so whether or not the pronoun follows an adjective or a transitive verb. To be sure, one sometimes says, or hears some other over-educated person say, "It is I." But who (Henry Aldrich possibly excepted) has ever said, or heard, "Who, I?," or "That's I"?

Similarly, no one ever accused Louis XVI of saying, "L'etat, c'est je." French grammar sensibly gives official blessing to what is common but apparently unblessed usage in English, by recognizing, in addition to cases, two "forms" for its pronouns: the "conjunctive" (je; I), where the pronoun is unstressed; and the "disjunctive" (moi; me) where it's stressed.

I seem to recall that Winston Churchill, in a speech that got some attention in the American press, used the phrase "It is us," and stirred up something of a grammarian's hornet's nest. Somewhat later, Pogo uttered the famous sentence, "We have met the enemy and he is us." (I may not have either quote quite right in its entirety; but I'm sure about the final pronoun.) Churchill's technical solecism may have been overlooked on the ground that he was a grand enough figure to rise above principle, and Pogo's on the ground that he was only using quaint patois, but the fact is that in both cases the usage was both natural and correct; it was simply unblessed by the academicians' conventions.

If, like the French, we had an academy charged with making official pro-

nouncements about our language, it could announce a new pair of "forms" for pronouns and resolve the matter. We don't have that, however; we have only language mavens like yourself. Limited though your authority necessarily is, you can surely endorse, at least, a principle broader than that a conjunction may in some circumstances be a preposition.

David B. Isbell
Washington, D.C.

The objective case may be beating out the nominative, as you say, but has the nominative taken up another line of defense? How about those "native speakers" I keep hearing who do say "between you and I," "Bill and myself," "He gave it to Tom and I"?

As for Sparrow the killer in a modern courtroom, would he say "Me. I killed Cock Robin"? I doubt it. I think he'd say: "I did. I killed Cock Robin." (Objective overruled and confession accepted in the nominative case?)

Stay flexible, you suggest. Stay loose? Again, those native speakers. Which ones? Those who prefer "those kind"? It's "breezier" than those "kinds," and I hear it everywhere. Distinguish between "amount" and "number"? The latter is fading. I hear about the amount of people, the amount of books, chairs, and so on.

And then there are those incomplete introductories such as "As far as Bill and Tom [are concerned], I think, etc." They're common too.

All by native speakers and widespread. Acceptable?

Lie and lay. The persistence of lie *in the game of golf, as in "a bad lie," is reassuring. If we ever come to "a bad lay," the game's up.*

James J. Napier
Springfield, New Jersey

What you have to say on this subject has been much better and clearer expressed by Frederick T. Wood in his English Prepositional Idioms *(Macmillan, London/St. Martin's Press, New York, 1967, p. 74), namely:*

> *Frequently, a nominative, though demanded by strict grammatical rule, sounds awkward or unnatural, especially after verbs of incomplete prediction [he means, of course, predication] like* to be, to seem, to become, *and in such cases usage sanctions the accusative form: "He is several years older than me"* . . .

As a rule of the thumb, this seems to me to be a much simpler and much easier to remember guide than yours, which, after all, demands some thinking be-

*fore we decide which of the two we ought to use, "I" or "me." And who wants to
be stopping in the midst of writing to consult your essay on this subject?*

> Roman T. Gerlach
> Oakland, California

The very grammatical are different from us.
  Yes, they are more irritated.

> Jan R. Harrington
> New York, New York

Ode on a G-String

Chief Justice William H. Rehnquist announced the judgment of the Supreme
Court in the case of *Barnes* v. *Glen Theater*—in which Justices Scalia and
Souter concurred—and delivered an opinion in which Justices O'Connor and
Kennedy joined. (You can *concur in* a judgment without *joining* an opinion;
you cannot *concur in* an opinion without *joining* in a judgment.)

"We . . . now hold," goes the law of the land, "that the Indiana statutory requirement that the dancers in the establishments involved in this case must
wear pasties and a G-string does not violate the First Amendment."

Justice Souter, who seemed in recent hearings to have led such a sheltered
life, concurs: "Pasties and a G-string moderate the expression to some degree,
to be sure, but . . . the limitation is minor when measured against the dancer's
remaining capacity and opportunity to express the erotic message."

Right judgment, but for the wrong reason, Justice Scalia held. "The State is
regulating conduct, not expression," he wrote, and First Amendment scrutiny
is not involved. Nor is the law's moral purpose to protect only nonconsenting
parties from offense: "The purpose of Indiana's nudity law would be violated,
I think, if 60,000 fully consenting adults crowded into the Hoosierdome to
display their genitals to one another, even if there were not an offended innocent in the crowd."

That aroused Justice White, who, in a dissent joined by Justices Marshall,
Blackmun and Stevens, thundered: "No one can doubt, however, that those
same 60,000 Hoosiers would be perfectly free to drive to their respective
homes all across Indiana and, once there, to parade around, cavort and revel
in the nude for hours in front of relatives and friends. It is difficult to see why
the State's interest in morality is any less in that situation, especially if, as Justice Scalia seems to suggest, nudity is inherently evil."

Let me step in at this point, as one who infrequently cavorts nude in front of relatives and friends but who looks forward to his next thrilling visit to the Hoosierdome. Although the Court's opinion twice included Indiana's no-holds-barred definition of nudity (which can be delicately summarized in family newspapers as "it ain't the teat, it's the tumidity"), nowhere in this landmark decision can the concerned public find the meanings and origins of *pastie* and *G-string.* It is as if the justices hastily assumed we all knew what these terms signify, or were determined to participate in an etymological cover-up.

Pastie. In John Ayto's *Dictionary of Word Origins,* the root of *paste* is traced to the Greek verb *passein,* "to sprinkle"; the noun originally meant a barley porridge. Late Latin borrowed it as *pasta* and Old French as the basis of *pastry;* both words are with us today and excite no outrage except among dieters. Sometimes pasta sticks together, leading to *paste* in the sense of a whitish flour-and-water mixture with the character of glue, which led to the adjective *pasty-faced* and brings us to the noun *pasties.*

Pasties are coverings for the nipples of a stripteaser's (or erotic dancer's) breasts and are affixed by paste, glue, stickum or other mild adhesive. They usually glitter as if dusted by reflecting particles, recalling the earliest Greek meaning, "to sprinkle." The first *Oxford* citation is from *The Washington Post* in 1961: "Miss Mason was lying on the floor with nothing on except the scantiest of brassieres, known in the trade as '*pasties.*' " However, Fred Mish at Merriam-Webster has just come up with an earlier citation: Earl J. Abbot wrote in *True Police Cases* in 1954, " 'Pasties'—adhesive coverings for breast points—sell at $1.50 a pair and up." (Mr. Mish adds, "*Breast points?*")

Got that, brother Souter? Now, brother Rehnquist, to *G-string.* This is not derived from (as they say at the Court, "bottomed on") the first string on a double bass, the third on the viola or the fourth on the violin. That musical term was first used in print in 1831, without a hyphen, in a review of a performance by the violin virtuoso Niccolò Paganini, extolling the "surpassing beauty of . . . his performance on the single string (the fourth, or G string)."

The origin is in the American frontier. The *geestring* was a loincloth, or the string or thong supporting a piece of cloth enclosing the genitals, worn by American Indians and some settlers unconcerned with conventions of dress. In *Western Wilds, and the Men Who Redeem Them,* John H. Beadle wrote in 1877: "Around each boy's waist is the tight 'geestring,' from which a single strip of cloth runs between the limbs from front to back." Fourteen years later, *Harper's New Monthly Magazine* may have confused the loincloth's name with the musical term: "Some of the boys wore only 'G-strings' (as, for some reason, the breech-clout is commonly called on the prairie)." The slanguist Robert Hendrickson speculates that the *G* stands for "groin," then considered a word not to be used in polite society.

A stripteaser (or *ecdysiast,* from the Greek for "one who molts," coined by H. L. Mencken at the urgent request of Georgia Sothern, the stripper, but rejected by Gypsy Rose Lee, author of *The G-String Murders*) is apt to call her costume a *gadget*. The G-string is unrelated to the space agency's *G-suit*, with its *G* standing for "gravity," and to *G spot*, an erogenous area on the upper vaginal wall first described by Ernst Gräfenberg, a gynecologist, and named after him.

My favorite verb in the Hoosierdome Follies, as Court-watchers call *Barnes* v. *Glen Theater*, is Justice White's *cavort*. It means "prance," and may come from *curvet*, a jump by a frolicking horse in which both hind legs leave the ground before the forelegs are set down. *Parade around* is vivid, too; while a sense of the verb *parade* means generally "to show off," the compound *parade around* nicely narrows the meaning to an individual showing himself or herself off, often in the nude.

The best use of language in the case was by Judge Richard A. Posner of the Court of Appeals for the Seventh Circuit, who concurred in the judgment that nude dancing can indeed be covered by freedom of expression, a decision later reversed by the Rehnquist majority: "The true reason I think for wanting to exclude striptease dancing from the protection of the First Amendment is not any of the lawyers' classification games . . . such as expression versus nonexpression, ideas versus emotions, art versus entertainment, or speech versus conduct. It is a feeling that the proposition 'the First Amendment forbids the State of Indiana to require striptease dancers to cover their nipples' is ridiculous."

Having made his point that "a striptease is not a speech," Judge Posner, one of the few Reagan appointees now writing with the force of the late Learned Hand, went to the heart of the matter: "Censorship of erotica is pretty ridiculous too. What kind of people make a career of checking to see whether the covering of a woman's nipples is fully opaque, as the law requires? . . . Many of us do not admire busybodies who want to bring the force of law down on the heads of adults whose harmless private pleasures the busybodies find revolting."

You write about the nude dancing case, Barnes v. Glen Theatre, *spelling "Theatre" Theater. "Glen Theatre, Inc.," the corporate name of the owners of the now defunct Chippewa Drive-in and Bookstore, the South Bend establishment where the nude dancing case originated, retains the once thought arty British spelling, "theatre," lending a spurious (perhaps self-mocking) cachet to the company's business. Changing the legal spelling of "Theatre," to "Theater," and thereby missing its implications, is a small thing, but so is a G-string.*

> William O'Rourke
> Notre Dame, Indiana

On Being Layered

Layering is in. This locution—not to be confused with *lawyering,* or "making it hard to sue and impossible to understand"—has taken hold in several industries.

Vidal Sassoon, the London hairdresser, sent ripples through the barbering dodge with his geometric, layered hair styles in the 1960's; we still see people with that organized shagginess shaping their heads today. The description soon dropped from the head to the body: Since 1976, when *Newsweek* reported that Sonia Rykiel "continued her layered sweater look over Bermuda shorts," the *layered look*—big skirts with tight pants, tiers of fabric, one color on top of the other, men's shirts over women's blouses over kids' pajamas—has been a fashion staple. Lately, according to my *Times Magazine* colleague Carrie Donovan, the *layered look* has been overtaken by a *put-together* look, less rumpled, not as defiant a statement as in the old hippie-reminiscent days; though layering continues, it is not all that chic.

Ah, but it is becoming the hot new locution in another world. In the mid-70's, a different sense of the term appeared in *Business Week:* "Because of the *layered* organizational design, it is hard to get feedback," complained a lumber company executive, frustrated at the impenetrability of government trade regulators. That meaning of *layering*—bureaucratic buffers—lay dormant under a layer of feminist fashion until recently.

A White House official was quoted by Ann Devroy of *The Washington Post* as saying that a new communications director was going to be chosen by the new chief of staff, Samuel K. Skinner. But "the same official cautioned that because someone new is coming in 'does not mean David Demarest is going out.' " Ms Devroy explained that "David F. Demarest Jr. is the current communications director and is likely to leave or *'be layered,'* as one source put it yesterday—given lesser duties and a different title."

I had heard of such layering in political circles but never saw it in print. "I first heard it in the Reagan Administration," Ms Devroy recalls. "They never fired anyone either. They just put a super-whatever on top. When they put somebody else in below, they call it *sandwiching.*"

Despite the indignity, executives or bureaucrats being deprived of an in-box are happy to keep at least the shadow of their jobs in tight times. Keep your eye on *layering,* an important new bureaucratic management tool.

Own Thing

This is the season of commencement rhetoric. Across this glorious land (the land is always glorious on Graduation Day), commencement speakers have been laying advice on the young people blowing tassels out of their faces.

At the Syracuse University commencement exercises, Robert B. Menschel of Goldman, Sachs accepted his honorary Ph.D. and took a different tack: "To be a success, you don't have to force yourself into doing what you think others expect of you. I never met anybody in business who made a success of what he hated to do.

"On the contrary," my former college roommate advised, "do what you know you're good at. . . . You'll find that what you enjoy doing is what you will do best." Mr. Menschel, who is a philanthropist of photography and president of the Dalton School in New York, bolstered his advice with this citation from Ralph Waldo Emerson: "Do your thing."

Emerson? Do your thing? Yop: In the first edition of the collection of his essays, the transcendentalist included *do your thing* in his essay on "Self-Reliance." Then he had second thoughts, and changed it to *do your work* in later editions.

Chaucer fans among the Syracuse graduates knew that Emerson had been preceded in his use of the phrase, now so central to youthful philosophy, in *The Merchant's Tale:*

> Hoom to hir houses lustily they ryde,
> Where as they doon hir thynges.

And in *The Nun's Priest's Tale,* too:

> "No dreem," quod he, "may so myn herte agaste
> That I wol lette for to do my thynges."

Thynges change, phrases take intensifiers—now it's "Do your *own* thing"—but there's no better advice to this year's class.

O Ye Gates

Everybody was waiting for somebody else to open up the *-gates.* The news was out that members of the House of Representatives had used their cooperative bank as a kind of kitty, paying out cash for some ten thousand bad checks a year, with no penalty. Interest-free loans; hot cash in $10,000 bites; a General Accounting Office report with key lines left out; the Speaker of the House declaring the matter closed. Obviously, it was a something-gate.

To start the bidding, I put "Housegate" in a headline over a political harangue. I'm often first out of the box with what other pundits mutter is a trivialization of Watergate. After *Koreagate,* which never got off the ground, there were *Lancegate* and *Billygate.* My best was the encapsulation of a minor White House expense-account scandal as *doublebillingsgate.*

The uninspired *Housegate* was soon superseded by the *Washington Times's Rubbergate,* assuming everyone knew that a bounced check was said to be made of rubber. *The Wall Street Journal,* which ordinarily resists the *-gate* construction, chimed in with *Kitegate,* adding insult to injury by describing it as Congress's B.C.C.I.—"the Bank for Check-Kiting Congressional Incumbents."

In underworld slang, *to kite* at first meant "to smuggle messages out of prison" as if by flying a kite, a hawklike bird; its first citation in the present meaning was in *Dialect Notes* in 1927, the same year *rubber check* first appeared in *The New Republic.* Today, some wheeler-dealers differentiate between a *rubber* check (one returned by the bank unpaid because of insufficient funds in the check-writer's account) and a *kited* check (one postdated to allow the check-writer to accumulate money to cover it), but most people use the terms interchangeably.

Perhaps the initial reluctance to label this scandal with the customary *-gate* construction was caused by possible confusion with the confirmation hearings of Robert M. Gates to head the C.I.A. *Gatesgate* was bruited about, but gained no traction because he was not the center of a scandal. However, those hearings turned up two terms of interest, the first to a general audience, the second to spy-novel fans.

Politicization, or "the coloring for political purposes" of intelligence, which presumably should be politics-neutral, was the crux of the Gates hearings. (If it's one day, it's a *hearing;* if you have to keep listening for days on end, it's *hearings.*) This mid-1930's word, which triumphed over its longer 1902 rival, *politicalization,* was first applied to the attempt to pull the German Protestant Church into Nazi politics; later, the "total politicization of man" was said to be the essence of Marxist theory. In the British publication *The Listener,* the word continued through the 70's to have religious overtones, as the church became "concerned with social morality rather than with the ethereal qualities of immortality."

In the United States "politically motivated" is said with a sneer, in contrast to motivations of altruism; here, *politicization* is a no-no. The title of an article in the current *American Speech* magazine about the way *black* is being replaced by *African-American* is titled "The Politicization of Changing Terms of Self-Reference Among American Slave Descendants" (even so, it's an interesting piece). In 1981, Martin Tolchin of *The New York Times* wrote that Senator Robert Byrd "believed in a bipartisan foreign policy and opposed politicization of the Awacs debate."

The word was popularized in the intelligence lexicon in 1987 by none other than Robert Gates, then Deputy Director of Central Intelligence, who told the Woodrow Wilson School at Princeton that "We intend to tell it as it is, avoiding bias as much as we can or the politicization of our product." (One reason Mr. Gates is not liked is that he takes an expression like *tell it like it is* and corrects its grammar, thereby being right on the detail but wrong on the concept.)

Of narrower but more delectable interest was the locution that appeared in a C.I.A. document that read: "most SOVA [Office of Soviet Analysis] analysts and managers preferred, at least in the early years, not to consider the 'seamy' side of Soviet policy—wet operations and the like."

A *wet operation* is not a naval maneuver, frogman stunt or soggy battle plan. According to the 1986 *Dictionary of Espionage* by Henry S. A. Becket (a pseudonym, based on the deniability of the vague condemnation of Thomas à Becket by Henry II), the *wet squad* was, and maybe still is, "a special K.G.B. assassination group, controlled by and dispatched from K.G.B. Central in Moscow." A related K.G.B. term, *wet work,* is defined as "an operation involving the shedding of blood." It cannot be plausibly denied that this term (though not, of course, the practice, as the continued good health of Saddam Hussein attests) has been adopted by the American intelligence community.

Kiting *is defined with its justifiably pejorative, sinister and criminal connotations in the American Bankers Association's* Principles of Banking *by Eric N. Compton as: "Attempting to draw against non-existent funds for fraudulent purposes. A depositor writes a check in an amount to overdraw the account in one bank and makes up the deficiency by depositing into that same account a check drawn on another bank in which there is also insufficient funds." And* The American Heritage Dictionary Second College Edition *states that a kite is "a negotiable paper, as a check, representing a fictitious financial transaction and used temporarily to sustain credit or raise money."*

Comparing these two versions to your tame one leads me to wonder if this is yet another indication of the ethical deterioration of a society that considers once fraudulent and fictitious activities now to be no more than mere allowances, accommodations or concessions to convenience. Perhaps the title of that column would have rung truer had its allusion to the biblical verse popularized in Handel's Messiah, *"Lift up your heads, O ye gates," been expanded and amended to read more accurately, "Turn your heads," or, more judgmentally, "Hang down your heads [in shame], O ye gates!"*

Michael F. Janczecki
Assistant Vice President
Banking Center Manager
AmeriFirst Bank
Plantation, Florida

Starting -Gate

The everlasting *-gate* combining form is back with us. It all began more than twenty years ago with *Watergate;* the final syllable was then clipped and applied to other words to denote scandal.

Not just political scandal: The dilution of Bordeaux wines in France was called *winegate,* and cost overruns in Hollywood were called *heavensgate.* But most writers evoked *-gate* for political purposes; when Mario Cuomo was a candidate for Mayor of New York City in 1977, he denounced Abe Beame's suppression of a Securities and Exchange Commission report about Big Apple finances as *Applegate.*

Since then, we have seen *Koreagate* and *Irangate.* Although the combining form was trivialized by calling complaints against a Congressman named Daniel Flood *Floodgate* and by dubbing a flap about White House expense accounts *doublebillingsgate,* it came back into its own with the abuse of the bank in the House of Representatives, which I tried last year to label *kitegate* but which this year emerged as *rubbergate.*

Now we may have another big one: *Iraqgate* was emblazoned on the cover of *U.S. News & World Report* on May 18, 1992, in a story by Stephen J. Hedges and Brian Duffy, which was subheaded "How the Bush Administration helped Saddam Hussein buy his weapons of war and why American taxpayers got stuck with the bill."

I missed the boat on the naming of this one. "The Lavoro Scandal" was my feeble headline in November 1989, using the name of the Italian bank whose Atlanta branch was being used as the conduit for illicit billions in grain credits, which Alan Freedman of *The Financial Times* suspected were being used to buy rocket technology for Iraq. But in September of that year, Brendan Murphy of United Press International had already reported from Rome that the Iraqi Embassy "criticized media coverage of the '*Iraqgate*' scandal."

David Rubinger of the *Atlanta Business Chronicle* kept the name alive in 1990, but only as it was known around Rome: "In Italy it is known as '*Iraqgate.*' " A year later, *The Toronto Star* asked editorially, "Will some investigative journalists, in the style of the Watergate scandal, uncover this mass deception by the U.S., which can be termed Bush's *Iraqgate*?"

The *Los Angeles Times* got a good chunk of the story first, but eschewed the obvious headline. In late February 1992, a series by Douglas Frantz and Murray Waas drew on secret documents being gathered by the House Banking Committee chairman, Henry B. Gonzalez. The intrepid San Antonio Congressman, whose district includes the Alamo, then unloaded a pile of documents still stamped "secret"—but now merely embarrassing—into the *Congressional Record,* where other journalists could examine them without having to credit the *Los Angeles Times.*

In Britain, *The Guardian* tried a variant in its takeout on the scandal, choosing *Saddamgate,* but that did not catch on. Soon afterward, *U.S. News & World Report* led the newsmagazines with its coverage of what it headlines unabashedly "*Iraqgate.*"

Why had I, an avid *-gate*-combining-form fan, not adopted the name long favored in Italy for the Lavoro story? Philological fustiness, I suppose; the *q* is not followed by a *u,* and that troubled my soul. We have seen the abnormally followed *q* used to express a velar sound in Qazvin, an Iranian city, but in English, *Merriam-Webster's Ninth New Collegiate* has only four entries for terms that start with *q* and are followed by a letter other than *u.*

In case the question comes up at your breakfast table, as it so often does at mine, these are *Q-boat* (an armed vessel posing as a fishing ship, also known as a *Q-ship*), *qintar* (Albanian money), *qiviut* (the wool from a musk ox's undercoat) and *qoph* (the nineteenth letter of the Hebrew alphabet). An entry that ends with *q,* unfollowed by the letter that helps to form the sound of "kw," is *Iraq.*

Iraqgate. Do not hyphenate; that would spoil the nice juxtaposition of two letters whose bottoms curl away from each other.

You betray a linguistic ethnocentricism, more than a "philological fustiness," in insisting that a q *should always be followed by a* u. *In English and the Latin-based Romance languages, this may be, but there are other languages in which, when they are written in Latin script, a* q *has a particular value or designates a particular sound that has nothing to do with "our"* qu *combination.*

While you refer to a mere four entries in Webster's of terms starting with a q *followed by letters other than* u, *a bit wider research would have led you to the Semitic family of languages, whose alphabets contain a letter (the* qoph *of Hebrew—mentioned in your Webster's—and the* qaf *of Arabic, for example) which for generations scholars, linguists and archaeologists from the West have chosen to transliterate as a* q *in order to differentiate its sound (an emphatic guttural velar) from a softer back-of-the-throat sound, also existing in these languages, that is closer to our own* k. *This "q" sound is also found in non-Arabic languages such as Persian and Urdu, which have borrowed heavily from Arabic through the spread of Islam.*

Some Arabic words with the distinctive q *sound have entered our own vocabulary—usually through intermediary languages such as Greek or Turkish—although in doing so, they have seldom retained the* q *when written in English. (Early lexicographers, like yourself, found that somehow distasteful. Indeed,* Iraq *itself was usually written as* Irak *in the bad old colonial days, before the pedantic Orientalists took over. The Iraqis themselves adopted the spelling* Iraq—*and* Iraqi—*when they achieved independence in 1958.) Some words familiar to us that conceal both their Arabic origins and their original* q *sounds include* coffee *(from the Arabic* qahwah, *through the Turkish* kahveh), caravan *(Arabic* qairawan *and Turkish* karwan), canal *(Arabic* qanah, *passed on to us through Greek and Latin),* canon *(as in law—Arabic* qanun, *directly received) and* cotton *(Arabic* qutun, *with that* u *vowel again, twice).*

So, my advice, Mr. Safire, is to eschew linguo-centrism and let not your soul be troubled by "abnormal" foreign-looking letter combinations in what are, after all, foreign *languages (especially, it would seem, to you!).*

William Lee
New York, New York

One English word having a "q" without a "u" in the middle of the word is "miqra."

It is on page 1566 of the Merriam-Webster Unabridged, *Second Edition, and has two definitions:*

> *a. The liturgical reading of the Bible.*
> *b. The Hebrew text of the Bible.*

Gene K. Edlin
Chicago, Illinois

I was surprised that in your confession of "philological fustiness" you came up with only four examples of q*'s without* u*'s and ignored the abominable* pinyin *system for romanizing Chinese which, of course, abounds with* q*'s without* u*'s, and causes Westerners to make some awful sounds that are like nothing in the Chinese language.*

You might be interested in how this came about. It happened in the 1950s when the Soviet Union was the acknowledged "elder brother" to the newly established Chinese Communist regime and was ready to be helpful in many fields, including alphabetizing the Chinese language. A team of Russian linguists arrived in Beijing, primed to talk the Chinese into adopting the Cyrillic script. The head of the Chinese team, Guo Morou, who was one of the few intellectuals Mao trusted, boldly rejected the idea, arguing that the Chinese had already invested far too much in learning and using the Latin alphabet. With that settled, the two teams proceeded to formulate the pinyin *system. When they came to the "ch" sound, the Russians, still making the case for their script, pointed out that the Cyrillic "ч" was exactly the right letter for the "ch" sound. Guo Morou looked at the character and said, "Why, that looks like a* q, *so why don't we just use a* q *for the 'ch' sound."*

And that is how we all were cursed with one of the quirkier features of pinyin, *and people who don't speak Chinese end up making the strangest sounds as they try to read, for example, "Qing," which is now the silly way of spelling the great Ching dynasty.*

I obtained this story from a couple of Chinese sources, and from one of America's leading Chinese language and literature specialists, Professor James I. Crump of the University of Michigan.

Lucian W. Pye
Cambridge, Massachusetts

Padding Pedantry

Alistair Cooke, a member of Olbom (On Language's Board of Octogenarian Mentors), writes, "In a newspaper that can print 'The tournament was suspended because of lightening,' don't you think you should rip into the English that is used routinely, every day, by United States Senators, university presidents, and C.E.O.'s?"

I lightn up to address myself to Mr. Cooke's bête noire, the rampant practice of verbal padding.

"To begin with," he begins with (I suppose we could drop the *with*), "how about *basis*? Absolutely nobody in America says or writes, 'He saw him every week' or 'I practice every day.'" Sooner or later it was bound to happen, and it did—about two months ago. *Doctor:* "Do you have bowel movements on a daily basis?" *A. Cooke:* "Well, I have a daily bowel movement." *Doctor:* "That's what I mean."

The man from Olbom has a point: *On a* (*whatever*) *basis* is padded prose, a locution we lapse into that gives a semiofficial tone or bureaucratic harrumph to a phrase more clearly expressed with an *each* or *every* or introduced with a *regularly.* It is a habit that afflicts everyone who makes an announcement over an airplane's loudspeaker (called a *public-address system*).

Nor is that all to pedant padding, stuffily coined on the analogy of *patent pending.* "I have asked several tv. viewers"—Mr. Cooke, who is viewed often on television and is usually in a smoking jacket, puts a period after "tv," presumably on the theory that it is an abbreviation—"to listen and tell me if they hear anybody ever say, 'It takes a long time' or 'during that time.' Today it's 'a long *period of* time' or 'during *that period of* time.' It suggests some interesting song titles: 'A Long Period of Time Ago.' "

What is it about *time* that attracts the paddists? "At that *point in* time" was academese long before it became famous in Watergate, and "during that time *frame*" seems to be a vague effort to put officious brackets around the past.

Alistair, a trained linguist, suggests we start a padding pedants' competition, using song titles as examples, "*on the basis* of Jack Teagarden's singing 'Stars Fell on the Alabama *Area.*' " Good idea: Let's Fall in the Love *Process.* Please Be Kind *in Nature.*

Parlour Game

"These are *parlous* times." You seldom hear that oratorical cliché anymore; *parlous* was a Middle English variant of *perilous,* meaning "hazardous," even "dangerous," but the variant has fallen by the linguistic wayside.

George Bush took a look at some research he had been handed by the campaign staffers who listen for mistakes by his opponent. The President then asked "what the heck he's talking about when he describes a President's— quote—here's what he called it: 'A President's *powerless* moments when countries are invaded.' "

The Clinton press secretary promptly handed out the text of the candidate's speech to the Los Angeles World Affairs Council: "The ultimate test of Presidential leadership . . . is the judgment a President exercises in those *perilous* moments when countries are invaded."

The ear is tricky; it sometimes hears what it wants or expects to hear. This confusion was our most recent example of a mondegreen—not of the magnitude of "I Led the Pigeons to the Flag" or "Gladly the Cross-Eyed Bear," but parlous enough in these political times.

Peace-ese

Though I was not present, and cannot get a definite, on-the-record confirmation from a source inside the room, I am told that at one point in the negotiations leading up to the Madrid conference, Secretary of State James A. Baker 3d said to a member of the Israeli team about a procedural matter: "This shouldn't cause any *tsoris.*"

This epochal understanding of Yiddish angst by a starchy diplomat from Texas augured well for the opening of the face-to-face meetings between Israelis and Arabs. The word *tsoris,* roughly rhyming with "Boris," is derived from the Hebrew *tsarah* and means "trouble, woe"; it can also mean "worries" or "minor suffering." Emphasis can be provided by adding *gehokteh,* meaning "chopped," as in "chopped liver"; *gehokteh tsoris* is "deep trouble," enough to derail talks (and to diplomats, that ain't chopped liver).

We are in the world of peace-ese, the language of Middle East peacemaking. Trying to bridge the gulf of age-old resentments is a serious business, and it is not to trivialize the *peace process* (a phrase whose coiner should come forward) that this department delves into the means of communication; on the contrary, great issues churn up new usage.

From that Yiddish beginning, we are lured into Latin: Fans of Latin plurals were turned on by President Bush's speech in Madrid. After referring to bilateral (between two) and multilateral (among more than two) meetings to come, he talked of "progress in these *fora.*" *The New York Times* has moved to the more widely understood plural *forums; Webster's New World Dictionary* lists *fora* as an acceptable variant of *forums,* but *forums* is preferred. Wherefore *fora*? Professor Richard N. Haass, on leave from Harvard, had a hand in the speech; academicians like to expound in a variety of *fora.* The use of the proper Latin plural sent a signal to hippopotami sending each other memoranda in the Charles River: Intellectual at work.

However, the President soon stooped to pleonasm. "No one can say with any precision what the end result will be." The Squad Squad's opening-gambit section immediately threatened to walk out of listening to the talks: *End result* is redundant, tautological and unnecessarily repetitive, not to mention prolix and wordy. "What the end will be" would suffice, though "what the result will be" is more specific, since the goal is a result, not an end.

Informal interchanges between delegates require explanation. "I want to eat hummus in your place," said the Israeli Yoash Zidon to the Palestinian Albert Aghazarian, "and you eat hummus in my place." Replied Mr. Aghazarian, who has apparently had enough hummus: "Well, I will eat maybe gefilte fish in your place." *Hummus* is a Middle Eastern spread made of puréed chickpeas with tahini, garlic, lemon juice and olive oil; *gefilte fish* is a cake of *gehokteh* (see *tsoris* above) fish, carp when you can get it, mixed with onion, seasonings and egg, simmered in a broth, and when made inexpertly can anchor a battleship.

A key word in the negotiations is the verb *impose,* as in Mr. Bush's "This conference cannot impose a settlement on the participants." This is a word that has been getting heavier with the years. Originally, it meant "to place upon"; then it was most often used to mean "to place a burden on," as "to impose a tax." You can also *levy* a tax, but that comes from "levitate," or raise, describing the method rather than the fact of burdening. *Impose's* sense of placing a burden assumed a metaphoric dimension in imposing, or unsought, company ("are you sure we're not imposing on your good nature?") and then extended to unwanted authority ("don't impose your cultural prejudices on me") and now to diplomacy ("no imposed solutions").

Most Israelis do not want a settlement dictated to them; contrariwise, most Arabs would prefer a settlement ordained by Israel's longtime ally, the United States; thus does *impose* become a hot-button word. In such cases, a synonym is sought to describe the action without carrying the pejorative weight; such a word is *facilitate,* rooted in "to make easy." Nobody goes on record in favor of an imposed solution, but nobody can object to a facilitated one. If the bilateral and multilateral talks proceed, and if the time comes that the United States intervenes in the face-to-face negotiations, the solution will be hailed as having been *facilitated* and attacked as *imposed.*

The long- or short-range outcome of the Middle East peace conference remains to be seen, but you touched upon the emergence of an important and basic commonality between the Arab and Israeli delegations in "Peace-ese." The way to a peaceful settlement may well be through the stomach, as the informal exchanges turned to talk of hummus and gefilte fish.

Eleanor S. Rubin
Watchung, New Jersey

You ask that the coiner of the phrase "peace process" come forward. That phrase may have been the contribution of the late President of Egypt, Anwar el-Sadat. It is a direct translation of the Arabic phrase "amaliyat as-salaam," a phrase Sadat used frequently.

The term "peace process" owes its success to its ambiguity. Today, it seems equally to suit Palestinian leaders, Israeli prime ministers and American secretaries of state.

Issa A. Nour
Brooklyn, New York

You wrote, "The word tsoris, *roughly rhyming with 'Boris,' is derived from the Hebrew* tsarah. . . ." *Secretary of State Baker may have pronounced it that way, but anyone who has actually heard the word used in conversation would know that it is more accurately transliterated* tsuris *and rhymes, more or less, with* tourist *minus the final* t.

Stephen Chernicoff
Berkeley, California

"Impose": The Constitution (ours, that is) uses the phrase "Imposts or Duties" to mean taxes or tariffs.

Boris I. Bittker
Yale Law School
New Haven, Connecticut

Perotspeak

The most urgent linguistic problem in the presidential campaign of Henry Ross Perot is what to call his supporters.

The suffix *-ites* is the most familiar combining form, as *McGovernites* and *Nixonites* discovered in 1972; however, we have no *Bushites*—personal followers of the President are more often called *Bushies,* on the analogy of *Yalies* and *preppies*—and we don't hear often of *Clintonites,* or even *Clintonians.* (If the Democratic contender is elected, we'll hear a lot about *Clintonomics.*)

Perotite is awkward because the name Perot has a French pronunciation, its last syllable "row," not "rot," and "row-ite" does not come easily to the tongue when the eye sees *rotite.* A frequent headline, "Waiting for Perot," is a play on the title of Samuel Beckett's 1952 play, *Waiting for Godot,* with the final sound also "owe." (Beckett was playing on the English word *God,* for whom all the play's characters are presumably waiting.)

One possibility for labeling the backers of the Texas billionaire is *Perotistas,* on the analogy of *Peronistas,* but that formulation is usually used in

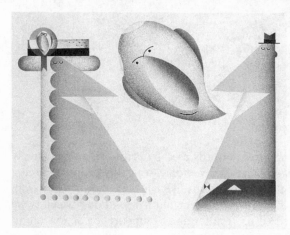

derogation, and *Perotniks* is unlikely. A snide, elitist media establishmentarian referred to them as *outrage groupies,* and I've had plenty of mail about that, but a more neutral characterization of angry, frustrated voters has appeared: the *radical middle.*

The phrase, coined in 1970 by Renata Adler to title a collection of reporting and criticism (*Time* magazine later called her fiction "middling radical"), was picked up in 1978 by Prime Minister Pierre Trudeau of Canada, who responded to a charge of a rightward turn by his Liberal party with "We are a party of the extreme center, the *radical middle.*"

Early in the 1992 presidential primary campaign, the *radical right,* a 1954 coinage, turned to Pat Buchanan, and the *radical left,* bordering on a redundancy, to Jerry Brown. Because Mr. Perot draws from both these antigovernment bases, and exploits the fierceness of "mad-as-hell" frustration, that position opened the field to the first *radical middle.* First to apply the term to Perot backers was Joe Klein of *New York* magazine. (My own *snarling center,* though alliterative, is too partisan to be adopted by academicians.)

Until a suitable one-word appellation that includes the candidate's name is introduced, we will have to make do with the lengthy *Perot supporters, Perot followers* and, perhaps, *members of the Perot movement.* The Perot campaign will surely stress *volunteers.*

On the matter of the candidate's name, however, we have universal agreement: At his request, the *H.* for Henry has been dropped. Deference to a choice of monikers is a courtesy the media traditionally extends to politicians: J. Danforth Quayle wanted his name written as Dan Quayle, William Clinton is the familiar Bill, and only those seeking to mock George Bush call him George Herbert Walker Bush.

And what of Perotspeak, the language of the radmids? (Note that it is not *Perotease,* which would call for pronunciation of the *t.*) In *Framewords,* a perceptive new newsletter about political rhetoric, edited by Edmund Blair

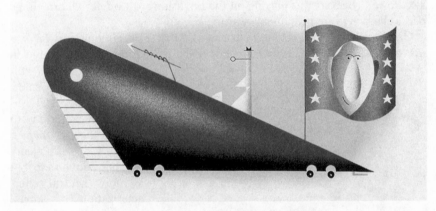

Bolles in New York, among the key words used by Perot are *action* (usually contrasted with *talk*); *broke* (America's economy, which he proposes to fix); *fix* (more action-oriented than fancy words like *empower, create, negotiate*), and *consensus,* meaning not so much "agreement on a solution," which is the way Lyndon Johnson liked to use the term, as "support for action on an agreed-upon problem."

Jerry Brown contributed *gridlock,* a traffic term coined in New York in the early 70's to denote an intersection blockage backing up traffic in all directions. In the political parlance adopted by Perot, it means "the special-interest support of incumbents in resistance to change." (Curiously, President Bush, the candidate of continuity, labels himself the candidate of *change;* evidently a hot-button word with focus groups that used to focus on *leadership.*)

Plans is big in Perotspeak, the product of *world-class experts* working on *problems*—never *injustices* or *wrongs,* only *problems* and *challenges*—on which there is a consensus. "Perot speaks of *plans* rather than *policies*," Mr. Bolles writes. He then notes the connotative difference: "*Policies* are the general result of political give and take, and provide a coherent guideline linking the activities of many separate legislators, cabinet members and civil servants. *Plans* are technical, focused, come from the top and are implemented by a hierarchy of managers."

Absolute freedom, in this context, can be a synonym for *absolute authority.* "We conduct pilot programs," Mr. Perot said, "in a way that the people running these pilot programs have absolute freedom to optimize it."

Then there is the complexity of *simple,* as central to Perotspeak as *clear* was to Nixonese. As Mr. Perot uses it about himself or his approach, it's good: "Look, it's simple." But when his interrogators ask him for specifics, the word takes on a sinister overtone: "I wish it were that simple."

The uniqueness of Perotspeak is its mixture of rustic metaphor with modern managementese. He proposes to improve the *process* by "sweeping the barn and taking out the trash," and promises not to "sit in the *bubble* and be *briefed*" when the deficit is "like a crazy aunt you try to hide in the basement."

Never before in a political campaign has down-home earthiness so combined with high-tech nerdiness. This department has absolute freedom to fix what's broke and has plans to observe the process problem at the grass-roots level.

You write that the presidential campaign of Ross Perot is having trouble deciding what to call his supporters. The answer is obvious: Perotselytes.

> *Erwin Klingsberg*
> *Mountainside, New Jersey*

The suffix 'ite or 'ites has a history of which you are unaware. It was first used by Stalin as an extremely negative suffix that was added to "Trotsky." To be a "Trotskyite" was the worst thing possible in the Soviet Union for decades.

If you want to simply indicate a follower, you use the suffix 'ist or 'ists, as in Trotskyist.

> *Anne Gregory*
> *Media, Pennsylvania*

You say that ". . . the media traditionally extends to politicians . . ."

Mr. Safire, as you better than almost anybody else should know, "media" is a plural noun and its verb should, of course, correspond to it.

Gerardo Joffe
San Francisco, California

As to Samuel Beckett having named his play Waiting for Godot *using the syllable "God" with some deific reference in mind; the work was originally written in French for the French theater with the title* En Attendant Godot, *and the word* Godot *would not have assumed any specific meaning for the initial audiences.*

It was not until the translated play was presented in England that the "allusion watchers" began to fumble around (and still are) trying to uncover Beckett's subtext of hidden intents—and with the first one naturally being God, especially when Godot is described in the latter portion of the play as being an old man with a white beard!

Perhaps a better theory, if such a thing ever exists when it comes to trying to define Beckett, might be found in a play called Mercadet *by Honoré de Balzac, the well-known French writer, with whom Beckett as a French scholar would have been familiar. In the play the arrival of a certain Godeau is awaited with much concern as this Godeau is the only one able to provide information that will satisfactorily (or not) conclude the story. Godeau never appears on stage, but the play ends with an announcement that Godeau has at last arrived.*

So much for Beckett, who once wrote to a friend saying, "My work is a matter of fundamental sounds (no joke intended) made as fully as possible, and I accept responsibility for nothing else. If people want to have headaches among the overtones, let them. And provide their own aspirin."

William S. Gegg
Tucson, Arizona

Perotmania vs. Perotphobia

Like *-philia, -mania* is a combining form for "being crazy about"; *-phobia* is a combining form for "being fearful of." Both *Perotmaniacs* and *Perotphobes* have responded to this department's request for a name for supporters of Ross Perot's candidacy.

Some pro-Perot people call themselves *Perotisans,* a play on *partisans,* in the sense of guerrilla fighters; others prefer *Perotesters,* pronounced "puh-ROW-test-ers"; still others have suggested *Perotians*, recalling militant Martians. Others advocating *Perotstroika* suggest *Rossniks*, while one former oarsman likes *Perowers*. Larry Bakst, writing from Cologne, Germany, suggests that supporters of a candidate who would clean out the four-flushers in Washington be called *Peroto-rooters*. Correspondents in the military like *Perotroopers*, while James H. Goulder Jr. of St. James, Long Island, submits a word to highlight moral firmness: *Perotcrusteans*.

Ethnic supporters of the candidate like *Perogies*, which Charles H. Willson of Allentown, Pennsylvania, describes as "a potato and/or cheese pastry turnover popular here in Lehigh County," and which Bruce Lercher of Binghamton, New York, says is a "Polish-Ukrainian knish, variously spelled *pirogi, piroghi, pirohi.*"

Opponents of Mr. Perot suggest his supporters be called *Perotsites*, or *Perotcrats;* John Morressy of East Sullivan, New Hampshire, and others like *Perobots*. Several also suggest *Perogies* but with a negative twist, recalling that delicacy's "doughy, half-baked nature." Lawrence Downes of East Norwich, New York, introduces an alienist element with *Perotnoiacs*.

Evenhanded readers will note this column's tone of scrupulous bipartisanship, or more accurately this year, tripartisanship. In a different forum, however, I cast a mild aspersion at Mr. Perot's thrice-changed story about why he sought early release from the Navy; when *TV Guide*'s executive editor, Barry Golson, and one of its correspondents, Peter Ross Range, asked the candidate about this situation, Mr. Perot responded with a noun phrase used as a compound adjective in a sense not spotted previously: "I'm not going to spend one minute today discussing that kind of unprofessional, Third World journalism."

Third world is a phrase coined by Charles de Gaulle—*tiers monde*—meaning "neutral in the struggle between the Soviet bloc and the 'free world.'" Now that the struggle is over, *third world* has come to mean "undeveloped nation," and in Perotspeak, "unprofessional" to the point of "scurrilous." As politics changes, so do the meanings of political terms.

-Auts, -Ites or -Ions

Will the followers of Bill Clinton follow the practice of George McGovern, Richard Nixon or Ronald Reagan?

If the first, we will see frequent references to *Clintonites*, modeled on *McGovernites*.

Another choice would be *Clintonians*, on the analogy of *Nixonians*.

A third would be *Clintonauts*, originating in *Argonauts* by way of *Reaganauts*.

The only other possibility that comes to mind is *Clinties,* modeled on *Bushies;* that won't fly.

Perotian Alert

I miss Ross Perot. Not only did he apply the traffic term *gridlock* to divided-party government, but also the jug-eared, thin-skinned executive generated the most derisive sobriquet of the current campaign, as his betrayed supporters called him "the yellow Ross of Texas."

In *Forbes* magazine's seventy-fifth anniversary issue, Peggy Noonan, the former Reagan-Bush speechwriter who has developed the art of impressionism in political prose, summarized the voters' view of the horseless head man in a poetic trope: "They looked at him and saw a hand grenade with a bad haircut."

Phrasedick Alert: Etymons Wanted

Three phrases in common current use are rooted in mystery.

"*Death by a thousand cuts* is vogue phrase of the month," Hendrik Hertzberg of *The New Republic* writes in a letter. "The Clarence Thomas nomination pushed it to its critical mass, but it's been building for most of this year."

In 1975, George F. Will wrote, "The myth of [Alger] Hiss's innocence suffers the *death of a thousand cuts,* delicate destruction by a scholar's scalpel." In grumping about the destructive leakage on John G. Tower during his nomination hearings in 1989, I used the phrase as well without bothering to cite a source. Now the earliest source I can find is a 1966 translation of *Quotations from Chairman Mao Tse-Tung,* cited by him as a Chinese proverb: " 'He who is not afraid of death by a thousand cuts dares to unhorse the emperor'—this is the indomitable spirit needed in our struggle to build socialism and communism." I suspect earlier usages in English can be found.

Phrasedicks have long been busting their chops over *No good deed goes unpunished.* I checked with Justin Kaplan, editor of *Bartlett's Familiar Quotations,* and he reports: "I haven't had any better luck than you. We'll list the quote as a 'saying' under *Anonymous.* It *may* be nineteenth century." In the *New Oxford Dictionary of American Proverbs,* Kansans are said to say: "There is no good that does not cost a price," but that's not it. Help wanted.

Now about *busting your chops,* "exhausting yourself, especially in a hopeless cause." The slang dictionaries are unhelpful. Here's a theory from James Redding, a trumpeter in New York: "*Chops* are not cheeks or jaws. They're what the wolf in 'Little Red Riding Hood' licked: lips. And to a brass player, the strength and endurance of the muscles thereof." He carries this toot on to a definition: "*To bust one's chops* means 'to become too fatigued to perform adequately.' "

Other theories are invited; the discoverer will be treated to death by a thousand cuts, because no good deed goes unpunished.

A complimentary truism to "No good deed goes unpunished" is "I don't know why that man hates me. I never did him a favor."

> Edward H.R. Blitzer
> New York, New York

My definition for "busting your chops" is distinctly different from "exhausting yourself, especially in a hopeless cause." I've heard the phrase used hundreds of times in the milieu of office work in New York City in the past 20 years, and while I'm not sure that I've never heard it used as you describe, the overwhelmingly more common meaning is "verbally harassing, especially with pressure to accomplish a task." A typical usage would be, "George, I don't mean to bust your chops, but that report has to be ready by four o'clock." One doesn't bust one's own chops, but someone else's: "The boss has been busting my chops all morning." There's no implication of the hopelessness of the cause, but rather of the (perceived) urgency of the task. A one-word synonym might be "nag."

> Alan C. Freed
> Bronx, New York

"Busting one's chops," no matter its origin, simply means "work hard." Whether or not that work is successful is irrelevant.

> Richard Chiaramonte
> Stamford, Connecticut

Poetic Allusion Watch

Lance Morrow is one of the classiest stylists in the news-magazine dodge, because he spices his prose with poetic allusions. He does this subtly, with no quotation marks or "as the poet says," expecting readers of *Time* to catch, appreciate and be intellectually enriched by the oblique references; if the allusion slips by unnoticed, no harm is done to the flow of communication.

This department conducts a periodic Poetic Allusion Watch (PAW), which is not to be confused with a periodical PAW limited to magazines. The PAW division of the Lexicographic Irregulars has been letting down the side lately, requiring me to clamber up to the crow's-nest myself.

Consider "The Trouble With Teddy." (*Time* magazine's headline writers capitalize *with* but few other prepositions and articles; sometimes they capitalize *of,* sometimes not, but hobgoblins pay this little mind.) In his essay-article about Senator Edward M. Kennedy's current nocturnal tribulations, Mr. Morrow uses the metaphor of a shadow cast across a luminous life. "Was all this unhappy transformation the influence of metaphysics? Or was it alcohol? In any case, *the shadow fell.*"

That's a fairly easy catch. In "The Hollow Men," T. S. Eliot used the line "Falls the Shadow." This passage, derived by Eliot from "There fell thy shadow" in Ernest Dowson's poem to Cynara, is followed by a line from the Lord's Prayer, "For Thine is the Kingdom," an apt reference to the Kennedy reach for power and glory.

The next was slightly more obscure. "Perhaps his life was cracked after Bobby died," Mr. Morrow wrote, "and Teddy found he was on his own and began to cross over from the powerful myth of his family into real time, which is intolerant of the bright and ideal."

Nice. *Real time,* with its computerese sense of "processes that respond immediately to user input," seems only to contrast with the preceding *powerful myth,* but the sensitized eye sees it connected by poetic allusion to the subsequent *intolerant.* Language mavens are especially likely to know that this comes from W. H. Auden's 1940 memorial to William Butler Yeats: "Time that is intolerant / Of the brave and innocent, / And indifferent in a week / To a beautiful physique, / Worships language and forgives / Everyone by whom it lives. . . ."

Mr. Morrow, or the *Time* copy editor, changed Auden's "Time that" to "time, which"; apparently they are especially sensitive at *Time* to relative pronouns that stand for their magazine's name. (They should devote that attention to taking a stand on the capitalization of *of* in headlines.)

When a writer makes two allusions in a piece, the odds are that he will make a third; some sort of inner need to accomplish a hat trick drives us all. I searched for the third, centered on "He had to soldier on in the messy world after Camelot floated away into memory," but found no Kipling reference under *soldier on* or *messy world* in any of the quotation-book indexes. (That's the trick in tracking poetic allusions; don't trust your memory.)

So I called Lance Morrow and laid the PAW on him.

"I only realized I was making the allusions afterward," he replied. "It wasn't entirely advertent. But then I said, what the hell, leave them in."

So where is the third one?

"*Cracked,*" he murmured.

Of course; that was an odd verb to use to describe a life, and PAW should have caught it. "Perhaps his life was cracked" is bottomed on the poet-philosopher Ralph Waldo Emerson's "There is a crack in every thing God has made." Whoso would be a PAWperson must be an Emerson student; he's the same fellow who linked the hobgoblin of little minds to a foolish consistency.

Oh great language maven, thou hast cleft my heart in twain! You used the term "quotation-book indexes" as a resource for tracking poetic allusions. As a physician used to reading about red cell and other indices, I am dismayed to see the passage of this Latinate plural form. My pet theory is that the "ices" form has hit the usage dungheap to accommodate such nouns as Kleenex, Windex, and other commercial preparations that end in -ex. True, it would be awkward to say "please pass the box of Kleenices," but I can report to you from the arcane world of medicine that the usage of red cell indices remains alive and well. Our colleagues in the world of finance, however, look at the Dow-Jones and other stock indexes and have abandoned the use of indices. To my chagrin, your recent column illustrates that you have thrown your lot in with the stockbrokers and have turned your back on the doctors, an unwise move in my view in this uncertain world.

Sidney P. Kadish, M.D.
Saint Vincent Hospital
Worcester, Massachusetts

Poetic Allusion Watch, Expanded

This department's unique contribution to uniculturalism, named the "Poetic Allusion Watch" but familiarly known to deep readers as PAW, has long exposed the devices that writers and speakers use to slip secret erudition past their audiences. Today we begin with poetry buried in the prose of the labor movement, and then give the envelope a hard shove: into allusions to biblical-

Shakespearean compounds, classical music titles, even to the heart of arcana—titles of economic treatises. No sizzling grounder gets through the Great Shortstop.

In a column about the rockiness of the marriage that makes up the Democratic party, David S. Broder of *The Washington Post* used as a source Lane Kirkland, president of the A.F.L.-C.I.O. The "new-age issues"—presumably matters that concern Shirley MacLaine a lot, and roil the waters of West Coast hot tubs—have come to define liberalism today, leaving workers, ethnics and other members of the classic New Deal coalition feeling out in the cold. My brother Broder quoted Mr. Kirkland—originally a maritime worker; but a speechwriter along the way—saying that Democrats need a candidate "who can *shake the barley* . . . on issues that are important to the traditional base."

O.K., who or what *shakes the barley*? Because Mr. Kirkland is a Carolinian whose great-grandfather led a rebel force in the Civil War, I searched the Southern folklore files; nothing. The indexes of quotation books were equally barren—"Rough winds do shake the darling buds of May," wrote the Bard, but barley's buds are spiky and hardly darling—nor could Nexis, the computerized morgue, turn up any citations in the past fifteen years of the verb *shake* within two words of the noun *barley,* that key ingredient of a good malt beer.

Going to the source is a loser's game, but I had no choice. Stumped, I called the A.F.L.-C.I.O. Its president was overseas, at a meeting of international labor, and could not be reached unless it was really important, and couldn't anybody else help? I explained the problem. They slipped him a note in the Geneva meeting, and back came the word: "It's from a Scottish bagpipe tune, 'The Wind That Shook the Barley,' probably rooted in a poem by Robert Burns." If any Cobbler Johnny–come-lately finds it, a fast and furious PAW accolade awaits.

To the classical music allusion: "No Grazing for Sheep, Safely or Otherwise" was the headline in *The New York Times* over the story from Orwell, Vermont, about a method of mowing the lawn down the steep, rocky hillsides of a couple of cemeteries. A local sheep farmer said her herd of twenty Dorset sheep could do for $250 what mechanized mowers were charging $3,000 to do. That seemed a great idea to the town manager, but struck many of the townspeople as disrespectful and decidedly not Orwellian; a few testy Vermonters threatened to spook the sheep. Hence the headline about the unsafe grazing.

"If you don't have a category for musical allusions," writes PAW member Deborah A. Stapleton of Palo Alto, California, "perhaps you can create one. This headline writer had in mind Bach's piece 'Sheep May Safely Graze.' I used to play it in eighth-grade orchestra."

Business is picking up. Here is a book title: *Coming to Public Judgment* by Daniel Yankelovich, latest production of the lively Syracuse University Press. That's a snap: If my first name were Daniel, I would long ago have written a book with that title. The reference is to Shakespeare's allusion to the biblical Daniel, whose name in Hebrew means "God is my judge"; in *The Merchant of Venice,* Shylock praises the disguised Portia with "A Daniel come to judgment! Yea, a Daniel! O wise young judge, how I do honor thee!"

Finally, this six-column headline across the top of the *Boston Globe*'s front page: "Consequences of the Economic Pinch." This may not be the sort of screaming banner that impels readers to snatch up the paper in New York's headline war between the *News* and the *Post,* but it got to at least one reader—James Zall of Revere, Massachusetts. "I seem to recall that you've devoted space to esoteric references by erudite editors," goes his aggregate demand. "I assume the *Globe* headline writer's reference is to John Maynard Keynes's 'Economic Consequences of the Peace.' "

Gotcha! Ms Stapleton, safely grazing through her newspaper, summed up the thrill of the allusion-catcher: "As with all good allusions in journalism or in speech, this one was a delight to those of us who caught it, and made no never mind to those who did not."

I have the song "The Wind That Shakes the Barley" on an LP album by the Clancy Brothers and Tommy Makem entitled Irish Songs of Rebellion. *According to the notes by Patrick Clancy on the dust jacket, the song refers to the Irish uprising of 1798. The words are said to be the work of Robert Dwyer Joyce, a professor of English Literature at Catholic University in Dublin, who spent some time in the United States to avoid arrest for rebel activities, but later returned to Ireland and died in 1883. The song is about a young man who joins the uprising after his sweetheart is killed by a stray English bullet. In the first stanza, the young man is sitting with his sweetheart "[w]hile soft the wind blew down the glen and shook the golden barley." Subsequent stanzas end with phrases such as "while soft winds shake the barley" or "the wind that shook the barley."*

Patrick C. Reed
New York, New York

I've read a couple of your poetic allusion watch columns and wonder if you have had occasion to discuss my own favorite example: the slogan "Now more than ever" during the Nixon reelection campaign. As you doubtless know, the phrase derives, wittingly or unwittingly, from Keats's line in stanza six of "Ode to a Nightingale": "Now more than ever seems it rich to die."

Around the English department it was something of a joke to use the slogan in the early 1970s, because of the unspoken menace endowed by the Keatsian source. Perhaps the slogan was a dirty trick perpetrated by a Democrat. Anyway, it deserves mention in any history of the poetic allusion in political discourse.

> Laurence Goldstein
> *Editor,* Michigan Quarterly
>   Review
> *The University of Michigan*
> *Ann Arbor, Michigan*

PAW Prince

Headline writers are the poets of the universe next door. These eye-strained wretches understand the restraints of space and meter that bind the writers of Shakespearean sonnets (three quatrains followed by a couplet) or of Japanese *haiku* (three lines, having five, seven and five syllables). Like the poet, the headline writer tries to shoehorn great messages into a few words; some, to show an affinity to poetry, slip allusions to famous poems into their everyday headlines.

Most of us miss these allusions; they are private communications to the cognoscenti, phrases out of our literary past scribbled by our horseless headmen across a newspaper page, put in a bottle and thrown out to the sea of faces. Thanks to the members of the Poetic Allusion Watch, these furtive expressions of our subliminal culture are spotted when washed up on the beach of this column.

Consider a piece by C. G. Cupic datelined Osijek, Yugoslavia, about the civil war between Serbs and Croats, beginning: "The River Drava flows lazily across the rich Slavonian plain." The International *Herald Tribune* headline writer capitalized on the sense of place in the feature lede by writing, "On a Darkening Plain, War and Reconciliation."

If Memory's fond deceiver serves, that comes from Matthew Arnold's "Dover Beach," published in 1867, perhaps written around 1848, to suggest the poet's concern with the third wave of the European revolution:

> And we are here as on a darkling plain
> Swept with confused alarms of struggle and flight,
> Where ignorant armies clash by night.

Let us be true to one another: When it came to the key word, the poetic allusioneer choked. *Darkling* was changed to *darkening,* perhaps by another editor unversed in verse, or by the original headline writer who didn't remember the line correctly or who thought the archaic word was too much for a modern audience. *Darkling* dates back to Middle English as an adverb for "in the dark," and by the eighteenth century it was used as an adjective for "obscure, lying in darkness"; James Russell Lowell, his horny hand toiling in an 1884 ode to the poet Oliver Wendell Holmes, used it this way: "As many poets with their rhymes/Oblivion's darkling dust o'erwhelms." But "on a darkling plain" is the most famous context of the moody word; the phrase was also the title of Clifford Irving's first novel.

Above Russell F. Weigley's review of *Fatal Decision: Anzio and the Battle for Rome* by Carlo D'Este, the *New York Times Book Review* headline writer chose "Someone Had Blundered." As Emil Kaczor of Detroit noted, this was from Alfred, Lord Tennyson's 1854 "The Charge of the Light Brigade," an apt allusion to the bloody beachhead at Anzio in World War II:

> "Forward, the Light Brigade!"
> Was there a man dismayed?
> Not though the soldier knew
> Some one had blundered.

In this allusion, the poet's two-worded *some one* was written in the modern style as *someone,* probably because someone hung up on the stylebook had goofed. (Theirs not to reason *that* . . .)

A nice literary, though not poetic, allusion was noted by Joel F. Studebaker of Princeton, New Jersey, in *The Times*'s headline over a sports-page story from Chicago that begins, "Mark Grace capped a three-run rally in the ninth inning with a two-out double." The head: "Grace, Under Pressure in 9th, Doubles to Cap Cubs' Rally." In *The New Yorker* magazine of November 30, 1929, Ernest Hemingway, one of the mighty minds of old, defined *guts* as "grace under pressure."

An Op-Ed page editor at *The Times* headed a piece by Ernesto F. Betancourt "Let Cuba Be Cuba"; this, as Jeffrey Page of the Passaic, New Jersey, office of the Bergen *Record* notes, "assumes that I associate the line with 'Let Reagan Be Reagan' and that I am satisfied with the secondary originality (it is from Jack Kemp, right?)."

This was a phrase popularized by then-Representative Jack F. Kemp, who disclaims coinage, in urging White House "handlers" to permit President Reagan to express his true nature. It had previously appeared in January 1982 as a theme of a United States Information Agency global broadcast directed at Soviet imperialists to "Let Poland Be Poland."

When Bhagwan Shree Rajneesh was arrested for some wrongdoing, the *Washington Post* editorialist Meg Greenfield was heard to murmur, "Let Bhagwans be Bhagwans," a play on *bygones* from Sir Francis Nethersole's 1648 "Let bygans be bygans." The usage about national character, however, was bottomed on a 1938 work by the poet Langston Hughes titled "Let America Be America Again."

Poetic allusions are not limited to headline writers, of course. In the ebb and flow of human misery, we have this literary allusion from a *New York Times* editorialist to cast doubt on Iranian denials of complicity in the murder of a translator of *The Satanic Verses,* Salman Rushdie's reputedly blasphemous novel: "Circumstantial evidence, like finding feathers in the cat's milk, can be highly persuasive."

See Henry David Thoreau's journal entry of November 11, 1854: "Some circumstantial evidence is very strong, as when you find a trout in the milk."

"The alteration is appropriate," finds Gary Muldoon of Rochester. "Thoreau's reference to fish has to do with milk that's been adulterated—not exactly one of big business's scams du jour. Only by knowing of the problems of yesteryear does one readily grasp Thoreau's reference. *The Times*'s mentioning of feathers makes the statement more accessible, conjuring images of Sylvester finally getting the jump on poor Tweety Bird."

Journalists are not alone in the poetic allusion dodge. In Arizona, before entering an airtight greenhouse called Biosphere 2 with seven other intrepid ecologists, Dr. Roy Walford, a gerontologist and survivalist, was quoted as telling the world: "Listen, there is a hell of a universe next door waiting to be born."

That was not an idle reference to nearby California or Nevada; as Arnold Henderson of Highland Park, New Jersey, points out, that is an allusion to a fictional doctor's line in the poet e.e. cummings's 1944 *1×1* (or "one times one").

You quote, without attribution, the beginning of the last stanza of "Dover Beach"—"Ah, love, let us be true to one another!"

The stanza then goes on and ends with the lines you cited.

Is this poem still read in its entirety, or are only the last lines known and quoted without really knowing the "note of sadness" the poem conveys?

Leonore S. Oberman
Forest Hills, New York

Sometimes the poet, like the headline writer, slips allusions to everyday headlines into his famous poem.

The phrase "some one had blundered" from "The Charge of the Light Brigade" came from an account of the event in The Times *of London, which served as Tennyson's inspiration for the poem.*

Edward J. Kelly
Brockport, New York

In Edmund Spenser's The Faerie Queene, *Book II, Canto xii, after overthrowing Acrasia's Bower of Bliss, Sir Guyon, the knight of Temperance, and his companion, the Palmer, come upon Acrasia's lovers. They have all been turned into beasts. With a stroke of his "vertuous staffe," the Palmer returns them to human form:*

> Yet being men they did unmanly looke,
> And stared ghastly, some for inward shame
> And some for wrath to see their captive Dame.
> But one above the rest in speciall,
> That had an hog beene late, hight Grille by name,
> Repined greatly and did him miscall,
> That had from hoggish forme him brought to naturall.

The Palmer's response to this "miscalling" is:

> . . . "The donghill kind
> Delights in filth and foule incontinence:
> Let Grill be Grill, and have his hoggish mind."

So you can see that those of us who admire Mr. Reagan and know a bit of Spenser (both of us?) cringe when we hear "Let Reagan be Reagan."

Paul G. Reeve
Houston, Texas

You didn't take "Let Poland Be Poland" back to its source. The phrase used by President Reagan in January 1982, after the imposition of martial law in Poland, comes from the title of a song by Poland's foremost political satirist, Jan Pietrzak. He wrote it in 1976, at a time of severe repression of striking workers in Radom, when leading opposition movements such as KOR (Workers' Defense Committee) were born.

Barbara Wierzbianski
New York, New York

Meg Greenfield's "Let Bhagwans be Bhagwans" was cute, but not as clever as the headline I remember in the Charlotte Observer *on the arrest of the guru by the INS: "U.S. Agent Bhagswan."*

Clif Cormier
Gainesville, Florida

Dear Bill:

I wish you had included a paragraph or two about mindless *poetic allusions, now rampant. The most recent is "sea change." Plain change no longer occurs and sea means big or sudden. It has nothing to do with the sea or Shakespeare, evidently unread or not understood. Others of the kind are: "dim religious light" for a back alley where drug dealing goes on, and "fine and private place," for any private place, the user not realizing that his allusion is to the grave.*

Jacques [Barzun]
New York, New York

Pop Goes the Marlin

President Bush's press secretary, the moon-faced Marlin Fitzwater, has brought a touch of class to the 1992 campaign. He has introduced poetic allusions to the daily press briefings.

The White House press corps, which prides itself on a sandpapered-fingertip sensitivity to political arcana, has been struck dumb by this phenomenon. Nobody who has worked his or her razor-sharp elbows into the most coveted assignment in Washington has ever started on the poetry beat.

Here is the White House closet intellectual's blast at those Democrats on the House Ways and Means Committee who have disdained the President's economic plan: "weasels going into a hole."

A member of the Poetic Allusion Watch (PAW)—Sam Abrams at the Rochester Institute of Technology—was among those who spotted Mr. Fitzwater's direct (if slightly inaccurate) allusion to "Nineteen Hundred and Nineteen," a 1928 poem by William Butler Yeats:

> We . . . planned to bring the world under a rule,
>   Who are but weasels fighting in a hole.

The subtlety and aptness of Mr. Fitzwater's slouching towards Yeats are astonishing: The poet presages Mr. Bush's New World Order in his plan to bring the disorderly weasel-nations, down in the hole-arena, under the rule of international law.

Mr. Bush and his staff are evidently planning to leap down in that weasel hole to get in the fight.

Yeats is big these days on Madison Avenue, too. Dominique F. Nahas of New York calls my attention to the decision by R. J. Reynolds to switch ad agencies, a move that caused John L. Mezzina, whose fledgling agency got the account, to say that the Camel brand "is easier for a small agency because what tends to happen in any large organization is that the falcon can't hear the falconer."

"The falcon cannot hear the falconer" is from "The Second Coming," in which Yeats refers to the wide sweeps that sometimes take the hunting bird beyond the call of the falconer. Coincidentally, it precedes a line that reflects a concern in the White House:

> The best lack all conviction, while the worst
>   Are full of passionate intensity.

> *I, the poet W. B.*
> *Will not abid the center e.*

> Daniel Patrick Moynihan
> Senator, New York
> United States Senate
> Washington, D.C.

Policy Wonkmanship

Meg Greenfield of *Newsweek* called the two men being nominated by the Democratic party "tough, ambitious, leadership-minded *policy wonks.*" Jonathan Alter, in the same publication, quoted an economist who believes that "barn burners and hell raisers don't get very much accomplished," adding, "If Clinton's elected, the country will finally learn whether the *policy wonks* can do any better."

Sidney Blumenthal of *The New Republic* was the first to use the phrase in print, just before the 1984 election, deriding Walter Mondale's "thralldom to the *policy wonks* and wise men of the Washington establishment." A year later, the same magazine quoted Fred Branfman, of the Center for a New Democracy, as saying about Senator Gary Hart: "You have to be credible to the voters. You can't just be a *policy wonk.*"

A *policy wonk* is a too-studious student of public affairs, often a legislative aide heavy on position papers and light on practical experience. Both Governor Clinton and Senator Gore have been known to delight in the minutiae of program development, earning them the dubious honor of the label.

A *wonk,* as old salts know, was nautical slang for a wet-behind-the-ears cadet. It may have been influenced by the Chinese *huang gou,* "yellow dog," applied to animals that scavenge or work slavishly.

In 1962, *Sports Illustrated* wrote, "A *wonk,* sometimes called a 'turkey' or a 'lunch,' roughly corresponds to the 'meatball' of a decade ago." The *Oxford English Dictionary* supplement, to which I have just turned, also notes a 1980 usage: "At Harvard the excessively studious student is derided as a 'wonk,' which Amy Berman, Harvard '79, fancifully suggests may be 'know' spelled backward. (In British slang, 'wonky' means 'unsteady.')"

Wait a minute; that citation is from this column. Here I am citing them on British slang as they cited me on American slang and I cited British slang. That's the convoluted, nose-inside-the-books way of lexical *wonks.*

The Prep-Droppers

"When did *in* go out?" wonders Mark Burde of St. Louis. He spotted a line in an unusually prescient foreign-affairs column ridiculing the simple-minded view that once Saddam Hussein saw we were serious, "he will cave." Not *cave in;* just *cave.*

Similarly, a CNN report warned that "troops may be pulled"; not *pulled out,* just *pulled.*

The pro-prep Mr. Burde adds: "I read a piece by a junior reporter in which he wrote that 'the press didn't *show*,' meaning it didn't *show up*. Prepositions are disappearing. Do you droppers realize this? Should we noticers care?"

Another charter member of the Gotcha! Gang, Preppy Unit, is Ernest Dzendolet of Amherst, Massachusetts. He spotted the clipping of the preposition *off* in my fulmination about calling Saddam "Mr." Hussein, as in "Behind the scenes, I fought using the honorific," and asks, "Is *honorific* a special weapon, resembling an ax?" O.K.; it might have been less ambiguous to write, "I fought off using the honorific."

Why is *in* out, *up* down, and *off* not on? (Although these words are used adverbially—to modify a verb—I see them primarily as prepositions.) I turned to Allan Metcalf of the American Dialect Society, who offers a soothing: "A purist never lacks something to complain about. *Show up* can be—has been—stigmatized as a colloquialism, at least for the better part of this century. But take away the supposedly unnecessary *up* and just say *They showed*, and you promptly have 'a sad casualism,' in the 1965 words of *The New York Times*'s Theodore Bernstein."

After consulting a secret usage adviser (my thumb, fount of much practical wisdom), I have decided to go with the purists who require *up* after *show* when the meaning is "appear." The preposition pins down the meaning; you would not say *he fouled* when you meant *he fouled up*. When we say *she showed* (I use the feminine here, as many jurists do, to assert anti-sexist correctness), we may mean *she showed up*, but we may also mean "she finished third in the race."

This keep-*up* decision must be made case by case. *Cave*, for example, like *fold*, needs no preposition once we extend the metaphor beyond the pressure of soil on the hole it surrounds. *He caved*, without the following *in*, meaning "he collapsed" or "the coward abandoned the rampart," is not likely to be taken to mean "he entered the cave and became a hermit." Nor does *fold* without its *up* invite ambiguity; indeed, the poker player who tossed in his cards with "I fold *up*" would be taken by his companions to be an undercover federal agent who has not fully learned the gambling patois, and it's Big Julie-bar-the-door.

The guide (and if you want to get prescriptive, the rule) is: When the preposition narrows the meaning and thereby avoids confusion, use it (as in *pulled out*); when the preposition is a useless appendage, clip it. I'll show up, but I'm not caving.

Dear Bill:
I hope you are aware of the controversy as to whether the words that you blithely refer to as prepositions are in fact prepositions. If you follow the tradition that reflects the etymology of the word and restrict the application of

"preposition" to words that have objects, then the in *of* He caved in *isn't a preposition, since it doesn't have an object. Likewise the* off *in the sentence that you chose not to write,* I fought off *using the honorific: there using the honorific is the object not of* off *but either of* fought *or of* fought off, *though it is the object of* against *in another sentence that you might have just not thought of writing, rather than choosing not to write:* I fought against *using the honorific. Note the differences between* fight off X *and* fight against X *that confirm that* against X *is a prepositional phrase while* off X *is not even a syntactic unit, let alone a prepositional phrase:*

Against whom did he fight? (but not: *Off whom did he fight?)

He fought both against a tax increase and against increased military spending. (but not: *They fought both off the cavalry and off the archers.)

It was against the Saracens that he fought. (but not: *It was off the attackers that he fought.)

He fought only against the Saracens. (but not: *He fought only off the Saracens.)

He fought the attackers off. (but not: *He fought the attackers against.)

(For an explanation of why these differences show what I say they do, see pp. 64–6 of my The Syntactic Phenomena of English, *which I trust is on a shelf in your office where it is in easy reach.) The* off *of* fight off *is what is occasionally called a "particle," and the above sentences illustrate a number of respects in which "particles" in English differ systematically from what a more traditional user of the term would call a preposition (or at least, what he would feel happy calling a preposition after his attention had been drawn to the facts that I've just drawn your attention to; the term "preposition," like most grammatical terms, has in fact been used with remarkable abandon by grammarians, who commonly forget their definitions once they have discharged their obligation to provide definitions).*

The controversy as to whether the off *of* fight off *might nonetheless appropriately be called a "preposition" relates to the proposal that prepositions might, like verbs, differ from one another with regard to whether they take an object, i.e., that "particles" might be appropriately regarded as "intransitive prepositions" while what are traditionally classed as prepositions would be "transitive prepositions." This proposal (found in Otto Jespersen's* The Philosophy of Grammar, *the most important linguistics book that is currently out of print) involves ignoring the etymology of the word "preposition" (not a bad idea, when you consider how ill-conceived and unsystematic much grammatical terminology is) and arguing that "particles" and the traditional "prepositions" make up a single part of speech and differ from each other in the way that transitive and intransitive verbs differ from one another (or transitive and intransitive adjectives for that matter—it is reasonable e.g. to speak of intransitive* happy *and* transitive glad, *since you can be just plain happy but not just plain glad: you can only be glad of or glad about something). This in fact makes considerable sense; for example, many "particles" are intransitive counterparts of prepositions:* He jumped over *vs.* He jumped over the fence, *and* He wiped the stains off *vs.* He wiped the stains off *(of)* the table.

One important thing bothers me about your guide/rule for using or omitting particles: to use it, you have to decide whether the version with the particle has a more specific meaning than the version without it, and very few of your readers have trained their semantic sensibilities enough that they are competent to make such a decision. You may recall some of our earlier correspondence in which I pointed out subtle but real contributions that up *and* out *made to various sentences (*check out *vs. just plain* check, *for example), and your readers can hardly be expected to see that the particle makes a difference in all the cases in which it does.*

Jim [James D. McCawley]
Department of Linguistics
University of Chicago
Chicago, Illinois

According to traditional grammatical definitions, your article should perhaps have been called "The Adverb-Droppers," since "an adverb is a word that modifies a verb, an adjective, or another adverb." But what we really need in English is a special grammatical term for the adverbs that function like what are called "separable prefixes" in German verbs. English has exactly the same thing, except that they are not separable *but* separate, *and therefore cannot really be called prefixes:* think up, think out, think over, think through, *like the German* ausdenken, durchdenken, nachdenken, *etc. I have never seen an English grammar that gave adequate treatment to this feature of our language, which so greatly enriches its expressiveness. I suspect the reason is that we derived our grammatical categories from Latin and therefore failed to recognize that we achieve the same enrichment of our vocabulary through the combination of verb plus adverb that all the Latin languages—and indeed, all the other European languages I am familiar with—achieve through verbal prefixation: for example,* describe, inscribe, prescribe, proscribe, subscribe—*all derived from the Latin* scribere. *Our English system can even express the kind of perfectivity that is a feature of the Slavic languages, where practically all verbs exist in pairs, one imperfective and the other perfective. When we think up a new plan, think through all its implications, work up an appetite, or work out a solution, we add the meaning of perfectivity, or completion, to the basic meaning of* think *or* work, *and are doing just what the Russians, Poles, and other Slavs regularly do with their verbs.*

The misguided writers you cited who pulled, fought, fouled, showed, folded, *and* caved *are impoverishing our marvelous English language. They should be* called forth, dressed down, *and if necessary* driven out *into illiterate darkness until they have* thought through *the implications of their error and* turned back *to a proper respect for our mother tongue.*

William Edgerton
Professor Emeritus of Slavic
   Languages and Literatures
Indiana University
Bloomington, Indiana

I think your "prepositions" are better viewed as particles, part of a verb-particle combination which forms a two-word verbal idiom. (See my The Verb-Particle Combination in English, *Academic Press, 1976, for more details than anyone would ever want to know.)*

Although the lineage of forms like in, out, on, off, *and* up *in two-word verbs may be prepositional, it is more often adverbial, with many coming from German separable suffixes. If they were prepositions, they could be expected to take objects and permit a preceding manner adverbial (??cave quickly in). They don't. Moreover, when the verb-particle combination has a direct object, the particle may usually move:* talk up the point/talk the point up. *Prepositions don't do this.*

Some of these particles systematically affect the meaning of the verb (e.g., burn/burn up; fence/fence in*), and these can often be omitted. But the majority do not permit this (e.g., the* out *of* figure out *and the* up *of* think up *must remain).*

Had you used the term particle *rather than* preposition, *you could have entitled the piece "A Particle of Difference."*

Bruce Fraser
Scituate, Massachusetts

What you call a preposition in your article is, strictly speaking, not a preposition, but a separated suffix or, if you will, a verbal adjunct. It is a characteristic of Indo-European languages that the lexicon of verbs is expanded, enriched and made more precise by prefixing what were originally prepositions to almost all native verbs, i.e., to the language in question.

In suffering this treatment, the prepositions traded status and became part of the meaning of the verb. They ceased to be prepositions. It is this phenomenon that generated the quaint rule: "Never end a sentence with a preposition." A preposition by definition is pre *placed, i.e., in front of a noun phrase. The distinction between pre-positioning and pre-fixing is not entirely clear cut, hence the inclination to designate the* down *in the locution "He fell down" as a preposition when in actuality it is historically a prefix that has become a separated suffix in usage.*

The Germanic languages had a tendency to separate some verbal prefixes when the verb was conjugated. German still does, e.g., auf*fallen, literally to fall* upon*; Er fällt auf. English has gone all the way and kept the prefixes as separated suffixes. This phenomenon is clouded in English by the fact that we have borrowed liberally from Latin/French, e.g.,* surprise. *This hides the prefix identity of verbal adjuncts. In the language of the linguists the free morpheme prepositions became bound to verbs both literally and connotatively and would never be called prepositions in Latin or Russian. In the German, they are sometimes bound and sometimes separated and in English they remain free. Thus, the* out *in the sentence "She looks* out *for the children" is not a preposition in the same sense that* out *is a preposition in "She looks* out *the window." The* look *in "look out for" is not the same lexical item as the* look *in "look out the window." The true preposition in "look out for" is* for. For, *by the way, is valenced to the verb, because* look out *cannot take an object without* for.

Thus, it is not prepositions that we are dropping, but adjuncts. In made a verb out *of* cave *and* out *made the verb to pull more precise in that it limited its action to the act of extracting, which is Latin for pulling* out. *We pull teeth and corks without* out *because we know what's going on. In the contexts cited in your column, the meaning of* cave *and* pull *were quite clear without the respective adjuncts.*

James A. Garvey
Moraga, California

By now you have certainly heard from many women and a few men that there is at least one other meaning to "She showed." My wife mentioned it.

"She shows" commonly refers to a woman in about her fifth month of pregnancy. (More often: "Does she show yet?" Or sometimes, "She showed quite early.")

In the sixth month, it's no longer necessary to wonder if she shows. She shows indeed.

Don Kent
Hurley, New York

It is unclear from the context but my guess is that you used the word jurist *as a synonym for the word* judge. *This usage has always annoyed me. A jurist is a scholar of the law. A law professor or a practicing lawyer may be a jurist and a judge may not be (and based on my unhappy experience most often is not) one.*

The distinction between a judge and a jurist is one that I believe should be preserved though I am afraid it is being lost to those who consider jurist *to be a fancy or upscale way to say* judge.

> *Leonard Sims*
> *New York, New York*

Quick, Henry, the Fix

"*Quick fix* still likely to tempt Bush, Congress," headlined the *Washington Times*, despite the advice of sobersided pundits that went, "Don't just do something, stand there."

Lawrence A. Kudlow, chief economist of Bear, Stearns & Company, argued that "the wrong tax cut is a temporary *quick fix* that puts money into people's pockets."

In a diplomatic context, Secretary of State James A. Baker 3d told Russians that "there are not *quick fixes* and there are no simple solutions."

And President Bush, commenting on indictments filed against Libyan terrorists, pointed out that the charges were not "some quick hit, *quick fix* on trying to find the answer."

Perhaps subconsciously, the President stumbled on the derivation of the phrase being used to decry a panacea for cure-alls. A *hit*, now widely used as slang for "assassination," has also been used since 1949 to describe the sensation of instant satisfaction experienced by the narcotics user; in *The Man with the Golden Arm*, Nelson Algren wrote about the way an injection "hit the heart like a runaway locomotive, it hit like a falling wall." Long before that, a shot of dope was called a *fix-up*, a compound first used in 1867 by the British historian William Hepworth Dixon, who wrote in his book *New America* about an "eye-opener, fix-ups, or any other Yankee deception in the shape of liquor." To get a *fix-up* changed to *get fixed* in the 1930's, and reverted to a shortened noun—to get a *fix*—a generation later.

The first use of *quick fix* has not been located, but in the mid-1970's *Newsweek* began applying the drug term to tax cuts. Soon it lost its drug sense; in 1986, the Canadian Labor Congress denounced drug testing as "a *quick-fix* solution," apparently unaware of the aptness of its choice of words.

The sense of *fix* in *quick fix* meaning "cure-all that cures nothing" is in competition with the slang sense of the verb *fix* as "to influence the outcome corruptly," as in *the race was fixed*, or in noun form, *the fix is in*. Curious, how

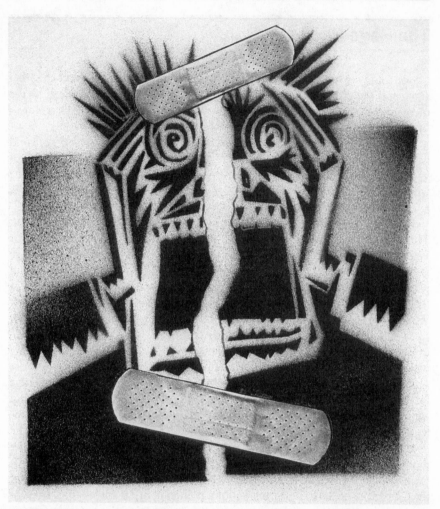

the standard verb *fix,* meaning "set, fasten, make firm or permanent," has been so often associated with corruption (*Mr. Fix-it* is an influence-peddler, and *price fixers* go to jail). The most voguish sense of *quick fix* is "any slapped-together solution doomed to failure." Word junkies pushing narco-derivations are freaked out because it's hard to get a quick fix on why.

Your suggestion that "fix" has come to mean "no-fix-at-all" is really very scary. In this case the old adage "If it ain't broke, don't fix it" must be retired in favor of something like "Don't worry if it ain't broke, fix it anyway."

Carl J. Turkstra
Hamilton, Ontario, Canada

The Rage Rage

"I don't know what to do about the depression and the inflation and the Russians and the crime in the street," the incendiary speaker announced to the media populace. "All I know is that first you've got to get mad. You've got to say, 'I'm a human being, goddamn it! My life has value!' "

This populist instigator looked the viewers straight in the television eye and gave them their marching orders: "So I want you to get up now. I want all of you to get up out of your chairs. I want you to get up right now and go to the window, open it and stick your head out and yell, '*I'm as mad as hell, and I'm not going to take this anymore!*' "

That speech was not from Jerry Brown or Pat Buchanan or Ross Perot. Those were the words of screenwriter Paddy Chayefsky on the lips of actor Peter Finch playing a news anchor in the 1976 movie *Network*. The message is being redelivered in this year's campaign to "take America back" (from plundering politicians, presumably), and to return power to the "owners" of the country. Curiously, the message is primarily associated not with network broadcasters but with local radio talk-show hosts who receive not calls but *call-ins*, usually from irate citizens eager to sound off at the *Beltway crowd*, formerly the *Establishment* or *power structure*. The adjectival phrase being widely used to describe these disaffected voters is *mad-as-hell*.

Meg Greenfield of *Newsweek* described what she termed "the current rage for *rage*" as an "explosive, antigovernment feeling, fueled by some real and some imagined evidence of arrogance and privilege on the part of the country's so-called public servants." Another polemicist wrote that "*rage* is all the rage."

Whence *rage*? It's from the Latin *rabere*, "to be *mad*," meaning "insane"; the root also led to the viral disease *rabies*, and its adjective *rabid*. But it took the Chayefsky of his day, writing about a politician of an ancient day, to popularize an early sense of the noun *rage*. Shakespeare's volatile Coriolanus, a military man seeking political power, uses the word in this comment to his mother, Volumnia:

> Desire not
> T'allay my rages and revenges with
> Your colder reasons.

That is the sense of the noun today: "a fit of wrath, usually violent; uncontrolled anger." It is married to the verb *to fly;* one never *enters, moves into, comes into* a rage; one sometimes *goes into* but usually *flies into* a rage.

But here is where the rage-purveyors and rage-knockers go wrong: A *rage* is not an *outrage*.

If you are *enraged,* you are incensed—removed from your good senses—

and are consumed by anger, which causes you to be red-faced and sputtering. But if you are *outraged,* you have not left your senses; on the contrary, you are morally offended, distressed by some sin or transgression of justice. The Latin *dignus,* which means "worthy" and is the root of *dignity,* leads as well to *indignant,* and to be *outraged* is to be "righteously indignant."

In the synonymy of the sorehead, *anger,* rooted in the Old Norse for "grief," is the general term; *wrath* carries a connotation of vengeance; *ire* is intellectual anger, leading to *irate* and, according to some authorities, possibly related to *Ireland* (which would explain "get your Irish up"). *Fury* is interchangeable with *rage,* meaning "uncontrolled, destructive anger"; the Furies, in Greek mythology, were the avenging spirits bringing plagues and torment to evildoers.

Rage, as a noun, has acquired a special meaning: "fashion," as in *all the rage,* perhaps derived from the metaphor of a person foaming at the mouth at the high cost of *haute couture.* As a verb, it gained a connotation of courage in Dylan Thomas's poem urging his father not to yield to death:

> Do not go gentle into that good night, . . .
> Rage, rage against the dying of the light.

But the central sense of the word, as both noun and verb, is that of a person flipping his lid. And who is the mad-as-hell voter's favorite candidate? *Uncommitted* is the formal primary word, but the phrase taking outraged-politics by storm is *none of the above.* This term entered the language in the 1920's, along with *all of the above,* as part of the language of the multiple-choice test. (Only the most smug or easily pleased citizen would vote for *all of the above.*)

The preposition *above,* so often rhymed with *love,* has been used elliptically as a quasi-adjective and noun for two centuries. The British historian William Russell, in his *View of Society* in 1779, wrote, "Just as I was concluding *the above,* I received yours." It was an improvement over *the foregoing,* which gives me fits.

As at least half a million letters have probably already advised, your comment on outrage(d) *is nothing short of outrageous.*

Outrage is not formed from out + rage: *it comes from French* outr(er), *"to push beyond bounds," from* outre, *"beyond," which is ultimately from Latin* ultra *and can be seen as a past participle in the common loan-word* outré + -age, *the common noun-forming suffix that occurs in* voyage, courage, triage *[tri(er) 'to sort' + -age].*

Laurence Urdang
Old Lyme, Connecticut

"Incensed," like all those related words—incense, incendiary and all the rest of them—has nothing to do with the senses, but rather, with fire. The O.E.D. *says that current usage, meaning to become enraged, dates from 1494. Sensational, no?*

Karen Wilkin
New York, New York

Your synonymy for "rage" conspicuously excludes "tantrum" [origin un-known], a fit of anger, i.e., relatively short, as the dictionary puts it. It best de-scribes not only the current mood but is a frequent reaction in American politics; it differs from the more durable fanaticism with which Europeans express their rages, though Buchanan and his ilk are pretty good copies. A slow or low-voltage tantrum is, of course, a kvetch *(the message and the messenger).*

Second, "ire" comes from Latin "ira" (anger), as in dies irae *(Day of Wrath) at the beginning of the mass. I would be curious by what convoluted philological* pilpul *"ire" could be related to Ireland. Not only was it called Hi-bernia in Roman times, but "getting your Irish up" is strictly an American ex-pression. I certainly never heard it when I lived in England.*

John E. Ullmann
Hempstead, New York

The Rap on Hip-Hop

"But the Czar Never Knew About Hip-Hop" was the headline in a recent *U.S. News & World Report.* The article was about the Siberian Cadets Corps in Novosibirsk, Russia, where students are learning the real history of Russia along with the cultural activities associated with that country before the rise of Communism.

"We are learning the mazurka, polonaise, waltz," says fifteen-year-old Yevgeny Kondratiev, undoubtedly a good dancer, possibly an avid cyclist. "Later, they promise to teach us the *hip-hop.*"

That opens some linguistic doors. First, to get hip on *hip-hop:* In the mid-70's, Love Bug Starsky and D. J. Hollywood and other pioneering rappers were developing a syncopation suited for improvisation. "[Hollywood] paced himself with a repeating refrain," wrote Robert Palmer in *The New York Times,* often "a variation on the nonsense formula 'hip, hop, hip-hip-de-hop.' " Rapping disc jockeys "created what were basically new musical accompaniments out of bits and pieces of funk hits."

Funk? I vaguely recall Louis Armstrong's singing "The Funkie Butt Boogie." Weren't smelly cigars called "funky butts"? "There was *funk* before there was *hip-hop,*" explains Jim Steinblatt of Ascap. "*Funk* is a variety of *soul,* from the James Brown school of soul. *Hip-hop* is an outgrowth of soul, yet it's very much related to *rap.* It's all connected, part of the R & B [rhythm and blues] tradition, which is related to gospel, country blues and jazz."

Hippity-hop has for centuries been a reduplication describing the motion of a rabbit. In its shortened form, *hip hop* (without a hyphen) first appeared in *The Rehearsal,* a 1671 play by George Villiers: "To go off hip hop, hip hop, upon this occasion."

Hip-hop is itself a prime example of a third-order reduplication. (First-order simply doubles a syllable, as in "boo-boo" and "bye-bye," and second-order changes the opening consonant sound, as in "bow-wow" and "mumbo jumbo"; third-order changes the vowel sounds, as in "flip-flop," "tip-top" and our subject today, *hip-hop.*)

A rabbit hops along, or bops along, sometimes rhythmically, often jerkily; the reduplication describing it has been given a new twist, or metaphoric extension, by musicians. They have taken over the word *rap* the same way.

Rap began in the fourteenth century as an echoic noun, imitating the sound of a sharp blow. Early American English applied *rap* to a sharp rebuke, perhaps also the source of the 1903 sense of a criminal charge, along with the hope of "beating the rap."

As a verb, *rap* has long meant "to express orally." The poet Sir Thomas Wyatt wrote in 1541, "I am wont sometime to rap out on oath in an earnest talk." British prison slang used *rap* for "to say" as early as 1879, and Damon Runyon may have picked up that *rap* to use in a 1929 story: "I wish Moosh a hello, and he never raps to me but only bows, and takes my hat."

According to one theory, this talking *rap* came from British English into the American language, perhaps transferred through Caribbean English; another theory suggests that *rap* is a clipped alteration of *repartee,* a 1645 noun from French for "retort."

However *rap* entered American usage, it was widely adopted in black English by the 1960's. Eldridge Cleaver wrote in a 1965 letter, "In point of fact he is funny and very glib, and I dig rapping with him." Clarence Major, in his 1970 *Dictionary of Afro-American Slang,* defined *rap* as both verb and noun: "to hold conversation; a long, impressive monologue." Within a decade, the noun was used attributively in *rap music,* labeling the rhythmic rhyming lines set to an insistent beat.

Covering this beat is Fred Brathwaite, known as Fab 5 Freddy, who hosts the weekly television show *Yo! MTV Raps.* This rapper-turned-lexicographer has collected hip-hop slang in *Fresh Fly Flavor* (Longmeadow Press), an alliterative title that joins three favorable terms.

Fresh, a shortened form of *fresh out of the pack,* is a compliment that's taken even higher by *fly,* a clipping of the 1960's slang *superfly* for "the brightest or flashiest." The noun *flavor* has a positive sense of "something good," but it also takes a neutral meaning of "the tone or vibe of a person, place or situation."

As the best baddies know, *bad* and *dope* have turned around into expressions of praise. Mr. Brathwaite explains the positive sense for a drug term like *dope:* "A key ingredient in ultra urban, contemporary counter-youth-culture is to flirt with what's wrong, take the negative vibe and power, and turn it all the way around to make it serve a new purpose, yet with the shock value still intact."

Like the hare's bounce in *hip-hop,* rap terms stress action or excitement. To start doing or performing something is to *kick it;* if it's done well, it's *slammin'* (a 40's bass player was Slam Stewart), which is also the term for playing loudly (the rhyming *jammin',* also eliding its *g* ending, means "partying" or "making good music"). *Pump it up* turns up that volume even higher.

The rap artist likes to clip words. *Dis* uses the first part of *disrespect* and means "to put down or show disrespect." Other terms, though, are clipped to their final syllable: *hood* for "neighborhood" and *tude* for "attitude," particularly a bad or negative disposition.

Rhyme and redundancy also have their place in hip-hop slang. In Tuesday's election, every candidate should have been *in it to win it,* a phrase using internal rhyme to express "trying your best." Deliberate redundancy rears its head in *quick, fast and in a hurry,* infuriating the Squad Squad.

Boxers on the losing end of a bout may be *down* and *out,* but those terms take other senses in this lexicon. *I'm down* means "I'm ready" (*get down* is "to become culturally adjusted"), and *I'm out* means "I'm leaving," probably a shortening of "I'm outta here." (*I'm Outtie 5000* is a more insistent term for departure, playing on the name of the Audi 5000 automobile.) Leaving quick, fast and in a hurry is a *breakout,* which has a curious parallel to the term used by arms-control negotiators for the sudden upsetting of a strategic balance.

Before I'm Outtie 5000, let me return to that *U.S. News* headline: "But the Czar Never Knew About Hip-Hop." That's bottomed on a phrase that reverberates through political history: *if the Czar only knew.*

"One of the oldest traditions in this nation's history," Murray Kempton wrote in a column from Russia in 1988, "is the voice of some victim of an administrative injustice, vast or little, saying that such things could not be 'if the Czar only knew.' "

This aposiopesis—leaving the remainder of the thought understood after "If the Czar only knew . . ."—is the classic way for a subject to excuse the inefficiency or barbarism of the highest authority. Many people prefer not to assign blame to the person at the top; thus the Czar, or President, or ruler can hip-hop away from responsibility.

Reach, Crescendo

"Demands to Fix U.S. Health Care Reach a Crescendo" was a recent *New York Times* subhead, under a teasing headline, "Say Ouch."

"Ouch, indeed!" retorts John Bloomfield of New York, who is coming to the end of his patience. "Can't you do anything about the flagrant and widespread misuse of the word *crescendo*? I have seen it used to mean 'climax' or 'critical point' in all sorts of respected publications."

That's because the climactic sense of *crescendo* has entered the GUZ—the Gray Usage Zone—somewhere between correct and incorrect, neither safely precise nor readily correctable.

Every musician knows that *crescendo,* Italian for "growing," means "increasing in loudness." As the metaphor extended, nonmusicians used it to mean "growing in volume, intensity, frequency or force." At the end of the *crescendo* comes the *climax,* when the guy with the cymbals gets the nod from the conductor and crashes them together, or when the steamy novelist suggesting the sex act starts a new paragraph with "Afterward," or when the outcry from hospital patients who want one more test reaches such a political pitch that legislators pop with a new law.

The essence of the word's meaning, as its etymology suggests, is the process of "increasing" and not the conclusion of increase—the balloon's stretching, not its pop. Why, then, are so many literate people using *crescendo* when they mean *apex, apogee, peak, pinnacle, zenith* or *culmination*?

Because they're not stopping to think, that's why. F. Scott Fitzgerald and William Faulkner led the way fifty years ago, and their sloppy assumption that the buildup also meant the climax has been adopted by lesser writers, including those responsible for our headlines. As a result, a new sense of *crescendo* has entered some dictionaries: Merriam-Webster admits "the peak of a gradual increase," while American Heritage resolutely holds the line with "gradually increasing."

With usage so obviously in flux, what's a poor language maven to do?

The answer is rooted in the preference for precision, in the reluctance to go along with the burgeoning of error, in the hope that the wall has not yet been finally breached, in the grim determination to try to do one's bit for clarity—and, in the face of fuzziness, despite the choking inexorability of permissiveness—to rise up, thrusting, twisting, to defy the momentum of mistakery, to clamber atop the ramparts of usage, straining ever upward, and to wholeheartedly, gloriously TAKE A STAND!

Afterward, we can discuss *diminuendo.*

Dear Bill:

Apropos of crescendo, *I think there is a psychological excuse for the mistake your correspondent deplores.* Climax *does not mean "the top" either; it means* ladder. *So there seems to be a hunch that once things start going up, the top will soon be reached. That is certainly assured with* crescendo: *when the musician sees the long "hairpin" pointing to the left, he knows that he is soon going to bang away full tilt or blow his lungs out—not that I want* crescendo *to become a needless synonym of* climax.

> Jacques [Barzun]
> New York, New York

If crescendo *is on its way to becoming* climax, *it is merely following* climax's *lead. As the attachment from F. Kinchin Smith and T. W. Melluish's text shows,* climax, *in classical Greek, was "originally 'a ladder,' later 'a gradual ascent to a climax'"* (Teach Yourself Greek. *U.K.: Hodder and Stoughton, 1968*).

> Frank Salvidio
> English Department
> Westfield State College
> Westfield, Massachusetts

The Retronymbles

An elite detachment of the Lexicographic Irregulars focuses on retronyms. These lexical units are created to revivify old nouns when those nouns, which used to be able to stand by themselves, have become too closely associated with other adjectives that describe a modern use.

For example, a *ball game* was something we all would be taken out to; then *night games* dominated the baseball world, to the point that games played in the daytime have to be called *day games.* Same with *wristwatch,* when *digital watch* required the coinage of *analog watch,* and an *electric guitar* required retronaming a plain old nonelectric *guitar* an *acoustic guitar.*

When the *push-button phone* was introduced, the *telephone* as we knew it became the *rotary phone,* but that was only the beginning; I was wondering what the retronym for *telephone* would be. The political analyst Michael Barone faxes in the latest retronym: a *talk phone.* You used to have a *telephone;* then you got a *fax phone;* now you need to call the phone you don't use for the fax machine your *talk phone.*

Retronymmetry is always brought to you in *real time.*

What bothers my husband the most is having to order a "gin martini."

> Gerry Muir
> (Mrs. Edward A. Muir)
> Larchmont, New York

Retronym Watch

The story is told of a modern mother laying a guilt trip on her grown-up son: "You never call, you never write, you never fax. . . ."

If he sends her a fax in response, we have a name for what she receives: *fax mail.* And if he leaves a message on her answering machine, that is becoming known as *voice mail.* But what of the stuff that comes in a paper envelope along with the greeting cards, bills, catalogues, charity solicitations and junk mail?

We can no longer call that plain *mail.* "Recently I received a fax message," writes Gary Muldoon of Rochester, "with the words '*land mail* to follow.' Mail is now *land mail.*" But that locution, evoking the days of the Pony Express, won't fly; so much domestic mail is sent by air that we no longer specify *airmail,* and *land mail* would be a misnomer.

This question has also puzzled John W. Nason of Jericho, Long Island: "*Mail* used to be what the postman (now letter carrier) deposited in your mailbox. Now that there's *voice mail* and *E-mail,* I wonder what all those bills and other stuff that come through the U.S. Postal Service will be called in the future. *Real mail?*"

Nope—*real mail* doesn't eat quiche. *Post* is a possibility, from the Italian *posta,* "a station along the way," from its Latin root, meaning "place"; it came to mean a series of places in a system of communication. As a verb, it gained a meaning of "to send," as in Hamlet's condemnation of Queen Gertrude for her willingness "to post with such dexterity to incestuous sheets" (don't fax that to your mother). *The post* is now British usage for "the mail," and might serve Americans well to signify old-fashioned mail.

But it lacks the quality of a retronym. We have two-word names now for many things that have been overtaken by events. The classic was *acoustic guitar,* which replaced *guitar* when the *electric guitar* came along; this change quickly led to *analog watch,* which showed its face when the *digital watch* threatened its existence. Recently, with the introduction of the *laser printer,* the plain old printer that used to stand next to your creaky old 286 computer became an *impact printer.* Now that fancy restaurants are advertising *free-range chicken,* I don't know how to order the other kind. *Domesticated chicken?*

The idea of a retronym is to downdate: to modify a familiar term in a way that calls attention to its not being the updated version. As Andrew Pollack wrote in *The New York Times* a few years ago, "Voice mail users now talk about two kinds of telephone communications—voice mail, which is communicating by message, and 'real-time' communications, once known as conversation, in which both parties are on the line at the same time." To use retronyms in a sentence: "The *female nurse* went to a *day game* and ordered *health food.*" (Don't look up *downdate:* I can't wait for the dictionaries.)

In some of these retronyms, the modifier mocks the noun: Tom Pribek of the University of Wisconsin at La Crosse notes the redundancy in *religious holiday* and *handwritten manuscript.*

Back to the handwritten, or hand-typed, or impact-printed mail. The emergent idea plays on the traditional contrast between *hard* and *soft.* In politics, *hard-liner* led to *soft-liner;* in computer lingo, *hardware* spawned *software;* contrariwise, the old *hard money,* meaning "specie" or "an anti-inflationary policy," led to the new *soft money,* meaning "contributions not counted against a candidate's limits in a campaign." In newsrooms, *hard copy* was printed out and available to be held in the hand as if to be read, while the newscaster read the *soft copy* on the prompter screen.

The solution: *voice mail* and its accompanying *voicephone number* to print on your business cards; *fax mail* (two words destined to become one) and its companion *fax number,* and the unreal-time communication that enlivens and enriches this column, *hard mail.*

You say post *has gained a meaning of "to send," as in Hamlet's condemnation of Queen Gertrude for her willingness "to post with such dexterity to incestuous sheets."*

You are clearly no horseman. Webster defines the verb post: *"To rise and sink in the saddle, in accordance with the motion of the horse, especially in trotting."*

Shakespeare, master of metaphor, had something more graphic in mind than just sending Gertrude to the sheets. The emphasis, Mr. Safire, is on dexterity. Get it?

> *Nardi Reeder Campion*
> *Hanover, New Hampshire*

The Whining Snail

In the fax age, what do you call the stuff the postal carrier (formerly postman or mailman) delivers? In a recent thumbsucker on this subject, I suggested *post* or *hard mail.*

It has taken a while to get here, but a barrage of letters in envelopes has informed me that a coinage has long been in use among hackers (a word that applies to all computer addicts, not just mischievous or larcenous ones).

"Communication with donors and researchers," writes Brian Wallace of the Computer Museum in Boston, "increasingly takes the form of electronic mail and faxes (now often transmitted directly from computer to computer). Mailed confirmation documents are invariably and disparagingly referred to as *snail mail.*"

The snail, for a thousand years a symbol of slow movement, was immortalized in simile by Shakespeare in his description of "the whining schoolboy" in one of man's seven stages, "creeping like snail unwillingly to school." The widespread usage of the sluggish mollusk in computer lingo is probably derived from *U.S. Mail,* the former name of the Postal Service, which quickly went from *smail* to *snail.*

The man from the Computer Museum (presumably where they preserve ancient 286's of the no-megahertz era) asks: "How does one spell the past tense of the verb *modem*? I would substitute it for my parenthetical 'transmitted' if I could only decide between *modemed* and *modemmed.*"

In the computer world, nouns like *modem* and *fax* become verbs in a nanosecond (which is one billionth of a second, a description of instantaneity almost as short as a *New York minute*). A *modem,* according to *Webster's New World Dictionary of Computer Terms* (fourth edition in paperback for a buyer-unfriendly $8.95), is an "acronym for *mo*dulator-*dem*odulator, a device that translates digital pulses from a computer into analog signals for telephone transmission, and analog signals from the telephone into digital pulses the computer can understand." Rather than use all the keystrokes it takes to write "send it by modem," the hacker writes "modem it."

It's nice that they turn to the old ink-stained wretch, with his quill pen poised, for spelling decisions that are not yet in their spell-checking programs. Here's the trick: When adding *-ed* to a verb, double the last letter when the accent is on the last syllable, as in *occur/occurred;* contrariwise, leave the last letter single when the accent is on the first syllable, as in *cancel/canceled.* On that analogy, and presuming *modem* to be pronounced "MO-dem," the past tense should be spelled *modemed.*

Objections to this decree will be entertained, but not if faxed and certainly not if fax-modemed. I prefer *snail mail.*

As a maven's maven, let me quote you the rule about doubling final consonants which my teacher, Mr. Allis, taught me in grade 6-B, at P.S. 184, Manhattan, in the Spring of 1922:

"Monosyllables, and polysyllables accented on the final syllable, ending in a

single consonant, preceded by a single vowel, double the final consonant when adding a suffix beginning with a vowel."

  Otherwise not.

Arthur J. Morgan
New York, New York

May I enter a mild demurrer to modemed? *The way I and my acquaintances pronounce* modem *is specifically "MO-dem," with a secondary accent on the second syllable, not "MOWED-'m," with a throwaway second syllable using a schwa vowel sound. Accordingly, if I could stomach the verbification of* modem *at all, I would prefer* modemmed *to* modemed, *on the underlying principle that the final construction should look most like the way it would be pronounced in real life. In support of my preference, I suggest your consideration of what I perceive to be the widely accepted precedent of* formatted *in preference to* formated—*a rather direct parallel. The conflict between our preferences could be resolved entirely by re-subdividing* modem *into the elements of its source construction. When one sends a communication using one's modem, one is actually using only (or at least primarily) the modulator, and not the demodulator. How about* modded *for* sent *and* demodded *for* received, *if the ordinary English words aren't* mod *enough for you?*

  I have a similar quarrel with people who write programed, *particularly since they rarely have the guts, or perhaps the linguistic sensitivity, to follow through and write* programer, *a parallel construction that makes it painfully obvious that* programed *is faulty. A voguish pronunciation among public-radio announcers and other people who wish to sound erudite, or at least British, would permit the un-doubled "m": they really do say "PROGUE-rum," instead of the vernacular "PRO-gram," with the secondary accent on the second syllable and the clear pronunciation of the flat-a sound. I have yet to hear anyone try to get away with losing the second syllable when they try to pronounce* programmer. *Q.E.D., I say.*

John Strother
Princeton, New Jersey

I wish your rule for forming the past tense of verbs applied universally. I am a copy editor and I am always eager to find rules that will save me the time spent in consulting a dictionary. But by your rule the past tense of "format" would be "formated," and the past tense of "mimic" would be "mimiced." After all, both verbs are accented on the first syllable.

  Why are the past tense forms "formatted" and "mimicked"? My guess is that the extra letter is inserted to avoid forming a final unit that looks and sounds like a different word. The short vowel sound in "-mat" becomes the long vowel sound in "-mated," and at first glance "formated" might look like it has something to do with procreation. Similarly, "mimiced" might seem to have something to do with rodents. But "formatted" and "mimicked" retain the same vowel sound and are instantly clear.

The British insert double consonants in past tense verbs much more often than we do. It almost seems that American streamlining led to the deletion of all repeats of final consonants except in cases where the word would look confusing. It also seems that the longer the word, say, three syllables or more, the less necessary it is to double the consonant, because the word is long enough to instantly register correctly, e.g., "diagramed." Conversely, one-syllable verbs always double the consonant, e.g., nabbed, hummed, sinned. The words are so short that even though "nabed" and "humed" are not words it would be impossible for the reader to get past the changed vowel sound and understand what the words are.

So if there is a rule for when to double the final consonant, and I doubt there is, it has probably more to do with how the word looks and possibly sounds without the double consonant.

David M. Kaplan
New York, New York

Seize the Hour, Day or Moment

As Richard Nixon, in the Great Hall of the People in Beijing, lifted a glass twenty years ago to toast the beginning of a new relationship between the United States and China, he quoted from a poem by Mao Zedong:

> So many deeds cry out to be done . . .
> Seize the day. Seize the hour.

When it came to titling his new book, however, about America's challenges in a "one-superpower world," the former President seized neither the day nor the hour. The title: *Seize the Moment.* That was no spur-of-the-day decision; Mr. Nixon wanted to instill an even greater sense of urgency, or to express the essence of the idea without slavishly following the cliché.

Others are willing to stick with the old form. In the final scene of Steven Spielberg's movie *Hook,* a sequel to *Peter Pan,* the rejuvenated old man named Tootles, after a liberal sprinkling of Tinkerbell's fairy dust, flies out the window and soars over London shouting, "*Seize the day!*"

Robin Williams, who plays the grown-up Peter, starred in an 1986 film based on a 1956 novella by Saul Bellow. Its title: *Seize the Day.*

The historian David McCullough, in his book *Brave Companions,* makes the same choice as Nixon. He relates an anecdote about the painter John Singer Sargent, who had been hanging around the White House hoping to talk Theodore Roosevelt into posing for a portrait. The two men met unexpectedly as the President was descending the stairs, and the artist asked when would be a convenient time to pose. Said Roosevelt, in his typically decisive way: "Now!" McCullough writes: "So there he is in the painting, standing at the foot of the stairs, his hand on the newel post. . . . Moments come and go, the President was telling the painter. Here is the time, seize it, do your best."

As should be apparent, moment-seizing is in, even more than day-seizing; hour-seizing seems to be missing its time. The phrase's origin, presuming there to be no earlier usage in Chinese literature, is in the Latin *carpe diem.* The verb *carpere* means "to pluck, grab, seize," from the Greek *karpos,* "fruit"; it's what you do to ripe fruit on the vine. There may be a connection between *carpere* and the verb *to carp,* of Scandinavian origin, "to pick on, find fault with," as in "those carping liberal Democrats" in Mr. Bush's what-recession rhetoric. The noun *diem* is "day," as everyone who puts in for *per diem* knows, though few expense-accounters pronounce it correctly: it's "DEE-em." and the whole phrase is "KAR-peh DEE-em."

There's a phrase that has changed its meaning radically. When Horace wrote his odes, *carpe diem, quam minimum credula postero* meant "seize the day, put no trust in tomorrow." Lord Byron, a swinging Romantic poet, wrote in an 1817 letter: "I never anticipate—*carpe diem*—the past at least is one's own, which is one reason for making sure of the present."

That live-for-today meaning was expressed in the 1867 novel *Under Two Flags* by "Ouida," the pseudonym of the English novelist Louise de La Ramée, writing of "the reckless life of Algeria" with its "gay, careless carpe diem camp-philosophy." The *Daily News* of London grumped in 1901: "The 'Carpe diem' philosophy is not the philosophy of happy people." Its synonymous expression is "Eat, drink and be merry," the advice of the worldly author of Ecclesiastes (8:15), to which the prophet Isaiah added a fatalistic note: "Let us eat and drink; for tomorrow we shall die."

The amalgam of hedonism and existential resignation, of the pursuit of pleasure and the anguish of transience—the only-come-this-way-once ambiance of beer commercials—is the opposite of the phrase's meaning today. Now we think of riding the tide in the affairs of men, which Shakespeare said could lead on to fortune; to change metaphors, *seize the day* has come to mean "strike while the iron is hot." No longer is *carpe diem* the what-the-hell attitude of the dwellers in the present; it has become the battle cry of the gutsy opportunist with an eye on the future.

I had to handle this topic today. You know what attitude drove me to it.

Wouldn't "a 1986 film" have been preferable to your "an 1986 film"?

Walter S. Rosenberry III
Englewood, Colorado

The Latin verb carpere *is not "from the Greek* karpos, *'fruit.' " Carpere and* karpos *are cognates; in other words, they are derived from the same Indo-European root, but neither is derived from the other.*

Furthermore, there is no etymological connection between carpere *and the Scandinavian-derived English verb* carp. *Indo-European initial* k *remains unchanged in Latin and Greek but is always represented by* h *in English, Scandinavian and the other Germanic languages.* Carpere *is cognate with English* harvest *("plucking time"). By way of further illustrating this sound law, English* heart *is cognate with Latin* cor *(stem* cord-*) and Greek* kardia, *English* horn *is cognate with Latin* cornu *and Greek* keras, *and English* hound *is cognate with Latin* canis *and Greek* kuon. *On the other hand, Germanic initial* k *corresponds to Latin-Greek* g, *which is unchanged from Indo-European. Thus,*

English kin *is cognate with Latin* genus *and Greek* genos, *English* knee *is cognate with Latin* genu *and Greek* gonu, *and English* corn *is cognate with Latin* granum.

Louis Jay Herman
New York, New York

The Seven-Year Itch

"At my in-laws' fortieth wedding anniversary party recently, someone asked about the origin of the phrase *the seven-year itch*. Do you know its provenance? Why seven years?"

This note comes from the office of the Vice President, signed "William Kristol, chief of staff (happily married for 16 years)."

"On Language" is not an advice-to-the-lovelorn column. (*Lovelorn,* a beautiful word, seems to survive only in that hyphenated phrase. Unrequited love now results in feeling *depressed,* a quasi-clinical term; it's dispiriting, but lovers are no longer *lovelorn,* and not even babies are sweetly *melancholy.*)

However, it's possible that Dan Quayle could make it all the way, and Kristol will be a White House big shot, and I will be able to get an advance text of Quayle's first inaugural address on the basis of having provided the provenance of *seven-year itch.* So:

Henry David Thoreau, different-drumming along to Walden Pond in 1854, wrote: "These may be but the spring months in the life of the race. If we have had the *seven-years' itch,* we have not seen the seventeen-year locust yet in Concord." He did not explain what the *seven-years' itch* was—a physical ailment or a marital wanderlust—nor did he explain why *year* was plural for the itch and singular for the locust (called the *cicada,* and not due back to my Washington lawn until 2004).

The poet Carl Sandburg, in his 1936 "The People, Yes," caught the cadence of American dialect by using the phrase in what seems to be a physical-annoyance sense: " 'May you have the *sevenyear itch,*' was answered, 'I hope your wife eats crackers in bed.' "

No doubt that the phrase had a sense of irritation: "What are you always tagging after me for?" *Dialect Notes* noted in a 1907 New Hampshire usage. "You're worse than the *seven years' itch.*"

The etymological question is: Where did the current sense come from? The phrase is now almost exclusively used to mean "the desire of a married person to stray from his or her spouse after seven years of marriage."

There is no doubt as to the source of its popularization. *The Seven Year Itch* (no hyphen, although *seven-year* really forms a compound modifying *itch,* as in *seventeen-year locust*) was the title of a 1952 Broadway play by George Axelrod, which was made into a movie three years later starring Marilyn Monroe and Tom Ewell.

I reached Mr. Axelrod in Los Angeles to find out what the phrase meant when he titled his comedy.

"At the time of the play, it was a kind of nonmedical term for a skin disease," he replies, "not, perhaps, unlike 'the Chinese zing,' and had never been used in, to use your phrase, a 'marital wanderlust' connotation."

How did he come across this Americanism? "I was writing jokes for a hillbilly comedian called Rod Brassfield," recalls Mr. Axelrod, "who starred with Minnie Pearl on the 'Grand Ole Opry' radio show." Mr. Brassfield liked cow jokes: "I probably know more cow jokes than any living human being. Why did the cow jump over the moon? The farmer had such cold hands. That kind of thing. I tried to write a few of my own: Did you hear about the cow that swallowed a bottle of blue ink and Mood Indigo? But Rod felt that was too 'uptown' for his people."

The hillbilly comedian also used ugly-girl jokes. "One of his favorite lines was: 'I know she's over twenty-one because she's had the *seven-year itch* four times!' That hideous line," says Mr. Axelrod, now sixty-nine, "was running through my head when I was desperately seeking a title for the play I had just finished that was free from cow jokes forever.

"In the first draft, the guy had been married 10 years (as had I) but the title, when it came, had a natural ring to it and I changed the number of years the hero had been married accordingly. Elliott Nugent, who co-produced the play, loathed the title and wanted to take an ad in *Variety* saying he was not responsible.

"The new usage caught on so fast," Mr. Axelrod says proudly, "that it seems to have seemed it was always thus. It wasn't. *Bartlett's,* where have you been?"

Thus is dialect etymology served. The phrase is current, as Mr. Kristol's letter demonstrates. Variants are proof that the phrase is in the language: A recent issue of *Variety,* writing about a movie producer who tries to keep budgets down in the seven-figure range, headlines "Former Studio Chief Has the $7 Million Itch."

Why seven years, not six or eight? Because seven years has a historical basis: In Genesis, Joseph interprets Pharaoh's dream of "seven years of great plenty" followed by "seven years of famine." Farmers who hate hillbilly jokes know about the *seven-years' apple* and *seven-years' bean;* military historians refer to the third Silesian war, of 1756–63, which confirmed Prussia as a major power, as the *Seven Years' War.*

Get cracking on that inaugural, Kristol; the presidential itch has no numerical limitation.

The "seven year itch" has its origins with a microbe known as Sarcoptes scabiei. More commonly called "scabies." The bug produces an itching skin irritation that, before modern drugs, lasted, on the average—you guessed it—seven years.

> Robert V. Fuschetto
> New York, New York

Sighted Supersession, Sank Same

Some spooky character answering a query about the theft of communication encoders and keys from the Department of Justice dumped a bunch of secret memos on my desk. I will mine the dump for news in another space, but cannot resist reporting immediately on the language of security bureaucrats.

Describing an inventory check, the man from DOJ COMSEC Central Office of Record writes "all items were *physically sighted.*" Presumably this means the items themselves—not pictures or descriptions or computer simulations—were seen by the inventory-taker's human eye. *Physically* is sometimes used to mean "I was there"; *sighted* can have the sense of being seen from afar, or the sense of not being blind. In normal human discourse, *physically sighted* would be put as *actually seen.*

"The destruction of *superseded key* is accorded high priority with N.S.A.," the security official notes sternly. (N.S.A. stands for National Security Agency, nicknamed No Such Agency.) *Key* is, I assume, code material; *superseded key* must be "old codes" superseded, or replaced, by new ones. (Comes from the Latin *supersedere,* literally "to sit on top of.") Thus, if you look at an old code and want to impress your superiors about it in a memo, you write you are *physically sighting superseded key.*

"Custodian failed to destroy over three hundred pieces of Top Secret operational and contingency STU-II key material," huffs the investigating officer, using *over* when he means *more than,* "within five days of supersession."

Although *supersession* was in use in 1790 to mean "the act of superseding," it has itself been superseded by the gerund *superseding.* He should have written "within five days of superseding"; a *supersession,* among the Ninth Street cognoscenti, connotes a fun time in the office of the Attorney General.

Slim Pickings

A member of the U.S. Embassy staff in Belgrade, capital of formerly-Yugoslavia, finds time to send the State Department's "travel advisory for Russia" from his hardship post.

Under "Crime and Personal Security," our government warns its citizens about what it considers a growing problem: "Crimes against tourists (primarily robberies, muggings, and pick-pocketings)."

"Note the State Department's choice of *pick-pocketings,*" our embattled diplomat writes. "Is the doer of such deeds a *pickpocket* or a *pocket-picker?*"

The gerund *pick-pocketing* does have a history (Charles Dickens used the term in his 1838 novel, *Oliver Twist*), but the more sensible *pocket-picking* dates back to 1662.

Grammar advisory for Foggy Bottom: The sentence should read "robberies, muggings and pocket-pickings." One picks pockets; nobody pockets picks.

If you say pocket-picking *was around in 1662 I have to believe you. I vasn't dere, Sharlie, but pickpockets weren't called* pickpockets *by most people. The "in" word was* cutpurse. *But was the gerund* cutpursing *or* purse-cutting? *I leave it to you, master.*

Arthur J. Morgan
New York, New York

Your preference for "pocket-pickings" over the State Department's "pick-pocketings" seems justified, but then you conclude with the astonishing assertion that "nobody pockets picks."

This is no picayune matter. Guitarists, mandolinists and banjoists routinely pocket picks, both of the "flat" (or "plectrum") or "finger" variety. Indeed, most of my friends don't leave home without them.

For his information, pickers pocket picks. Is this nitpicking?

Denis J. Hynes
Fresh Meadows, New York

Stulte Agitur Oeconomia

Headline writers, who thrive on the short and recognizable, have a formulation for the 90's: an identification of a noun, followed by the derogation "Stupid!"

James Carville, the Clinton political strategist, put up a sign in his Little Rock headquarters: "It's the Economy, Stupid!" That was supposedly his answer to the question "What's the campaign about?" The sign, and the stories about it, helped keep the central attack issue constantly in focus.

Now comes Ethan H. Siegal of Prudential Securities with a headline over his financial newsletter: "It's the *Deficit,* Stupid!" A David Twersky column in *The Forward* headlines: "The Mideast, Stupid!" Op-editors are preparing "It's Health Policy, Stupid!" or "It's the Inaugural Address, Stupid!"

Stupid (from *stupere,* "to be stunned") in direct address is certain to become the most commonly used adjective-turned-noun of the coming year. And then, as suddenly as it appeared, it will vanish. Why? Formulation overload. It's the fast-changing vocabulary, Rocket Scientist!

Your subhead "Stulte Agitur Oeconomia" will not do as a representation of "It's the economy, stupid" (which, by the way, is a variation of the sports adage "Keep it simple, stupid"). What you wrote, with no comma, grammatically forces stulte *to be an adverb. This makes perfect sense but gives a campaign slogan: "The economy is being managed stupidly."*

William C. Waterhouse
University Park, Pennsylvania

The Take on Voice

On the soap opera *Santa Barbara,* an irate father complains about his teenage daughter's relationship with a newspaper publisher. The publisher's girlfriend, Angela, quickly straightens the father out: "You think they were sleeping together? You have the wrong *take* on this situation."

I had originally filed that citation under "archaic euphemisms," because *sleeping together* now seems to be in the category once reserved for *holding hands;* the couch-potato generation, which knows more about copulation than copulative verbs and whose eyes glaze over at terms that used to be shocking, must wonder if *sleeping together* is some new kind of communal family value.

But it is fortunate that I squirreled that sound bite away. *Take,* as in "the wrong take," is roaring through the language.

"Is it mere coincidence," *U.S. News & World Report* wrote during Johnny Carson's last days on the air, "that as Carson's *take* on Bush has grown rougher, the President's standing has shrunk?"

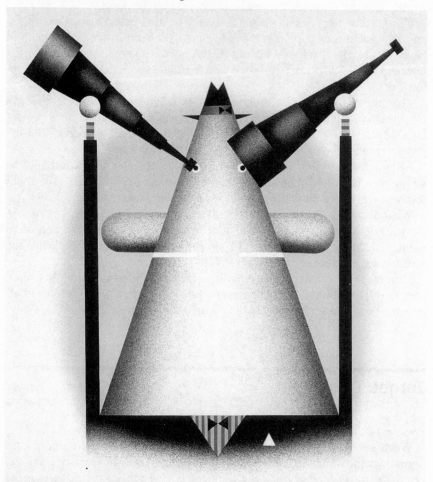

In a *New York Times* review of James Brady's novel *Fashion Show,* Deborah Mason wrote, "Mr. Brady again attempts a juicy insider's *take* on the vanities and inanities of the fashion-society-publishing axis."

In this sense, *take* is a noun meaning "view, understanding, perception, perspective," or in popular usage, "slant." The lexicographer Cynthia Barnhart has a 1988 citation from *The Guardian* on the novelist Thomas Pynchon (specifically "Pynchon's *take* on things"), but she suspects that the usage may be much older.

How did the functional shift from *take* as a verb—"to grab, seize, snatch, remove"—come about?

Sir Edward Nicholas, in 1654, was struck by the notion that he could use the word to mean "something that is taken or received," and nobody told him that was a functional shift: "The *take* off 200,000 crownes is now sett," he wrote, "and the Emperor declared his present shall be apart."

Using this sense, printers in the nineteenth century began using the noun to mean "a portion of copy taken at one time by a compositor to be set up in type." (As I write this today, an editor who wants to sneak away early for the weekend is asking, "Can't you send us a first *take* so we can let the artist get to work?")

Then the use of *take* as a noun took off. It can mean "proceeds" ("the *take* from the rock concert"), "share" ("If I don't get a bigger *take*, it's a cement footbath for you"), "catch" ("today's *take* of fish") and "response" ("don't just give me a delayed *take*, Cary, give me a full *double take*").

Although *takeoff* has been eclipsed by *sendup* as slang for "parody," to be *on the take* is still current among grafters, and casino operators talk about today's *take;* the noun retains a slightly larcenous connotation.

What accounts for its present popularity? Its Hollywood use, I think. As early as 1922, a continuous run of film was referred to as a *take*, and often numbered: "Take 1!" A refilming of a scene or shot was "Take 2." When the director was satisfied, he would say, "That's a *take*."

I am inclined to end this entry with a finalizing "That's a take," but when filming or recording is ended, the expression is "That's a wrap," on the analogy of a wrapped-up package (which is my take on *wrap*).

Target: Declinism

Pessimist-bashing is again with us.

When people feel irritable about the lack of bounce in the economic rebound; when words like *malaise* and phrases like *triple dip* and *creeping decrepitude* are bruited about—the moment is ripe for yeasayers to pop the pessimists.

As Republicans in 1936 charged that the New Deal had failed to lift the nation out of sustained Depression, supporters of F.D.R. called them *disciples of despair* floundering in a *fountain of fear*. As Republicans in 1952 blazed away at Harry Truman's "mess in Washington," Democrats—led, I think, by Adlai Stevenson—derided the *prophets of gloom and doom*.

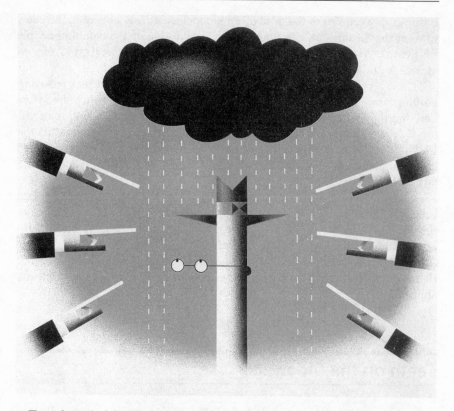

Turnabout is fair play: In 1956, Clare Boothe Luce led the Republicans in denouncing Democrats as *troubadors of trouble* and *crooners of catastrophe.* As Democrats expressed their dissatisfaction with the lingering war and slow economic growth in 1970, a Republican wordsmith, recalling Mrs. Luce's alliterative ripostes, fed Vice President Spiro T. Agnew a nice bit of alliteration with which to castigate the castigators: He called them the *nattering nabobs of negativism.* (I was that wordsmith; that year, I was big on *n*'s.)

Here we are, a generation later, with the ouching outcasts of outrage again in full cry, complaining that it's late afternoon in America. What affirmationist will turn the tables and smite them (perhaps with a little innuendo that it is unpatriotic to "run down America"), and with what catchy new phrase?

George Bush has volunteered. He took the 1987 book by Paul Kennedy, *The Rise and Fall of the Great Powers,* which offered a gloom-and-doom view of our future, and married it to Edward Gibbon's *History of the Decline and Fall of the Roman Empire* to come up with a new class of pessimist: the *declinists.*

Here it is in context, from President Bush's commencement address at Southern Methodist University in Dallas [May 1992]:

"I realize that I might not be taking the fashionable view." (This approach is how a speaker strikes the pose of an iconoclast, gutsily opposing the elites who set the fashions and settling instead on the side of the common people who vote.) "Much of the conventional wisdom these days portrays America in decline and its energy dissipated, its possibilities exhausted. . . .

"These *declinists,* as they are called, will hate to hear it, but they're saying nothing new." The President then recalled how even Walt Whitman had worried that the United States would "prove the most tremendous failure in history" only a few years before the dawn of the American century. "In the 1930's," Mr. Bush went on, "the *declinists* told us the Great Depression had made capitalism outmoded. Our victory in World War II put an end to that talk."

Declinist, labeled a "nonce word" in the *Oxford English Dictionary,* had been used in 1831 by a British philosopher, William Whewell, in discussing the decline of science: "The only professor who has written at all on the subject is Babbage, the leader of the *Declinists.*"

Rhetoricians wonder: Will an anti-pessimist coinage work without either rhyme or alliteration? It's a daring move, but the speechwriters are optimistic about it.

Teeth on the Sidewalk

Newsweek, in "The Inside Story" of the '92 campaign, points out proudly that "Mark Miller was given extraordinary access to the inner workings of the Clinton campaign, thanks to the permission of the candidate himself."

Miller reports an episode of interest to students of vivid figures of speech in general, and of Southern American dialect in particular.

When the Bush campaign suggested that Clinton's "People first" economics would mean higher taxes for everyone who makes more than $36,000 a year, Clinton, according to *Newsweek,* blew up. Speechwriter Paul Begala sought to assuage his anger, Mr. Miller reports, but Governor Clinton said: "I want to put a fist halfway down their throats with this. I don't want subtlety. I want their teeth on the sidewalk."

This is not the cherubic, resolutely respectful Clinton that a plurality of American voters came to know and love. Historians and biographers will look at that direct quotation and ask: Was the reporter present to hear the words? Was his source Mr. Begala or someone else who was present, and was the source, if firsthand, paraphrasing or quoting directly? Was this quotation relayed to the reporter from vivid memory, contemporaneous notes—or from general recollection weeks afterward? Will President-elect Clinton confirm that these figures of speech—even if spoken on inside-background rules for publication after election—are indeed his own?

If so, we have a challenge to dialect etymology. First, *to put a fist halfway down their throats*—qualified violence, not so strong as *to put a fist all the way down their throats*—was presaged by Shakespeare in a Hamlet soliloquy: "Who calls me villain, . . . tweaks me by the nose, gives me *the lye i' the throate* as deepe as to the lungs?" Earlier, in *Titus Andronicus,* the Bard pioneered the metaphor of fist-toward-larynx: "Till I have . . . *thrust these reprochfull speeches downe his throat,* that he hath breath'd in my dishonour heere."

The image split in American dialect usage: *to ram down the throat* means "to force acceptance," while *to jump down (someone's) throat* means "to criticize suddenly." A third variant, *to cut (someone's) throat,* became a trope for intense competition.

Teeth on the sidewalk was presumably coined on the analogy of the more familiar *blood on the floor,* both are horrific images meant to exaggerate "severe consequences." The nautical word picture *a shot across the bow* has been replaced with the less cautionary, more forthright *a shot in the teeth.* False teeth are used in dialect as the basis of *to drop one's teeth,* calling up the picture of gaping in surprise and losing one's dentures.

The two strands—throat and teeth—combine in the hyperbolic threat *to knock your teeth down your throat.*

According to Joan Hall at the *Dictionary of American Regional English* (*DARE*), a black, Spanish-speaking informant from Florida is cited in the *Linguistic Atlas of the Gulf States* (Lee Pederson's great work at Emory University) as saying, "You'd be picking up your teeth off the floor with a broken arm." Ms Hall's colleagues at the University of Wisconsin recall, but cannot immediately cite, a detective novel line, "All I could think of was how good his teeth would look on the floor." (Says the woman from *DARE:* "We could really use a concordance of Mickey Spillane.")

Will the President-elect, once ensconced in the White House, lose connection with the figures of speech of his campaign trail? Or will he emulate Harry Truman and Lyndon Johnson and retain them, as he likes to say publicly, *until the last dog dies*?

Assuming the quotations attributed to him in *Newsweek*'s "Inside Story" are accurate, we can await future memoirs by aides along the same revealing lines. Sooner or later, there will be a confrontation between President Clinton and the Senate majority leader, George Mitchell, who has an especially toothy smile. Dialecticians can't wait for a confirming citation.

The classic detective-novel line about teeth comes out of the mouth of Marlowe in Raymond Chandler's The Big Sleep: *"You know what Canino will do—beat my teeth out and then kick me in the stomach for mumbling." (Chapter XXVIII).*

Peter A. Sundelin
West Barnstable, Massachusetts

I have come across a toothsome ancient reference to your "teeth on the sidewalk" column.

The reference is in C. S. Lewis's The Allegory of Love *(Oxford University*

WATCHING MY LANGUAGE · 243

Press, 1936), page 67 of the 1971 paperback reprint. Lewis is quoting the Spanish poet Prudentius (A.D. 348–c. 405) from his description of gladiatorial combat between the virtues and the vices in an early example in the West of allegorical poetry, "Psychomachia":

> Chance led the stone, shattering the ways of breath
> To mingle lips with palate; the rent tongue,
> With gory gobbets and the wreck of teeth
> Dashed inward, stuff'd the lacerated throat.

I spare you the Latin translation of a footnote, but the key words "Dentibus introrsum" leap across the centuries with the immediacy of the modern phrase from our sidewalk-pounding President-elect. I cannot help but be reminded of your recent exegesis of ol' Job shaking his fist at the Lord, and am led to muse that all social intercourse must spring from the teeth and fists of our biology and all our philosophizing is just whistling in the dark.

> Pat Winter
> New York, New York

"Until the last dog dies" is a dog's age older than the Clinton campaign. In David McCullough's fine biography, Truman (p. 973), the author quotes HST, in connection with his opposition to John Kennedy's nomination in 1960: "I am not a pessimist and always fight until the last dog dies." I guess the expression existed on either side of the Ozarks.

> Philip Weinberg
> Jamaica, New York

More on "Teeth on the Sidewalk"

"I want to put a fist halfway down their throats with this," an irate Bill Clinton was quoted as saying by Mark Miller in *Newsweek,* adding, "I want their teeth on the sidewalk."

In a recent column, I noted the richness and unexpected power of this dialect use by the President-to-be and wondered if the reporter was on the scene when the words were spoken.

Turns out he was right there. Mark Miller called to say he heard the expressions with his own ears and made contemporaneous notes. Thus is history served; few other statements by the campaigning Clinton will be noted as lip-smackingly by historians.

Mr. Miller says, "The figures of speech are not an affectation—he really talks that way; he's comfortable with Arkansas slang. When I once beat Governor Clinton at hearts—a rare thing for me—I got him to sign the score sheet, and he wrote, 'Even a blind hog can find an acorn.' "

Razorbackese is in.

You cite (from Mark Miller) an Arkansas proverb used by Bill Clinton: "Even a blind hog can find an acorn." Like most proverbs it has ancestors and parallels in various parts of the world. In Poland it's a blind hen that happens across a grain. A version from 1618 reads: "I ślepej kokoszy ziarno się nadarzy." In Rome it was a blind dove or pigeon that sometimes found a pea: "Invenit interdum caeca columba pisum."

The blind hen also finds a grain in the Estonian proverb "Pime kana leiab vahel ka tera," which is cited in an article by the Tartu paremiologist Arvo Krikmann. Krikmann, writing about the "semantic indefiniteness of proverbs" in the journal Proverbium *(vol. 2, 1985), points out that the proverb about the blind hen can be used in more than one way. If a person is generally viewed as clumsy, incompetent, prone to failure, the proverb can be used to encourage that person's attempt to do something (or to answer criticism of that attempt). On the other hand, if a person has accomplished something, the proverb can be used to depreciate the accomplishment by suggesting that it was an accident and came about despite clumsiness, incompetence, etc.*

Robert A. Rothstein
Slavic Department
University of Massachusetts
Amherst, Massachusetts

Tense Encounter

The British interviewer David Frost likes to give the impression of relaxation when interrogating world leaders on television. Yet in his most recent annual chat with President Bush, the key word was *tense.*

"Do you sometimes wish," Mr. Frost wondered as if innocently, "that as a condition of the cease-fire you had asked for Saddam Hussein to be handed over?"

The President gave what to some might have been a puzzling reply: "I don't know about 'handed over,' but 'out of there' would have been nice—expluperfect past tense, I mean, sure."

In Baghdad, Iraqi translators blanched at having to render *ex-pluperfect past tense* into Arabic. In American schoolrooms, English teachers stopped banging together computer erasers to wonder: Is there such a tense as the *ex-pluperfect past*? Did the "education President" have more of an education in grammar than anyone suspected?

Let us begin the deconstruction of Mr. Bush's syntactical pyrotechnics with the word *perfect*. In its most common sense, that word means "flawless, impeccable, having zero defects," a sense that slops over to "absolutely right, appropriate, just so." A *perfect martini,* for example, contains one-eighth dry vermouth, one-eighth sweet vermouth, six-eighths gin and geddoutahere with the olive, because that is what purist bartenders consider the flawless martini. (I'll get mail on that, as I did on the recipe for perfect gefilte fish.)

An earlier sense of *perfect,* however, is "whole, completed, finished"; the Apostle Paul, in the King James translation of his first letter to the Corinthians, defined love of God: "But when that which is perfect is come, then that which is in part shall be done away." That meaning of completion lingers in the verb *to perfect,* which means "to bring to a satisfying conclusion." That's the sense of the adjective *perfect* used in grammar: "completed; done in the past."

Only in grammar can you be more than perfect. (Tell that to the crowd that tears its hair out at *very unique.*) The Latin *plus quam perfectum* means "more than perfect," and the French pronunciation of *plus* is close to "ploo"; that gave us *pluperfect*—not merely completed at some vague time in the past, maybe just now, but completed at or before a certain time. For another biblical example, Luke writes of the prodigal son: "And when he *had spent* all, there arose a mighty famine." The little auxiliary word *had* does the perfecting trick, locating the action just after the spending of all.

Perfect refines the past tense, which is why some grammarians like to call the *pluperfect* the *past perfect;* I had gone along with this new name until I decided *pluperfect* was more archaically distinctive, even if it does not contain the word *past.* (In that sentence, *had gone* is in the pluperfect tense; the past has a time frame, ending with my gutsy decision to embrace the old *pluperfect.*) The perfecting of the simple past, present and future tenses began in Old English and has long enriched the language, helping spot events in time.

David Frost used the pluperfect in his question: "Do you sometimes wish . . . you *had asked* for Saddam Hussein to be handed over?" Without the *had,* the tense would be simple past, meaning that Mr. Bush could have been asking that right up to the moment the show began; with the *had,* the question locates that asking back at the fateful time Mr. Bush let Saddam off the hook.

The President must have recognized the pluperfect tense being used in the question, and saw the trap closing to get him to admit a mistake; instead, he answered in the past conditional tense: ". . . 'out of there' *would have been* nice." He then stunned us all and caused panic among the Iraqi interpreters by identifying the *would have been* as "ex-pluperfect past tense."

There is, of course, no "ex-pluperfect past tense." As we have seen, there is a *pluperfect,* which can also be called *past perfect* (" 'out of there' *had been* nice"); there is a *present perfect,* which means it was completed just now (" 'out of there' *has been* nice"), and there is a *future perfect* (" 'out of there' *will have been* nice"). It's not complicated: *had* is past, *has* and *have* are present, *will have* is future—and all are used to make the tense perfect, or complete, or more specific.

Mr. Bush undoubtedly knows this; he went to Phillips Academy in Andover, Massachusetts, where they still teach this stuff. Why, then, did he characterize Mr. Frost's question ("you had asked," in the pluperfect) or his own response ("would have been," in the past conditional) as "ex-pluperfect past tense"?

For the same reason he drops his participial *g*'s ("I don't know what dramatic change that would . . . have made in terms of *gettin'* Saddam out of there"). For the same reason he munches pork rinds and swills beer at campaign time. For the same reason many educated speakers adopt self-mocking, shucks-I'm-not-one-of-those-grammatical-types mannerisms: to avoid the appearance of elitism.

Pluperfect, with its nice enclosure of retrospection, is a word that fairly reeks of grammar; it is a misused staple of old jokes about hungry visitors to Boston asking cabbies where to get scrod ("first time I heard that in the pluperfect, mister"). By derogating his own understanding of tenses, the patrician Mr. Bush adopts a reg'ler feller pose. (Remember when George McGovern took a flock of photographers with him into a kosher deli in Brooklyn and ordered a hot dog and a glass of milk? Same cross-cultural awkwardness.)

The President, sensitive to the powerful "iffiness" of Mr. Frost's question in the pluperfect, chose to characterize his own past-conditional response in a self-derogating, grammar-spoofing way. He is equally sensitive to labels that would be welcomed by centrists. When reminded by the interviewer that a right-wing columnist had described him as a "moderate," and asked if he liked that description, Mr. Bush replied: "No; it depends what it relates to. I'm basically conservative and I've always been that way."

Have always been is the present perfect; *had always been* would be pluperfect.

I write to take issue with your grammatical analysis of David Frost's question to President Bush. In English, when one says one wishes that he had done something, that verb had is in the subjunctive, a mood employed to express those situations that are contrary to fact. The confusion with the pluperfect results from the fact that the subjunctive is supine in modern English, i.e., that it is not fully conjugated, and thus the poor overworked had must play a multitude of roles.

Your own explanation offers the correct criterion for a pluperfect: it is a tense prior to some other past act or condition. "Oscar avoided the party because his wife had warned him beforehand not to go." The Frost question does not require a pluperfect since the act of wishing is clearly in the present.

Joseph C. Voelker
Professor of English
Franklin & Marshall College
Lancaster, Pennsylvania

You (and President Bush) have confused pluperfect subjunctive with the pluperfect indicative. David Frost, in his question, was uttering a counterfactual when he said ". . . you had asked for . . ." in the subjunctive mood. Mr. Bush replied as though Frost had spoken in the indicative (another example of subjunctive use. In neither case had Mr. Bush asked for Saddam Hussein to be handed over, nor had Mr. Frost spoken in the indicative).

Unlike most inflected languages, the subjunctive is hard to spot in English. In fact distinctive subjunctive forms exist only in the case of the verb "to be," which has a present subjunctive form (I insist that you be home by 8:00 P.M., or [more rarely] If this be true . . .), a past tense which is used with present tense meaning in counterfactuals (If I were President . . . [and I am not]), and a pluperfect with a simple past tense meaning in counterfactuals (If I had come earlier [but I did not]).

In English we tend to substitute a periphrastic modal phrase for the simple subjunctive (I insist that you should go to bed earlier) except in the case of present or past counterfactuals, where the simple subjunctive is always used, even though you only notice it in the apparent substitution of "were" for "was"; and in England, of course, even this distinction has become muddied, and you will more often hear "If I was President Bush . . ." than the older (and more logical) American usage "If I were President Bush . . ."

John Foster Leich
Sharon, Connecticut

You refer to the phrase "it would have been nice" as being in the conditional tense. To me it would seem this is a past subjunctive, since it is a contrary-to-fact statement. I would regard a conditional statement to be one such as "If my old friend is still alive he must be eighty now." The condition here being "If he is still alive."

James F. Rogers
Tucson, Arizona

You recently discussed the way George Bush adjusts his speech to sound like a "reg'ler feller," and pointed out that the president often "drops his participial g's." You mention Mr. Bush's phrase "gettin' Saddam out of there" as an instance of this usage, and thereby fall into a common trap.

The sound represented by "ng" in the normal spelling of "getting" is not composed of an "n" plus a "g," rather the two letters have been assigned the convention of representing one sound, one of the three nasals available in English, the others being "n" and "m."

What Mr. Bush, and most of the rest of us, does, is substitute one nasal sound for another, not simply drop a letter. Phonology is what counts; spelling, to commandeer Yeats, is "but a spume that plays upon a ghostly paradigm" of sounds.

James Owens
Haysi, Virginia

It'll be interesting to see the response to the martini reference, which reminded me of this old wheeze I heard during the Korean conflict:

A sergeant is explaining to his squad what to do if separated in battle and lost somewhere in the field. "If you are lost and alone out in the middle of nowhere, reach into your mess kit. You'll find a small bottle of gin, a smaller jar of dry vermouth and an olive wrapped in foil. Put all of them into your canteen, swish them around with your spoon and, men, I guarantee that within 30 seconds an American will walk up to you and say, 'That's no way to mix a martini!'"

William G. Clotworthy
Westport, Connecticut

You correctly predicted you would get mail on your formula for a "perfect martini."

I'm not surprised that you got it wrong. Anyone with the chutzpah to propose the perfect gefilte fish deserves disaster martini-wise.

I'll help you by citing impeccable authority. In the mid-'70's, among the many articles written on the occasion of the 30th anniversary of the liberation of Paris was an account of Ernest Hemingway's contribution. It recalled his leading an advance guard to liberate the bar (Harry's?) at the Ritz, bellying-up and ordering a martini (by definition the perfect one). In his advance guard was a young officer by the name of David Bruce.

Since I was Deputy Director of NATO Affairs at State while David Bruce (one of the small handful of great American diplomats) was U.S. Ambassador to NATO, I had the chance to ask him if the story was true (he confirmed it) and how the martini was made. Ambassador Bruce replied 15–1 (gin to dry vermouth), adding that it was the only civilized way to construct a martini.

As the Talmud would say, Safire, learn from it! Next week, the perfect gefilte fish according to a chasidic fishmonger in Antwerp.

Gerald B. Helman
Alexandria, Virginia

There's No Wearware

Let the speaker beware: The combining form -*ware* is everyware.

According to Howard Gardner, a professor of education at Harvard, a new use of the ubiquitous -*ware* popped up in connection with a recent meeting of the Cognitive Science Society that concentrated on artificial intelligence.

Gary Lynch, a neurobiologist investigating the mysteries of memory, I forget at what school, recalled he felt completely out of place at the conference, "a student of *wetware* among the computer hackers."

Since the early 80's, *wetware* has meant "the human brain," presumably because it is moist when removed from the cranium. Other coinages were possible—*skullware, grayware,* even *noodleware* leap to the mindware—but *wetware* has been adopted by neuroscientists to differentiate the working of the human mind from the *software* that drives the *hardware* in a computer. Alan Stern of Hastings-on-Hudson, New York, suggests that *dryware* may soon be used to denote the entire hardware-software spectrum in comparisons with human thinking.

The term *ware* for "manufactured thing" has been kicking around for the better part of the millennium after making its debut in the English abbot Aelfric's *Homilies* circa 1000. Robert K. Barnhart's dictionary of etymology makes a guess at the origin: Perhaps the original meaning was "object of care," related to *waer,* "aware, cautious," akin to *beware.*

A peddler showed his *wares,* and in the fourteenth century decided to call the place he stored them a *warehouse.* (That word suffered pejoration when it was used to mean "the unkind storage of people" or "the dark and airless storage of goods," but has been given a happy connotation in the promotion of new "food warehouses," discount supermarkets.) By 1440, tools and parts of machines were *hardware;* that led to *chinaware* and *earthenware* (we're in the seventeenth century), *kitchenware* and *glassware* and *tableware.* In this century, every generation has its ware: first *giftware,* then in 1921 *housewares,* in 1943 *spongeware*—that's earthenware with color spattered or sponged on— and then, in 1950, the trademark *Tupperware.*

That eponymous trade name is based on Earl S. Tupper's original line of molded plastic tumblers, canisters and soap holders, marketed at gatherings in private homes. In Thomas Pynchon's 1966 novel, *The Crying of Lot 49,* the word was immortalized in the literary world: "Mrs. Oedipa Maas came home from a Tupperware party whose hostess had put perhaps too much kirsch in the fondue."

With the *software* explosion in our generation came *courseware* ("programs written to teach"), *firmware* ("programs implanted in a read-only-memory device," combining hardware and software for a specific task), *shareware* ("copyrighted software to be used and copied without charge, but not on a regular basis"), and *freeware* ("software in the public domain" to be used as freely as a good metaphor in a presidential speech).

What about the *wear* in *men's wear, sportswear, swimwear, sleepwear* and the new *dancewear* (replacing the eponymous *leotards*)? No; that *wear* and the other *ware* are homophones, words that sound the same but are spelled differently and have different meanings. Until there is a special uniform chosen by the users of *softwear,* there is, as Gertrude Stein would say, no *warewear.*

The Third Way

Jack Kemp, his "empowerment" policies thrust into the national limelight after the Los Angeles riot, characterized them on David Brinkley's TV show as "the *third way.*"

That phrase is also a favorite of Bill Clinton's. "I saw people who want a *third way,* a different way, a new approach to our problems, not a big new bunch of top-down money coming from Washington, not twelve more years of neglect coming from Washington. They want basic empowerment."

Clinton is using Kemp's *empowerment,* and Kemp has Clinton's *third way;* fair enough. But *third way* has some fascinating echoes.

The *Baltimore Sun* reported in 1956 on a faith healer who was said to influence politics in the Netherlands: "The healer . . . is closely connected with a movement called the *Third Way,* something like the Third Force, which swept Europe after the war. The movement is strongly neutralist and pacifist."

Other uses abound. "Peronist philosophy seeks a '*third way*' between capitalism and communism," Edward Schumacher of *The New York Times* wrote from Buenos Aires in 1981, "with a heavy state role in unions and industry."

A year later, John Vinocur wrote a piece from Bonn, West Germany, quoting Walther Kiep, a Christian Democratic candidate, who used the term in derogation of moral relativism. Mr. Kiep wanted to express a "clear no to those in our country who are seeking a *third way,* who set the United States and the Soviet Union on the same level, and who demand equal distance between them."

Also in 1982, President Ferdinand E. Marcos of the Philippines tied the phrase to the *third world* (a de Gaullism) with "What we ask of the developed countries is to let the third world find a *third way.*"

In the United States, speaking to businessmen at the height of his 1984 Democratic primary campaign for President, Senator Gary Hart rejected both parties' traditional economic policies and put together two thirds by putting forward "a *third way* for the nation's third century."

The phrase has had a tryout in the Soviet Union, too. In 1990, wrote Peter Passell of *The New York Times,* "most Western experts were still dithering over the design of a '*third way,*' some hybrid of socialism and capitalism that would ease the Soviet Union's entry into the world economy."

That third way didn't work, either. Serge Schmemann of *The Times* wrote from Moscow in 1991 that economist Grigory A. Yavlinsky "tried to convince Mr. Gorbachev that in economics, as compared with politics, there can be no compromise, no marriage of 'left' and 'right,' no '*third way*' between the past and the future."

Can the center ever hold? Will there ever be a *third way* between Scylla and Charybdis, or between right and wrong? Of course there will; the *third way*'s time will come, somewhere, on some subject.

At that point, every farseeing phrase maker will hold his hand aloft, concealing his thumb and spreading his other digits, and say: "The much-heralded *third way* has failed. I have a better approach. . . ."

You know what he'll call it.

–30–

Nothing goes unnoticed and nothing is unnamed.

"What do you call the mark at the end of an article that means there ain't no more?" asks Robert A. Clark, M.D., of Elkins Park, Pennsylvania. "The body of *The New York Times* uses a little black square, while the *Book Review* has an empty square. *Common Cause* magazine has a black diamond. *Smithsonian* magazine leaves the reader to guess whether or not its articles have ended. Is there need for uniformity on this matter?"

At *Esquire, Rolling Stone* and *Popular Mechanics,* the concluding symbol is called an *end slug. Working Woman* calls it a *dingbat,* though others use that term to mean "a decorative mark before a paragraph." At *The New York Times Magazine,* editors call it a *ballot box* or a *square bullet.*

In case you wonder what they're talking about, and want to be present at the first time in recorded history that an article is properly concluded with a colon, here it comes: ■

I question the parallelism of the term "dingbat" with those such as "end slug," "square bullet," etc. Isn't "dingbat" a generic term for novelty shapes, of which the others are special cases?

Paul Bogrow
Glendale, California

This Ol' House

I was having some trouble with a leaky copper gutter, and the beams in the basement looked bent out of shape, so I called Martha Stewart.

This author of cookbooks and guides to weddings and other entertainments has a book out—*New Old House*—dealing with *restoration* and *renova-*

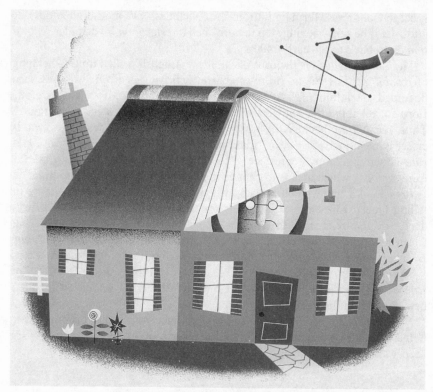

tion. Actually, not gutters but leaders are my problem; during Washington's interregnum, the synonymy of *renewal* was bothering me.

She writes in the book, after consulting the Random House dictionary: "It is my understanding that a *restoration* is a pure, line-for-line replication of a space or object, as nearly as possible to its original state. A *renovation* is a rebuilding of a space or object, with less attention paid to authenticity than to making it new again."

I wanted to hear a less formal differentiation from her own lips. "*Restoration* is putting things back the way they were," Martha Stewart says. "It's making a house like a museum, the way it was when first built—taking new paint off old paneling, taking it back in time.

"*Renovation* is making something new again—putting in bathrooms, knocking out walls, making an old house more livable for today."

And what about *rehabilitation, remodeling* and *refurbishment*? "You're going to have to work those out for yourself," she said invitingly.

Where did I put that ruler with the bubble in the middle? Here we go:

The noun *restoration* dates back to the fifteenth century. In British history, the *Restoration* (which ended the interregnum) began in 1660 when Charles II returned to England and reestablished the monarchy. George F. Will uses the term to title his new book on congressional reform, intended to restore respect to Congress. "Term limitation," he concludes, "is a measured, moderate and—let it be said—loving step toward such a *restoration.*" The older *renovation* dates back to the early 1400's.

The Latin *habilitas* is the root of "ability"; English picked up the meaning of *rehabilitate* in 1580, as "to re-establish the privileges of one who has been degraded or attainted." A Scottish register announced, "Our Soverane Lord . . . rehabilitattis and restoris the said Robert . . . to his gude fame." Thus, *rehabilitate* is close to "*restore* to a previous state," while *renovate* is closer in meaning to *renew,* or "make new again," but not necessarily to *replicate*—meaning "copy, reproduce"—the house that used to be. Both are far from *remodel,* which means to change the floor plan or alter the structure.

Refurbish, a word much mocked when used by Walter H. Annenberg in telling Queen Elizabeth of his plans for the American Ambassador's residence, originally meant "to repolish"; now its meaning lies somewhere between *redecorate,* "to redo the style of interior furnishings," and *spruce up,* perhaps from *spruce leather,* a smart item once imported from Prussia.

So what is Martha doing to her house in East Hampton, Long Island? "I'm *renovating* the inside and *restoring* the outside," she says, "while working on a new book about homekeeping."

Homekeeping? "It's not just *housekeeping;* once your house becomes your home, you have more at stake." (It takes a heap of livin' to make a housekeeper a homekeeper.)

To Remind

The invitation seemed eerily robotic:

The Offices of
The Attorney General
and
The Deputy Attorney General
request the pleasure of your company
at a
holiday reception.

I had heard of office parties, but—a party given by offices? This was a matter for Miss Manners.

Judith Martin does for the nation's etiquette what I try to do for its grammar. (Run it.) I shot the curiously worded invitation on to her at United Feature Syndicate, with the query "Should an office invite a person to a party? Even an office party?"

Miss Manners's (yes, that's correct) reply, in the most beautiful writing hand I have ever seen:

"Although I never much cared for talking furniture—rulings from chairs, messages from desks 'of'—I welcome the clarification that a party is actually being given by offices, rather than people.

"If the Attorney General and his deputy want to give a party, they may not have to make the hors d'oeuvres, but they should pay for them, and they should sustain the illusion that they invited people they happened to like, not those from whom they expect any professional advantage.

"Guests of an office need not reciprocate, as they have incurred no social obligation. There is far too much confusion about this sort of thing (although I admired the thank-you letter a friend wrote the President's wife after a State dinner—'Let's do this again real soon'), which is why I am willing to approve the crude admission that a party is being given by an office."

Tossing Our Cookies

The humorist Sam Levenson used to tell of a little boy who reported that all the children in his class had been asked to stand up and do a turn on their first day at school. "And what did you do, Johnny?" asked his parents. Replied the boy: "I vomited."

This homely anecdote convulsed audiences because (a) children do it all too often in real life, and (b) the verb *to vomit* packs such a punch.

When George Bush, during his state visit to Japan, was afflicted with "stomach flu," as White House aides called it, or "intestinal flu" as it was called more formally, or "gastroenteritis" as preferred by Lawrence K. Altman, M.D., medical correspondent of *The New York Times,* many radio and television news readers shied away from the distasteful verb to describe what the President did. First reports were that he "*was taken ill* and collapsed" or "became *sick to his stomach* and fainted"; later, the broadcasters added that he had *thrown up.*

Print reporters were more inclined to come up with the hard word. When Marlin Fitzwater, the White House press secretary, announced that the President "was feeling weak and was helped to the floor by Secret Service agents," a reporter introduced the V-word: "Was the President nauseous when he slumped to the floor, or was there any vomiting?" Mr. Fitzwater, being helped to the truth by inquiring journalists, said: "Yes, he was nauseous. He did vomit just before he slumped to the floor."

But he adopted the questioner's use of *nauseous,* which most dictionaries say means "causing nausea or disgust; sickening." (Pronounce it "NAW-

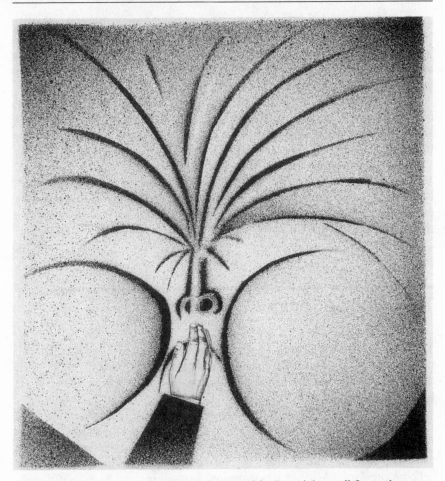

shus," not "NAW-zee-us.") *Nausea* is rooted in "seasickness," from the same Greek root as *nautical;* for years, good usagists have insisted that the feeling you get before vomiting should be *nauseated,* not *nauseous.*

As a card-carrying lexicographer and self-styled usagist, I always say, "I am *nauseated,*" before clapping a handkerchief over my mouth and racing to talk to Ralph on the big white phone, but I don't know anybody else who says that. They all say, "Gawd, I feel *nauseous,*" or offer a telegraphic "*Nauseous, gonna go whoops,*" and they actually take offense when I correct them with "No, you are *nauseated*"; in one instance, my lap then became the target of a power boot. Since that time, I have accepted *nauseous* as a synonym for *nauseated,* and when I need a word to denote "causing nausea," I rely on *disgusting.* I realize this caving-in to common usage is permissive and descriptive—*nauseous* to prescriptivists—but it has saved me from the fallout of upchucking friends.

The slightly green reader will note my use of such modern euphemisms as *boot, upchuck* and *talk to Ralph on the big white phone,* as well as the Shakespearean favorite *puke;* I might have turned to a dignified-sounding *regurgitate* or *reverse peristalsis,* tried the latest *hurl,* or added *tossing your cookies, blowing your doughnuts* and *losing your lunch.* More modern power booters use *driving the porcelain bus* and *laughing at the carpet;* my personal choice in describing the embarrassing act when it happens to me is *yawning in Technicolor.*

Probably the preferred slang verb to describe the evacuation of the stomach was used by Johnny Carson just after the episode involving the President: "If you had to eat raw fish while you looked at Lee Iacocca, you'd *barf* too."

I grew up in Oklahoma, where the word "nauseated" is the standard for "the feeling you get before vomiting," to quote your definition. After college and marriage, my husband and I went to New York and lived there (in the suburbs) for more than 30 years. I think "nauseous" was the only word I ever heard in the New York area for "the feeling you get before vomiting." I learned long ago that one must use the locally approved word in order to be understood, but I could never bring myself to use "nauseous" for that definition. I had to invent some other combination of words to convey that meaning.

Now we live in California. We have lived here only three years, but in that time I have never heard anyone say "nauseous" to convey the meaning of "the feeling you get before vomiting." In fact, I think that in three years I have never heard anyone use the word at all. I am once again comfortable using "nauseated" for that meaning, because everyone else uses "nauseated" also.

In these three years of living here, I have come to the conclusion that these two words must be used in different areas of the country to express the same meaning. This would be a parallel usage to the words "tonic," "soda," and "pop," for example, which mean the same thing in different parts of the country.

Anniebeth Young
Coronado, California

Dear Bill:

I am glad to read that you have "caved in to common usage" with regard to nauseous *in the sense of "experiencing nausea," though I am puzzled to read that you rely on* disgusting *when you need a word to denote "causing nausea": there's an obvious and completely transparent alternative, namely* nauseating.

Actually, I'm puzzled that nauseous *in the sense of "causing nausea" has retained even a tenuous hold on a place in current English vocabulary. Adjectives of the form X-ous generally mean roughly "be/have/do X" (or something corresponding to X—the X often isn't a whole word by itself, as in* cautious*), and* *hardly any of them mean "cause one to be/have/do X." I have just skimmed the roughly 2,200 words ending in* -ous *that are listed in the* Rückläufiges Wörterbuch der englischen Sprache *(11 pages, each of 50 lines and 4 columns) and found (aside from hundreds of medical terms whose meanings I don't even want to know) mainly words like* courageous, courteous, porous, glamorous, mischievous, cautious, envious, pompous, loquatious, amorous, ambitious, superstitious, penurious, curious, sagacious, audacious, punctilious, conscious, delirious, industrious, ostentatious, anxious; gelatinous, numerous, fictitious, miraculous, mysterious, hetero-/homogeneous; libelous, treacherous, sacrilegious, cancerous. *The only words I noticed that could be conceived of as having a meaning "cause one to be/have/do X" (I say "could be conceived of," because there often is more than one way that you could take a given meaning as breaking up into parts) were* suspicious, injurious, infectious, noxious, *and perhaps* riotous. *One word in this list, namely* suspicious, *deserves the attention of prescriptive grammarians, since it has an ambiguity that at times can be pernicious ("have suspicions" vs. "incite suspicions").*

Jim [James D. McCawley]
Department of Linguistics
University of Chicago
Chicago, Illinois

Another authority in your corner: Woody Allen, whose movie Sleeper *closes with a line about sex and death—"two things that come once in a lifetime, although at least after death, you don't feel nauseous."*

John H. Taylor
Yorba Linda, California

My favorites are: "Barking at ants," and "Calling Europe."

Steven M. Denenberg, M.D.
Omaha, Nebraska

"Sick up" (Brit.)
  "Flash your hash" (U.S., fifties/sixties)

Edward Brown
Medford, New Jersey

An Unstaid Heads-up

When called to account by a *Washington Post* reporter, Susan Schmidt, for his personal stock and bond trades, which were said to average twice a month over the past four years, the Comptroller of the Currency, Robert L. Clarke, expostulated: "There is no requirement for putting these investments in a blind trust." He added, in words that were blown up in a "bank" on the front page (apt journalese, as Mr. Clarke is the nation's top banking regulator): "I don't find anything the slightest bit *unsobering* in those dealings."

I tried to figure that out. *Insobriety,* the state of not being sober, means "drunkenness"; could Mr. Clarke have been protesting that he was not throwing his money around like a drunken sailor? That doesn't track (and if sensitive naval personnel want to strike the *drunken sailor* simile from the language, they can leap overboard).

In the fourteenth century, *unsober* was used as an adjective to mean "uncontrolled, unregulated," certainly an appropriate term for the Comptroller of the Currency to be familiar with, and the verb form was used at least once in the nineteenth century to mean "to make unstaid," in "We are getting hugely into debt to the greatness . . . of God's mercies, and this at times unsobers us." Was the Comptroller resuscitating a useful old word?

Or did he mean, instead, *sobering,* an 1831 coinage meaning "tending to make one thoughtful"? That would be closer to a denial of concern, but it still would get a funny look from Norma Loquendi.

"He's generally very careful with his words," says Leonora Cross, deputy comptroller for communications, "but he was starting to get angry at the reporter's implications that he's a high-rolling speculator. I think he was trying to say *sobering.*"

I think it was just one of those days: Some banks were tottering, his broker was on the phone touting a hot junk bond, and when a nosy reporter started pestering him, he meant to say, "I don't find anything the slightest bit *unsettling* in these dealings," and the wrong word popped out—and onto the front page, then into the Nexis computer system, where it will be associated with his name forever.

Perhaps this was a fortunate (not a *fortuitous*) error. We need a word to denote a relaxation of stern demeanor; when, for example, the slightly inebriated football star John Riggins advised Supreme Court Justice Sandra Day O'Connor at a black-tie dinner to "loosen up," he might more formally have suggested, "Unsober yourself." What causes us to lighten up, to shake off care or responsibility, has an *unsobering* effect.

You use "average" in a way that sounded very odd to my ear. The relevant portion of this sentence, somewhat untangled: "Robert Clarke's personal stock and bond trades were said to average twice a month." There is no doubt as to your meaning ("occur on average"), but "average" as an intransitive verb followed by a frequency, as opposed to a rate or an amount, looked unusual.

I work in the area of corpus lexicography; we're building software tools to assist lexicographers from Oxford University Press to produce definitions for the forthcoming Oxford Dictionary of the English Language (ODEL), where the name of the game is to base decisions about word-senses on actual usage (mostly). We have a preliminary, 7-million-word corpus of British-English text (American-English text will appear in the final, 21-million-word corpus), so I looked at all the occurrences of "average." There were 876, including inflections (e.g., "averaging"). Indeed, there were no uses of "average" as an intransitive verb followed by a frequency.

Webster's Third gives three "examples" of "average" as an intransitive verb. (I put quotes around "examples" because, having studied a little lexicography at Oxford, I know that these are often made up by well-meaning lexicographers who haven't the slightest idea whether the example reflects reality. I confess to being a "corpus" zealot.)

> *Example 1: "the fish average larger." Well, there weren't any examples in the corpus of that usage, either.*
>
> *Example 2: "losses will average $5,000 a year." This usage is quite common, and probably holds the key to my discomfort with your sentence. "$5,000 a year" is a rate, a ratio of an amount (a number, 5,000, and a unit, dollars) and a unit of time. A frequency, such as "twice a month," is a ratio of a pure number ("two") and a unit of time. Perhaps the convention, then, is that since there is such a strong expectation of seeing a rate after the intransitive "average," we express frequencies in some other manner. Sure enough, in the corpus, all the examples with frequencies use "on average."*
>
> *Example 3: "these poles average 10 feet in length." This is simply an amount. The corpus contains examples where the amount is temporal: ". . . the chairman of the hoteliers' federation estimated that some 500,000 bookings were possible with visitors averaging seven days each." (Personally, I'd prefer the non-metonymic "visits" to "visitors.")*

Oddly enough, Webster's gives "averages 2 days per week on the golf course" as an example of "average" as a transitive verb. The subject is presumably human, and I fail to see a distinction between "Lee averages $5,000 per year in commissions," which is presumably intransitive in Webster's book, and "Lee averages 2 days per week on the golf course," which is intransitive.

James R. Meehan
Digital Equipment Corp.
Systems Research Center
Palo Alto, California

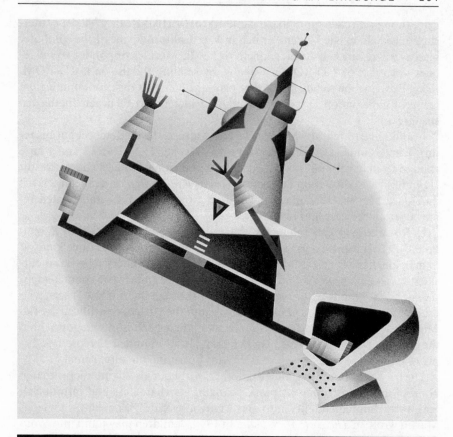

Virtual Reality

There you sit, a *real person* (my readers are neither robots nor androids nor phony-balonies) reading this in *real time* (meaning "now," not photographing it in your mind for perusal later) and secure in the knowledge that the real you and the real information you draw from the real page you hold in your real hand at this very moment constitute *reality.*

Don't let anybody shake that certainty out of you. Cling to it. You'll need it as we pass into the world of *virtual reality.*

Virtual has come to mean "almost"; when we say "virtually everyone," we mean "everybody except a few jerks who never get the word and they don't count." Purists insist on its old meaning, now its second sense, of "in effect but unadmitted," like "I wanna be a virtual usage dictator." Let's stick with the first sense here, as virtually everyone does. (Do not use it to mean "near" or "bordering": A suburb is not "virtually in the city.")

Here in my real hand right now is an invitation from Alan Meckler of Meckler Managing Information Technology (presumably the name of his

firm, though it reads more like a caption) to "Virtual Reality '92," a conference to be held in late September in San Jose, California, one of the computer
meccas where our Cupertino runneth over. Mr. Meckler responded to my request for a list of CD-ROM's available by sending the list on a CD-ROM,
thereby forcing me to buy a unit that plays the compact disk containing great
reams of information. (I spell *disk* with a *k,* which is why I'll never win the dis-
cus throw.)

I would like to tell Mr. Meckler I cannot attend the conference, but his return E-mail address is listed as "Internet: MecklerJVNC.NET" and I have
enough trouble with old-fashioned stamps and elongated ZIP codes already.
He publishes the monthly newsletter *Virtual Reality Report,* and can tell the
difference between that phrase—familiarly known as VR—and related re-
movals from the here and now.

"VR is a way of enabling users," he writes, "to participate directly in real-
time, 3-D environments generated by computers." He describes three kinds of
immersion: first, the toe-in-the-water experience of beginners, who stand outside the imaginary world and communicate by computer with characters inside it. Next, wading up to the hips, are the "through the window" users, who
use a "flying mouse" to project themselves into the virtual, or artificial, world.
Then there are the hold-the-nose plungers: "first-person interaction within
the computer-generated world via the use of head-mounted stereoscopic dis-
plays, gloves, bodysuits, and audio systems providing binaural sound."

The trick is not only to simulate another world but also to interact with it—
pouring in data affecting its plots, changing its characters and introducing
real-world unpredictability into this "mirror world." "Someday," Douglas
Martin wrote in *The New York Times* in 1990, "children may jump into Won-
derland with Alice or put Humpty Dumpty back together."

Coiner of the phrase *virtual reality,* according to Howard Rheingold, who
wrote a book in 1991 using the title, is Jaron Lanier, a computer scientist
whose company developed the Dataglove. It triumphed over its synonym, *artificial reality,* because *artificial* means "fake" and *virtual* means "almost." (I
tried to reach Mr. Lanier, but apparently he stepped out of the real world for
a few days.) A related term is *telepresence,* the déjà-voodoo that helps virtual-
ists feel they are actually present in another place or time.

Mr. Rheingold, reached in San Francisco, helped differentiate among real-
ities:

"*Virtual reality,* the illusion of being in an artificial world, differs from *alternative reality,* which could be a hypnotized state," he says. I presume it
could also be a state of self-delusion or a drug-induced condition.

Cyberspace, a word derived from Norbert Wiener's *cybernetics,* was coined
by William Gibson in his 1984 sci-fi novel, *Neuromancer* (which my son the
software developer informs me is "the definitive work of cyberpunk fiction").
According to Mr. Rheingold, it is "a larger, abstract space that virtual reality
allows you to enter, which also includes the communications field."

That loses me in cyberspace. Peggy Weil, an M.I.T. graduate now living in Los Angeles, writes: "The entire field is in its infancy and badly needs a linguistic referee. We don't know what to call the stuff. Is it hypermedia, multimedia, interactive computer graphics, interactive media, electronic publishing—books without pages, paperback movies? The field is very exciting now, but I'm not happy with all these *inter* and *hyper* and *multi* words."

Wonks, hackers, computer scientists, cognitive psychologists, graphic artists and mirror-worldly philosophers are happily engaged in this linguistic melee. The comforting part of it all is that the creative argonauts of artificiality world have this real-life, real-time problem with a realistic vocabulary—and are now writing themselves a reality check.

I've been in the software business for 25 years and never heard "virtual" used as "almost." It's always used as the antonym of "real" and means "something that does the right thing and you could swear exists, but doesn't." A computer might have 1 MB of real memory and 50 MB of virtual memory, that looks like memory but is simulated. A virtual disk is an imitation disk that is really a section of memory.

"Imitation" is probably the closest English word, although it misses the non-existence connotation. By "virtual memory" we mean "imitation memory," and by a "virtual disk" we mean an "imitation disk." "Virtual reality" doesn't mean "almost reality," it means "imitation reality."

You could think of "virtual" as the opposite of "transparent." "Transparent" means it's there but you can't see it; "virtual" means you can see it but it isn't there.

Richard A. Stone
Westborough, Massachusetts

Voice Over

When people begin to accustom themselves to a new columnist, they say, "He found his voice."

When the legendary editor Kate Medina was displeased by a writer's chapter, she crystallized her criticism in "But it's not in your voice."

Literary criticism has become hoarse with *voice;* now *Road & Track* magazine is quoted in an automobile advertisement as saying, "This confident 'new' Audi has a distinct voice."

What's this vox, Pop? And how does this literary sense of *voice* differ from *style?*

Do not confuse this hot new voice with grammatical voice, which determines the direction of the action in a sentence. In an *active voice,* the subject is performing the verb's action, with the object at the receiving end: "I lit-critted John." In a *passive voice,* the object becomes the doer of the action: "John was lit-critted by me." Professor James D. McCawley at the University of Chicago, now writing a preface to the new edition of Otto Jespersen's *Philosophy of Grammar,* writes of this grammatical sense: "I think 'voice' is a lousy term and greatly prefer Jespersen's 'turn' (the idea being that active and passive clauses are the same thing but turned around in different ways)."

Let's hear a different voice. T. S. Eliot explained the new sense in his 1953 *The Three Voices of Poetry.* First was the *persona,* or mask-voice, that a poet adopts for a particular poem, as Robert Browning did hiding behind the Duke in "My Last Duchess." Second was the familiar *stylistic voice* of the poet, as in the rousing lilt of Kipling, that causes the reader to say, "That's Kipling, all right." Third was the *archetypal voice,* supposedly using the poet as a medium in a trance.

That second voice—the distinctive mode of expression, the expected quirks and trademark tone, the characteristic attitude of writer toward reader and subject—has taken over as the meaning of *voice* in writing today. Hemingway had a voice: spare, selective, easily parodied because readily identifiable.

This is not necessarily the natural voice of the writer; for example, I knock myself out in these language pieces to adopt a scholarly breeziness, respectfully flip and deliciously tedious—a darting-about voice far different from my march-over-the-cliff, calumnious polemics on the Op-Ed page. Voice is not essence, but is essential to separate the writer from the pack. (That sentence is in a didactic, op-ed voice, and has no place in this light and airy space.)

The meaning of *voice* overlaps *style,* but is different from that familiar term. The playwright Sam Shepard told an interviewer: "Style is the outer trappings. . . . But a voice is almost without words. . . . It's something in the spaces, in between."

Warlords, Bandits, Thugs and Regional Leaders

"Why is the word *warlord* employed for the gunmen in Somalia," asks Herb O'Connor of ABC News, "as opposed to other places in the world? It seems a Draculian kind of term."

I like *Draculian,* imputing bloodiness, somewhat on the analogy of *Draconian.* And I agree that *warlord* is a word that seems out of place in Africa.

The word was coined in 1856 by Ralph Waldo Emerson: "Piracy and war," he wrote, "gave place to trade, politics and letters; the *war-lord* to the *law-lord.*" Between 1916 and 1928, that word was used in translation of the Chi-

nese term *junfa,* meaning "regional military commander, ruling with little re-gard to orders from a central government"; said *The New York Times* of De-cember 31, 1922, "His regard for the Peking Government is proportioned inversely to the size of his army and his distance from the capital."

The word and its variations in English gained a distinctly Chinese conno-tation by the 1960's. "Throughout his struggles with provincial *warlordism,* 'communist-bandits' and finally with the Japanese," wrote Edgar Snow, an early apologist for the Communist Mao Zedong against Chiang Kai-shek, "Chiang remained essentially an old-fashioned militarist."

Toward the end of that decade, the word was applied elsewhere in the Far East. "Is Indonesia now in for a spell of *warlordism?*" *The New Statesman* asked in 1966. By the late 70's, the word made its way into Middle East coverage: "Petty *warlordism,* protection rackets," *The Guardian* wrote in 1979, ". . . have alienated the natural allies of the Palestinians."

Now we have *Somalia's rival warlords* and their "clan-based followers." Some find the cultural shift bothersome: "*War lord* is a term I associated more with medieval Japan," writes Richard Johnson, a columnist for the *Daily News.* "In Africa they have *tribal chiefs.* Then it occurred to me. Tribal chiefs are armed with spears. War lords carry rifles." He finds a touch of political correctness in the usage: "A war lord is a tribal chief who has been armed by colonialists. Now that we've sold them guns, we have to go in and take them away, turning the war lords back into more peaceful tribal chiefs."

Because the leaders of these clans, vying for power, stole food supplies and blocked the distribution of relief to the starving, Western journalists denounced them as *bandits*—rooted in the Germanic verb *bannan,* "to command," the noun now meaning "outlaw, plunderer"—and as *thugs.* This 1810 noun came from the Hindi word *thag,* for a member of a gang of professional murderers who specialized in strangling their victims. *Time* magazine called them "Mad Max characters . . . conducting an experiment in anarchy," referring to a 1979 Australian film, starring Mel Gibson, about violent and vengeful characters.

As the gang chiefs in Somalia became individuals with whom to negotiate, the term *warlord* was dropped from the official vocabulary of American spokesmen. Ted Koppel of ABC, broadcasting from Mogadishu, started to use the word twice one night and ostentatiously caught himself, saying they were now to be known as *"regional leaders."* Particularly helpful ones, whatever their age, are called *elders.*

Washington Tense

"Obviously, some mistakes were made," said the White House chief of staff, John H. Sununu, in a statement I suspect was beaten out of him by Bush Administration damage-controllers late one night in a room not far from the Oval Office.

"Washington has invented a new tense," observes William Schneider, resident fellow at the American Enterprise Institute. "This usage should be referred to as the *past exonerative.*" True; the passive voice acknowledges the errors, but it avoids the blame entirely, though in this case Mr. Sununu went on to accept his small portion of the general mistake-making. Bureaucrats use the past exonerative all the time: "The program was implemented" is their way of not quite saying, "I did it."

Mr. Schneider believes that this useful invention can be adopted for household use, much as research on insulating materials for spacesuits can be applied to keep-cool tote bags. He offers *dishes were broken,* an announcement that can be made with a suitable "who me?" expression. When deniability is impossible, dissociation is the way, and the past exonerative allows the actor to separate himself from the act.

Schneider's "exonerative" is right on target, but "tense" is off. It is voice that exonerates, not tense, and Mr. Schneider might better call the usage in question "exonerative voice."

> James Merriam Howard Jr.
> Westport, Massachusetts

Would not voice *be a better designation than* tense? *After all, the ducking of responsibility is not limited to the past.*
　　Hindi already delightfully contains such a voice. *It is called* causative. *I do prefer* exonerative, *however, and hope that it becomes the preferred designation. Its uses are really often delightful. It is far gentler to speak to a child about something that broke when it is not necessary to attribute causality to the agent of breakage. Similarly for problems of the car, the train schedule, the weather, the state of one's belly. These things just occur.*
　　Documentary footnote:

I cut it.	Maine wuh kata.
It was cut.	Wuh kat gaya.
It just seems to be cut!	Wuh katwa gaya.

> David H. Barnhouse, M.D.
> Pittsburgh, Pennsylvania

The "exonerative" is a whole mood, *comparable, perhaps, to the indicative and subjunctive. A speaker may use the exonerative mood to disclaim personal responsibility for his or her past, present, or future actions. Institutions may similarly use the exonerative to evade or deny responsibility. The exonerative has not only a past tense, but also present and future tenses. The exonerative is usually in the passive voice, but can be in the active.*
　　At the beginning of the Gulf War, a government spokesperson might have said, "Iraq's aggression against Kuwait forces the United States to intervene." This is the present exonerative, active voice. President Bush was not making a

choice based on considerations of national interest, morality, and political ad-
vantage, but "the United States" had no choice. When a hapless fellow misses
several house payments, the mortgage company writes, "We are compelled to
commence foreclosure proceedings." This is the present exonerative, passive
voice. The mortgage company is not making a choice based on considerations of
economic self-interest, but is "compelled" to foreclose.

> Bruce A. Campbell
> Professor of Law
> University of Toledo
> Toledo, Ohio

There is, I think, a more appropriate designation for President Reagan's "Mis-
takes were made" and Mr. Sununu's "Obviously some mistakes were made"
than past exonerative. *I much prefer the term* passive evasive.

> Helene Bell
> Oceanside, New York

Did you know the past exonerative is part of Spanish usage (not by that term, of
course)? Despite the pronouncements of high school athletes, "Oh yeah, Span-
ish is easy," Spanish is an extremely subtle language. (I never heard anyone who
spoke it well call it easy.) An example of its subtlety, apart from the use of the
past subjunctive, is the avoidance of placing the blame for ordinary actions. In
English we say, "I dropped the books"; in French "J'ai laissé tomber les livres";
but in Spanish one says, "Se me cayeron los libros." Not "I dropped the books,"
but, literally, "the books dropped themselves on me." "On me" in this sense
doesn't mean they fell on top of the speaker, but that the speaker was a victim of
the books falling, as in "that's a joke on me."

> Frank Ruddy
> Chevy Chase, Maryland

While spending a year in Tegucigalpa, Honduras, on a United States Informa-
tion Service English Teaching Fellowship during 1975 and 1976, I had occasion
to not only improve my Spanish, but to make certain observations about lan-

guage as an indicator of the psychology of its speakers. The past exonerative comes into use at all levels of Spanish-speaking society. I noticed that when a person dropped a fabulously expensive crystal vase, the Spanish expression he used (at least the more printable one) translated not as "I dropped it," but as "It fell to me." Personal responsibility could be avoided with similar grace in the event one was late—a not infrequent occurrence in that part of the world. The phrase, which translates rather clumsily into English, is: "It was to me a delay."

Can we conclude from the emergence of this new tense in English that the growing size of the Hispanic population is making its influence felt in Los Estados Unidos?

If in fact it is a reflection of new linguistic clout on the part of the Latino community that this grammatical form is making an appearance, we may be able to look forward to the infusion of still more diverse cultural innovations that will continue to modify the American syntactic mosaic.

Miriam Imerman
Bloomfield Hills, Michigan

The Way the Poll Bounces

"It's partly a *convention bounce,*" Governor Bill Clinton said after his poll ratings shot up in July.

As August ended and the Republicans had convened in Houston, the Bush-Quayle ratings improved somewhat and *The Christian Science Monitor* wrote, "It represents a routine *convention bounce.*" *Newsweek,* in its Conventional Wisdom Watch, asked, "Why does the CW worry about the '*convention bounce*' if the CW also says the bounce dissipates within two weeks?"

The much-discussed *convention bounce* is a temporary rise in the opinion polls caused by the television exposure and print commentary during a party's national convention. As the Associated Press reported in 1988, "The *convention bounce* usually settles down as voters focus on the issues of the race."

Bounce has triumphed over the variant *bump.* Who coined the phrase? In 1980, the Carter presidential spokesman, Jody Powell, used the term to mean a psychological lift: He said that the increase in President Carter's rating was "the post-convention bounce we hoped for." In a dozen years, the *post-* prefix has worn off.

Weaning Weenie

When does a mistake become a new sense of a word?

Viola Novicki of Niles, MI (MIchigan, MIssissippi, only the postal computer knows), sends in a couple of recent citations. One is Tom Brokaw of NBC talking about "children *weaned* on television"; another is a vituperative clayfoot writing in *The New York Times* about the background of the new Secretary of Education, Lamar Alexander: "Lamar was politically *weaned* by Bryce Harlow."

The verb *to wean,* Mrs. Novicki notes, means "to cause to give up suckling and accept other food" and by extension "to detach from the accustomed." The essence of the meaning is removal; a baby is weaned away from mother's milk to hearty meals of mashed bananas. The verb, which may be rooted in the Latin *Venus,* has never meant *to suckle;* just the opposite, it has meant "to withdraw from suckling."

Yet here are two influential language nurses, Brokaw and Safire, using the word in the sense of "brought up on, reared, raised." Are they mistaken or on the cutting edge of new usage? Let us fearlessly dip our elbows into that tub.

"Perhaps it was a simple case of confusion about the meaning of *wean,*" writes *Merriam-Webster's Dictionary of English Usage,* citing a dozen examples, from Fred Allen in 1931 ("Babies are being weaned on aspirin") to a 1985 *New York Times* book reviewer ("a writer weaned on the short story"). "The new sense of *wean* has established an independent existence for itself, apart from the literal meaning of the word," says the anything-goes usage guide. "Its eventual appearance in dictionaries is just a matter of time."

True enough; *Webster's New World,* Third Edition, already has it as a third sense: "to be raised on or brought up with; to become accustomed to."

Wait a minute. Are the Language Snobs going to let the Language Slobs take over without a fight? Granted, *weaned on* is in use by solecists, mainly men who never offered a hungry baby a nurturing teat. But are there no defenders, besides Mrs. Novicki, of *weaned away from* as the meaning insisted upon by educated users of the language?

I think the misuse of *weaned on* came about as a euphemism for *suckled on,* as if that beautiful term were somehow too intimate for ordinary discourse. Let's reject that cowardly linguistic prissiness.

My advice: If you mean *raised by,* use that term (for animals, of course; for humans, it should be *reared by*). If you mean *suckled on,* use that vivid term to refer to the milk, or *suckled by* to refer to the mother. Same with the figurative extension: "Lamar was politically suckled by Bryce." You, too, Tom: "children suckled on television."

Use *weaned* with *away* or *from* to avoid the new confusion. (In buying a puppy, however, a simple "Is it weaned?" is acceptable. "Is it wormed?" and "Is it housebroken?" do not enter into this controversy.)

My ambition is to avert overweaning. When next you hear a media biggie boast of having been "weaned on Watergate" or whatever, snicker ostentatiously. Join the Gotcha! Gang; send a postcard. If this informed correctness fails; if the weaning barbarians cannot be driven from the temple—then from the nurturing breasts of clarity and precision we'll all be suckled away together.

Tom Brokaw's use of the word weaned *is incorrect. Yet, it carries a thrust of meaning occurring in common usage. The word* wean *clearly means to accustom a child or other young animal to the loss of mother's milk. Normally, this occurs through substituting solid food. It is common to hear people who raise animals refer to the solid food as in the phrase, "The calves were weaned on mashed oats."*

Once upon a time, young mothers would discuss the various solid foods given to their newborn in phrases such as, "I weaned Jimmy on mashed potatoes, but my sister Sarah thought Mom's recipe for mashed peas was the best thing she found for weaning her son." When the mother's milk is removed, there is an emphasis placed on the substitute. As a result, weaning takes place on mashed oats, mashed potatoes and strained cooked peas. The broader meaning used by Tom Brokaw and Webster's New World, *Third Edition, is one which circulated in common currency for years. The reason it was never identified by lexicographers was because most people for years refrained from using the word in polite company (except in the most correct manner) and its everyday common usage occurred only in animal husbandry and in intimate conversations between nursing mothers. In the era of post-frontal nudity in the arts and every other form of communication, the word* wean *is no longer relegated to hushed private conversations and its long-practiced common use is exposed to the world.*

David Allen
Sacramento, California

Under natural conditions, babies of most species are gradually weaned by their mother. In some farm situations, weaning occurs at an earlier age when the young are weaned abruptly by the farmer. This is analogous to Lamar Alexander being politically weaned by Bryce Harlow. Presumably Harlow gave Alexander something solid to chew on.

G. I. Christison
Professor of Animal and
Poultry Science
University of Saskatchewan
Saskatoon, Canada

"Wean" means to take off of the breast or bottle, but "weaned on," in my memory, at least, has always been used to indicate what was given as an inducement to accomplish the weaning. In the late '40s, in sixth grade, we read that Pecos Bill was so tough because he was "weaned on snake venom." I remember bad guys in the western movies having been "weaned on whiskey." The phrase, by its nature, has a meaning nearly opposite the word alone. It is useful and traditional, and I think it should be correct. Otherwise the bad guys would have to be "weaned away from milk by the substitution of whiskey," and that would never do.

> *Walter Darby Bannard*
> *Coral Gables, Florida*

There is noooo way that the humble little word wean, *with its impeccable Anglo-Saxon lineage, is "rooted in" Latin* Venus. *When the etymological note in Webster's New World Dictionary says that* wean *"< IE base *wen-, to desire, attain, be satisfied," that means that it goes back in a direct line to this Indo-European base (or root). When the etymological note states further that the base *wen- "> L venus, love," that means that the Indo-European base is also the source of the Latin word.* Wean *(as well as* win, wish, wont*(ed) and (*over*)ween(ing)!) and* venus *are thus cognate words having a common origin in Indo-European, but* wean *is not "rooted in"* venus *any more than* venus *is "rooted in"* wean. *Since the word* cognate *might leave your readers scratching their heads, you can make the point quite nicely by saying in such cases that the English word is "akin to" the Latin (or Greek) word.*

Incidentally, if you're in the market for an English word that is really "rooted in" Latin venus, *I strongly recommend* venereal*!*

> *Louis Jay Herman*
> *New York, New York*

Wedges and Bounces

America is back up on wedgies. Remember those triangulated, high-soled shoes of the 40's that incorporated the heel and turned the fashionable woman into an endangered species? They're back—not merely in the form of platform soles, but planks in political platforms.

In 1990, as Bush White House aides fought over the degree to which affirmative action guidelines became quotas, the former Carter adviser Stuart E.

Eizenstat said with some prescience that the Republicans had "a need to give the Reagan Democrats red meat at a time when the economy is going into the tank, and they see civil rights and quotas as a *wedge issue.*"

Recalling this early usage and perhaps coinage, Mr. Eizenstat tells me: "I was looking for a phrase to illustrate the attempt to split the coalition of working-class whites and blacks, the two constituencies Roosevelt unified on economic grounds. The image came to mind of a wedge being driven."

It filled a political-linguistic need for fresh labels. Another Democrat, the Clinton strategist James Carville, charged two years later that President

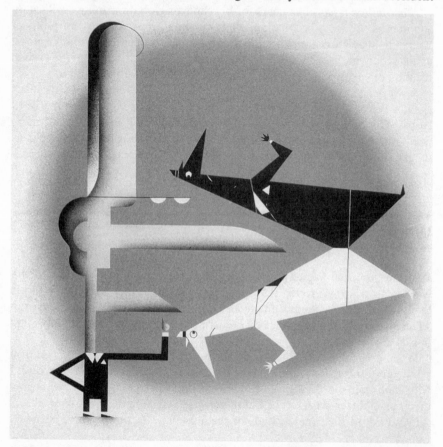

Bush's advisers, bereft of an agenda, had to "dust off the Republican manual, which is to go to *wedge issues:* 'We can't lead the country so maybe we can divide it.' "

As a phrase, *wedge issue* is related to the 80's *hot-button issue,* which was an updating of the 70's *polarization. Wedge,* with earthy Indo-European roots as both verb and noun, strikes me as an improvement over the Latinate *polarize* and *polarization.*

Wedge issue is a political attack locution, usually used by liberals and moderates, aimed at politicians on the right who bring up sensitive cultural and social subjects during political campaigns. The dividing wedge, however, need not be racial: Free trade is seen by the right as a wedge issue to use to divide workers and environmentalists on the left.

Here is a synonymy of the issues issue: A *switcher issue*—like gun control or abortion—is a single subject that will cause a minority of voters to change their vote regardless of other patterns, urges or habits (resulting in a *bullet vote*).

A *hot-button issue*—like perks for big shots or global warming—will cause a potential voter to become agitated, but not necessarily to the point of switching allegiance; touching this button causes audiences to roar or hoot, and is synonymous with *red meat,* the figure of speech drawn from the excited reaction of carnivorous animals when food is thrown into their cage.

A *gut issue* has a wider visceral appeal: The intestinal matter on this year's agenda is the slow growth of the economy, expressed in the single word "jobs." This *bread-and-butter issue* can also be the *burning issue* if it is dramatized, but if the opposition fails to ignite it, the subject is better described as the *paramount issue.* As an issue fades, it becomes characterized as a *yawner.*

Whacking the Suits

Wearing his usual Western attire—a plaid shirt, jeans and a quilted down waistcoat—a former rodeo rider named Cy Baumgartner paid a visit to the St. Louis Art Museum and made an interesting discovery: the horseman in "The Bronco Buster," a bronze by Frederic Remington, was wearing his spurs upside down.

When the real broncobuster (now one word, on the analogy of *gangbuster*) pointed out this gaffe to the curator, his embarrassing revelation was received with a disdain bordering on condescension. Mr. Baumgartner, who now drives an eighteen-wheel truck but retains his interest in the Wild West, cheerfully waved off the frigid attitude of the museum official with "I've been lied to by *suits* all my life."

This episode was recounted to me by Eliot Porter of the *St. Louis Post-Dispatch* with the suggestion that I explore "the metonymical use of *suit.*" He enclosed an early citation in print of a 1984 A.P. Laserphoto (formerly wirephoto) of a bunch of executives marching with briefcases, beneath the title "*Suits* in Step."

First, he is right about "*metonymy,*" pronounced "Muh-TAHN-uh-mee," which is the figure of speech that identifies a person or thing by referring to something closely associated with it. Older examples include *the brass* for high military officers and *the crown* for the only royalty not headed for the divorce courts.

Metonymy is not to be confused with *synecdoche,* which is pronounced correctly only in Schenectady and uses the part to refer to the whole. ("I'm using the *wheels,* Pops, to go get a new *tube*" means your high-definition son is borrowing the car to obtain a new television set.) A *suit* is associated with, but is not part of, a person, and *suit* as the figure of speech is therefore metonymic.

Its sense as "the sort of person who wears a suit"—meaning "formal, stiff, conventional"—is apparently only a decade old. (You've got a 70's citation? Send it in.) However, its sense as "game, racket" was noted in Grose's 1785 *Classical Dictionary of the Vulgar Tongue,* and a *suit-and-cloak* was Cockney cant for a "good store of brandy or any agreeable liquor."

Although a *suit* can be an executive of either sex, the term is more often applied to men; during the Clarence Thomas hearings, female commentators often referred to the male-only panel of Senators as "that pack of *suits.*" Although women wear suits, most often the word in its metonymic sense refers to men.

What follows is speculation, but this new sense may be bottomed on *an empty suit,* the derogation of a person as hollow. Snide, unfeeling right-wing commentators have been applying that term to Senator Ted Kennedy for years. The earliest usage supplied to me by Sol Steinmetz of Random House was from a *Cagney and Lacey* TV show in 1982, in which a character referred slightingly to "some *suit* from the Mayor's office." He included a 1990 print citation from *Hit Men,* a book by Fredric Dannen that described CBS executives as "the *suits* upstairs."

A more specific term, *a fifteen-hundred-dollar suit,* has been noted here earlier, describing the Mafia don John Gotti's attire at his recent trial.

Whack, You're Dead

"I was in jail when I *whacked* him," John Gotti seemed to say on a secretly recorded tape.

The defense suggested that the usage meant merely "I beat him up," and it is true that *whack,* a verb of echoic origin, means "to strike, hit with a sharp blow." However, to *whack out* has a more serious new slang sense: In *Wilderness,* a 1979 novel by Robert B. Parker, a character warns, "You come into a town and try to whack the guy out first thing, you're not likely to get ahead."

Laurie Goodstein, in *The Washington Post,* defined the verb *whack,* and its extended variant *whack in the mouth,* as "to execute; usually—but not limited to—a close personal friend, a brother-in-law or a business partner who holds an inconvenient percent share in your lucrative concern."

In this sense, *whack* is synonymous with *pop.* "Like, I just wouldn't say nothing about *popping* people," said Mr. Gotti, in the context of speaking in a room suspected of being bugged. Like *whack,* the slang also has a more innocent sense; when columnists *pop* politicians, this act is considered less severe than *zapping* them, but both *pop* and *zap* are less than lethal.

A *yellow dog,* in the latest gangland slang, is an informer or *rat.* A yellow dog is considered the definition of a cur; in labor terminology, it is applied to an agreement signed by employees not to join a union. In politics, curiously, the words form a compound adjective meaning "loyal"; a *yellow-dog Democrat* is a voter who cannot be swayed from voting the straight ticket, "even if the candidate is a yellow dog."

What to Call the Russians

Happy 1992, C.I.S.!

Or should that be—Welcome to the list of the names of nations, S.N.G.!

Oh, the heavy problems of disunion. Segments of the former Union of Soviet Socialist Republics (or *internal empire,* as American hawks called it) have become the Commonwealth of Independent States. The initials for the English words are C.I.S.; the initials for the Russian words are S.N.G., for *Sodruzhestvo Nezavisimykh Gosudarstv.*

I would say to go with C.I.S., or as space-conscious *USA Today* would write it, CIS; the acronym sounds like "Sis," with a warm sororal connotation. (You are unfamilial with *sororal*? So was I; a call to Fred Mish at Merriam-Webster got the answer to "What's the feminine for *fraternal*?") S.N.G., on the other hand, would be pronounced like *snig,* a clip of the verb *snigger,* a variation of *snicker,* meaning "to laugh derisively," of echoic origin; it would also lend itself to pronunciation as *snag,* the noun meaning "minor obstacle, hitch," and would conflict with the Society of North American Goldsmiths.

I realize that meat is scarce in Moscow this winter and the ruble overhang is a terrible threat to the economy, and observers should pause before adding to the burdens of the new gathering of sovereignties, but we cannot ignore this problem: What seemed like a great idea for a name when the three Slavic nations gathered at Minsk last month has a substantial linguistic drawback or snag. As the far-flung membership of the Squad Squad will hasten and hurry to say and declaim, the chosen name—in both its English and Russian forms—is redundant. A *commonwealth* is "an association of independent states"; the C.I.S. is "an association of independent states of independent states."

Granted, the namers had a problem. Boris Yeltsin of Russia, Leonid Kravchuk of Ukraine and Stanislav Shushkevich of Byelorussia wanted to use the word *sodruzhestvo,* which we may translate as *commonwealth, community* or *concord* (related terms that are not the same), because it was not the word the old unionists in Mikhail Gorbachev's Kremlin wanted: *union,* or at the very least *federation.* The leaders of the republics within the disintegrating union would not even stand for the murky *confederation;* they wanted a word that clearly broke with the center forever.

Hence, *sodruzhestvo*. Our translation into *commonwealth* uses a word that began as *common weal,* or "public good," expressed in our Constitution's preamble as "general welfare"; it came to mean "body politic," or "the whole people," and later "a loose association of sovereign nations, often with a common history as parts of an empire." What we have in mind is the equivalent of the *British Commonwealth of Nations* (not quite as redundant), linked by tradition, language and sometimes a sentimental allegiance to the British Crown, and with formal communications and meetings but no dominance over one another.

When this word is translated as *community,* you have more of an economic than a political common denominator, in current global usage. The pundit Walter Lippmann in a 1944 book coined *Atlantic community* as a description of the common interests of Britain, the United States and Canada, and the term was later extended to all the members of the North Atlantic Treaty Organization; that community was political.

As early as 1888, the Earl of Carnarvon, an English statesman, was using the word in that political sense: "We are part of the community of Europe, and we must do our duty as such." In our generation, however, the European Economic Community was formed and colored the word; now all communities, in the international diplomatic sense, are presumed to be economic alliances or zones. (In Europe today, the argument is over making an economic union into a political one.)

So there you are in Minsk, naming this form of cooperation and coordination within a nonunion. You cannot call it the Russian Commonwealth, on the analogy of the British Commonwealth, because Ukraine is tired of Russian domination; you cannot call it the Ukrainian Commonwealth, because everybody knows that Russia is the senior partner in terms of land and population. The reason you are meeting in Minsk is that this Byelorussian, or White Russian, capital is neither in the dominant Russia nor in the obstreperous Ukraine, but you cannot very well call the new grouping the Byelorussian Commonwealth. So you reject all national adjectives, call it the Commonwealth (or Community) of Independent States, and to hell with the Squad Squad.

A commonwealth is useful because it does not need a capital. What about Minsk? (My own maternal grandfather, Harris Panish, emigrated from Minsk at the turn of the twentieth century, accompanied by his wife, Jennie, from nearby Pinsk; that makes my hyphenation Polish, Russian or Lithuanian, depending on the century in which the territory was governed.)

The term chosen to describe the function of Minsk, a half-Jewish city largely destroyed by the Nazis, was not the word for "capital," but the term for "meeting place"—*mesto vstrechi.* The capital of Russia is Moscow, which is where most of the action will remain, but the home of the inter-republic committees is, for the time being, Minsk, whose residents are *Minchane.*

The English-speaking world can roll with the punch of renaming the fragmented union. For generations, we called the U.S.S.R. "the Russians"; nobody warned, "The Soviets are coming." In the 1960's, under linguistic pressure from Moscow, American Presidents began substituting *Soviet* for *Russian;* speechwriters at summits were told to use the plural "Soviet peoples." By the 80's, the term *Soviet,* Russian for "governing council," was misapplied to individuals: we went from "He's a Soviet citizen" to "They're Soviets." Now *Soviet* will be used in the historical sense only, as in "the former Soviet Union" (already being shortened to F.S.U.).

A formulation attributed to Andrei D. Sakharov, and belatedly endorsed by Mikhail Gorbachev, was "Commonwealth of European and Asian States." This would have the advantage not only of describing the specific geographic area of the new agglomeration, but also of avoiding half the redundancy. In this independent state of flux, and with our eye on the remaining possibility of C.E.A.S., we will now desist.

What to Do With "Soviet"?

We have a word that is no longer attached to a thing. In philologese, that could be put this way: The sign is detached from the fractionated referent. Such linguistic severance requires immediate outplacement efforts on behalf of the replacement, or in plain words: If *Soviet* doesn't work anymore, what do we call the several groupings of the newly separated former Soviet republics?

Soviet was first a Russian noun, meaning "local council"; the word was thrust on the world scene with the Leninist slogan "Power to the Soviets!" Later, it became an adjective, as in "the new Soviet man," and was treated by many as a modifier of *union* in "Soviet Union," though it could still be considered a noun meaning "union of soviets."

In this generation, "the Russians"—as in "containing the Russians" or "the Russians are coming!"—was replaced by "the Soviet peoples" or "the Soviets." Language thus helped the process of centralization desired by Moscow, even as the strains of separation were developing.

But when the Soviet Union was dissolved, what happened to the word? First, we stopped saying "Soviets" when we meant "Russians" or "Ukrainians" or the new conceptual amalgam, "Turkic-speaking peoples" or "Muslim republics."

Next, we made a valiant effort to adopt the Commonwealth of Sovereign States, or C.I.S., in referring to the association of the Slavic states—Russia, Ukraine (no "the") and Belarus (not Byelorussia anymore)—and eight non-Slavic republics, but that military cooperation pact is not the commonwealth

it was cracked up to be, and nobody says "C.I.S." these days. I would use the capitals as helpers: "Moscow, with Minsk in tow but with Kiev dragging a foot, is likely to . . ."

But some unifying word is needed to designate these three Slavic republics, and another to designate the rest of the nations on the land mass covering eleven time zones. "Former Soviet Union," or F.S.U., won't do.

The Central Intelligence Agency, constantly on the lookout for useful things to do these days, has provided us with its approach to the linguistic head-scratcher. We outsiders can noodle it around, but bureaucrats have to have a sign painted on a real door, a need that adds urgency to their quest for a solution.

"The former title of our Soviet department," says a C.I.A. spokesman, Mark Mansfield, "was Office of Soviet Analysis. Obviously, now that there is no more Soviet Union, we have to change the name."

The envelope, please.

"The new name is Office of Slavic and Eurasian Analysis," he tells me, on the record, no cover at all. "That name more accurately reflects the current situation, but it still covers the same area."

The acronym is OSEA. (As a special favor to my new friends at the former Lubyanka prison on the former Dzerzhinsky Square, I report herewith the proper pronunciation: "oh-SEE-uh.") Presumably, spies from the former K.G.B. getting paid by Moscow, Minsk and Kiev and seeking to penetrate our defenses at Langley are "Slavic moles," while their counterparts from Kazakhstan and the other Turkic-speaking republics are "Eurasian moles." This development is too recent to be included in David Wise's *Molehunt*, an indispooksable new book about the C.I.A.'s self-policing, even if it is a bit hard on Jim (Harlot) Angleton.

"Slavic" is a branch of the Indo-European language family; the language dodge is important in this. Like all Gaul, it is divided into East Slavic (Moscow-Minsk-Kiev and environs), West Slavic (Polish, Czech and Slovak) and South Slavic (Serbo-Croatian, Bulgarian and Macedonian); there seems to be no North Slavic, and the Baltics like it that way. If you want to separate groups of republics, one way is to use "the Slavic republics" and "the Turkic republics."

Eurasian is a geologic way of describing "everything from London to Vladivostok." The Eurasian tectonic plate is what geologists think of as the Big Enchilada; the word has another sense, meaning "of European and Asian ancestry." I think *Eurasian* covers much more than the area our geo-spooks intended, and those in search of a word to characterize "the former Soviet republics minus the Slavic-speaking nations" should come up with something else. Send your suggestions to Robert M. Gates, Director of Central Intelligence, Central Intelligence Agency, Washington, D.C. 20505, and you will receive a reply from that newly taxpayer-friendly organization.

Our intelligence communitarians are relieved to be rid of C.I.S., however. The informally named Commonwealth of Independent States Office, or C.I.S.-Office, was being pronounced "kiss-off," something that troubled budgeteers.

The folks in Ljubljana will be miffed at your failure to include Slovenian among the South Slavic languages!

Louis Jay Herman
New York, New York

When Putsch Comes to Coup

In the tumult of what has come quickly to be called "the Second Russian Revolution" (soon to be shortened to RR II), the most memorable line spoken by the deposed and reimposed Soviet President Mikhail Gorbachev was to the Parliament Speaker, Anatoly Lukyanov. When that fellow traveler of the failed coup's plotters came to try to explain away his perfidy, Mikhail Sergeyevich snapped: "Don't hang noodles on my ears."

"Not quite 'Et tu, Tolya,' " wrote Serge Schmemann of *The New York Times* in Moscow, "but it made the point." He reported that the phrase was an "earthy Russian saying" drawn from Mr. Gorbachev's agrarian childhood. A check with local Russian speakers confirms that the figure of speech means "Don't hand me any of that guff" or, more precisely, "Don't try to make a fool of me."

Noodles is a humorous word, and its yodeling sound has been jocularly extended to *oodles o' noodles.* When the comedian Henny Youngman wanted to encapsulate craziness in a one-liner, he relied on the word: "Man comes in to a psychiatrist with a bowl of noodles on his head, running down his ears, says, 'Doc—I want to talk to you about my brother.' " That humorous connotation has been noted by restaurateurs, who now refer to their more serious *pasta.*

As a noun, *noodle* also means "head," from confusion with the earlier slang *noddle,* and has led to *off your noodle* and *noodle around,* which means "think over" to most of us, but to musicians means "tune up" and to Australian jewelers "to mine for opals."

Mr. Gorbachev's use of the figure of speech shows the linkage of languages: As in English, the notion of draping one's own self or one's target in noodles creates an image of foolishness; the disgraced Mr. Lukyanov may be wearing his noodle earrings for a long time.

Another high official, Foreign Minister Aleksandr Bessmertnykh, was relieved of his duties not for having joined the plotters, but for a nefarious activity that Mr. Gorbachev called *maneuvering.* He could have been charged with the similar *opportunism,* but if every opportunist in Moscow or Washington were fired, nobody would be left to turn out the lights.

A *maneuver,* from the French based on Latin "to work by hand," initially denoted an adroit military movement, later coming to connote a deceptive movement or feint, and now often meaning "a trick." Thus, a *maneuverer,* while not so bad in Communist terminology as an *adventurer,* is too clever by half, and who wants a Foreign Minister known as Tricky Al? Still, to be fired for maneuvering is new to the American ear.

A euphemism had to be found for a switch in British-American diplomatic conduct. For months, officials who wanted to strengthen the hand of Mr. Gorbachev and *the center*—a word now substituted for "Moscow, the Kremlin, the Union"—had hoped to send food (usually called *foodstuffs* by the stuffy) to the national government.

The New York Times ran a "reefer," or paragraph on the front page referring to a story on an inside page, with the new term for "change of mind" subtly noted: "President Bush and Prime Minister John Major of Britain announced that some increased food aid to the Soviet Union would bypass the central authorities and be sent directly to republics struggling for greater autonomy. The step was called 'a natural evolution of policy.' "

And now to the event itself, so often mismodified by *abortive* ("tending to be cut short"), better modified by *aborted* ("terminated early") and best by *failed, unsuccessful* or the breezier *fizzled:* "It was described as a *coup,*" writes the Reverend Donald Hendricks of Yonkers. "Should it not be a *putsch* or, more correctly in Marxist terms, a *Blanquist putsch*? Historically, I prefer the term *insurrection.* I suppose it might also be a *barracks revolt.*"

I called the priest who lives in the place where true love conquers in the wilds to find out about *Blanquism.* The eponym is Louis Auguste Blanqui, a French Communist of the nineteenth century; in Isaac Deutscher's 1949 biography of Stalin, the word's origin is given: "To the Menshivists this sounded like an ominous repetition of Blanquism, the doctrine of the leader of the Paris Commune, who believed that the only method of achieving revolution was direct action by a small conspiratorial minority ignoring the will of the majority."

A *coup*, Blanquist or not, started out as a blow or stroke. A *coup de main*, literally "a blow of the hand," is a sudden attack in force; a *coup de grâce* is a finishing shot; a *coup d'état*, from which we get *coup* in this political sense, is a sudden overthrow of a government by a small group, usually including some who are already in or near power. (The closest the United States came to a coup was when a group of unpaid Revolutionary War officers met in Newburgh, New York, in 1783 to discuss ousting the Congress and taking over; General Washington, poignantly putting on his spectacles to show how he had given his eyesight for his country, talked them out of it.)

Father Hendricks's point—that a *coup* connotes a well-executed, successful takeover—is well and decisively taken. Although "failed coup" is not incorrect, there's something wrong with it: Why use a modifier to set straight a not-quite-right noun when the right noun is available?

The right word, used by Boris Yeltsin from the start, perhaps for its Nazi beer-hall associations, is *putsch.* The German word also means "blow, thrust," same as the original French *coup,* but has the connotation of "attempt" rather than "successful quick completion." A *rebellion* is a *revolution* that failed; a *putsch* is a *coup* that did not come off.

But what of a *Potemkin coup*? The Center for Security Policy in Washington faxes a "decision brief" to opinionmongers with the latest hard line; it reported "speculation that Gorbachev may not have been quite the innocent victim of the *putsch,*" adding, "whether one buys the 'Potemkin coup' theory or not." Move over, Blanqui, for Grigori Potemkin, Catherine II's counselor-lover, who was said to have built sham villages along the Dnieper River to fool the Empress about his regional development. The name now means "phony"; a *Potemkin coup* would have to have Mr. Gorbachev as an orchestrator of his own victimization, which requires conspiracy theorizing to tax a Cassius.

The second-best pun of RR II was the headline by Leon Wieseltier of *The New Republic* over an article by Tatyana Tolstaya: "When Putsch Comes to Shove," which inspired the headline of this piece.

The best was Washington superlawyer Len Garment's description of the family of bungling plotters: the *Coup Klutz Clan.*

You state that "noodle around" to musicians means "tune up." Not so. "Noodles" are many notes in one measure, played very fast (on the page, they resemble spaghetti—many thin dark lines in a tightly confined space). A musician may noodle around, i.e., practice noodles (especially difficult passages) while others tune up. That musician is not tuning up. As a member of the woodwind quintet Prevailing Winds of Connecticut, I thought I'd set your noodle straight.

Stewart I. Edelstein
Southport, Connecticut

My dad is a classical musician (who has also some substantial experience in jazz), and I grew up hanging around players. To a musician, "noodling around" does not mean "tuning." It describes the activities of musicians who are casually improvising, especially with regard to whimsical melodic excursions. It's a little bit like jamming (there's a word to examine!) although jamming is something that requires two or several players whereas noodling around can be performed solo.

There's likely to be quite a bit of noodling around in a jam session even if a lone player cannot quite properly be said to be jamming.

Richard Walter
Los Angeles, California

Wholly of Whollies

"I think the key to my plan is that it is *holistic,*" Governor Cuomo said during his consideration-of-running phase, which may be over by the time this appears. He was discussing his ideas of a "progressive free-enterprise economy" to "fuel an investment-led recovery" when he used *holistic.* "I told the Fortune 500 C.E.O.'s, 'Think of it as *holistic*—but don't use that word; they'll think you smoke marijuana.' I'm afraid some of them looked it up and started with *w* and got lost."

Those dopey C.E.O.'s; they make up one of the few groups that can be derogated as a group without the derogator having to fear being accused of a slur. (Schwarzenegger could star in *The Derogator,* dotted-lining the despised C.E.O.'s to smithereens.) As an aid to those pitiful boardroom dolts, here is the bottom line on *holistic:*

Holism was coined in 1926 by Jan Christiaan Smuts, who first served as Prime Minister of the Union of South Africa from 1919 to 1924. In his book, *Holism and Evolution,* he expounded a theory that evolution was a process of units constantly integrating into systems, applying it to politics in the cases of the British Empire and the League of Nations. "The whole-making, *holistic* tendency, or *Holism,*" he wrote, dropping the *w* for no known reason, "operating in and through particular wholes, is seen at all stages of existence."

A generation later, some nutritionists adopted the word to advocate an approach to health and medicine on a broad, unorthodox front, and the word was used in derision by traditionalists. In time, *holistic,* in contrast to *analytic,* was extended to mean a way of thinking that emphasized the meaning of the whole as more than the sum of its parts. Thus, Governor Cuomo's "it has to be a total plan. You have to do everything." The word is in vogue in international economics, applied to the formation of tariff-free communities, but on the political level, nationalists have been giving it a kick in the head.

Evolution is at the root of another allusion made on *This Week with David Brinkley* that Sunday morning. Mr. Donaldson, trying to be analytic about Mr. Cuomo's holism, said, "Well, Governor, as you know, the devil is in the details." (A similar phrase, "God is in the details," is attributed to the Bauhaus architect Ludwig Mies van der Rohe, but the coiner is still being sought.) To which Mr. Cuomo, eager to keep his questioner off-balance, cracked, "I'm trying to stay with the angels."

"Is man an ape or an angel?" Benjamin Disraeli asked rhetorically in 1864 at the Oxford Diocesan Conference, which was disturbed about Charles Darwin's theory of evolution. "I, my lord, I am on the side of the angels. I repudiate with indignation and abhorrence those newfangled theories."

Darwin's newfangled theory was what we came to call *holistic.* Governor Cuomo will have to make up his mind: A politician cannot be both *holistic* and *on the side of the angels.*

Whole *comes from the Greek* holos, *so it's the "w" in* whole *that's an interloper.*

> Arthur J. Morgan
> New York, New York

J. C. Smuts didn't "drop the w *for no known reason" in coining* holism; *he formed it from the Greek* holos, *"whole," as English-speakers had been doing for 300 years, starting with* holograph *in 1623, according to the* Oxford English Dictionary. Holocaust *("whole fire") was in the language from Middle English times, via Latin. Some writers, usually for New Age publications, have in fact lately engrafted a* w *onto Smuts's word, apparently wishing to give it a handwoven or homebaked feeling.*

You might wish to search for a holophrastic *(summing up a phrase in one word) description of your emotions on learning in what company this places you.*

> D. R. Bensen
> Croton-on-Hudson, New York

I can give you some clues concerning "God is in the details." Mies probably got it from Aby Warburg, the German art historian. Mies studied architecture in Berlin with Peter Behrens and would have been well educated in art history. I am currently writing a book on Erwin Panofsky, the German art historian who taught at Hamburg University and worked with Warburg at his library in Ham-

burg in the 1920s. Panofsky later emigrated to the U.S. and was at the Institute for Advanced Studies at Princeton, 1935–68. Panofsky liked to quote Warburg's famous dictum, "The good God is in the details," which Panofsky believed came from Flaubert.

Panofsky not only was a brilliant art historian, he was also a brilliant philologist. He would have loved your column, although not your politics. After his emigration in 1934, he carried on a long correspondence with another Hamburg refugee, Richard Salomon. Salomon was a philologist in the old classical tradition, specializing in Slavic languages at Hamburg University and in medieval history at the Divinity School at Kenyon College. In 1959, they had an interesting discussion about "God is in the details." Panofsky quoted it to Salomon in regard to William Heckscher's book on the Rembrandt painting, the "Anatomy Lesson of Dr. Tulp," a good exemplar of detailed research. Salomon wrote back to Panofsky: "A chance find ad vocem 'God almighty in the details' follows here: 'Crede vel in minima parte latere Deum' / Barlaeus.'" Salomon found this, apparently, (I haven't checked it) in Heckscher's footnotes to the Rembrandt book, p. 113. Panofsky wrote back that he now feels the origin of Warburg's phrase becomes more and more enigmatic. He was sure he had found it in Flaubert as "Le bon Dieu est dans le détail." But he can't find it. And he can scarcely imagine Flaubert reading Barlaeus. He concludes that it will someday be found in a Nominalist source. Heckscher is still alive and resides in Princeton.

Since these scholars were trained in a tradition of philology no longer available to anyone, I am willing to bet they are right. Happy hunting!

> Joan Hart
> Bloomington, Indiana

I had no idea I would have to go to the Art Library at Indiana University today for another errand and find myself looking up William Heckscher's Rembrandt's Anatomy of Dr. Nicolaas Tulp *(Washington Sq.: NYU Press, 1958). Salomon's quotation of the "good God is in the details" from Caspar Barlaeus looks even better to me now that I see the original and the translation on pp. 112–113 of Heckscher's book. The context is: Barlaeus was considered "the greatest orator and poet of our age" by Dr. Tulp and others living in Amsterdam in the 17th century. Barlaeus was professor of philosophy and medicine at Amsterdam's university. Barlaeus's quote* "Crede vel in minima parte latere Deum" *(Heckscher translates "in the smallest part God is enshrined") comes from a poem to celebrate the opening of the Amsterdam Anatomical Theater. Heckscher believes that the poem, explicitly referring to Tulp, must also refer to Rembrandt's painting, which was commissioned for the new anatomical theater. To cite more of the poem: "Here addresses us the Eloquence of learned Tulpius while with nimble hand he dissects livid limbs. Listener, learn for thyself, and as*

thou proceedest from one to another, believe that even in the smallest part God
is enshrined."

*I would guess that this is a common little saying (topoi) that probably does
have a more ancient source. It is nice that it refers to a painting and Mies popularized it later in regard to architecture.*

> *Joan Hart*
> *Bloomington, Indiana*

*Concerning the phrase "God is in detail": This expression is one of the bywords
at the Warburg Institute in London, and there are various attributions for its
source. One of the founders of the Institute, Aby Warburg, had a favorite dictum:* "Le bon Dieu est dans le détail" *(which suggests that he thought of the
transmission through the French tradition). But other possible origins have been
attributed: the literary historian Ernst Robert Curtius and the first director of
the Warburg after it had been transmigrated to London, Fritz Saxl.*

Virginia W. Callahan has brought forward a Latin passage of ca. 1640: Crede
vel in minima parte latere Deum *("Believe me that in the smallest particle God
is enshrined"), an inscription composed by Caspar Barlaeus that appeared in a
new anatomical theatre (thus V. W. Callahan in* Moreana *89 [February 1986],
90–1, writing on William Heckscher).*

But the concept may be traced back to Hugh of St. Victor's encyclopedic Di-
dascalicon, *which celebrates learning everything, for then "you will see afterward that nothing is useless"; and Hugh saw God in every detail of the creation
of the world (see F. Vernet, "Hughes de Saint-Victor" in* Dict. Theol. Cath.,
VII).

> *Richard J. Schoeck*
> *Lawrence, Kansas*

Who Trusts Whom?

"Who do you trust?" George Bush asks, changing the subject from the Democrats' "change." This is a slogan that reverberates in the souls of the slickness-
averse, but it drags a piece of chalk along the blackboard with a loud squeak
in the English classrooms of America.

"I don't trust any educated person who deliberately breaks the rule on pronoun case," writes Florence Withheld of Tallahassee, Florida (a school-teacher who has asked that her name be withheld). "*Who* is a subject pronoun, but the subject in President Bush's question is not *who* but *you.*"

She's right; there goes the purist vote. Change the question "Who do you trust?" into a statement—"You do trust *him*"—and the use of *whom* is inescapable. You would never say, "You do trust *he*," and you should not ask, "*Who* do you trust?" Those traditionalists who believe in linguistic values insist on "*Whom* do you trust?"

The only trouble with that is it runs afoul of Safire's Law of Who/Whom, which forever solves the problem troubling writers and speakers caught between the pedantic and the incorrect: "When *whom* is correct, recast the sentence."

Thus, instead of changing his slogan to "Whom do you trust?"—making him sound like a hypereducated Yalie stiff—Mr. Bush would win back the purist vote with "Which candidate do you trust?" Hard to get that on a bumper sticker, I know, but I cannot solve all his problems.

In the spirit of nonpartisanship that has always drained the juice from this column, let us turn now to the same mistake—the corruption of the pronoun case—by the Democratic candidate.

"If you're tired of being heartbroken when you go home at night," says Bill Clinton in the peroration of his stump speech, "and you want a spring in your step and a song in your heart, you give Al Gore and I a chance to bring America back."

In the independent clause that ends that sentence, both "Al Gore" and "I" are indirect objects of the verb "give." The word *I* is a subject, not an object; the word *me* is the pronoun to use in the objective case. Therefore—and I hope he's briefed on this before he blows it with the purists in debate—whatever he wants us to give, he should ask us to give to "Al Gore and *me.*"

Which candidate will be first to get off our pronoun case? Between you and me—never you and I—to the question "Who do you trust?" the best answer is "Give I a break."

As Hemingway should have said, "Don't ask who the bell is ringing for." Whom cares?

Allan Leedy
Portland, Oregon

The Winged Frog

F.D.R. rejected what he called "iffy questions"; he saw them as reportorial traps. President Bush, too, dismisses hypothetical questions; asked about extending unemployment benefits if the economy sinks again, he replied, "If a frog had wings, he wouldn't hit his tail on the ground."

This vivid construction was cited in the 1942 *Dictionary of Quotations* by H. L. Mencken as "If a frog had wings, he wouldn't bump his backside every time he jumps." It was an American variant of the English "If my aunt had been a man, she'd have been my uncle" and the German "If my aunt had wheels, she would be an omnibus."

In this tall-talking construction, the subordinate or "iffy" clause is called the *protasis* (pronounced "PRAH-tuh-sis"), from the Greek for "premise of a syllogism"; the main clause is the *apodosis* ("uh-PAH-duh-sis"), from the Greek verb for "to deliver." Together, they form a hypothetical situation that has been described as *suppository,* which strikes me as a poor choice of a word; Fred Cassidy at the *Dictionary of American Regional English* calls it a *counterfactual trope;* I call it the *comic conditional.*

Don't you wish you could coin one? (As they said in the seventeenth century, "If wishes were horses, beggars would ride.")

You may have heard another version of the "If . . ." routine that was broadcast over a New York City radio station some time in 1949, I think by the late great Henry Morgan: he maintained that "If my grandmother had tubes, she'd be a radio," which I immediately categorized as an easing, as the linguistic types have it, of an older version, "If my grandmother had balls, she'd be my grandfather," which, unfortunately, he couldn't use on the air.

Bernard W. Kane
Ridley Park, Pennsylvania

Wise Guys Finish Last

To strike an ingratiating pose of fallibility, I occasionally insert a metaphoric mistake or usage error in a political essay or language column.

"Did you really mean to say," writes Mark Lasswell of New York, "that in failing to keep Saddam Hussein's helicopters grounded, President Bush 'suddenly *choked up*'?"

Baseball players *choke up* on their bats—sacrificing power for accuracy by allowing an inch or two of wood below the grasp—but this was not the image I had in mind in this polemic. Nor was *choke up* intended to mean "become emotional or sentimental" in my usage. "I doubt you were saying," writes the relentless Mr. Lasswell, "that Mr. Bush got all *choked up* about rebellion," since his reaction at first was dismayingly dry-eyed.

My mistake was in the use of *up.* "I believe you meant to say that Mr. Bush *choked*—minus the *up*—meaning that when presented with a stern challenge, the President collapsed on a sofa and began fanning himself. Uncharitable observers usually illustrate this inability to deliver in the clutch by grabbing their throats while their eyes bulge and their tongues loll out of their mouths. I think I saw General Colin Powell doing it on television the other day when Mr. Bush's back was turned."

For slang synonymists outside of baseball, this lesson: *To choke up* means "to become visibly affected, on the verge of tears"; *to choke*—without the *up*—means "to flinch from a challenge."

In suggesting that the United Nations Security Council choose a troika of Margaret Thatcher, Yaqub Khan and Eduard A. Shevardnadze to be the next Secretary General, I wrote in my political column: "This modest proposal will be met with hoots and harrumphs from the dovecote on Turtle Bay."

I was so transfixed with the allusion to Jonathan Swift's satiric "modest proposal" as well as the use of *harrumph*—a throat-clearing onomatopoeia from the comic strip "Major Hoople" ("Hak! Fap! Harrumph!")—that I did not stop to think of the sounds emanating from a *dovecote.*

"I have been around dovecotes for years," writes Arnold Beichman of the Hoover Institution at Stanford (but not *of* Stanford), "but never, never, never did I ever hear 'hoots and harrumphs' coming from such informed quarters. What kind of dovecote do you have, or is it one of those mixed-up metaphors?"

Of course, the sound that comes from a dovecote is described as "cooing," with an occasional little liberal "peep" from the newly hatched. (If doves live in a *dovecote,* where do hawks live? In a *hawkery,* coined in 1832 on the analogy of *rookery,* where rooks—also known as crows—live. Hawks issue *cries,* an apt phrase for reactions to billions in aid for the Soviet Union. Eagles live in lofty *aeries,* which can be metaphorically applied to sharp-eyed executives in their skyscraper offices; you cannot use *harrumphs* as the sound from aeries, either—only *screams, shrieks* and authoritative *peeps.*)

Finally, a passing reference to Secretary of State James A. Baker 3d in my Essay used a word that scrapes a fingernail across the blackboard: "The President has learned something that his manager-mentee has not."

"*Mentee?*" writes the shocked James B. McCloskey of Norfolk, Virginia. He had heard this word used by broadcast journalists, and had dismissed it as the misnomer for a beneficiary of the efforts of a *mentor,* a word meaning "trusted counselor or teacher" derived from the name of the teacher to whom Odysseus entrusted the education of Telemachus, his son. But "surely,

William Safire wouldn't misconstrue the meaningless final two letters of a proper name—Mentor—as representing the -or suffix denoting one performing the act described by the root verb." Because *ment* is not a verb that led to *mentor,* it cannot lead to *mentee.* "Whence came this abomination?"

I was hoping to get good mail on that. *Mentee* was first used in letters from Linda S. Benedict and Bonnie K. Shimahara published in *Business Week* on November 20, 1978. In 1986, I noted that Citibank had issued a "Mentor/Mentee Profile," and opined that "the use of -ee as the automatic complement to -or should be resisted." This especially applied to eponymous words and things to which good labels had already been attached; in the case of *mentee,* it seemed an unnecessary addition to *protégé* or *fellow.*

I know how Gorbachev feels after issuing a decree. Thirty-three citations come leaping out of the Nexis morgue, from some of our more literate publications, in the five years since I told you all to cut it out. Perhaps my authority would better be maintained by now switching to Yeltsinesque reform.

For "one who is under a mentor's wing," *fellow* does not work. In academia and at think tanks, fellowships abound, but in ordinary speech, *fellow* is too often associated with a male person. (Sorry, fellas.) *Protégé* has a musical-world connotation and means "one being promoted or put forward"; that French word is not taking root in the business world. People there seem to prefer being known as *mentees.*

This does not mean I will run out and buy *sponsor/sponsee* or *metaphor/metaphee,* but let's suspend the abominating of *mentee.* Give it a break. Help it along.

You are too quick to assume that James B. McCloskey of Norfolk, Virginia, knows what he's talking about when he warns you not to "misconstrue the meaningless final two letters of a proper name—Mentor—as representing the -or suffix denoting one performing the act described by the root verb."

Like most proper names, Greek Mentor *was originally a word. It means "adviser" and is cognate with Sanskrit* mantar, *"thinker," and Latin* commentor, *"inventor." The first syllable,* men-, *is from the Indo-European verbal root meaning "to think" (see English* mental *and* mind*), and* -tor *is an agent suffix (see Latin* actor *from* agere, *monitor* from* monere*) which is every bit as common as* -or. *(Some of this information is in* Webster's New World Dictionary, *and the rest can be found in Julius Pokorny's Indo-European etymological dictionary [actual title:* Indogermanisches etymologisches Wörterbuch*], page 727.) Thus, once you're on an* -ee *kick,* mentor/mentee *is perfectly acceptable.*

At the end of your column, you say: "This does not mean I will run out and buy sponsor/sponsee *or* metaphor/metaphee." *It so happens there's nothing wrong with the first of those pairs:* Sponsor *is a Latin agent noun (meaning "bondsman") derived from the verb* spondere *"to go bail (for someone)," so that* sponsee *is A-OK. In the case of* metaphor, *on the other hand,* -phor *is the root (from the Greek verb for "to carry"), so that* metaphee *would definitely be, as Mr. McCloskey might put it, an abomination.*

Louis Jay Herman
New York, New York

The English noun form ending in "ee" has developed from the French past participle, which takes the end "é" or "ée" depending on gender. Thus, the form not only presupposes a verb; it presupposes a transitive verb or at least a reflexive one, which can give rise to a passive form (hence the need for gender marking in a language that has genders). For example, "Je me suis fiancée" or "Il est fiancé. . . ."

"Mentee" is doubtless an abomination, and beyond the pale, but more common barbarisms are "attendee," "escapee" and other similar words. How people can be attended (unless they are ill in bed perhaps, or royalty) or escaped, I cannot fathom. Attended to, yes, or escaped from, certainly, but otherwise, forget it.

Grace Kenny
London, England

Word Needed

No discipline can be disciplined without a name.

Joseph A. Califano Jr., architect of the Great Society, has kicked over the life of a Washington superlawyer to run the new Center on Addiction and Substance Abuse at Columbia University.

Getting hooked on dope, booze and smoking is bad for us. Getting doctors, law officers, teachers and executives together to create a new social-scientific field to combat addiction is good for us. Joe wants to give professional work in this area the same kind of panache as work in the areas of, say, cancer or heart disease.

"I want parents to be as proud of saying, 'My son (or daughter), the expert on addiction and substance abuse,' " Califano writes, "as they are of saying, 'My son, the oncologist,' or 'My daughter, the cardiologist.' "

The problem: We have no word for those who find their calling in the anti-addiction-and-abuse discipline. His request: "How about giving the new profession the right name?"

Inundate him with suggestions, Lexicographic Irregulars. Years from now, you can say to your grandchildren asking what you did in the drug wars, "I named the whole field."

Hookology Won't Do

A word-wanted ad was run here last year by Joe Califano, president of the Center on Addiction and Substance Abuse at Columbia University. He sought the name for the study of addiction, received 155 responses from Lexicographic Irregulars and is mulling over these finalists:

Addictionology, which is quickly understandable but seems long and banal.

Pharmacosiology, from *pharmaco-,* "drug," and *-osis,* "disease." I don't like the "cosy" in the middle.

Deditology from the Latin *deditus,* "addicted to," and has a warning connection to "dead" in the first syllable.

Etheology, from the Greek *ethos,* "habit."

If you want to vote, or top these, write to Joe at CASA, 152 West 57th Street, New York, N.Y. 10019. Help your fellow person; be a coiner.

Words of Wisdom

Phrase junkies are always on the lookout for political axioms, adages and proverbs.

Bert Lance's "*If it ain't broke, don't fix it*" has become a source of inspiration to anti-activists. Dwight Morrow's "*Any party which takes credit for the rain must not be surprised if its opponents blame it for the drought*" is being ruefully repeated by supporters of George Bush. Economists eager to fine-tune the economy turn to the wisdom attributed to the gangster Al Capone: "*You can get a lot more done with a kind word and a gun, than with a kind word alone.*"

A subcategory in this field is "forgiveness, political," headed by the quotation attributed to the Kennedy brothers: "*Forgive but don't forget.*" An addition to this store of sophisticated sagacity has been provided by the newscaster Jim Lehrer, in his new, breezily profound memoir, *A Bus of My Own* (Putnam). He notes in passing that some former associates tried to do him in, and then forgives them, but not completely: "As a prominent Oklahoma politician says a lot," Lehrer writes, " '*Show me somebody who can't tell his friends from his enemies and I'll show you somebody who's going to end up with no friends.*' "

Zipping the Lip

The baseball manager Leo Durocher is widely quoted by business managers of today for coining the phrase "Nice guys finish last."

Did he say that, or did history help him along by editing his remark? A reader in Mount Kisco, New York, wrote to *The New York Times* recalling—without citation—that Durocher, managing the Brooklyn Dodgers in the mid-1940's, was asked how the Giants would finish that year. The reader, Jack A. Thaw, remembers the reply as "The Giants. Gordon, Mize, Kerr, Jansen, Ott. Nice guys. They'll finish last," and the New York *Daily News* headline the next day: "Nice Guys Finish Last: Leo."

Writes Mr. Thaw: "As Casey Stengel (or was it Damon Runyon) might have said, 'You could look it up.' " It's a good lead to a historical verification; I would trust Mr. Thaw's recollection a little more if he remembered that it was James Thurber who had one of his baseball characters say, "You could look it up."

Durocher never said it. He always said he hadn't (to me, too, in a phone conversation two years ago [in 1989]), and he was telling the truth. On July 6, 1946, he was sitting in the Brooklyn dugout before a game with the Giants at the Polo Grounds. Red Barber was there, and Red kidded Leo, asking him why he couldn't be a nice guy once in a while. Frank Graham was also there. Graham, who was then covering the Giants for the old Journal-American, *had a near-photographic memory, and he wrote up what Durocher said as follows:*

> *"Nice guys!" he said. "Look over there. Do you know a nicer guy than Mel Ott? Or any of the other Giants? Why, they're the nicest guys in the world! And where are they? In seventh place!" He waved toward the Giants' dugout again. "The nice guys are all over there," he said. "In seventh place."*

A month later, Graham's piece was picked up by Baseball Digest, *whose editor, Herb Simons, abridged it for the September issue. By now, the Giants were last, and Simons made a significant change, possibly to heighten the dramatic effect. Each time Graham quoted Durocher as saying "seventh," Simons substituted "last." It's Simons's version of Durocher's comment that eventually evolved into "Nice guys finish last." Here, as it often has, myth superseded history, and accuracy took a backseat to journalistic enterprise.*

Peter Williams
Caldwell, New Jersey

ACKNOWLEDGEMENTS

Who put the *ac* in *acknowledgement*?

This is a matter of controversy among etymologists. In *Merriam-Webster's Tenth Collegiate*, we see "[*ac-* (as in *accord*) + *knowledge*]." But when you look up the prefix *ac-*, it sends you to *ad-*, which it tracks though Middle English to Old French to Latin to mean "to, toward," noting that *ad-* is usually *ac-* before a *c, k* or *q*, all of which represent the same sound.

Then you take the *ac-*, meaning "toward," and marry it to *knowledge*, "awareness of information" (not "sexual intercourse"—that's an archaic sense), and you get the verb *acknowledge*, "to recognize" or "to disclose knowledge or note receipt of" or "to thank."

But *The Barnhart Dictionary of Etymology* comes at it differently. It takes the Middle English word *acknow*, "to admit," which combined with *knowleche* to produce *acknowledge*.

That sent me to the *Oxford English Dictionary* to find the obsolete *acknow*. There it is, spelled *oncnáwan* in Old English, divisible into *on* and *cnáwan*, "to know." The lexicographer explains the shift from *on* to *ac-:* "ON, in, on + *cnáwan* to know (by the senses), to recognize; the prefix afterwards reduced, as usual, to *o-, a-*, and at length corruptly written *ac-* in imitation of *ac-* before *c- k- q-* in words adopted from Latin."

Thus (a great word for explicators, shunned as pedantic for types who want to seem with-it), the root of *acknowledge* is *acknow*, "on knowing," and its earliest meanings are (1) "to come to know," or "recognize"; (2) "to admit or show one's knowledge, to confess," and then the much-later meanings about telling people you got their E-mail or, in my case at this point, admitting a debt of gratitude to people who help me in writing language columns.

For example, I called Frederick C. Mish at Merriam-Webster to wonder about the difference between his etymology and the *O.E.D.*'s, and he put the question to his specialists in etymology. In turn, they sorted through the Old English and Middle English derivations of the term for the acknowledged facts.

That's the way it works. I get a subject, like thanking people at the end of the book; I want to get away from *credits,* which I have been using for years to free me from *acknowledgements;* I look up *acknowledge,* focusing on the stuff in brackets, and spot some unargued argument; I (or more frequently, Jeffrey McQuain, my research arm) call up a lexie buddy, and get the most knowledgeable help. (Do I like *acknowledgement* with that third *e*? Nah; drop it, on the analogy of *judgment.*)

Here is what Fred Mish reports from his etymology team: "The *O.E.D.* presents two possibilities for *acknowledge,* the second of which is the same as ours. We simply give the one that seems likelier to us. . . . *Acknowledge* was created by adding the *ac-* of *acknow* to the already existing *knowledge.*

"*Acknow* is obsolete in modern English," Dr. Mish adds. "It was originally *aknow,* the *a-* representing the vestige of the Old English *on-*. This *a-* is the same as the one found in 'a-hunting we will go.' "

Then comes the big question: Who cares? How many people are interested in etymology?

The answer is: Plenty of people care about the origins of words, *provided the word is "hot."* At the moment, writing this farewell, I find that *acknowledgment* (yeah, that looks better) is in the forefront of my attention, and the reader's as well. More often, an unfamiliar word in the news gets hot: *reconfiguration* of forces in the Balkans, for example. That's when I move in, satisfying a curiosity, going into the *figure* that is the shape that the *re-* and the *con-* are re-forming.

What separates *information*—that endless stream of data—from *knowledge* is awareness of the possession of that knowledge, and experience in dealing with similar information. In the case of *acknowledge,* I just found out about it and am delightedly passing it along. It brightened a tedious job of listing my thank-yous. Neither you nor I will ever look at that word as blankly as before. Now we acknow.

The thankees are: Fred Mish of Merriam-Webster, Sol Steinmetz of Random House, Mike Agnes of Webster's New World and Anne Soukhanov, formerly of American Heritage. The "On Language" Board of Mentors—Olbom—comprises (not "is comprised of") Jacques Barzun, Fred Cassidy of the *Dictionary of American Regional English,* Alistair Cooke and Allen Walker Read.

Others called upon for lexicographic service include John Algeo, David K. Barnhart, Cynthia Barnhart, William A. Kretzschmar Jr. of the *Linguistic Atlas* project, James McCawley (the philological heavyweight of the University of Chicago), and Allan Metcalf of the American Dialect Society. Quotation assistance came from James Simpson of *Simpson's Quotations,* Justin Kaplan of *Bartlett's,* Fred Shapiro of Yale Law School and Jeanne Smith at the Library of Congress.

My editors at Random House include Kate Medina, Jonathan Karp, Beth Pearson, Adam Davies, Sean Abbott, Mina Samuels, Margaret Wimberger,

Janet Wygal and Patricia Abdale. These columns first appear in *The New York Times Magazine,* where my editors are and have been Jack Rosenthal, Harvey Shapiro, Michael Molyneux, and Rob Hoerburger. In addition to Jeffrey McQuain's and Elizabeth Gibbens's language support, my help at the *Times* Washington bureau includes my assistant, Ann Elise Rubin, who keeps a watch on current words, and Todd Webb, who tries keeping up with the mail. The copy editors of my political column, who often lead me to language topics, are Steve Pickering, Linda Cohn and Sue Kirby. The bureau's chief librarian, Barclay Walsh, and the librarians Monica Borkowski and Marjorie Goldsborough are as helpful as ever.

My final thankees are the Lexicographic Irregulars, from the redundancy reducers of the Squad Squad to the nit-picking troops of the Gotcha! Gang. Their helpful corrections and incessant nagging keep "On Language" going, and they deserve every acknowledgment.

INDEX

Wattenberg, Ben J., xiii, 79
Watts, Doug, 144
Wayne, John, 85
wean, weaned on, 270–72
wear, 250
Weaver, Sigourney, 38
Webb, Todd, 299
wedge issue, 273–74
Weed, Thurlow, 63
Weeks, Albert L., 140–41
we have no evidence, 3
Weigley, Russell F., 205
Weil, Peggy, 262–63
Weinberg, Goodwin G., 81
Weinberg, Philip, 243
Weinberger, Caspar, 4
weird, 14–15
Weissberg, Melissa, 174
Weitzner, Walter B., 16
Welch, Rupert, 93
Wells, Michael T., 25
Weseen, Maurice, 109
wet operation, 184
wet squad, 184
wet work, 184
Weymouth, Elizabeth Graham "Lally,"
    11
whack, whack out, 275–76
whaddya, 133
Whewell, William, 240
White, Byron, 178, 180
White, Edmund, xiv
White, Joan, 88
White, Stewart Edward, 40
Whitman, Walt, 57, 240
who, whom, 128–29, 288–89
Wickenden, Hermione, 128
Wiener, Norbert, 262
Wierzbianski, Barbara, 208
Wieseltier, Leon, 284
Wilkin, Karen, 220
Will, George F., 137, 167–68, 198,
    253–54
Williams, Peter, 295

Williams, Robin, 229
Willson, Charles H., 197
Wilner, Judith, 101
Wilson, Pete, 11
Wimberger, Margaret, 298
Wines, Michael, 164
winnability, winnable, 63
Winter, Munroe A., 81
Winter, Pat, 242–43
Wise, David, 281
"Withheld, Florence," 288–89
Wodehouse, P. G., 171
wonk, 210
Wood, Frederick T., 177
Wood, J. S., 45
Wood, Peter, 74
Wood, William, 126
*World Almanac Guide to Good Word
    Usage, The* (Manser and
    McQuain), 162
Wyatt, Thomas, 221
Wyclif, John, 84
Wygal, Janet, 299

Yankelovich, Daniel, 202
Yavlinsky, Grigory A., 251
Yeats, William Butler, 200, 209, 248
yellow dog, 276
Yeltsin, Boris, 277, 284
Yingling, Charles D., 139
y'know, 116, 117
yobo, 23
Yoder, Edwin, 23
you know, 115–16
Young, Anniebeth, 257
Youngman, Henny, 282

Zall, James, 203
zar, 16
Zeitlin, Lynn G., 153
Zidon, Yoash, 191
Zimmer, Elizabeth, 73
Zuckerman, Mort, 96
Zweig, Jason, xiii

ABOUT THE AUTHOR

WILLIAM SAFIRE is a writer of many incarnations: reporter, publicist, White House speechwriter, historian, novelist, lexicographer, and provocative pundit.

His primary occupation since 1972 has been political columnist for *The New York Times,* usually taking the point of view of a libertarian conservative; in 1978, he was awarded the Pulitzer Prize for distinguished commentary. His column "On Language" in *The New York Times* is syndicated around the world and has made him the most widely read and vociferously argued-with writer on the subject of the English language.

Mr. Safire is married to a jeweler, is the father of a multimedia software developer and a graphic artist, and is able to communicate with all of them.